The NEW ENCYCLOPEDIA *of* SOUTHERN CULTURE

VOLUME 3 : HISTORY

Volumes to appear in

The New Encyclopedia of Southern Culture

are:

Agriculture and Industry *Law and Politics*

Art and Architecture *Literature*

Education *Media*

Environment *Music*

Ethnicity *Myth, Manners, and Memory*

Folk Art *Race*

Folklife *Recreation*

Foodways *Religion*

Gender *Science and Medicine*

Geography *Social Class*

History *Urbanization*

Language *Violence*

The NEW

ENCYCLOPEDIA *of* SOUTHERN CULTURE

CHARLES REAGAN WILSON General Editor

JAMES G. THOMAS JR. Managing Editor

ANN J. ABADIE Associate Editor

VOLUME 3

History

CHARLES REAGAN WILSON Volume Editor

Sponsored by

THE CENTER FOR THE STUDY OF SOUTHERN CULTURE

at the University of Mississippi

THE UNIVERSITY OF NORTH CAROLINA PRESS

Chapel Hill

© 2006 The University of North Carolina Press

All rights reserved

Designed by Richard Hendel

Set in Minion types by Tseng Information Systems, Inc.

Manufactured in the United States of America

The paper in this book meets the guidelines for permanence and durability of the Committee on Production Guidelines for Book Longevity of the Council on Library Resources.

This book was published with the assistance of the Anniversary Endowment Fund of the University of North Carolina Press.

Library of Congress Cataloging-in-Publication Data

The new encyclopedia of Southern culture / Charles Reagan Wilson, general editor ; James G. Thomas Jr., managing editor ; Ann J. Abadie, associate editor.

p. cm.

Rev. ed. of: Encyclopedia of Southern culture. 1991.

"Sponsored by The Center for the Study of Southern Culture at the University of Mississippi."

Includes bibliographical references and index.

Contents: — v. 3. History.

ISBN-13: 978-0-8078-3028-4 (cloth : v. 3 : alk. paper)

ISBN-13: 978-0-8078-5691-8 (pbk. : v. 3 : alk. paper)

1. Southern States—Civilization—Encyclopedias. 2. Southern States—Encyclopedias. I. Wilson, Charles Reagan. II. Thomas, James G. III. Abadie, Ann J. IV. University of Mississippi. Center for the Study of Southern Culture.

V. Encyclopedia of Southern culture.

F209.N47 2006

975.003—dc22

2005024807

The *Encyclopedia of Southern Culture*, sponsored by the Center for the Study of Southern Culture at the University of Mississippi, was published by the University of North Carolina Press in 1989.

cloth   11 10 09 08 07   6 5 4 3

paper   10 09 08 07 06   5 4 3 2 1

Tell about the South. What it's like there.

What do they do there. Why do they live there.

Why do they live at all.

WILLIAM FAULKNER

Absalom, Absalom!

CONTENTS

In 1989 years of planning and hard work came to fruition when the University of North Carolina Press joined the Center for the Study of Southern Culture at the University of Mississippi to publish the *Encyclopedia of Southern Culture*. While all those involved in writing, reviewing, editing, and producing the volume believed it would be received as a vital contribution to our understanding of the American South, no one could have anticipated fully the widespread acclaim it would receive from reviewers and other commentators. But the *Encyclopedia* was indeed celebrated, not only by scholars, but also by popular audiences with a deep, abiding interest in the region. At a time when some people talked of the "vanishing South," the book helped remind a national audience that the region was alive and well, and it has continued to shape national perceptions of the South through the work of its many users—journalists, scholars, teachers, students, and general readers.

As the introduction to the *Encyclopedia* noted, its conceptualization and organization reflected a cultural approach to the South. It highlighted such issues as the core zones and margins of southern culture, the boundaries where "the South" overlapped with other cultures, the role of history in contemporary culture, and the centrality of regional consciousness, symbolism, and mythology. By 1989 scholars had moved beyond the idea of cultures as real, tangible entities, viewing them instead as abstractions. The *Encyclopedia*'s editors and contributors thus included a full range of social indicators, trait groupings, literary concepts, and historical evidence typically used in regional studies, carefully working to address the distinctive and characteristic traits that made the American South a particular place. The introduction to the *Encyclopedia* concluded that the fundamental uniqueness of southern culture was reflected in the volume's composite portrait of the South. We asked contributors to consider aspects that were unique to the region but also those that suggested its internal diversity. The volume was not a reference book of southern history, which explained something of the design of entries. There were fewer essays on colonial and antebellum history than on the postbellum and modern periods, befitting our conception of the volume as one trying not only to chart the cultural landscape of the South but also to illuminate the contemporary era.

When C. Vann Woodward reviewed the *Encyclopedia* in the *New York Review of Books*, he concluded his review by noting "the continued liveliness of interest in the South and its seeming inexhaustibility as a field of study." Research on the South, he wrote, furnishes "proof of the value of the *Encyclopedia* as a scholarly undertaking as well as suggesting future needs for revision or supplement to keep up with ongoing scholarship." The decade and a half since the publication of the *Encyclopedia of Southern Culture* have certainly suggested that Woodward was correct. The American South has undergone significant changes that make for a different context for the study of the region. The South has undergone social, economic, political, intellectual, and literary transformations, creating the need for a new edition of the *Encyclopedia* that will remain relevant to a changing region. Globalization has become a major issue, seen in the South through the appearance of Japanese automobile factories, Hispanic workers who have immigrated from Latin America or Cuba, and a new prominence for Asian and Middle Eastern religions that were hardly present in the 1980s South. The African American return migration to the South, which started in the 1970s, dramatically increased in the 1990s, as countless books simultaneously appeared asserting powerfully the claims of African Americans as formative influences on southern culture. Politically, southerners from both parties have played crucial leadership roles in national politics, and the Republican Party has dominated a near-solid South in national elections. Meanwhile, new forms of music, like hip-hop, have emerged with distinct southern expressions, and the term "dirty South" has taken on new musical meanings not thought of in 1989. New genres of writing by creative southerners, such as gay and lesbian literature and "white trash" writing, extend the southern literary tradition.

Meanwhile, as Woodward foresaw, scholars have continued their engagement with the history and culture of the South since the publication of the *Encyclopedia*, raising new scholarly issues and opening new areas of study. Historians have moved beyond their earlier preoccupation with social history to write new cultural history as well. They have used the categories of race, social class, and gender to illuminate the diversity of the South, rather than a unified "mind of the South." Previously underexplored areas within the field of southern historical studies, such as the colonial era, are now seen as formative periods of the region's character, with the South's positioning within a larger Atlantic world a productive new area of study. Cultural memory has become a major topic in the exploration of how the social construction of "the South" benefited some social groups and exploited others. Scholars in many disciplines have made the southern identity a major topic, and they have used a variety of methodologies to suggest what that identity has meant to different social groups. Literary critics have adapted cultural theories to the South and have raised the issue of postsouthern literature to a major category of concern as well as exploring the links between the literature of the American South and that of the Caribbean. Anthropologists have used different theoretical formulations from literary critics, providing models for their fieldwork in southern communities. In the past 30 years anthropologists have set increasing numbers of their ethnographic studies in the South, with many of them now exploring topics specifically linked to southern cultural issues. Scholars now place the Native American story, from prehistory to the contemporary era, as a central part of southern history. Comparative and interdisciplinary approaches to the South have encouraged scholars to look at such issues as the borders and boundaries of the South, specific places and spaces with distinct identities within the American South, and the global and transnational Souths, linking the American South with many formerly colonial societies around the world.

The first edition of the *Encyclopedia of Southern Culture* anticipated many of these approaches and indeed stimulated the growth of Southern Studies as a distinct interdisciplinary field. The Center for the Study of Southern Culture has worked for more than a quarter century to encourage research and teaching about the American South. Its academic programs have produced graduates who have gone on to write interdisciplinary studies of the South, while others have staffed the cultural institutions of the region and in turn encouraged those institutions to document and present the South's culture to broad public audiences. The center's conferences and publications have continued its long tradition of promoting understanding of the history, literature, and music of the South, with new initiatives focused on southern foodways, the future of the South, and the global Souths, expressing the center's mission to bring the best current scholarship to broad public audiences. Its documentary studies projects build oral and visual archives, and the New Directions in Southern Studies book series, published by the University of North Carolina Press, offers an important venue for innovative scholarship.

Since the *Encyclopedia of Southern Culture* appeared, the field of Southern Studies has dramatically developed, with an extensive network now of academic and research institutions whose projects focus specifically on the interdisciplinary study of the South. The Center for the Study of the American South at the University of North Carolina at Chapel Hill, led by Director Harry Watson and Associate Director and *Encyclopedia* coeditor William Ferris, publishes the lively journal *Southern Cultures* and is now at the organizational center of many other Southern Studies projects. The Institute for Southern Studies at the University of South Carolina, the Southern Intellectual History Circle, the Society for the Study of Southern Literature, the Southern Studies Forum of the European American Studies Association, Emory University's Web site Southernspaces.org, and the South Atlantic Humanities Center (at the Virginia Foundation for the Humanities, the University of Virginia, and Virginia Polytechnic Institute and State University) express the recent expansion of interest in regional study.

Observers of the American South have had much to absorb, given the rapid pace of recent change. The institutional framework for studying the South is broader and deeper than ever, yet the relationship between the older verities of regional study and new realities remains unclear. Given the extent of changes in the American South and in Southern Studies since the publication of the *Encyclopedia of Southern Culture*, the need for a new edition of that work is clear. Therefore, the Center for the Study of Southern Culture has once again joined the University of North Carolina Press to produce *The New Encyclopedia of Southern Culture*. As readers of the original edition will quickly see, *The New Encyclopedia* follows many of the scholarly principles and editorial conventions established in the original, but with one key difference; rather than being published in a single hardback volume, *The New Encyclopedia* is presented in a series of shorter individual volumes that build on the 24 original subject categories used in the *Encyclopedia* and adapt them to new scholarly developments. Some earlier *Encyclopedia* categories have been reconceptualized in light of new academic interests. For example, the subject section originally titled "Women's Life" is reconceived as a new volume, *Gender*, and the original "Black Life" section is more broadly interpreted as a volume on race. These changes reflect new analytical concerns that place the study of women and blacks in broader cultural systems, reflecting the emergence of, among other topics, the study of male culture and of whiteness. Both volumes draw as well from the rich recent scholarship on women's life and black life. In addition, topics with some thematic coherence are combined in a volume, such as *Law and Politics* and *Agriculture and Industry*. One new topic, *Foodways*, is the basis of a separate volume, reflecting its new prominence in the interdisciplinary study of southern culture.

Numerous individual topical volumes together make up *The New Encyclopedia of Southern Culture* and extend the reach of the reference work to wider audiences. This approach should enhance the use of the *Encyclopedia* in academic courses and is intended to be convenient for readers with more focused interests within the larger context of southern culture. Readers will have handy access to one-volume, authoritative, and comprehensive scholarly treatments of the major areas of southern culture.

We have been fortunate that, in nearly all cases, subject consultants who offered crucial direction in shaping the topical sections for the original edition have agreed to join us in this new endeavor as volume editors. When new volume editors have been added, we have again looked for respected figures who can provide not only their own expertise but also strong networks of scholars to help develop relevant lists of topics and to serve as contributors in their areas. The reputations of all our volume editors as leading scholars in their areas encouraged the contributions of other scholars and added to *The New Encyclopedia*'s authority as a reference work.

The New Encyclopedia of Southern Culture builds on the strengths of articles in the original edition in several ways. For many existing articles, original authors agreed to update their contributions with new interpretations and theoretical perspectives, current statistics, new bibliographies, or simple factual developments that needed to be included. If the original contributor was unable to update an article, the editorial staff added new material or sent it to another scholar for assessment. In some cases, the general editor and volume editors selected a new contributor if an article seemed particularly dated and new work indicated the need for a fresh perspective. And importantly, where new developments have warranted treatment of topics not addressed in the original edition, volume editors have commissioned entirely new essays and articles that are published here for the first time.

The American South embodies a powerful historical and mythical presence, both a complex environmental and geographic landscape and a place of the imagination. Changes in the region's contemporary socioeconomic realities and new developments in scholarship have been incorporated in the conceptualization and approach of *The New Encyclopedia of Southern Culture*. Anthropologist Clifford Geertz has spoken of culture as context, and this encyclopedia looks at the American South as a complex place that has served as the context for cultural expression. This volume provides information and perspective on the diversity of cultures in a geographic and imaginative place with a long history and distinctive character.

The *Encyclopedia of Southern Culture* was produced through major grants from the Program for Research Tools and Reference Works of the National Endowment for the Humanities, the Ford Foundation, the Atlantic-Richfield Foundation, and the Mary Doyle Trust. We are grateful as well to the individual donors to the Center for the Study of Southern Culture who have directly or indirectly supported work on *The New Encyclopedia of Southern Culture*. We thank the volume editors for their ideas in reimagining their subjects and the contributors of articles for their work in extending the usefulness of the book in new ways. We acknowledge the support and contributions of the faculty and staff at the Center for the Study of Southern Culture. Finally, we want especially to honor the work of William Ferris and Mary Hart on the *Encyclopedia of Southern Culture*. Bill, the founding director of the Center for the Study of Southern Culture, was coeditor, and his good work recruiting authors, editing text, selecting images, and publicizing the volume among a wide network of people was, of course, invaluable. Despite the many changes in the new encyclopedia, Bill's influence remains. Mary "Sue" Hart was also an invaluable member of the original encyclopedia team, bringing the careful and precise eye of the librarian, and an iconoclastic spirit, to our work.

INTRODUCTION

The Southern Historical Association began its work in 1934, bringing a new professional spirit to analyzing the American South's past, a past in which history has long been a key academic discipline in understanding the region. A structure of state archives, historical societies, journals, and academic historians has long promoted an interest in the events and people that were responsible for the South's sense of identity as a distinctive place. This historical focus has not been just a matter for professional academic historians. Genealogists and Civil War buffs, as well as academic historians, are tenacious researchers and vigorous discussants of the South's past. C. Vann Woodward's phrase "the burden of southern history" captures the profundity for many observers of a region whose past seems to make it forever different from other American places.

Cultural history is a relatively recent genre of southern history, and the *Encyclopedia of Southern Culture* was a significant contribution to its emergence. The search for meanings, the existence of complex worldviews, the interrelations of cultural attitudes and behaviors, attention to the linguistic basis of cultural systems, the role of material culture, the central importance of identity — all are among cultural history's concerns. The field naturally overlaps with other disciplines, drawing from theories and methodologies to illuminate the South's cultures rooted in social groupings and differing geographies within the region.

The study of history always dwells on time, the continuities and changes that give any society its character. The South's turbulent history includes the violent marginalization of an indigenous population, a biracial population often in conflict, attempts to force unity out of much diversity, fighting and losing a bloody Civil War on southern soil, migrations across and outside the region, a late but then rapid modernization, and a dramatic civil rights movement that brought fundamental change to the South's social order. With this background, historiographical debates over continuity and change in southern history have long been important. The new cultural history reimagines categories, though, to move beyond such debates. Politics, for example, is now political culture. Politics thus involves not just white men campaigning for government office but also the redrawing of the domestic sphere after emancipation with meanings for public life. Black women emerge in scholarship now as important figures in the political culture of the Progressive Era South, even though they could not vote.

The new cultural history looks at the positioning of the South in overlapping contexts. The South can appear to have been a premodern society with a slave workforce or a modern capitalist economy expressed in the plantation fields rather than the factory floors. Some scholars characterize it as postcolonial, but others see it as the leading edge at times of an imperial America. The South surely was a sectional historical concept defined against "the North," but southerners themselves always understood that local places and regions within "the South" complicated the region's identity. Today, we are attuned to positioning the South beyond North-South comparisons to see southern history in international contexts, whether the transatlantic South, the global Souths, or contemporary globalization.

The history volume provides a chronological and interpretive spine for *The New Encyclopedia of Southern Culture*. It focuses on key events, movements, and organizations. Civil War generals and civil rights leaders are here, as are southern-born U.S. presidents. The *Encyclopedia*, in general, focuses less on early southern history and more on its later development, but the editors have added material to reflect major historiographical issues in early southern history, including extensive coverage of Indians of the Southeast, an entry on the Atlantic world that explores the South's early international context, and several articles on slavery. The overview article has been extensively revised to provide a historical narrative for Southern Studies, stressing how collective memory has been at the heart of southern identity.

The NEW ENCYCLOPEDIA *of* SOUTHERN CULTURE

VOLUME 3 : HISTORY

HISTORY

The American South emerged as a particular geographic and imaginative place over the course of thousands of years of settlement, growth, and periodic transformations. Physiographic areas and ecological systems provided the foundation for developing regions within the southeastern part of North America, but a distinctive mix of peoples from differing ethnic backgrounds shaped the land and its human societies. Whether living in the uplands or lowlands, in the Alabama Black Belt or the Tennessee hill country, the Florida coast or the south Louisiana swamps, people in the American South developed particular cultural systems that reflected their cultural inheritances and adaptations to particular ecologies. People who lived in the South, and outsiders as well, constructed a compelling place of the imagination.

The development of the South as an identifiable socioeconomic region and cultural entity was a slow process, with complex meanings. Southern culture includes the dominant public culture of the region, expressed in officially sanctioned rituals and discourse. From the differing memories of the South's peoples some narratives became adopted as the authorized version of the past, institutionalized, and taught as the essential history of the region, a cultural component of the exercise of power by some southerners over others. The term also includes the folkways that grew out of the long demographic dominance of peoples from Western Europe and Western Africa, the centrality of an agricultural economy, and the rural context for the life of most of the region's people until recently. The cultural interaction of the region's people grew out of this face-to-face society. Southern culture also includes the alternative cultures that were nurtured in ethnic, racial, gendered, and socially classed communities across the South. The cultures of the American South have never been static or uncontested in their claims of authenticity and influence. Recent scholarship has expanded the time frames of southern cultural studies, going back in time beyond the early-19th-century sectional conflict that promoted a regional consciousness. Historians and other scholars also are breaking down the borders of the South to focus on regions within the larger South and to explore border areas, as well as core zones, of southern culture. Observers now go beyond the usual North-South dichotomy within North America to position the South as a part of the Atlantic world system of the 18th and 19th centuries and within the global world of the contemporary era.

Ruins of Windsor, antebellum mansion, in Port Gibson, Miss. (Marion Post Wolcott, photographer, Library of Congress [LC-USF-34-54814-D], Washington, D.C.)

Anthropologist Clifford Geertz argues that culture is a "historically transmitted" pattern of meaning, suggesting the central importance of historical experience and the collective memory of it in providing a sense of identity and purpose to a culture. Two points are central in exploring the relationship between southern history and culture. The first is the connection between history and the sense of identity among southerners as a distinct people. The southern people have had characteristic assumptions, values, and attitudes apart from other Americans. When did that identity arise and how was it transmitted to future generations? How did historical events and forces create a sense of common purpose among people in the South, and how was that purpose passed on from generation to generation, adapting to new circumstances? How did a sense of history in itself contribute to the identity? The second broad point to explore is the way of life at the heart of southern culture, the complex pattern of institutions, rituals, myths, material objects, and other aspects of a functioning culture. This pattern reveals how the region differed from other areas of the United States in behavior, as well as attitude. It also shows the degree to which cultural integration occurred over time, despite formal attempts to maintain racial separation between whites, blacks, and Native Americans.

Origins. The narrative starts with prehistory, with the Native Americans settling in environments that would someday become known as "the South." Indians were not just forerunners of later peoples who would call themselves southerners. Native Americans marked geographical spaces as cultural places, parts of what archaeologists and anthropologists label a southeastern culture area. Through prehistory and protohistory, Native Americans in the Southeast created a context of environmental adaptations, material goods, and mythic representations that the southeastern culture area embodied. Local geographies were already apparent. Archaeologists identify five environmental zones—proto-regions—in the late-prehistoric South: Appalachian Highlands (where indigenous people combined women's farming with men's hunting in isolated mountains and valleys); Piedmont Plateau (sizable populations lived off plentiful game from forests and from farming in the alluvial valleys); Mississippi Alluvial Valley (which had the largest populations of the Southeast and the most productive lands); Coastal Plain (a place of piney woods, alluvial valleys, abundant rivers and streams, and sandy coastal areas); and Subtropical South Florida (whose marine and estuarine resources made dense settlement possible).

The Mississippian tradition (A.D. 1000–1700) was particularly notable for the rise of powerful chiefdoms in the Southeast. Ritual centers appeared around platform mounds that were places for the performance of the Southeastern Ceremonial Cult, which provided unifying artistic and mythical features across the region. In the early 13th century, the Mississippian tradition began to decline, with the depletion of timber and game, chronic tribal warfare, and loss of population. Southeastern tribes adapted and reorganized. The arrival of Europeans in the 15th century and after challenged Native Americans of the Southeast who were undergoing, in many places, societal reorganization, and new diseases and warfare contributed to their decline. Tribes nonetheless combined into new groupings, and through much of the colonial era, powerful confederacies still controlled the lands south of the Ohio and Potomac rivers and east of the Great Plains. Peter Wood has shown that seven out of ten Indians in 1685 lived in seven non-English regions of the South: Florida, Georgia and

Alabama south of the Appalachian foothills, southern Appalachia, Mississippi, lower Louisiana, east Texas, and an area below the Ohio River known as the "Shawnee interior." By the mid-18th century Indians were no longer effectively challenging white authority in Virginia and the Carolinas, but in the interior and border areas the Indian population was twice as large as the combined white-black population. Still, though, the Indian population of the South had declined overall from 199,400 in 1685 to 55,600 in 1775.

Spanish and French explorers were on the leading edge of European incursions into Indian lands of the South. The legend of the new Andalucia helped shape Spanish exploration and colonization along the Gulf Coast. Lucas Vázquez de Ayllón claimed to have discovered in 1521 a new land along the same latitude as the province of Andalucia in Spain, a place of abundance that could produce those Iberian essentials, olive oil and wine. The Spanish thus were drawn to Florida, founding settlements there in the 1560s, including at St. Augustine. Spanish Florida extended northward to South Carolina and became a focus for the European imperial rivalries and close Caribbean ties that would influence the emergence of the American South. France laid the groundwork for opening up European development of the Mississippi River valley through early explorations from the north and by founding the colony of Louisiana in 1699, aiming to secure claims to the Mississippi River, extend the French fur trade into the South, and establish a maritime presence along the Gulf.

The English first attempted a colony in North America in 1587 when settlers arrived in Roanoke Island off the coast of present-day North Carolina, but Jamestown in Virginia was the first successful English colony, established in 1607. Other southern colonies would follow, but they had separate identities, leading historian Wesley Frank Craven to note that historians of the colonial South have "to write about the South when there was no South." When southern self-consciousness emerged, it grew out of concrete differences in institutions and attitudes that had appeared earlier.

The early South differed from the northern colonies in physical environment and motives for settlement. The first settlers in Virginia were charmed by the sights and smells of the new land. Observers focused on the climate as a key factor in the region. The climate favored a long growing season, which promoted an agricultural economy based on tobacco, rice, and indigo and, later, on cotton and sugar. The climate and environment affected architecture, clothing, and seemingly even the very pace of life and speech. Geography, however, unified neither the early nor the later South. The region is divided by mountain ranges and rivers, and its plains and valleys run north and south, connecting with land in other regions. Partly because of geography, different societies developed in the colonial South: an aristocratic society along the Chesapeake Bay; a second elite-dominated society in the Carolina Lowcountry; a frontier land to the west of the Tidewater; and perhaps another, loosely formed society in central North Carolina. The Chesapeake and Carolina Lowcountry were distinctive regions for African slaves in the colonial era. Their numbers were greater in the Low-country, as they formed a majority of the overall population by the 1770s. The nature of slave work differed in the two regions (task work in South Carolina and gang labor in the Chesapeake), as did the possibilities of preserving aspects of African culture. The Sea Islands off the Carolina Coast would long represent the hearth of African cultural influence in the South. Mechal Sobel has found evidence of considerable white-black interaction among premodern European and African settlers in the early Chesapeake.

The motives of early Virginia settlers and of later southern colonists differed significantly from those of the North. Although both groups were predomi-nantly middle-class English, the southern colonists came primarily for eco-nomic reasons, seeking opportunities not available in England. If the Puritans established New England to be a City on a Hill, the early southerners portrayed their area as a new Garden of Eden. The first signs of an emerging southern self-consciousness appeared couched in this mythic outlook. But ease of environ-ment seemed to promote a decline in the moral character of the people. Resi-dents south of Chesapeake Bay compared themselves with northern settlers, sometimes to their own disadvantage. William Byrd II, for example, saw New Englanders as "Frugal and Industrious," whereas those in the southern colonies had "very loose and Profligate Morals." Blessed with a beneficent land, south-erners seemed to give in to the environment and failed to live up to another part of their cultural legacy—the demands of a Christianity heavily tinged with Calvinism.

The colonial South had already begun to develop in distinctive ways. New England made a partial commitment to public education as early as the 1640s, but the South did so only much later. Eight colleges existed in the North by 1776, compared to only one (the College of William and Mary) in the South. The colonial South lacked not only schools and colleges but libraries, books, and periodicals as well. Religion was also institutionally weak, lacking the inten-sity, idealism, and organization of that in the North. Anglicanism, an American version of the English national religion, was predominant in the southern colo-nies, providing a degree of unity through religious worship services, a common theology and moral values, and education. Anglicanism embodied an influential social model that shaped southern development. Anglican ministers allied themselves with the gentry, and upper-class southerners accepted an ethic of social class differences, along with paternalistic responsibilities.

The origins of distinctive southern social relations lie in the colonial era. At the top of the social structure was a small class of large planters who dominated society through control of land, wealth, and political power. Prominent southern colonial planter families included the Byrds, Randolphs, Carters, Burwells, Pages, Beverleys, Lees, Masons, Fitzhughs, and Wormsleys in Virginia and the Rutledges, Pringles, and Draytons in South Carolina. Their names have reappeared throughout the ages of southern history as symbols of social prestige and southern style. The life of the English country gentry was their model, and their mansions are symbolic of southern gentility. The planters dominated the imagination of the region, symbolizing social success.

Family and neighborhood networks were informal but effective community institutions, which bolstered white unity and, especially, white elite male authority. The household patriarchy that hardened in the 17th century made white women increasingly subservient. Bacon's Rebellion (1676) was a watershed in the consolidation of elite male power. Wealthy planters had gradually gained control of the best Virginia lands in the 16th century, leaving poorer sorts frustrated. Without many community ties, they became followers of Nathaniel Bacon in a conflict with social class, race, and gender implications. The planter elite used its political authority to put down the unrest and assert a new level of control over society, subduing blacks and white women more authoritatively than before. Women were excluded from roles in public life, but increased prosperity and genteel living standards provided privileged compensations.

Members of the middle class were sometimes related by blood or marriage to the wealthiest planters. They enjoyed a degree of social mobility themselves and aspired to be seen as gentry. Beneath the middle class were the poorer whites. This group included landless farmers, farmworkers, unskilled laborers, indentured servants (who agreed to work a period of time for a colonial employer in exchange for passage to America), and craftsmen who were not self-supporting. A separate, peculiar group known already in the 1700s as the "poor whites" also existed. They appear in colonial writings as a defeated people, subject to disease, beset by illiteracy, given to laziness (in middle-class eyes), and living in physical isolation on the worst lands.

African southerners were at the bottom of the social structure. A system of white racial dominance developed as soon as Europeans, Indians, and blacks encountered each other in the early days of Virginia. A Dutch ship brought 20 Africans to Jamestown in 1619, the same year that Virginia established the

The Plantation (c. 1825), artist unknown (Gift of Edgar Williams and Bernice Chrysler Garbisch, 1963, Metropolitan Museum of Art [63.210.3], New York, N.Y.)

House of Burgesses, embodying the hope of political liberty. The slave population expanded throughout the late 1600s and early 1700s, creating economic prosperity but fueling whites' fear of blacks. The Stono Rebellion (1739) in South Carolina was a landmark that led to increased regulation of slave life and efforts to restrict the slave trade. Southern whites saw slavery as a method of racial control, as well as an economic system. Although powerless, blacks became one of the central factors in early southern society, both passively and actively.

Early southern culture developed in a context of transatlantic influences. Historians have long written of the triangular trade between the Caribbean, New England, and the South, and European and African cultures were surely formative ones on the South. The Atlantic world provided economic connections for southern planters raising staple crops in the emerging capitalist world system. Slaves from Africa represented the degree to which commodification could go, but they became a formative influence in an emerging creolized southern society. European intellectual life, from Enlightenment ideas to evangelical Protestant faith, provided worldviews for southerners who embraced them passionately. When Barbados planters came to South Carolina, they stamped the Lowcountry with what became tenacious, if evolving, connections to the Caribbean Islands.

Scholars have only recently begun a serious study of the cultural integration that began in the South in the colonial era. The history of the South begins, in fact, with the role of the American Indians as pioneers of cultural patterns in the southern part of North America. Early Indian cultures established many of the patterns involving use of natural resources and location of settlements and transportation routes that Europeans later exploited. Indians introduced Europeans and Africans to New World ways of living, and many white and black southerners have Indian ancestry. The Indians named rivers and states. They influenced the agricultural and dietary habits of later southerners, and folk medicine used by southerners is a mixture of Indian herbal knowledge and European and African elements. Many of the folk tales in southern oral tradition are influenced by Native American lore.

English colonists adapted their institutions and customs to the American environment and combined them with native ways. British social hierarchy, European musical and literary forms, Christian institutional forms and worldview, European agricultural methods—all of these became a part of early southern culture. Upper-class, elite culture from the colonial period to contemporary times has been based on values and behavior of the English gentry. In exploring the cultural contributions of previously overlooked groups in the South, recent scholars have shown little interest in English cultural contributions, but these contributions were surely crucial. Later generations of influential southerners often acted as though English culture was the South's culture.

By the beginning of the 18th century African slaves mediated between Indian and European cultures. West Africans and Indians, who were more familiar with the South's kind of environment than the English, shared a similar body of customs and knowledge. As Indians declined in power and numbers, blacks helped preserve traditional Indian lore and passed it on to Europeans. Africans also brought useful knowledge with them from their homelands. They were familiar with techniques of herding livestock and cultivating rice and indigo, which became key early crops in the early Carolina Lowcountry. Some crops may even have been introduced from Africa, and plants such as okra surely were. Europeans realized the economic advantages of slaves with such knowledge and made use of them. Despite the rigid legal boundaries of an emerging caste system, cultural integration was beginning through the transfer of knowledge, customs, and ways of separate peoples.

While cultural integration of a sort was occurring among white Europeans, African blacks, and Native Americans, a distinctive African-southern culture was also appearing. Before 1700, black cultural life was restricted by the relatively small numbers of slaves in North America and by their wide geographical distribution. The 18th century saw the forging of a rigid racial caste system and the creation of a separate black culture by slaves. South Carolina was the center of this emerging black culture because it contained a critical mass of Africans concentrated in a relatively narrow, coastal, rice-growing area.

About 60 percent of all slaves brought to what would be the United States came between 1720 and 1780, and these years represent the cultural watershed for black southerners. Africans from different areas and tribal backgrounds learned in the New World to communicate through pidgin languages and found a common identity in the South. The common factor brought from Africa was an intellectual outlook, a worldview with definite attitudes about the deity, time, social relations, and rituals of life. Slaves preserved African notions about kinship, the individual's place in the cosmos, musical forms, and concrete skills such as metalworking and wood carving, herding, boat making and navigation, and rice cultivation. Where slaves were concentrated in significant numbers, blacks created distinctive southern cultural traditions involving everything from music and dance to customs of child raising, crafting, and even speaking. The planter's mansion was recognized from the colonial era on as a symbol for one aspect of southern culture; the slave quarters deserve recognition as the hearthstone for another central aspect of that culture.

The frontier experience was also crucial to the formation of a southern character. In the late 1600s and early 1700s settlers flocked west, and sectional tensions appeared between Tidewater aristocrats and backcountry farmers. These were class conflicts, reflecting the social divisions between frontier and Tidewater. The Upcountry Piedmont frontier was the scene of Bacon's Rebellion in Virginia in 1676 and the Regulator movement in western North Carolina in 1766–71 on the eve of revolution.

Some disputes on the frontier were also ethnic conflicts. Land-hungry Scots-Irish and German settlers migrated from western Pennsylvania into the Piedmont and later crossed the Appalachian Mountains. The Scots-Irish represented the other large ethnic tradition introduced into southern life in the colonial era, one that became closely associated with the frontier. If the Tidewater aristocracy was English in style and outlook, the frontier was predominantly Scots-Irish. Like the Africans, this group brought distinctive institutions and customs, which reflected long-held attitudes about kinship, work, religion, music, and herding and farming skills. By the end of the colonial era, the Scots-Irish had established communities in what would become Tennessee and Kentucky. This was the "dark and bloody ground" of legend, with brutal warfare between white settlers and Indians and a struggle for survival in the lush wilderness of the Great Meadow. Daniel Boone was the romantic symbol of this phase of southern life.

The frontier experience promoted both individualism and communal neighborliness, impatience with formal institutions, and allegiance to family; it encouraged hard work; it promoted violence, and yet evangelical religion flourished there. Most southerners lived in frontier conditions up to the time of the Civil War. Recent migrants to the areas they lived in, they engaged in subsistence or small-scale commodity farming, used rivers and streams for transportation, and vividly remembered the Indian wars that preceded settlement. They lived in simple log cabins, which became another major symbol of southern culture. Many of the traits now called "southern" were nurtured in these isolated outposts. The frontier experience was common in America, but perhaps nowhere else in the nation did frontier attitudes and ways persist over so many generations through the preservation of a rural folk culture permeated by the effects of the frontier.

The backcountry was one center of the cultural diversity that characterized the colonial South. Colonists from Germany, Switzerland, the Netherlands, France, Scotland, and Ireland joined with the larger numbers of English and Africans, often mingling on the frontier. Charleston became a center of cosmopolitan life, with communities of French Huguenots and Sephardic Jews adding to a multicultural mix. Native Americans met these colonists in stages of advancement onto the frontier: first the coastal tribes, then such stronger nomadic tribes as the Yamassee, and finally such advanced tribes as the Creeks, Cherokees, Chickasaws, Seminoles, and Catawbas. The interaction of Indians, deerskin trappers, traders, and herdsmen and farmers promoted cultural exchange, the remnants of which would remain long after the South ceased attracting this diversity of immigrants in the 19th century.

By the late colonial period, authors of various texts had created the beginnings of a southern literature that promoted a sense of collective memory about the past. Although southern colonists lacked the spiritually driven introspection of New Englanders, they did reflect on their communal role. John Smith, the early governor of Jamestown, wrote a book about only two decades of Virginia's experience and called it a "Historie." Robert Beverley claimed the same sense of renewing the past in his *History and Present State of Virginia* (1705), and

William Stith's *History and First Discovery of Virginia* (1747) looked back on the colonial founders as a heroic group and the past as better than the present — the beginnings of a familiar southern lament. With the Indians effectively subjugated in the English colonies, writers began romanticizing the tribes as a vanishing part of the emergent South.

Historians do not agree as to when a self-conscious southern identity appeared. The American Revolutionary era (1775–89) was, though, one landmark in its definition. John Alden referred to it as the time of the "First South," which was at that time geographically defined toward the west by the Mississippi River with major settlements along the Atlantic Coast. The phrase "southern states" was frequently used in those years. At the beginning of the period, though, the term "southern" was used to describe all the colonies except those in New England, from New York to Georgia. When Charles Mason and Jeremiah Dixon drew a surveyor's line between Pennsylvania and Maryland in the 1760s to settle a boundary disagreement, there was no understanding that a "North" and a "South" were being divided. But "southern" soon acquired a more restrictive meaning, as "middle states" was increasingly used to describe New York, New Jersey, Pennsylvania, and Delaware. There was the abiding problem of definition, with some observers including Maryland as southern and others excluding it. By the end of the Revolution the common view was that the northern boundary of the South was the Ohio River and the Mason-Dixon line. The southern population in the first census of 1790 showed approximately 1,900,000 people (over a third of whom were black) below that line and 2,000,000 above it.

The Revolutionary War gave the colonists a common enemy and served to draw northern and southern colonists together. Many unifying forces existed: a common language, a predominantly British and Western European background among colonists (except for the politically powerless slaves), a clear cultural and political heritage, and transportation, communication, and trade ties among the colonies. The term "American" was increasingly used both in the colonies and outside of them to describe the residents of the 13 colonies.

Nationalism surely triumphed in the Revolutionary era. White southerners played a crucial role in events from the First Continental Congress in 1774 to President George Washington's administration in the 1790s. Yet nationalism was a necessary precondition for the appearance of sectionalist concerns. The Revolution, for example, created heroes who were national but also local and regional. Disagreements between the North and South appeared as early as the conflict over the embargo sponsored by the First Continental Congress, and as John Alden has written, "that body during the years 1781–1787 was often rived by strife between South and North. Southern fears of Northern domination appeared in the Philadelphia Convention of 1787, and were frequently and forcefully asserted in the contests over ratification of the Constitution which took place below the Mason-Dixon line."

Economic conflicts emerged over regional interests, especially those related to trade and to the protection of slavery. The Revolutionary ideology expressed in words such as "liberty" and "equality," in documents such as the Declaration of Independence, and in emerging antislavery sentiment made southerners aware of their dilemma as slave owners in a democratic republic and thereby helped to promote regional self-consciousness. Events that dramatized the South's racial situation included the debate over slavery during the Philadelphia Convention in 1787, the slave uprising in Santo Domingo in the early 1790s, and Gabriel Prosser's slave conspiracy near Richmond in 1800. These events connected southern identity to peculiar racial concerns and promoted racial fears. They helped to crystallize the South's commitment to slavery as a system of race control. By 1800 southerners felt threatened by outsiders, generating the siege mentality that would later characterize the evolving southern identity.

Thomas Jefferson, with his party and supporters, was the central political and intellectual force in the South during the years from the Revolution to the 1820s, and he is crucial to understanding southern developments. The South in this era, according to Clement Eaton and others, appeared to be a liberal, humane society. Southern leaders such as Jefferson and Madison reflected the intellectual influence of the Enlightenment, expressing belief in the natural rights of human beings and confidence in human reason. Freedom of thought and expression was respected, and the rhetoric of liberty and equality was articulated not only by Jefferson but by many other southerners.

Racial fears did not disappear, though, nor did the commitment to the maintenance of white supremacy. Slavery was not dying out, contrary to the hopes of some earlier southern leaders. Most southerners saw it as a profitable system when well managed; the planter's lifestyle depended upon it; social success—the southern version of the American dream—was defined within its parameters; and the fear of black equality without slavery remained. Racism was the dark underside of the luminous Jeffersonian dream of a chosen agrarian people. Jefferson's own relationship with his slave Sally Hemings symbolized the complex separation and connectedness of southern whites and blacks in an evolving slave society.

The Jeffersonian era experienced an economic transformation that contributed to southern identity. The invention of the cotton gin in 1793, the emergence of sugar growing in Louisiana in the mid-1790s, and the rising prices for frontier lands in the early 1800s brought an increased commitment to an agriculture of staple crops. Outlandish profits could be made by a few people, further strengthening the power of the elite planters. Cotton became the prime symbol of the South's expansive development into the Old Southwest in this era. Like Faulkner's Thomas Sutpen in *Absalom, Absalom!*, the pioneer planters of the Deep South carved slave plantations out of frontier forests. The mentality of the planter was thus transferred to the frontier; in the Southwest a rough-hewn character such as Andrew Jackson could become a self-made man and take on the trappings of an elite planter. The raw materialism of the frontier challenged the paternalism of the Tidewater planters as a cultural ideal.

Old South to New South. The Civil War has generally been seen as the crucial watershed in southern history. For the cultural historian, though, the period from 1830 to 1910 can be seen as a single era. After 1830 the self-conscious identification with "the South" notably increased, and a distinctive pattern of institutions, values, myths, and rituals took shape, reflecting a southern worldview that developed but never fully matured before the Civil War. The war and Reconstruction stand as the crystallizing events that promoted the postbellum development of a peculiar regional culture.

The years 1830 to 1832 were particularly important in the growth of a southern regional consciousness. Sectionalism dramatically appeared in politics during the preceding decade with the Missouri Compromise of 1819–20. After a bitter debate, Congress admitted Missouri as a slave state and Maine as a free state, and drew a 36° 30' line of latitude, prohibiting slavery above the line. The Missouri controversy awakened southern fears over the region's position as a minority section in the Union and pointed the way to an emerging regional consciousness that took form after 1830.

A minority psychology developed as the northern population outgrew that of the South. North-South conflict developed over control of the national government and the direction of national policy. A southern states' rights philosophy and the fears underlying it were seen in the nullification crisis of the late 1820s and early 1830s. South Carolina challenged the national government, specifically over the issue of the national government's power to pass a tariff, but more generally over the rights of the majority to legislate over a minority—defined as a regional population. John C. Calhoun emerged as the premier figure of antebellum southern politics, a defender of southern rights, one of the nation's greatest political philosophers, and a symbol of the southern consciousness.

The driving force propelling southern identity was racial fear. Rumors of slave unrest periodically appeared, reinforcing white uneasiness. The Nat Turner rebellion in 1831, a slave uprising led by a visionary slave preacher, killed 60 whites in Southampton County, Va., and became a symbol thereafter for the potential for slave rebellion. It solidified white fears and led to new restrictions on the activities of slaves and free blacks. William Lloyd Garrison, one of the chief devil figures to southern whites, also stirred racial fears in 1832 when he began publishing the *Liberator*, a Boston antislavery newspaper that called for immediate, uncompensated emancipation of the slaves. He led a strident new antislavery movement that stressed the immorality of slavery. The southern reaction was an equally strident intellectual defense of the "peculiar institution" — a proslavery argument that justified the institution as a positive good, using religious, scientific, and historical arguments.

Displacement of the southeastern Indian tribes was also a part of an emerging southern white identity that drew boundaries. The Louisiana Purchase (1803) opened the possibility of new western space for Indian reservations, and the Removal Act (1830) made clear the federal government would not shield the Indian tribes from state efforts to remove them and would open tribal lands to aggressive white frontier settlers.

By the 1840s southern attitudes toward history were beginning to change with the growing sense of regional self-consciousness. More and more southerners after 1830 began questioning the national republican tradition as the proper framework for telling the regional story. The conflict with the North caused southern whites to stress their belief in a common historical experience and to play down differences within the South. The Virginia Historical Society appeared in 1831, the first such organization in the South, and other historical societies proliferated in the region during the next two decades of growing North-South tensions. By the 1850s southern histories had shifted from focusing on the national contributions of southern states to documenting the differences in the historical experiences of the South and the North. Southerners believed, moreover, that only they could be trusted to write their history. Dates of historic events in the South were ritually honored with celebration that praised the South's noble history. National Revolutionary heroes such as Patrick Henry and Francis Marion were seen after 1830 as state or regional heroes. The refocusing of American history into southern history was a factor in forging a self-conscious regional identity.

Religion emerged in the early 19th century as a defining feature of the South, a crucial part of a growing regional self-consciousness. Evangelical Protestant groups emerged as small sectarian groups in the late 18th century, at first antislavery, egalitarian in promoting new gender roles, and generally questioning of existing authorities. This evangelical counterculture challenged the South's hierarchal social order, though, and within a few decades Baptists and Methodists began their drive to convert southerners, white and black, to the gospel of Jesus. This faith began on the frontier, and evangelicalism's impact was felt in the Midwest and Northeast, as well as the South.

The sectional conflict entangled ministers and laypersons in North-South politics. Northern ministers joined reform efforts and injected considerable moral passion into the antislavery movement. Southern preachers, meanwhile, provided the biblical arguments for the proslavery movement. In the mid-1840s, southern Baptists and Methodists split from their northern religionists and formed separate southern denominations, as the Presbyterians from the South did once the Civil War began. These regional churches remained carriers of the regional identity and repositories of southern folkways long after the war ended.

The 1830s also witnessed the emergence of a new mythic center for the southern identity: the Cavalier image, which embodied the belief that southerners were descendants of aristocratic Royalist exiles from Cromwell's England in the 1600s. Northern colonists, according to the legend, were Puritans by origin. Many Americans came to believe that these two "types" generated northerners and southerners with differing temperaments, psychologies, and concerns.

John Pendleton Kennedy's *Swallow Barn* appeared in 1832 and became a prototype for the romantic plantation legend. Kennedy and other writers portrayed the southern plantation as an orderly, feudal world of harmonious, static, hierarchical relationships between master and slave. The southern planter was a noble, honorable figure, and the southern lady, a vital part of the myth, was chaste, saintly, sacrificial, and spiritual. Slaves were childlike and loyal. The contrast between the Cavalier planter and the grasping Yankee was popular among conservative northerners and had remarkable power among southern whites.

Northerners and southerners still shared much in this era, but belief in the differences between northerners and southerners had some basis in reality. The slave-based plantation system was uniquely southern, and its crops were distinctive to the region. The nature of the southern population was different from that elsewhere, with English, African, and Scots-Irish elements remaining dominant at a time when the northern population was being transformed through immigration. Southerners remained rural, while industry, immigration, urbanization, and reform were changing the North.

The southern social structure was the background against which a distinctive culture appeared. Planter hegemony over society was based partly on control of the South's wealth. Wealthy planters owned the best farming land, and the productivity of these lands was greater than that of smaller farms. The planter elite included two groups: those traditional southern families whose wealth extended back several generations or more, taking on the refinements and prestige of "old money," and a larger group of self-made men, humble in origins, who had seized opportunities and luck to amass fortunes from cotton. Eugene D. Genovese has portrayed the planter elite as paternalist and precapitalist, but other historians point out their essentially bourgeois outlook. Their cultural significance was in their control of cultural and social values in the South. The "big house" was the tangible symbol of their power over the southern imagination.

The yeoman farmer, the independent landowner, was the Jeffersonian ideal and W. J. Cash's "man at the center." Historians overlooked the importance of the "plain folk" until Frank L. Owsley in the 1930s showed they were the largest class in the Old South. White racism brought a shared racial solidarity between the wealthy planters and the yeoman farmers. The commitment of the South was to both slavery and democracy. The term "Herrenvolk democracy" describes the southern system of democracy for the master class and repression for a subordinate group. The region's political rhetoric said that all white men were created equal with inalienable rights, which depended, though, on black subjugation. Seeing slaves around them led whites to value their own freedom and to celebrate their bond with whites in other classes. This ideal triumphed in the period of Jacksonian democracy in the 1830s and promoted a sense of internal southern white solidarity in facing the North.

The yeoman ethic was an individualistic belief system that valued self-reliance, material acquisition, private property rights, and honorable behavior. A sense of community was nurtured by logrollings, house-raisings, dances, camp meetings, political barbecues, and neighborly visiting. Yeomen sometimes owned slaves, but they worked beside them in the fields, ate similar food, and lived in similar houses. Owning slaves defined social success in the South, and aspiring landowners were often ambitious to rise into the more substantial planter class.

Slaves were another crucial social group in the antebellum South. White polemicists labeled them the "mudsill," the working class whose labor made the plantations and farms operate. Slavery rested on force, with occasions for violence and brutality. African Americans responded to its demands in many ways—some openly rebelling, some with small daily resistance, and others acquiescing to its realities. Slaves developed a rich culture that sustained them. Part of the appeal of evangelical Protestantism was its spiritual egalitarianism

—everyone was equal in God's sight, providing dignity and empowerment to the disfranchised. Spirituals gave a musical vision of freedom and the hope of eventual eternal peace. While slave marriage was illegal throughout the South, slaves developed a "fictive family" tradition, with parents, grandparents, extended kin, and communal responsibility within the slave quarters for all children. The slave quarters rank with the log cabin and the mansion as a hearth of southern culture.

African Americans in the South asserted their own collective identity, as they tried to make sense of issues of slavery and freedom. For example, through memories of the past, African Americans put themselves in the history of Virginia. White and black writers lauded the sacrifices of Revolutionary War slaves who reported on British activities and contributed to American independence. Blacks remembered Gabriel's planned slave rebellion and the Nat Turner rebellion with songs and novels. Both the American Revolution and the remembered slave rebellions represented the ideals of liberty and equality upon which African Americans maintained they had a special claim. The Bible, with its images of God's chosen people and of Moses and Jesus as liberators, offered innumerable passages that suggested God's Word was especially meaningful for an enslaved people.

North-South tensions became an urgent national issue during the 1850s. The debate over slavery in the western territories, which were gained as a result of the Mexican War, stirred sectionalism to a new pitch in the late 1840s. The Nashville Convention, an expression of southern consciousness during this debate, met in 1850, but moderates controlled it, and the situation was diffused by the Compromise of 1850. A litany of laws and events polarized the nation throughout the decade: the publication of *Uncle Tom's Cabin* (1851), the Kansas-Nebraska Act (1854), the civil war in Kansas (late 1850s), South Carolina congressman Preston Brooks's beating of Massachusetts senator Charles Sumner in Congress (1856), the death of the Whig Party and emergence of a northern-based Republican Party, the Supreme Court's *Dred Scott* decision (1857), John Brown's raid on Harpers Ferry, Va. (1859), and the election of Abraham Lincoln (1860).

The Civil War was the crucial event cementing the southern white identity. The experience of fighting and losing a war would isolate the region's people. As C. Vann Woodward has written, losing the Civil War became a central burden of southern history.

The Confederate States of America stands as the supreme statement of the southern desire for self-determination. The Confederacy aimed at preserving a traditional life that seemed threatened by outside intervention. It did not at-

Ambrotype of two Confederate soldiers from Georgia
(Georgia Department of Archives and History, Atlanta)

tempt any utopian transformation for the future but represented instead a conservative political revolution aimed at preventing social and economic changes in its fundamental institutions. White southerners did not simply justify the war as crusade for slavery. Orators emphasized not race but the issues of self-determination, localism, righteous holiness, and constitutional rights. Nonetheless, there is no escaping the racial dimension of a war fought by a slave society; the conflict was a logical culmination of the proslavery argument. The Confederate vice president Alexander Stephens even admitted that slavery was the cornerstone of the Confederacy. As the war and its suffering went on, deep social cleavages appeared. Bread riots occurred in cities, and yeoman farmers came to believe that they were suffering more than wealthy plantation families.

White southerners asserted a long collective memory in forging a new Confederate identity. They put forward the American Revolution as their heritage, with the Confederacy an attempt to reclaim its legacy from a United States that had become corrupt and tyrannical. They called the Confederacy the Second American Revolution and Jefferson Davis the Second George Washington. Northern soldiers were said to be Hessians, referring to the German mercenaries the English hired during the Revolution. Southerners changed the title of the "Star-Spangled Banner" to the "Stars and Bars." They continued to celebrate the Fourth of July as a reminder that southern ancestors had helped win American independence. As the war went on, a new pantheon of specifically Confederate heroes emerged as symbols of an emerging new Confederate identity based in wartime experience and becoming the basis for the postwar memory of the Lost Cause.

Historians generally agree that southerners during the Civil War developed only a limited sense of political nationalism and that a romantic cultural nationalism may have been more a product of the war than a cause for it. Novelist Robert Penn Warren wrote that the Confederacy became immortal, a "City of the Soul," when it expired, and the memory of it has had a tenacious hold on the southern imagination. No southern *War and Peace, Guernica*, or "Gettysburg Address" came out of it. Its tragedy, however, surely shaped postwar southern life. Southerners learned the lessons of defeat, the lessons of human limitation and mortality, and the virtues of upholding the basic human values of family, community, and economic survival. The war was a tremendous bonding experience for southern whites who had tried and failed at independence; that separate history would forever differentiate the region from others in the nation.

The economic base of southern culture had been transformed by the end of the war. A $2 billion investment in land had been destroyed, a $3 million cotton crop confiscated, factories dismantled, banks closed, public buildings damaged, and cities leveled. The physical landscape had changed. Throughout the South there were damaged bridges, roads, and railroad tracks, and burned cotton gins, factories, fences, and barns. Chimneys stood without houses. Few horses, mules, sheep, cattle, or hogs could be found. Items necessary for daily living had vanished, and no replacements could be found. Lack of tools, livestock, and seed made even good land useless.

The human toll was even more awesome. There were 258,000 dead and

150,000 disabled. Every third household saw one of its members dead, a rate that was four times that of the North. Lingering wounds and illnesses plagued the surviving soldiers; the number of widows and orphaned children was uncounted. A spiritual depression settled on the region, as its people tried to understand how they could lose a war they had been told was a holy one. The South was cast back into subsistence living, into frontier life, "the frontier the Yankee made," said W. J. Cash. The North moved into a new modern era after the war while the South reverted to a primitive, violent, individualistic, provincial life. A culture of poverty appeared that would haunt the region.

The Reconstruction era from 1865 to 1877 was nearly equal to the Civil War in forging a self-conscious white southern identity. It marked white southerners against northerners on the one hand and against southern blacks on the other. Fear, grievance, defensiveness, and the memory of hardship and bitterness—all were central to cementing this identity. The southern white view of Reconstruction was preserved and passed on for generations by the South's official history books, by literature such as Thomas Dixon's *The Clansman* (1905), and by family stories told generation after generation. Eventually the southern white legend of Reconstruction was nationally reinforced by D. W. Griffith's film *The Birth of a Nation* and academic histories produced by William A. Dunning and his students at Columbia University.

Journalist Hodding Carter called Reconstruction "the angry scar," and it was a major setback for black-white cultural integration in the South. Under slavery there had been much social interaction because of the intimate role blacks played in the lives of southern whites. Blacks helped in the birthing, nursing, and raising of white children; they tended to white men and women throughout their lives and were there at high moments of marrying and dying. Blacks continued that intimate role but under very different circumstances. There was less paternalism and less institutional, public contact.

Developments in religion were revealing. Blacks had once worshipped as members of the same churches as whites. To be sure, slaves had their "invisible institution," the religion they practiced in their slave quarters, outside the bounds of Christian institutions. Nonetheless, their Christian worship was a shared communion, where baptism, the ritual of church worship, and the ecstasy of revivalism were shared with whites. During Reconstruction blacks withdrew from white churches and set up independent congregations. They joined the northern-based African Methodist Episcopal Church or the African Methodist Episcopal Church Zion in large numbers. Others joined the Colored Methodist Episcopal Church, an organization created with the assistance of southern white Methodists. Thousands of independent black Baptist churches emerged logically from the Baptist heritage of local church autonomy. These churches were often established with the encouragement and active support of white congregations, and fraternal ties remained. This development was one of the most significant results of Reconstruction and was vital for the emergence of a distinct black culture. It was a peaceable separation; the violence seen in politics was not reproduced here. But in terms of a culturally integrated southern life, it was a setback. Ironically, white and black southerners shared many beliefs, but the region's spiritual life was now segregated.

The mind of the white South after the Civil War was dominated by myths — the romantic legend of the Old South, the tragic Lost Cause, and the pragmatic creed of a New South. The myth of the "moonlight-and-magnolias" Old South originated in the antebellum era, but the idealization of the plantation world received its most influential expression in the 1880s and after in the local color stories of Thomas Nelson Page and others. The myth of the Lost Cause described heroic men from plantations and farms crusading for the Confederacy against invading forces of evil. Ministers and religious groups created a civil religion that tied regional patriotism and religion together so that the remembered Confederate cause took on spiritual significance.

After the Civil War southerners worked hard to preserve the memory of their regional historical experience. The sense of history was given a tangible meaning through memorial celebrations, the erection of monuments, and the expansion of historical societies. Paintings of Robert E. Lee and Jefferson Davis were hung in schoolrooms across the region. Folk ballads, poems, and storytelling by the old passed on to the young the region's memory of the Civil War. Patriotic societies such as the United Confederate Veterans and the United Daughters of the Confederacy campaigned for the teaching of southern history in schools and for the preservation of historical records. The Southern Historical Society was organized in 1873 and soon accumulated an archive of Confederate history. Southerners complained of the bias against the South in textbooks written by northerners and began writing their own histories and lobbying for southern school boards to adopt them. In all these efforts white southerners wanted to explain their view of the past, especially the Confederate and antebellum eras, confident of their ultimate vindication. "Lest ye forget," which appeared on countless Confederate monuments, was an apt motto for southerners of that era. The intense cultivation of an interest in history surely helped preserve the self-conscious southern identity. The history was more a cultivation of myth than a critical examination of the past. The historical record, though, became a prime foundation for the preservation of southern ways.

The Reconstruction years witnessed a ferocious contest for control of the

South's public spaces and the memory of the southern past. Confederate widows began to honor wartime southern heroes in graveside rituals during the year after the end of the Civil War, beginning the religion of the Lost Cause that sacralized the Confederacy and became the focus for large commemorations. African Americans and some northern whites staged hundreds of commemorative celebrations in the Reconstruction years. Before the war, large public spaces in such towns as Richmond, Charleston, and New Orleans were banned for use by slaves or freed blacks, but in the new postwar circumstances African southerners paraded, posted banners, waved flags, said an "amen" to prayers of thanksgiving, and applauded speeches in these public spaces. Black churches and civic organizations also became important sites for blacks in a new southern public culture.

Whites waved the Confederate flag and sang "Dixie" at their rallies, while blacks waved the U.S. flag and sang spirituals that spoke of freedom. The Lost Cause spoke of the tragedy of Confederate defeat, while Emancipation Day commemorations spoke of the blessedness of freedom that came as a result of that war.

One phase in the contestation over public culture in the South effectively ended with Redemption, which was the regaining of control of southern governments and southern public culture by whites in the late 1870s. This was achieved through voter intimidation, fraud, and outright violence to ensure that black votes would not be counted in elections. Northerners, who had once pressed for remaking the South, now acquiesced to white dominance over African southerners. Sectional reconciliation promised economic progress, albeit at the expense of black rights. Black leaders like Frederick Douglass would continue to campaign for Americans to embrace the African American vision of the war's meaning as an expansion of human freedom.

The New South embodied the hope of change. The key word was progress. The central historiographical issue of the period was continuity versus change. C. Vann Woodward in *The Origins of the New South, 1877–1914* (1951) made the case for the significance of the Civil War as a profound break in southern history; Carl N. Degler in *Place over Time: The Continuity of Southern Distinctiveness* (1977) makes the case for continuity. Recent historians focus on the planter and the sharecropper as the main symbols for the issue. Agriculture after the Civil War seemed very different from before, but new institutions simply emerged to accomplish aims similar to those before the war. The plantation survived, albeit transformed, and blacks were held in near peonage as sharecroppers. During Reconstruction the crop-lien system emerged, providing a way for landowners with little cash or credit and laborers without land or money to restart the economy. Sharecroppers and tenants made the crop and shared the harvest with the landowner. Credit for food, tools, livestock, seed, and living necessities was based on the tenant's mortgaging a crop that had not yet been planted. This credit system involved great risk for all concerned, and it opened the way for severe exploitation of the poor.

The postwar planter remained a crucial southern character, and recent studies by Dwight B. Billings, Jonathan Wiener, and others suggest the antebellum planter class continued to exercise considerable power in the New South. But other cultural figures also emerged. The planter himself had to rely frequently on the storekeeper. T. S. Stribling wrote of the merchant in *The Store* (1932), and William Faulkner created a portrait of a mercenary family of merchants in his Snopes trilogy. Newspaper editors such as Henry W. Grady of the *Atlanta Constitution*, Henry Watterson of the Louisville *Courier-Journal*, Richard H. Edmonds of the *Manufacturer's Record* in Baltimore, and Francis W. Dawson of the *Charleston News and Courier* became especially prominent supporters of a New South. The businessman as hero became a new part of the folklore of the South in this era. Businessmen were typically self-made men from the middle class. The lumber, tobacco, textile, furniture, iron and steel, and mining industries expanded in the 1880s, generating wealth and a new privileged class. Lawyer-politicians were powerful figures in the New South, dominating courthouse rings, monopolizing public offices, and supervising public expenditures.

If the nature of the New South can be conveyed through these social types, its meaning can also be seen through the appearance of newly important institutions on the landscape. Textile mills had existed before the Civil War, but in the 1880s southerners went on a veritable crusade for industry, which focused mainly on the mills. W. J. Cash called it "a mighty folk movement," the "dream of virtually the whole southern people." The cotton mills were to be the salvation for the South's poor whites, providing employment opportunities for them but not for blacks. By 1915 the South produced more textiles than the rest of the nation combined, but this production was achieved at a great cost in human misery, in the form of desperately low wages, 72-hour work weeks, and the exploitation of women and children. The mills exacerbated the culture of poverty rather than ending it.

Mill villages became the locale where rural southerners met the modern world. The old paternalism of the plantation became intertwined with the new logic of industrial capitalism. The mills used child labor, offered long, often grueling work weeks, and paid low wages. Their cash payments were tangible, though, and mill life was likely a better one than many had known as sharecroppers or hardscrabble small farmers. Many of the millworkers would later remember the sense of community in the villages and their pride in work.

Railroads became as important a symbol in the southern psyche as they had been in the North generations earlier. They nurtured ties with the regional past by hiring Confederate generals such as Jubal Early as representatives. In fact, though, northerners controlled the South's expanding rail system after the Civil War, with southerners usually involved only in support positions. Ambitious young southerners were now allied with Yankee businessmen, not fighting them as their fathers had. Railroads helped bring the development of cities such as Atlanta, Birmingham, and Durham, which emerged as New South industrial and commercial centers.

Despite these changes, race in the late 19th century was still the central theme of southern identity. Legalized racial segregation began in the 1890s, the result of the decline of northern support for protecting black rights, the rise of a virulent white racism, and the growing assertiveness of African Americans. Cultural historians put particular stress on the last factors. Changes in race relations in the post-Reconstruction years resulted from white male perceptions of black male threats to their control of the social order, representing an endangered white masculinity. A generation of young African Americans had grown up in freedom and challenged attempts to impose second-class citizenship in the 1880s. Racist fears about black male violence against white women led to the white communal ritual of spectacle lynchings, as whites bonded over black bodies. Recent scholarship suggests the codification of segregation laws in the 1890s was not so much the end result of earlier trends as much as it was a serious reordering of southern society. A culture of whiteness became a new way to deal with a modernizing society that threw whites and blacks together in urban settings that challenged older racial folk customs. The New South was thus achieved at the expense of blacks. Life for southern blacks reached its lowest point between the end of Reconstruction and the beginning of World War I. Economically, they were prisoners of a sharecropping system that kept them in near bondage to the land. They lost political power as disfranchisement was achieved through poll taxes, residency requirements, literacy tests, "understanding the Constitution" tests, grandfather clauses basing the right to vote on ancestors having voted, and whites-only primaries. Jim Crow laws sought to establish a rigid caste system. Unwritten customs of racial etiquette also hardened. The economy segregated black jobs and white jobs. The Supreme Court case of *Plessy v. Ferguson* (1896) gave federal approval to southern actions by declaring "separate-but-equal" facilities to be legal. Railroads, schools, theaters, hotels, restaurants, restrooms, water fountains, parks, public offices, and even cemeteries were segregated by the early 20th century. The landscape itself reflected this aspect of the New South—"colored" and "white" signs were soon pervasive. In spite of this terrible setback for black-white cultural interaction, daily occasions often arose for contact between blacks and whites, especially in the region's small towns and rural communities.

The late 19th century was perhaps the age of the most cohesive regional culture and an identifiable, distinctive southern way of life. In addition to the peculiar racial system, a host of customs and cultural ways were associated with southern blacks and whites. Poverty and rural isolation promoted the persistence of attitudes and customs. Blacks and whites placed a high value on family and kinship. People dined, entertained, lived, and visited, all within the boundaries of the family. The family sheltered maiden aunts, distant cousins, and respected grandparents. Household matters were central concerns. Distinctive culinary styles of the typical family were noted by southerners and others as well. On a less positive note, violence was common in the South, which had a high homicide rate, lynchings, public executions, and in general a visible culture of accepted violent behavior. Southerners upheld an ancient ethic of honor. If race relations were rigid, so were gender roles. Patriarchy characterized privileged and plain-folk families.

Churches became even more important institutions in southern culture after the war. Whites joined evangelical churches, and separate black churches emerged. Religious institutions were racially segregated, yet black and white worshippers shared a Protestant, predominantly Baptist and Methodist, orientation. Southern Baptists, Methodists, and Presbyterians did not reunite with their northern brethren after the Civil War but instead worshipped in regionally organized churches. Southern whites remained evangelical and fundamentalist at a time when northern religion was becoming pluralistic in denominations and liberal in theology. Churches extended a pervasive moralism into southern culture through crusades for prohibition of alcohol, for blue laws honoring the Sabbath, and for restrictions on gambling.

Southern culture was also transmitted through distinctive regional rituals such as Confederate Memorial Day, Sunday dinners on the church grounds, political campaign barbecues celebrating the Democratic Party, religious camp meetings, and revivals. On such ritual occasions one heard storytelling and swapping of folk sayings, proverbs, and superstitions; ballad singings; and the formal oratory of the political rabble-rouser and the fiery itinerant evangelist. Sports were a central part of living for southerners. Hunting and fishing had long been regional favorites and remained so for a people who were predominantly rural.

The emergence of agrarian political and economic protest in the 1890s marked the beginning of nearly 30 years of efforts at reform and represented the most serious challenge to southern orthodoxy. Efforts for change began in the Grange, and then the Farmers' Alliance spread over the South, gaining 3 million white members by 1890–91, with over a million more in the Colored Alliance. The Alliance was significant in southern history in trying to forge a class coalition by overcoming racial divisions. Its reformers called for structural changes in the economy to give the federal government a greater role in regulating and controlling an economy increasingly dominated by corporate power. Agrarian protesters attempted to substitute economic issues for racial issues as the dominant concerns in public policy. It was a direct class appeal to the poor, articulating the profound grievances of farmers and forging a democratic political culture. Some historians argue that the agrarian movement represented the last chance for true structural reform in American society, while others see the movement as backward looking, parochial, and conspiratorial. In the latter view, agrarian reformers sought a black-white coalition out of convenience, not principle, and only a minority of reformers used a rhetoric of class appeal across racial lines. Agrarian radicals were thus not entirely alienated, in other words, from the southern way of life. Radicals accepted the color line, used the words and teachings of evangelical Protestantism in demanding reform, and did not challenge the sharecropping system.

The existence of agrarian protest suggests also, though, that the southern way of life was not monolithically conservative. Southern reformers developed a political culture that reflected the abiding democratic and religious style of the South. Southern culture has periodically produced charismatic spokesmen demanding reform for an oppressed people. Rural protesters such as Pitchfork Ben Tillman in South Carolina and James H. "Cyclone" Davis and H. S. P. "Stump" Ashby in Texas used the incendiary language of itinerant democratic ministers and politicians. With the failure of serious reform by the turn of the 20th century, racial extremism appeared. Political demagogues blamed blacks for the failure and exploited the emotions of poor whites.

The Progressive Era presented a social type seldom seen in the earlier South — the middle-class, liberal reformer. Like Progressives in other regions, southern Progressives favored reform to deal with political corruption and irregularities, to rationalize society along more businesslike and scientific lines, to limit business monopoly and the abuse of society, and to restore traditional moral values. They accepted racial segregation and disfranchisement, regarding them as forms peculiar to the South. Southern Progressives thus attempted to achieve reform at the expense of blacks. Lynchings and race riots were ironically at a peak in this era of reform. The appearance of biracial groups such as the National Association for the Advancement of Colored People (NAACP) and the Commission on Interracial Cooperation (CIC) did lay the basis for future change.

Black cultural attitudes in this period were symbolized by two leaders—Booker T. Washington and W. E. B. Du Bois. Born a slave, educated at Hampton Institute in Virginia, and appointed director of Tuskegee Institute in Alabama in 1881, Washington expressed the predominant black view favoring economic self-help. Rather than directly challenge segregation, Washington proposed that blacks work toward building community strength. Washington was one of the most influential southerners in the nation. He communicated with blacks and whites, northerners and southerners, and advocated postponement of political and civil rights and concentration on individual self-improvement. Washington secretly challenged features of the southern system, but publicly he strongly supported black economic development through jobs, landowner-ship, training in business leadership, and vocational skills. Du Bois came to maturity in the early 20th century and reflected the outlook of the Progressive Era. He helped found the NAACP and urged concentration of black efforts on gaining political and civil rights. His book *The Souls of Black Folk* (1903) was an evocative description of turn-of-the-century black southern life.

Americanization. The major theme of the years from 1910 to 1980 was the Americanization of the South. Woodrow Wilson was a southerner by heritage and training, and his election as president in 1912 (along with the election of a Democratic Party–controlled Congress) marked the reappearance of southern political influence on the national scene.

While Wilson was president, World War I promoted patriotic nationalism in the South. The Spanish-American War (1898–99) had been an earlier land-mark reincorporating southerners into the nation, and by 1917 memories of the Lost Cause and Reconstruction had diminished enough to make southerners enthusiastic about the nation at war. Soon southerners were honoring fallen warriors for the nation rather than the region.

The outbreak of war in 1914 led to economic advancement for the South be-cause of a rising demand for agricultural goods. The employment picture in the region improved, and cash incomes rose. The war-related changes also pro-moted mobility. Southerners had been a relatively static people in the late 19th century, but they now flocked to southern and northern cities seeking jobs. The South was the setting for the training of American troops after the United States entered the war in 1917. Northerners came south, and almost a million southerners served in the army and naval forces, helping to diminish the isolation characteristic for generations of southern life. Blacks in particular began leaving the plantations to seek work elsewhere.

Change in the post–World War I South became apparent with the decline in the price of cotton in 1921. On top of that, the boll weevil entered the southern landscape and psyche, devastating cotton in the 1920s and thereafter. The specter of starvation was especially significant in further spurring black migration from the land to northern cities. The southern economy, in general, made some improvement in the 1920s, with an increase in the number of textile mills, a growing chemical industry that had been stimulated during the war, expansion of coal and iron production, and advancement of hydroelectric power. Nonetheless, the southern economy as a whole was in decline well before the stock-market crash of 1929 set off the Great Depression.

The Depression was more devastating to the South than to any other region. A federal government report referred to the region as "the nation's number one economic problem." Franklin D. Roosevelt's New Deal directed a disproportionate share of programs to the region, as symbolized best perhaps by the Tennessee Valley Authority (TVA), relief and public-works projects, and farm and crop-control efforts. The southern populace generally supported the New Deal, although many regional political leaders became critical of it as an experiment in socialism. They especially feared the effects of social experimentation on the region's racial caste system. Overall, New Deal farm programs and farm mechanization combined to promote a revolutionary exodus of sharecroppers and tenants from the land.

Modern southerners have been migrants. African Americans began leaving the South increasingly during World War I, as the hardening of the southern racial context and increasing economic problems in the 1920s pushed them out of the rural South and toward industrial employment in the North and West. Three million African Americans left the South from 1920 to 1960. Hundreds of thousands of whites from the southern mountains, the hill country, and the southern plains also migrated, most between 1930 and 1960, seeking opportunities elsewhere. The migration took southern culture to the nation, leading to soul food cafés in south Chicago, honky-tonks in Detroit, and stock car races in Bakersfield, Calif.

The South's cities became increasingly significant for new southern ways. A civic elite, including bankers, builders, insurance brokers, real estate agents, and professionals pushed for urban growth. The Rotary Clubs and chambers of commerce, expressions of a discourse of progress, attracted ambitious young southern whites.

The Americanization of the South brought a crisis in the southern identity. The years from 1920 to 1945 were creative ones for southern culture, but the creativity came out of a period of transition. The identity crisis especially affected the region's intellectuals and artists who felt the impact of the region's transition from a traditional society to a modern one. What did the regional identity—being southern—mean in the context of world wars and international, modernist intellectual currents? During the 1920s the region appeared to the nation as, in George B. Tindall's phrase, the "Benighted South" symbolized by the Ku Klux Klan, hookworm and pellagra, chain gangs, lynchings, the Scopes Trial, and the Fundamentalist movement in religion. The leadership of the South was in the hands of those of the booster mentality. Intellectuals realized they could no longer take the southern identity for granted. Literary critic Louis D. Rubin Jr. called the 1930 Agrarian manifesto *I'll Take My Stand* "an assertion of identity." The South to the Agrarians represented the last hope of the Western world to tame industrialization and the forces of modernization and dehumanization. Generations of material deprivation had given a spiritual strength that should be used. Intellectuals began questioning and rejecting the romantic and sentimental view of southern culture.

From this period of transition came the Southern Literary Renaissance and a flowering of studies in the social sciences. Journalism, literary criticism, history, fiction, and poetry were all affected by the new spirit of self-criticism, which set the stage for changes after World War II in the southern identity and way of life. The years from 1920 to 1945 witnessed such a creative outpouring that the period should be seen as a southern cultural renaissance. The same period that produced acclaimed writers also produced Louis Armstrong and Fletcher Henderson in jazz, Robert Johnson and Muddy Waters in blues, and Jimmie Rodgers and the Carter Family in country music.

The Harlem Renaissance was a cultural outpouring by African Americans in the 1920s, and it drew from southern black folk culture for inspiration. Such southern African Americans as Zora Neale Hurston, Sterling Brown, and Walter White were key Renaissance figures, with their work drawing from fusing music and poetry, folklore and fiction. Jean Toomer taught in Georgia in 1921, and his observations there led to *Cane*, a poetic evocation of southern black life that stressed the beauty of the natural world and the vernacular culture, while also portraying the violence that lurked in everyday life. Harlem Renaissance writers and artists portrayed the American South within a bigger context of new appreciation of Africa and of comparisons of the South with the Caribbean and awareness of the opportunities and limitations the North presented to African American creative spirits.

These changes also affected the South's folk culture. Small-town, rural folk culture had survived longer in the South than in other regions of the nation. It nurtured distinctive musical, painting, and craft traditions. In the years from 1920 to 1945 the folk culture provided materials for the expansive achievements in popular culture that would flourish in the era after World War II. Authentic, traditional folklife has survived in the South despite the commercialization of mass culture. That folk culture combined black and white contributions became increasingly clear after World War II. Southern ideology had never sanctioned such cultural miscegenation, yet two races living for 300 years on the same soil, often isolated in rural areas from outsiders, had exchanged much specific knowledge and skill and had developed shared attitudes on such matters as religion, the family, recreation, and the importance of land and community.

The South since World War II has experienced a revolution. World War II itself was central to change in the region; it may prove to be even more significant for the region than the Civil War. The pace of economic development stepped up as the federal government poured defense-related investment into the South. The region's lingering isolation was broken as the war encouraged mobility. Many blacks and whites left the South to serve in the military, and civilian workers left rural areas to work in southern cities or left the region to work in northern and western defense industries. Millions of nonsoutherners came into the region, exposing southerners to new influences. The war turned the South's interests outward.

The war laid the basis for postwar economic development and the emergence of the Sunbelt. The decade of the 1960s was the key period, an era of extraordinary growth. Incomes and the standard of living rose. There was still a gap with the rest of the nation, but the once-pervasive poverty was broken. Agriculture was transformed. There was a drastic decline in the number of farms and the farm population. Cotton no longer was king. Mechanization helped to displace rural tenant farmers and sharecroppers. Farming became agribusiness, a commercial enterprise, not the activity promoting the agrarian life urged by the contributors to *I'll Take My Stand*. The southern economy diversified, and industry is now more economically important than agriculture, even in the most predominantly rural state, Mississippi. To be sure, problems remain. Southern economic development has been based on exploiting extractive resources, such as coal or oil, or on low-wage industries such as textiles. Tax and wage policies have left fewer economic benefits than advocates of those policies earlier claimed. Much of the growth has been through branch plants controlled by national firms. Moreover, the growth has been uneven, with Texas, Florida, Georgia, and North Carolina the major beneficiaries. Pockets of poverty remain in states such as Mississippi, Alabama, and Arkansas and among Appalachians and rural blacks. The Sunbelt image of regional prosperity became, though, a new myth of southern success.

The southern landscape has changed as a result of the dramatic economic developments. Gangs of cotton pickers are gone, and tenant shacks are torn down or covered with kudzu. Today soybeans and peanuts, as well as cotton, grow in southern fields, and rural homes have television satellite dishes. Southern cities look much like those elsewhere, and the modern highway strip, mobile home parks, and shopping malls are more typical of the region's urban areas than the once powerful symbol of the county courthouse. The nation's communications and transportation systems have drawn the South in and ended its isolation. If one had to pick a symbol of the modern South, it might be the sight of the bulldozer on a construction crew where once the mule or later the tractor worked.

Another major development since World War II is the decline of race as the central theme—and obsession—of the South. In the 1950s black activists entered a new stage of the struggle to end the region's caste system. The NAACP's traditional strategy of working through the judicial system led to a legal victory over segregation in *Brown v. Board of Education* (1954), which overturned the *Plessy* decision of the 1890s legalizing racial segregation. Southern white conservatives responded with a strategy of massive resistance, and legalists such as journalist James J. Kilpatrick revived interposition theories from the 19th century. The 1950s witnessed a resurrection of Confederate symbolism and die-hard racism. Groups such as the Ku Klux Klan and the White Citizens' Councils led the opposition to change. They proposed once again associating southern identity with race alone. Moderate whites stood on the sidelines and offered little constructive leadership, with a few notable, brave exceptions.

Black civil rights activists, led by the eloquent Martin Luther King Jr., took the offensive, with a campaign of nonviolent resistance based partly in regional religious tradition. Civil rights leaders faced economic and physical intimidation, mean-spiritedness, and outright violence. The height of violence was 1963–68, when 97 people were killed in racial conflict in the South, according to figures compiled by the Southern Regional Council. Through television the world witnessed sit-ins, freedom rides, boycotts, marches, and freedom summers. Little Rock, Selma, Oxford, Montgomery, Birmingham, Neshoba County, and Greensboro may one day rank as great battlefields in the southern imagination, along with Shiloh, Manassas, Antietam, and Gettysburg. The Southern Christian Leadership Conference may take its place beside the Army of Northern Virginia in the southern mind.

External pressure from the federal government, along with the internal pressure of civil rights reformers, led to the passage of the Civil Rights Acts of 1964 and 1965 and the Voting Rights Act of 1965. These laws destroyed the legal basis of caste, overturning the segregation laws and promoting the return of blacks to southern politics. Belief in white supremacy was surely not destroyed, but the South's racial picture by the 1980s resembled the nation's pattern more than its own once-distinctive system. An emerging myth of the redemptive biracial South even suggested the region would achieve true integration before the rest of the nation.

Recent South. The modern South has experienced dramatic change—the end of the one-crop cotton economy, the growth of industrialization and the end of its culture of poverty, the rise of the Republican Party and the end of the one-party Solid South, the draining of the rural countryside and the growth of cities, the end of isolation and the incorporation of the region's peoples into the national culture, and the end of the peculiar racial caste system embodied in Jim Crow laws. Despite the changes, a degree of continuity with the region's past remains—regional traditions in literature, music, sports, eating, and the appreciation of leisure time, outdoor life, family activities, and community life remain vital; and the willingness to use violence and force in certain situations is still a regional trait. The average contemporary southerner has more money, lives in a larger urban area, goes to better schools, and goes to church in bigger buildings than his or her ancestors. Prosperity has dramatically affected traditional southern culture. Material advances have promoted cultural achievements such as art galleries, symphonies, universities, and libraries. Studies by sociologist John Shelton Reed suggest that a profile of the future southerner has already appeared—he or she is well educated, well traveled, middle class, attuned to the nation's communications systems, lives in a suburb, and has the strongest sense of regional identity of anyone living in the South. The locus of southern identity has thus shifted from the rural plantation and small farm of more than a century ago to the most modern form of residential living, the suburb.

Historians increasingly use the concept of collective memory to analyze how societies construct a meaningful past and how issues of power are worked out among dominant and subordinate groups. The contemporary South has witnessed a ferocious contest over its cultural symbols and the collective memories they represent. Many of the region's cultural images come out of the 19th century, and public culture has long used the Lost Cause mythology to represent the continued memory of the Confederacy as a sacred experience for white southerners. Defenders of the Confederate battle flag and the playing of "Dixie" believe they honor the region's past and its ancestors, including family forebears. Opponents of the imagery see it as veiled racism, since the defeat of the Confederacy extended human freedom to African Americans in the South. The Lost Cause symbols were adopted as public icons of the South at a time when black southerners were powerless to shape such symbolism, but the challenges to them in the contemporary South reflect the redefinition of the South's public culture in a desegregated society. Still, despite efforts to change the symbols, the Confederate flag still flies over the Capitol grounds in South Carolina and remains on the state flag of Mississippi. Meanwhile, the memorialization of the heroes of the civil rights movement is vigorously proceeding, with monuments to Medgar Evers in Jackson, Miss., and Rosa Parks in Montgomery, Ala., and with Dr. King's image widespread throughout the region, reinforcing a new collective memory for the South.

Racial reconciliation reflects the efforts to bridge divides in the South's biracial society. Mississippi was the bloodiest of states in its racial history, yet developments there are revealing. The William Winter Institute for Racial Reconciliation at the University of Mississippi works in local communities to foster interracial cooperation, while Mission Mississippi focuses its efforts around evangelical religion, holding rallies with the theme "Grace, not Race." Local communities in the South sometimes sponsor modified versions of South Africa's truth and reconciliation forums, designed to provide healing confrontations with painful memories of the past. The South Africa model is significant in recognizing that the South's story is connected with international efforts at reconciliation among people with differing memories of the same collective past.

The South's global connections have always been a part of the regional economy, especially for a place so dependent on the world market for its cotton and other commodity prices. The global context has grown even more salient in the last two decades. German, Japanese, and Korean automobile makers have taken up residence in the region, with Nissan in Mississippi, BMW in South Carolina, and Mercedes-Benz, Honda, and Hyundai in Alabama. State governors recruit overseas, selling the cultures of their states, as well as their workforce potentials. The new immigrants to the United States are coming increasingly to the South. Hispanics are coming in greatest numbers, but one finds Vietnamese, Cambodians, Haitians, and others in significant enough numbers to influence local cultures throughout the region.

Popular culture keeps the South alive, drawing from old typologies. Browsing the newsstand one finds such magazines as *Southern Lady*, *Southern Bride*, *Southern Football*, and hunting and fishing periodicals galore dedicated to the southern woods. Distinguished filmmakers like Robert Altman and the Coen brothers turn to the South for their imaginative takes on the region, while films like *The Dukes of Hazzard* resuscitate television stereotypes. Music remains a carrier of the southern identity, whether country music from Nashville or hip-hop from Atlanta. The World Wide Web seems too technical to have a sense of place, but southern sites make it easy to find the virtual South. Tourism commodifies the southern past, with historic places the scenes of pilgrimages, tours, and souvenirs for sale.

The southern identity remains alive and well, though perhaps shrinking. One public opinion survey concluded that from 1991 to 2001 the number of people living in the South who identified themselves as southerners declined from about 78 percent to 70 percent. Another poll looked at the years 1992–99 and concluded that residents of Deep South states had the highest identification as "southerners." Ninety percent of Mississippians claimed the label, followed by those from Alabama (88 percent), Tennessee (84 percent), South Carolina (82 percent), and Georgia (81 percent). The percentages declined for Virginia (60 percent) and Florida (51 percent), suggesting differences between core and marginal Souths. The latter poll included African Americans indicating a high identification with the South among blacks, especially in the Deep South. The end of Jim Crow segregation enabled African Americans to embrace the South as their homeland and to work for continuing reform. The black population of the South grew in the 1990s by 3.5 million, which represents a surprising 58 percent of the increase in the nation's African American population. Much of the increase resulted from a return migration of blacks to the South — a population shift that began in the 1970s, when 1.9 million blacks came to the region, and continued in the 1980s, with 1.7 million returnees. Blacks have been especially significant in keeping alive the sense of the South's history. Understanding black identity often means "going into the Black Belt" to understand the origin of African American history. Memoirs, histories, journalistic accounts, travel accounts, fiction, poetry, painting, and music are among some of the cultural forms that blacks have used to explore their complex love-hate relationships with the American South.

CHARLES REAGAN WILSON
University of Mississippi

Stephen Anthony Aron, *How the West Was Lost: The Transformation of Kentucky from Daniel Boone to Henry Clay* (1996); James Axtell, *The Indians' New South* (1997); Edward L. Ayers, *The Promise of the New South after Reconstruction* (1992); Peter W. Bardaglio, *Reconstructing the Household: Families, Sex, and the Law in the Nineteenth-Century South* (1995); Numan Bartley, *The New South, 1945–1980* (1995); Nancy Bercaw, *Gendered Freedoms: Race, Rights, and the Politics of Household in the Delta, 1861–1875* (2005); Ira Berlin, *Many Thousands Gone: The First Two Centuries of Slavery in North America* (1998); Roger Biles, *The South and the New Deal* (1994); Merle Black, *Politics and Society in the South* (1987); David Blight, *Race and Reunion: The Civil War in American Memory* (2001); John B. Boles, ed., *A Companion to the American South* (2002); Charles C. Bolton, *Poor Whites of the Antebellum South: Tenants and Laborers in Central North Carolina and Northeast Mississippi* (1994); Taylor Branch, *Pillar of Fire: America in the King Years, 1963–1965* (1998); Kathleen M. Brown, *Good Wives, Nasty Wenches, and Anxious Patriarchs: Gender, Race, and Power in Colonial Virginia* (1996); W. Fitzhugh Brundage, *Where These Memories Grow: History, Memory, and Southern Identity* (2000); Dan T. Carter, *The Politics of Rage: George Wallace, the Origins of the New Conservatism, and the Transformation of American Politics* (1995); Bill Cecil-Fronsman, *Common Whites: Class and Culture in Antebellum North Carolina* (1992); Paul A. Cimbala, *Under the Guardianship of the Nation: The Freedmen's Bureau and the Reconstruction of Georgia, 1865–1870* (1997); James C. Cobb, *The Most Southern Place on Earth: The Mississippi Delta and the Roots of Regional Identity* (1992), *The Selling of the South: The Southern Crusade for Industrial Development, 1936–1980* (1982); Peter A Coclanis, *The Shadow of a Dream* (1989); William Cohen, *At Freedom's Edge: Black Mobility and the Southern White Quest for Racial Control, 1860–1915* (1991); Pete Daniel, *Lost Revolutions: The South in the 1950s* (2000); Charles B. Dew, *Bond of Iron: Master and Slave at Buffalo Forge* (1994); John Dittmer, *Local People: The Struggle for Civil Rights in Mississippi* (1994); Daniel S. Dupre, *Transforming the Cotton Frontier: Madison County, Alabama, 1800–1840* (1997); William Dusinberre, *Them Dark Days: Slavery in the American Rice Swamps* (1996); Charles W. Eagles, *Outside Agitator: Jon Daniels and the Civil Rights Movement in Alabama* (1993); Laura F. Edwards, *Gendered Strife and Confusion: The Political Culture of Reconstruction* (1997); Douglas R. Egerton, *Gabriel's Rebellion: The Virginia Slave Conspiracies of 1800 and 1802* (1993); Geneviève Fabre and Robert O'Meally, eds., *History and Memory in African-American Culture* (1994); Adam Fairclough, *Race and Democracy: The Civil Rights Struggle in Louisiana, 1915–1972* (1995); Drew Gilpin Faust, *The Creation of Confederate Nationalism: Ideology and Identity in the Civil War South* (1988), *Mothers of Invention: Women of the Slaveholding South in the American Civil War* (1996); Paul Finkelman, *Slavery and the Founders: Race and Liberty in the Age of Jefferson* (1996); J. Wayne Flynt, *Dixie's Forgotten People: The South's Poor Whites* (1979); Eric Foner, *Reconstruction: America's Unfinished Revolution, 1863–1877* (1988); Lacy K. Ford Jr., *Origins of Southern Radicalism: The South Carolina Upcountry, 1800–1860* (1988); Gaines M. Foster, *Ghosts of the Confederacy: Defeat, the Lost Cause, and the Emergence of the New South, 1865–1913* (1987); Elizabeth Fox-Genovese, *Within the Plantation Household: Black and White Women of the Old South* (1988); William W. Freehling, *The Road to Disunion: Secessionists at Bay, 1776–1854* (1990); Sylvia R. Frey and Betty Wood, *Come Shouting to Zion: African American Protestantism in the American South and British Caribbean to 1830* (1998); Gary Gallagher, *The Confederate War* (1997); Patricia Galloway, ed., *The Hernando de Soto Expedition: History, Historiography, and "Discovery" in the Southeast* (1997); David J. Garrow, *Bearing the Cross: Martin Luther King Jr. and the Southern Christian Leadership Conference* (1986); Eugene D. Genovese, *The Slaveholders' Dilemma: Freedom and Progress in Southern Conservative Thought, 1820–1860* (1992), *A Consuming Fire: The Fall of the Confederacy in the Mind of the White Christian South* (1998); Glenda Elizabeth Gilmore, *Gender and Jim Crow: Women and the Politics of White Supremacy in North Carolina, 1896–1920* (1996); Frederic W. Gleach, *Powhatan's World and Colonial Virginia: A Conflict of Cultures* (1997); David Goldfield, *Black, White, and Southern: Race Relations and Southern Culture* (1990), *Still Fighting the Civil War: The American South and Southern History* (2002); Michael A. Gomez, *Exchanging Our Country Marks: The Transformation of African Identities in the Colonial and Antebellum South* (1998); Virginia Meacham Gould, ed., *Chained to the Rock of Adversity: To Be Free, Black, and Female in the Old South* (1998); Richard Gray and Owen Robinson, eds., *A Companion to the Literature and Culture of the American South* (2004); Jack P. Green, *Pursuits of Happiness: The Social Development of Early Modern British Colonies and the Formation of American Culture* (1988); Kenneth S. Greenberg, *Masters and Statesmen: The Political Culture of American Slavery* (1985); James R. Grossman, *Land of Hope: Chicago, Black Southerners, and the Great Migration* (1989); Grace Elizabeth Hale, *Making Whiteness: The Culture of Segregation in the South, 1890–1940* (1998); Jacquelyn Dowd Hall, *Revolt against Chivalry: Jesse Daniel Ames and the Women's Campaign against Lynching* (1979); Jacquelyn Dowd Hall et al., *Like a Family: The Making of a Southern Cotton Mill World* (1987); Randall Lee Hall, *William Louis Poteat: A Leader of the Progressive Era South* (2000); Paul Harvey, *Freedom's Coming: Religious Culture and the Shaping of the South from the Civil War through the Civil Rights Era* (2005), *Redeeming the South: Religious Cultures and Racial Identities among Southern Baptists, 1865–1920* (1997); Christine Leigh Heyrman, *Southern Cross: The Beginnings of the Bible Belt* (1997); Samuel S. Hill Jr., *The South and the North in American Religion* (1980); Sarah H. Hill, *Weaving New Worlds: Southeastern Cherokee Women and Their Basketry* (1997); Michael F. Holt, *The Rise and Fall of the American Whig Party: Jacksonian Politics and the Onset of Civil War* (1999); Thomas C. Holt, *The Problems of Freedom: Race, Labor, and Politics in Jamaica and Britain, 1832–1938* (1992); James Horn, *Adapting to a New World* (1994); Charles Hudson, *The Southeastern Indians* (1978); Tera W. Hunter,

To 'Joy My Freedom: Southern Black Women's Lives and Labors after the Civil War* (1997); Douglas R. Hurt, ed., *The Rural South since World War II* (1998); Samuel C. Hyde Jr., ed., *Plain Folk of the South Revisited* (1997); John C. Inscoe, *Mountain Masters: Slavery and the Sectional Crisis in Western North Carolina* (1989); John C. Inscoe and Gordon B. McKinney, *The Heart of Confederate Appalachia: Western North Carolina and the Civil War* (2000); Anne Goodwyn Jones and Susan V. Donaldson, eds., *Haunted Bodies: Gender and Southern Texts* (1998); Robin Kelley, *Hammer and Hoe: Alabama Communists during the Great Depression* (1990); Cynthia A. Kierner, *Beyond the Household: Women's Place in the Early South, 1700–1835* (1998); Jack Temple Kirby, *Rural Worlds Lost: The American South, 1920–1960* (1987), *Poquosin: A Study of Rural Landscape and Society* (1995); Rachael N. Klein, *Unification of a Slave State: The Rise of the Planter Class in the South Carolina Backcountry, 1760–1808* (1990); Allan Kulikoff, *Tobacco and Slaves: The Development of Southern Cultures in the Chesapeake, 1680–1800* (1988); Jane Landers, *Black Society in Spanish Florida* (1999); Ronald L. Lewis, *Transforming the Appalachian Countryside: Railroads, Deforestation, and Social Change in West Virginia, 1880–1920* (1998); Leon F. Litwack, *Trouble in Mind: Black Southerners in the Age Jim Crow* (1998); Ann Patton Malone, *Sweet Chariot: Slave Family and Household Structure in Nineteenth-Century Louisiana* (1992); Charles Marsh, *God's Long Summer: Stories of Faith and Civil Rights* (1997); Stephanie McCurry, *Masters of Small Worlds: Yeoman Households, Gender Relations, and the Political Culture of the Antebellum South Carolina Low Country* (1995); Neil R. McMillen, *Dark Journey: Black Mississippians in the Age of Jim Crow* (1989); Sally G. McMillen, *Motherhood in the Old South: Pregnancy, Childbirth, and Infant Rearing, 1800–1860* (1990); W. K. McNeil, ed., *Appalachian Images in Folk and Popular Culture* (1994); James M. McPherson, *Battle Cry of Freedom: The Civil War Era* (1988); Grady McWhitney, *Cracker Culture: Celtic Ways in the Old South* (1988); D. W. Meinig, *The Shaping of America: A Geographical Perspective on 500 Years of History: Atlantic America, 1492–1800* (1886); Philip D. Morgan, *Slave Counterpoint: Black Culture in the Eighteenth-Century Chesapeake and Lowcountry* (1998); Christopher Morris, *Becoming Southern: The Evolution of a Way of Life, Warren County and Vicksburg, Mississippi, 1770–1860* (1995); Peter S. Onuf, ed., *Jeffersonian Legacies* (1993); Ted Ownby, *Subduing Satan: Religion, Recreation, and Manhood in the Rural South, 1865–1920* (1990); George C. Rable, *Civil Wars: Women and the Crisis of Southern Nationalism* (1989), *The Confederate Republic: A Revolution against Politics* (1994); Bruce A. Ragsdale, *A Planter's Republic: The Search for Economic Independence in Revolutionary Virginia* (1996); Beth Barton Schweiger, *The Gospel Working Up: Progress and the Pulpit in Nineteenth-Century Virginia* (2000); James Sidbury, *Ploughshares into Swords: Race, Rebellion, and Identity in Gabriel's Virginia, 1730–1810* (1997); Timothy Silver, *A New Face on the Countryside: Indians, Colonists, and Slaves in South Atlantic Forests, 1500–1800* (1990); Anastasia Sims, *The Power of Femininity in the New South: Women's Organizations and Politics in North*

Carolina, 1880–1930 (1997); Mechal Sobel, *The World They Made Together: Black and White Values in Eighteenth-Century Virginia* (1987); Daniel H. Usner Jr., *Indians, Settlers, and Slaves in a Frontier Exchange Economy* (1992); Samuel L. Webb, *Two-Party Politics in the One-Party South: Alabama's Hill Country, 1874–1920* (1997); Daniel Weber, *The Spanish Frontier in North America* (1992); Charles Reagan Wilson and Mark Silk, eds., *Religion and Public Life in the South: In the Evangelical Mode* (2005); Peter H. Wood, in *Powhatan's Mantle: Indians in the Colonial Southeast*, ed., Peter H. Wood, Gregory A. Waselkov, and M. Thomas Hatley (1989).

Abolition

American abolition spanned two centuries, comprised numerous activists, and helped mold the nation's understanding of racial justice. Indeed, though the majority of Americans were never abolitionists, the abolition movement (like the civil rights movement of the 20th century) assumed a significance beyond numbers. "When we get a little farther away from the conflict," Frederick Douglass once proclaimed, "some brave and truth-loving man, with all the facts before him . . . will give use an impartial history of the grandest moral conflict of the [19th] century."

How does one define abolition? For reformers of the 18th and 19th centuries, an abolitionist was someone who either joined a movement to end slavery or worked actively to convince slaveholders to emancipate their slaves. Thomas Jefferson may have thus opposed slavery, but he was not an abolitionist. American abolitionism actually took root in the colonial era, first among Quaker groups (particularly in Pennsylvania, where on the eve of the American Revolution they were the first to ban slaveholding among members) and then among a coterie of abolitionist organizations in the new American union. The leading abolitionists of the early republic were located primarily in northern urban locales: the Pennsylvania Abolition Society in Philadelphia and the New York Manumission Society in New York City. Abolitionist groups also formed in Connecticut, Rhode Island, and New Jersey in the North, and in Delaware, Maryland, and Virginia in the South. In 1794 these early organizations met for the first time in a convention to plan and coordinate abolitionist activities.

Early abolitionism was characterized by two important traits: gradualism and segregated membership. The first abolitionists sought to end slavery gradually. Emancipation statutes passed in northern states at the close of the 18th century provided that slaves would be liberated at a certain age — often 21 for men, 24 for women. Pennsylvania adopted the inaugural gradual abolition law in 1780; every northern locale passed similar statutes over the next 20 years to end slavery gradually within state borders. Only Massachusetts ended slavery by judicial decree, in 1782. The total number of slaves that could have been liberated in the North was roughly 40,000, although devious masters often sold slaves in the South before emancipation statutes matured.

Nevertheless, early abolition societies were quite important. For one thing, they guarded against efforts to rescind abolition laws. For another, early northern abolitionists represented kidnapped blacks and runaway slaves in court of law. Virginia masters became so concerned about abolitionist legal meddling that they helped close down early emancipation societies in the Old Dominion prior to 1810. During the 1820s the Maryland legislature petitioned Pennsylvania to curtail abolitionist legal maneuverings that affected plantation discipline there. In this sense, by the early 19th century abolitionism had already become a part of sectional politics. Abolitionist footing in southern locales was usually tenuous, but southern abolitionists did nevertheless manage to survive, if not thrive, particularly in parts of the Upper South.

Although formally excluded from early abolitionist societies, black activists formed a parallel abolitionist movement during the early republic. Led by the first generation of free black activists to emerge in American culture (Prince Hall in Boston, Lemuel Haynes in Connecticut and Vermont, Richard Allen and James Forten in Pennsylvania), African American reformers before 1830 created a distinct brand of abolitionism revolving around public protest tactics and moralizing strategies. Centered largely in newly independent black churches in Philadelphia, New York City, Boston, Providence, and Baltimore, African American reformers gave antislavery speeches, published abolitionist pamphlets, and aided fugitive slaves. "My bosom swells with pride whenever I mention the name of James Forten," Frederick Douglass once declared of one of his abolitionist heroes.

The 1820s and 1830s witnessed great transformations in American abolitionism. Background factors are quite important here. First, the slave and the free black populations had doubled since the founding of the country. Slaves numbered 700,000 in 1790 and free blacks 6,300; by 1830 there were two million slaves and 250,000 free blacks. By 1860, those numbers would double yet again, intensifying concerns about both slavery's place in the republic and African Americans' claim to equality. Second, religious revivals erupted in many parts of the country; one of their central concerns was eradicating sin (such as slavery) from secular society. Third, colonization became one of the fastest-growing reform movements, its aim of transporting liberated blacks from America popular among northern, as well as southern, whites. While gradual-abolition societies responded with little or no opposition, the threat of colonization galvanized free black activists as never before. They mobilized mass protest meetings and founded the first black newspapers in response. The heyday of early abolitionist organizations, which focused on ending slavery at the state level and limited their activities at the federal level, thus ended by the late 1820s.

A whole new group of "immediate" abolitionists emerged during the 1830s. Located largely in the North and Midwest, they embraced more radical strategies and tactics: slavery, they declared, must be ended immediately and black Americans must be accorded full civil rights. New abolitionists also believed that they must wage a public war against bondage. William Lloyd Garrison's militant paper, the *Liberator*, is often cited as the key shot fired in this new war against bondage, but black activist David Walker's *Appeal* (a militant pamphlet from 1829 condemning slavery's expansion, as well as white colonizationist designs) was equally important. Immediate abolitionists also swept into local towns, holding large public meetings and debates and circulating petitions against slavery, and published thousands of antislavery documents and slave narratives for public consumption. Indeed, they spent many times more money than did early reformers on publishing and disseminating abolitionist materials. As one Massachusetts reformer put it in the 1830s, "We wish to turn the whole of the American people into one abolition society."

In addition, these new abolitionist societies formed interracial alliances. When the New England Anti-Slavery Society formed in 1832 in Boston, 25 percent of its members were African American. At the American Anti-Slavery Society's founding meeting in Philadelphia the following year, black activists were a similarly prominent presence. Finally, women joined immediatist societies in impressive numbers, the first time that female abolitionists formally worked in abolitionist organizations with men. Together, these groups overtook and overhauled American abolitionism after 1830.

After a few years of optimistic activity, however, abolitionism fragmented into various factions. One key division occurred over racial matters. The second revolved around political strategies. Still a third dividing line was the role of female activists. On the first matter, by the 1840s black activists felt marginalized within the new abolitionist movement. Frustrated at whites' continuing condescension, some black activists moved toward autonomous protest. In 1843, for example, African Americans revived the black convention movement. Blacks held dozens more conventions at the local, state, and national levels through the Civil War era that did whites, bolstering Henry Garnet's claim that "ours is the battle" to end slavery.

Abolitionists also divided over political action between 1840 and the Civil War. Some activists agreed with William Lloyd Garrison, who viewed American politics as anathema to abolitionism (the very Constitution was an evil compact, he famously declared). Other abolitionists — both black and white — embraced political action at the state and federal levels. The Liberty Party became the first abolitionist political party when it ran former Kentucky slaveholder James Birney for president in 1840. Advocating abolition in the District of Columbia, no extension of slavery in the West, and black equality, the group received only 7,000 votes. In 1844 it received 40,000 votes — including 15,000 in New York State (enough to help defeat Henry Clay's bid for the presidency).

Black activists such as Henry Garnet and Samuel Ringold Ward even ran for state political office. Ultimately, abolitionist political action would not be successful in and of itself; rather, key abolitionist ideas would be transmuted into party platforms for groups such as the Free-Soil and Republican Parties (which were far from abolitionist parties, though they did seek to stop slavery's expansion in western territories).

Women's role in the antebellum abolition movement became still another contentious concern before the Civil War. Although female activists were a key part of abolition's new wave in the 1830s (serving as local organizers, editors, and petition signatories), some male reformers felt they had overstepped their bounds. In 1840 the American Anti-Slavery Society split apart over the issue. Nevertheless, female activists assumed an even greater importance in the years leading to the Civil War.

American abolitionism reflected the intensifying sectional debates of the 1850s, particularly on the matter of violence. While some reformers embraced nonresistance (a denunciation of violent tactics), many black activists supported the right of self-defense, particularly after the new Fugitive Slave Law of 1850 gave masters more power to hunt down fugitive slaves in northern states (slave catchers were known to kidnap free blacks instead). In New York City, Philadelphia, and Boston, blacks formed vigilance societies to protect fleeing slaves and endangered free blacks. On the other hand, the Underground Railroad became more active in the 1850s, and slave rescues (such as the Jerry rescue in Syracuse and the Anthony Burns case in Massachusetts) attracted national attention as never before. On the eve of the Civil War, relatively few Americans were abolitionists — but most Americans knew what abolition was about.

Although never comprising more than a small percentage of the American population (perhaps two to five percent of the population in the most optimistic accounts), abolitionists helped articulate rationales for black freedom that eventually influenced American statesmen and the passage of constitutional amendments Thirteen through Fifteen. In the early republic, gradual abolitionists not only secured America's first emancipation laws but protected them in the face of a surprising amount of opposition from even northern masters. Early reformers also argued consistently that ending slavery was compatible with the principles of the American Revolution, as well as Christian fellowship. Later generations of abolitionists (black, white, male, female), while revising early reformers' tactics, amplified their predecessors' basic assumptions: slavery was wrong and must be dismantled via some form of activism. Moreover, antebellum reformers insisted that racial justice for free blacks was a necessary corollary to abolitionism. While the Civil War—and not abolitionists' exertions—ultimately led to slavery's demise, abolitionists provided the pathway to Americans' evolving understanding of equality. Without generations of abolitionist activism prior to 1860, Abraham Lincoln would not have had the wherewithal to declare "a new birth of freedom" for the American nation.

RICHARD NEWMAN
Rochester Institute of Technology

Gerda Lerner, *The Grimké Sisters from South Carolina: Pioneers for Women's Rights and Abolition* (1998); Henry Mayer, *All on Fire: William Lloyd Garrison and the Abolition of Slavery* (1998); Richard S. Newman, *The Transformation of American Abolitionism: Fighting Slavery in the Early Republic* (2002).

Anglo-American Antebellum Culture

The Old South's high culture was marked by two strong currents: it began and remained an Anglo-American culture in its tastes and loyalties, and it was sustained by an agrarian economic system partially supported by black slave labor. The first was seen in a strong taste for goods from abroad, and the second created tensions and anxieties about man's relation to man.

White colonial settlers in the South were northern Europeans, predominantly from the British Isles, who were not always seeking the same religious and political freedoms as their Puritan contemporaries in the North. The cultural evolution of the Old South proceeded as a logical extension of the English squirearchy, the Whig mentality wherein communal political authority was held in less regard than the customs of the local aristocracy. This aristocracy respected men of ability who became men of means, the type of "natural aristocrat" Thomas Jefferson espoused. Save in Virginia, the most English of the southern states, a hereditary aristocracy did not develop. Indeed, as Clement Eaton has written, "With few exceptions, the ruling families were developed on the native soil from middle class origins."

Affiliation with the Church of England through the colonial period in the South resulted in a consensus code of behavior. Abstract codes of honor and decency coalesced into an Anglo-Saxon common law of human behavior. Unlike the Puritans who felt they were living in a time of declension from the virtues of a distant past, southern whites, according to Bertram Wyatt-Brown, "believed that they had made peace with God's natural order." By and large southern culture was at odds with the national culture and was inclined to regard property and local option as the most important aspects of a democratic society and disinclined to respect external elective authority. These attitudes led inevitably to theories of nullification, actual secession, and war.

The southern antebellum economy was agrarian, stratified into large and small farms, many of which were called, in the archaic fashion of the 17th century, plantations. One lingering colonial trait within the culture was a factor system of exchanging agricultural produce for manufactured commodities from abroad or the North. This exchange system had a significant effect upon the market for local commodities and may have retarded the growth of the southern plastic arts.

Any understanding of southern plastic arts prior to 1861 must involve the integration of architecture, furnishings, and the exotic within the home. Coastal colonial architecture was by and large built of brick in the English manner of the 18th century, broadly fenestrated and preferring rear or side galleries to frontal porticoes. As the South moved west, builders used timber available from the virgin forests being cleared for farm lands and developed the first high-style frame architecture in the West. The rage for Greek Revival architecture, which seized most of the Western world in the first 50 years of the 19th century, was especially strong in the South.

The English gentry were fascinated with the classical age, as were southerners of a comparable class. Southern states were also dotted with towns named Troy, Athens, and Rome, and southern children were called Lucius, Cassius, Marcus — even Valerius Publicola in several Tennessee families. Collegiate education emphasized classical studies, not mechanical arts. Clearly, in the midst of an awesome controversy over slavery and its moral ramifications, some southerners thought of themselves as living in an ancient agrarian utopia, enshrined in white-columned temples.

Initially excellent and recently neglected traditions emerged in the plastic arts of the South. Superior cabinetmaking developed in the Coastal Plains, especially in Baltimore and Charleston. Baltimore remained through the period an important source for crafted and imported goods, though later in the period rivaled by New Orleans in influence and significance as a source for manufactured goods. Equally strong rural cabinetmaking traditions emerged in North Carolina and Kentucky, using cherry and hickory woods. Southern cabinetmakers tended to favor existing English styles, notably those to be seen in the pattern books of Thomas Sheraton, Thomas Shearer, and George Hepplewhite. An exception to the English taste was found in New Orleans, which introduced the French Empire and Rococo Revival styles to the Lower South.

Silversmiths excelled in the South, especially Samuel Kirk & Sons in Baltimore, Frederick Marquand in Savannah, James Conning in Mobile, and the Hyde and Goodrich firm of New Orleans. Many local craftsmen rendered silver coins into a variety of cups, pitchers, and spoons, but the works of Kentucky silversmiths, such as Asa Blanchard, were particularly prized.

In keeping with the tastes of England, portraiture was more esteemed than landscape painting, although a few painters, such as Granville Perkins (1830–95) and George Cooke (1793–1846), attempted to depict the scenic splendors of the region. George Caleb Bingham's (1811–79) river and political paintings are vivid documents of southern life and work.

Much of the portraiture of the Old South was rendered by itinerants, who established seasonal studios in favored urban areas like Natchez or Richmond. Some traveled from plantation house to plantation house, entertaining and depicting several members of a family at once. Under the influence of Gilbert Stuart (1755–1828) and Thomas Sully (1783–1872), a strong neoclassical portrait tradition emerged in Lexington, Ky., represented by William Edward West (1788–1857), Matthew Harris Jouett (1788–1827), Joseph Henry Bush (1794–1865), and Oliver Frazer (1808–64). New Orleans was a major center for portrait activity, especially by French academicians working there between 1820 and 1850. These artists, including Jean Joseph Vaudechamp (1790–1866) and Jacques Amans (1801–88), influenced several generations of southern itinerant painters, most notably C. R. Parker, who painted in Alabama, Mississippi, Georgia, and Louisiana.

Oratory was esteemed and well attended, favorites being the fire-eating secessionist speeches of William Lowndes Yancey (1814–63) and Robert Barnwell Rhett (1800–76). Chautauquas were held on the subjects of natural science, historical curiosities, and female education. "Camp meetings" by religious fundamentalists were particularly popular in the Upper South and were attended by as many as 15 to 20 thousand people at a time. Although a certain amount of speaking in tongues and writhing in the Holy Ghost took place at these gatherings, Clement Eaton felt that "beneath the tumult and excitement of the camp meetings can be discerned the craving of lonely frontier people for human companionship."

The literary tastes of affluent southerners mingled English influences with more homespun products. Romances of the medieval period, especially those of Sir Walter Scott, were wildly popular. So, too, were the humorous sketches of frontier southern life written by Augustus Baldwin Longstreet (1790–1870) and William Tappan Thompson (1812–82). Historical fiction by William Gilmore Simms (1806–70) assuaged the southern desire for a cavalier past, while the morbid gothic musings of Edgar Allan Poe made little impact. Literary journals, such as *De Bow's Review* and the *Southern Literary Messenger*, combined humor, political speculations, and natural history articles.

The 40 years following the Missouri Compromise of 1820 saw the southern mind become increasingly paranoid, hysterical, and preoccupied with the slavery issue. Paternalism "accepted by both masters and slaves," says historian Eugene D. Genovese, "afforded a fragile bridge across the intolerable contradictions inherent in a society based on racism." Southern culture was conservative and deeply suspicious of the Industrial Revolution, an attitude it shared with the English intelligentsia of the same period, several of whom, including Thomas Carlyle and Charles Darwin, supported the South in secession.

The material culture that evolved from English influences on the antebellum South reflected the tastes of local aristocrats. The ruling families, most of whom came from middle-class backgrounds, sought tangible expressions of their good fortune and their aspirations. A strong cultural belief in the sanctity of private property prevailed, obscuring for many southerners the moral issue of keeping other human beings in bondage.

ESTILL CURTIS PENNINGTON
The Filson Club
Louisville, Kentucky

Frances Gaither Blake, ed., *Mary Savage Conner of Adams County, Mississippi: A Young Girl's Journal, 1839* (1982); Clement Eaton, *The Freedom of Thought Struggle in the Old South* (1964), *A History of the Old South* (1964); Elizabeth Fox-Genovese, *Within the Plantation Household: Black and White Women of the Old South* (1989); Eugene D. Genovese, *Roll, Jordan, Roll: The World the Slaves Made* (1974); Robert Manson Myers, ed., *The Children of Pride: A True Story of Georgia and the Civil War* (1972); Estill Curtis Pennington, *Look Away: Reality and Southern Sentiment in Southern Art* (1989), *Southern Quarterly* (Fall 1985); Jessie Poesch, *The Art of the Old South: Painting, Sculpture, Architecture and the Products of Craftsmen, 1560–1860* (1983); William R. Taylor, *Cavalier and Yankee: The Old South and American National Character* (1961); Bertram Wyatt-Brown, *Southern Honor: Ethics and Behavior in the Old South* (1982); Jeffrey Robert Young, *Domesticating Slavery: The Master Class in Georgia and South Carolina, 1670–1837* (1999).

Atlantic World

The circulation of people, goods, and ideas throughout the Atlantic Ocean during the early modern period created an Atlantic world that shaped the societies that developed on the four continents of the Atlantic rim. That circulation began with Columbus's expeditions and continued into the 19th century. It was responsible for creating the particularly rich American cultures, including that in the American South, resulting from the mixture of various groups of Europeans, Africans, and Indians.

The roots of distinctively southern cultures lie in the Atlantic migrations of the 17th, 18th, and (to a lesser degree) 19th centuries. Spanish colonists from the Caribbean and Spain established the colony Florida in the 16th century. English colonists migrated from England and the Caribbean to Virginia and Carolina beginning in the 17th century. In the 18th century French colonists moved from Arcadia, the Caribbean, and France to Louisiana, and Scots and Scots-Irish settled in the western reaches of English colonies. Florida, Carolina, and Louisiana each maintained ties to Atlantic locales beyond their respective imperial centers (Cuba, Barbados, and St. Domingue and Canada, respectively). Most important for the definitions of southern culture, enslaved Africans came to all of these locales. Some came with their masters from the Spanish, French, or English Caribbean. Most, especially in the 18th century, came directly from Africa. They influenced the nature not only of African American culture that developed in each place but of the regional cultures more broadly. The individuals who arrived via these continuing Atlantic migrations brought with them from their European, African, and Caribbean points of origin knowledge and sensibilities that shaped southern culture, including its work patterns, architecture, language, food, and music.

Atlantic markets for staple crops such as tobacco, rice, indigo, sugar, and cotton encouraged the South to develop as a region focused on the export of agricultural products, helping to maintain its rural character into the modern period. Atlantic commercial ties with Europe and with other American colonies in the Caribbean and on the mainland facilitated the circulation of ideas and goods that further shaped the South's cultural development in the 18th and 19th centuries. A consumer revolution in the 18th century raised the material standard of living throughout the Atlantic world. That explosion in consumption depended in part on the productivity of enslaved Africans in the southern colonies and resulted in the proliferation of European manufactures in the South, as well as in the rest of the Atlantic world. Those goods connected southern colonies to changing European fashions in clothing, food, furnishing, and entertainment. Colonists' resulting ability to imitate English consumer fashions strengthened their cultural ties to Europe as the 18th century progressed.

Eighteenth-century intellectual currents also circulated throughout the Atlantic world. These included religious transformations such as latitudinarianism among Anglicans that so influenced the South's political elites at the end of the 18th century. The Atlantic diffusion of Baptist, Methodist, and Presbyterian believers and beliefs in the 17th and 18th centuries contributed to the development of a distinctly southern religious sensibility by the end of the 18th century. Atlantic intellectual currents also included the Enlightenment ideals that inspired independence wars in the United States, in Haiti, and in Latin American republics. In each of those places, strengthening abolitionism intertwined with that Enlightenment ideology. The connection between the American Revolution and abolition changed southern culture notably. Because it prompted states north of Delaware to provide for gradual emancipation, it demarcated a boundary between north and south for the first time (while at the same time separating Britain's Caribbean colonies from its mainland colonies). Most important for southern culture, the connection between Revolutionary ideology and abolition required for the first time that slave owners who intended to maintain the institution defend it against moral attack, not just from northern states, but from other Atlantic world residents such as Europeans and newly freed Haitians. Their defenses of slavery developed into the articulation of strong proslavery sentiment that for many southern whites developed into a presumed prerequisite of southernness. Southern slave owners' 19th-century cultivation of paternalistic behavior toward slaves, behavior that would affect race relations into the 20th century, was in part a response to the challenges to slavery that accompanied the spread of Enlightenment ideology throughout the Atlantic in the previous century.

While Atlantic migrations and commerce continued to affect the South from the middle of the 19th century to the present day, the Atlantic world possesses less explanatory power for this later period, as the circulation of goods, people, and ideas became increasingly global.

APRIL LEE HATFIELD
Texas A&M University

David Armitage and Michael J. Braddick, *The British Atlantic World, 1500–1800* (2002); Bernard Bailyn, *Voyagers to the West: A Passage in the Peopling of America on the Eve of the Revolution* (1986); Ira Berlin, *Many Thousands Gone: The First Two Centuries of Slavery in North America* (1998); Jack P. Greene, *Pursuits of Happiness: The Social Development of Early Modern British Colonies and the Formation of American Culture* (1988); Christine Heyrman, *Southern Cross: The Beginnings of the Bible Belt* (1997); James Horn, *Adapting to a New World: English Society in the 17th-Century Chesapeake* (1994); James Horn and Ida Altman, *"To Make America": European Emigration in the Early Modern Period* (1991); Jane Landers, *Black Society in Spanish Florida* (1999); Gary B. Nash, *Race and Revolution* (1990); Mechal Sobel, *The World They Made Together: Black and White Values in Eighteenth-Century Virginia* (1987);

John Thornton, *Africa and Africans in the Making of the Atlantic World, 1400–1680* (1992); Peter H. Wood, *Black Majority: Negroes in South Carolina from 1670 through the Stono Rebellion* (1974).

Battlefields, Civil War

The Gray and the Blue engaged in more than 10,000 armed conflicts from 1861 to 1865, and, except for Lee's Pennsylvania campaign in the summer of 1863 and an occasional Confederate raid into enemy territory, all occurred below the Mason-Dixon line. Although most concentrated in the border states, Tennessee and Virginia, battlefields ranging in size from a few acres to several dozen square miles dotted every corner of the Confederacy by war's end. Significant cities such as Vicksburg, Atlanta, Charleston, and Richmond had been the scenes of fierce and protracted combat. Looking out across a wilderness of roofless houses, blackened chimneys, crumbling walls, and shell-perforated buildings, Russell Conwell, a Union veteran touring the South in 1869 as correspondent for a Boston newspaper, described Fredericksburg as "a sample of an ideal battlefield." Yet it was not in urban areas but at strategic points along the rivers, roads, and rail lines connecting them that the bloodiest and most decisive fighting had taken place. The war was won and lost in the cornfields, cow pastures, craggy mountain passes, and sweltering swamps of the southern hinterland.

Civil War battlefields have long been regarded as sacred ground by many Americans. Sanctified by the blood of heroes who fought and died there in the triumphant defense of the Union and its hallowed tenets of liberty and democracy, these historic sites inspire patriotism and are enduring national symbols of right, might, and victory worthy of the highest form of veneration, to be set aside from surrounding secular space in perpetuity. But for southerners, especially white southerners who lost the war, living and making a living among, even on, these battlefields in the near century and a half since Appomattox has engendered a certain deep-seated ambivalence toward permanent preservation of their place in the landscape.

Shortly after Lee's surrender, a former officer in the Army of the Potomac remarked that since so much of the war had been waged on Virginia soil, the state "should be enclosed with a high fence and kept sacred." Yet the battlefields' first stewards were southerners, and in Virginia and elsewhere the sanctity of the sites began to be defiled almost as soon as the armies withdrew. With the South's economy in shambles, conquered Confederates swiftly beat their swords back into plowshares and looked to the land to sustain existence in the hardscrabble postbellum years. For the countless families unlucky enough

Battlefield Graveyard, Vicksburg National Military Park
(Vicksburg National Military Park, Vicksburg, Miss.)

to have lately had hostile military forces clash in their backyards, that meant breaking ground on a battlefield. Farmers from Maryland to Mississippi leveled breastworks, filled entrenchments, and returned desolate killing fields to cropland. Landless freedmen, who as slaves had been made to throw up fortifications along the coast and around cities, now tore them down in search of lead shot to sell as scrap. As he traveled through Virginia, Conwell noted that "the earthworks . . . are in some places nearly obliterated—especially at Manassas, Ball's Bluff, Winchester, Cedar Mountain, and the fields near Washington. A stranger to the country, however well he might be acquainted with the history of those early campaigns, could not trace at these places the works of either army, although numerous mounds and pits still remain." On the Georgia Piedmont north of Atlanta, "the transformation from earthworks, tents, signal and picket posts to fields of cotton and sweet potatoes" was equally striking.

Nearly two-thirds of a million American soldiers lost their lives in the Civil War, and despite the best efforts of the U.S. Army and Ladies' Memorial Associations of the South in the immediate postwar years to provide proper burials, for thousands upon thousands, most of them Confederates, the ground on which they fell became their final resting place. At Fort Harrison near Richmond, Conwell encountered a "most terrible" sight all too common in his travels, a farmer tilling a field littered with human skeletal remains and soldiers' accouterments. When asked how he could be party to such a "sacrilegious act," the farmer pled poverty. The land was the richest piece he had, and as for the bones, he "'didn't put 'em there nohow.'"

Not surprisingly, the earliest efforts to preserve Civil War battlefields as such came from the victors. At the urging of aging Union veterans anxious to uphold their martial accomplishments in posterity, Congress authorized federal acquisition of five battlefields in the 1890s—Chickamauga and Chattanooga, Antietam, Shiloh, Gettysburg, and Vicksburg—to be operated as public parks by the War Department. Each incorporated an existing national cemetery, and except for Chickamauga, all were the sites of important northern triumphs. Some enterprising ex-Confederates saw battlefield preservation as an opportunity to foster reconciliation between North and South and offered old enemies their support in hopes of building political and economic ties that might benefit both themselves and their section. More often, however, southerners simply saw the new battlefield preserves as attempts by despicable blue-bellies, the same ones who had once killed their kinsman and marched across their country burning and pillaging, to rub their noses in defeat. Generations of 20th-century Vicksburgers, for instance, disdained their city's national battlefield as a "Yankee park."

By the time southerners began to create battlefield shrines, the Civil War was barely a memory. One of the first, appropriately enough, was at Manassas, site of two of the Confederacy's most stunning victories. In 1927 a local grassroots organization called the Manassas Battlefield Confederate Park, Inc., the Sons of Confederate Veterans, and the Commonwealth of Virginia purchased outright the 128-acre Henry Farm, scene of heavy fighting during both battles. During the 1930s, President Franklin Roosevelt's Resettlement Administration acquired an additional 1,600 acres of the Manassas battlefields as the Bull Run Recreational Demonstration Area, and in 1938 the Manassas Battlefield Corporation deeded its property to the federal government. Despite lingering reservations in Congress over establishing a park that would commemorate a pair of stinging Union losses, in 1940 Manassas National Battlefield Park became a unit of the National Park Service, a Department of the Interior agency that had assumed the management of national military parks in 1933.

For the better part of a century after the demise of the Confederate States of America, the poverty-stricken South remained overwhelmingly rural and agrarian, and whether as open farmland or woods, into the 1960s the vast majority of Civil War battlefields continued to look much as they had in the 1860s. But in the decades that followed, as unprecedented population growth and economic expansion recast the cultural landscape of the region, the number of battlefield sites that a participant in the battle would still recognize began to decline precipitously. C. Vann Woodward described the landscape changes wrought by dramatic post–World War II industrialization and urbanization as Dixie's "Bulldozer Revolution," and indeed the giant earthmover — roaring and groaning and raising great clouds of dust — became a common sight on the outskirts of every southern city. A powerful symbol of progress in the not-so-New South, the bulldozer was warmly welcomed wherever it went, bringing in the wake of its lowered blade new jobs, increased tax revenue, and overdue social amenities. But Sunbelt prosperity meant metropolitan sprawl, and by the mid-1980s, as the suburban frontier expanded rapidly into the countryside, southerners were paving over portions of battlefield after battlefield to make way for commercial, industrial, and residential development. Some, such as Chantilly in Virginia, were blotted out altogether beneath mushrooming gas stations, superstores, and tract houses.

In early 1988, Virginia real estate developer John T. ("Til") Hazel's plan to build a 1.2-million-square-foot regional shopping mall on land adjacent to the Manassas National Battlefield Park awoke America to the effect that the emergence of the Sunbelt was having on the historical integrity of its Civil War battlefields. An upstart coalition of celebrities, politicians, historians, and concerned citizens from across the country rallied to save Stuart Hill, the proposed mall site where Lee had made his headquarters during Second Manassas, but were disappointed to find state and local government officials siding with the developers in the interests of economic growth. The public campaign soon caught the ear of Congress, and in November 1988, President Ronald Reagan signed into law a bill authorizing, through a rarely used procedure called "legislative taking," federal outlay of more than $130 million to acquire the contested 558-acre tract from the Hazel/Peterson Companies for incorporation into the Manassas battlefield park.

The so-called Third Battle of Manassas proved a watershed in battlefield preservation in the United States. Congress responded in 1991 by creating the Civil War Sites Advisory Commission, a 15-member body that would "identify the significant Civil War Sites, determine their condition, assess threats to their integrity, and offer alternatives for their preservation." According to the commission's landmark 1993 report, 19 percent (71) of the Civil War's 384 "principal" battlefields were already lost as coherent historic landscapes. Existing national or state parks contained some part of 32 percent (95) of the remaining sites, but of those only about a dozen held enough of the core battlefield area for it to be considered adequately protected. Of the 235 principal battlefields judged to be in good or fair condition, half were experiencing high or moderate threats. "Most of these sites," the report concluded, "will be lost or seriously fragmented within the coming 10 years, many very soon."

Infused with a sense of urgency by the events at Manassas, the nation's historic preservation community—both within the federal government and in the private sector—swiftly mobilized in the late 1980s and early 1990s to meet the crisis. At the same time that the Department of the Interior was initiating the National Park Service's American Battlefield Protection Program, a groundswell of grassroots interest led to the formation of two private, nonprofit organizations devoted to protecting Civil War battlefield lands endangered by development, the Association for the Preservation of Civil War Sites and the Civil War Trust, which merged in 1999 to become the Civil War Preservation Trust. Other national nonprofits like the National Parks Conservation Association and the Conservation Fund also promptly made battlefield preservation a priority.

Public and private efforts during the 1990s managed to preserve thousands of threatened battlefield acres through the purchase of land and conservation easements. Even so, these groups often had their work frustrated at the local level by the very people who they felt should be the sites' foremost advocates, the southerners abiding among them. As one leading preservationist lamented,

"We don't have a way to save these places where [local] people with control over them don't care about saving them, whereas there is a large constituency across the United States that favors them." By the end of the decade, Civil War battlefields were disappearing more rapidly than ever—at a rate of one acre every ten minutes, by one estimate.

While the burgeoning popularity of battle reenactments, recent environmental initiatives aimed at conserving open space in an increasingly suburbanized landscape, and the dollars drawn by heritage tourism have begun to build broader support for the movement in states below the Mason-Dixon line, the majority of modern southerners remain ambivalent about battlefield preservation. Like the characters in a Bobbie Ann Mason short story, they still enjoy an occasional visit to Shiloh; but frequenting the new strip mall and fast-food franchises off the interstate and dreaming of an attractive home in a new subdivision on the edge of town, they also embrace the affluence and amenities of the advancing metropolis that is fast obliterating so many of the other battlefields. Since Woodward first wrote of it in the late 1950s, the South's "Bulldozer Revolution" has only gained momentum with each passing decade. Fueled by the march of economic development and mounting population pressures, it rages on, encroaching "upon rural life to expand urban life," demolishing "the old to make way for the new," and insuring that in the 21st century the number of southerners with Civil War battlefields in their backyards will continue to decline.

MATTHEW A. LOCKHART
University of South Carolina

Georgie Boge and Margie Holder Boge, *Paving Over the Past: A History and Guide to Civil War Battlefield Preservation* (1993); Tony Horwitz, *Confederates in the Attic: Dispatches from the Unfinished Civil War* (1998); James A. Kaser, *At the Bivouac of Memory: History, Politics, and the Battle of Chickamauga* (1996); Frances H. Kennedy, ed., *The Civil War Battlefield Guide* (2d ed., 1998); Edward Tabor Linenthal, *Sacred Ground: Americans and Their Battlefields* (2d ed., 1993); A. J. Meek and Herman Hattaway, *Gettysburg to Vicksburg: The Five Original Civil War Battlefield Parks* (2001); John T. Trowbridge, *The South: A Tour of Its Battlefields and Ruined Cities* (1866); Joan M. Zenzen, *Battling for Manassas: The Fifty-Year Preservation Struggle at Manassas National Battlefield Park* (1998).

Civil Rights Movement

After the Civil War, many black leaders worked for equal status between blacks and whites. The most prominent spokesman for this aspiration in the early 20th century was W. E. B. Du Bois. The National Association for the Advancement of Colored People was founded in 1909, and a year later the National Urban League was organized. In *Buchanan v. Warley* (1917) the Supreme Court invalidated residential segregation laws as a deprivation of property rights without due process of law. During the 1930s the Court started to condemn the discriminatory administration of criminal justice in the South. Despite these early victories against racial discrimination, the nation made little progress in the field of civil rights until the end of World War II.

The emergence of New Deal social programs and the egalitarian rhetoric of World War II produced a change in American thought and helped to undermine the intellectual justification for racial segregation in the South. In turn, this development produced a gradual but significant shift in the role of the federal government. President Harry S. Truman identified his administration with the movement for equal rights. In 1948 Truman issued an executive order eliminating segregation in the armed forces. He also called for a Fair Employment Practices Commission and a ban on poll tax requirements for voting. Although Congress rejected Truman's legislative program, he established civil rights as a national issue. Moreover, the federal courts began to adopt a broader reading of the equal protection clause of the Fourteenth Amendment. During the late 1940s several Supreme Court decisions outlawed segregation in interstate transportation and higher education. This trend culminated with the historic 1954 decision in *Brown v. Board of Education*, which proscribed compulsory segregation in public schools as a violation of the equal protection clause.

Important new developments also took place at the state level and in the private sector. Several northern states passed laws against racial discrimination. In 1946 Jackie Robinson became the first black to play major league baseball. Four years later diplomat Ralph Bunche became the first black to win the Nobel Peace Prize.

The NAACP led the legal battle against segregation, working for civil rights legislation and instituting litigation to compel desegregation of public schools in the South. Despite the *Brown* ruling and pressure from the NAACP, only a limited amount of racial integration occurred in southern schools between 1954 and 1964. Most southern states rallied to the banner of "massive resistance" and sought to obstruct implementation of racial desegregation. President Dwight D. Eisenhower did not envision an active role for the federal government in promoting school desegregation. Nonetheless, he did send federal troops to Little Rock in 1957 when state authorities attempted to block implementation of a court-ordered desegregation plan.

Other organizations also struggled for equal rights. Foremost among these was the Southern Christian Leadership Conference, headed by Dr. Martin Luther King Jr. Late in 1955 blacks in Montgomery, Ala., under King's guidance, began nonviolent protest by instituting a successful boycott of the city's segregated bus system.

During the early 1960s the civil rights movement underwent several important changes. After a period of hesitation, President John F. Kennedy placed the executive branch of the federal government squarely behind desegregation efforts. In 1963 Kennedy endorsed a broad civil rights proposal to outlaw segregation in public accommodations. At the same time, many blacks grew impatient with the slow progress in achieving desegregation. Blacks increasingly resorted to direct forms of protest. There were sit-ins at segregated lunch counters and Freedom Rides that challenged segregation in transportation facilities. Defenders of segregation often employed violence against blacks or civil right workers in an attempt to halt their activities.

The civil rights movement may have reached its climax in August of 1963 when more than 200,000 persons took part in the March on Washington. King, who had emerged as the leading spokesman for the civil rights movement, delivered an impassioned plea for racial equality. President Lyndon B. Johnson responded to this initiative by calling upon Congress to enact sweeping civil rights legislation. The resulting Civil Rights Act of 1964 required equal access to public accommodations and outlawed discrimination in employment. The Voting Rights Act of 1965 suspended literacy tests in several states and strengthened federal protection of the right to vote. The Twenty-fourth Amendment, ratified in 1964, barred poll tax requirements for participation in federal elections. Subsequently the Supreme Court declared unconstitutional the poll tax in state elections. Thus, by the mid-1960s the civil rights movement had attained most of its original objectives, which concerned conditions in the South.

The late 1960s saw a marked shift in the goals of civil rights leaders. The large-scale migration of blacks to northern cities, which had begun by World War I, produced recurrent ethnic conflict in urban neighborhoods. Accordingly, the movement increasing focused upon racial discrimination in the North. In particular, black leaders challenged residential segregation, poor schooling, high unemployment among members of racial minorities, and alleged police brutality. Given the heavy concentration of impoverished blacks in the inner-city areas, resolution of these problems proved extremely difficult. Indeed, civil rights gains hardly affected the living conditions of many northern blacks. A wave of urban riots across the North highlighted racial tensions and also served to alienate white opinion.

In addition, by promoting new remedies for discrimination, civil rights activists moved well beyond the national consensus in favor of equality. The busing of pupils from one neighborhood to another in an effort to integrate schools, although endorsed by the Supreme Court in 1971, threatened traditional neighborhood schools and was opposed by the vast majority of whites. Congress debated numerous proposals to restrict this practice. In *Milliken v. Bradley* (1974) the Supreme Court ruled against busing across school district lines to achieve integration between suburban areas and the inner city.

Initiated in the late 1960s, affirmative action policies in employment and university admissions were often perceived as favoritism to members of minority groups and proved highly controversial. In 1978 the Supreme Court outlawed the use of quotas to aid racial minorities in the university admissions process but ruled that race was a factor that could be considered in the admissions process to further the goal of diversity. In a line of decisions in the 1980s the Court similarly sustained the legality of race-conscious remedies to remedy racial discrimination in the employment context. Thereafter, the Court seemed to shift course by tightening the evidentiary rule for proving employment discrimination, thereby making it more difficult for complainants to prevail in such cases. Moreover, in *City of Richmond v. J. A. Croson Co.* (1989) the justices held that a municipal plan awarding a set percentage of construction contracts to minority-owned businesses classified persons on a racial basis in violation of the equal protection clause. With the Civil Rights Act of 1991, however, Congress rejected a number of Supreme Court decisions that curtailed employment discrimination lawsuits, expanded the definition of discrimination, and reaffirmed its commitment to affirmative action.

Criticism of affirmative action in higher education mounted in the 1990s. In *Grutter v. Bollinger* (2003) the Supreme Court upheld a state law school's use of race, along with other factors, to obtain a diverse student body. Yet in a companion case the justices limited reliance on affirmative action by striking down a policy of automatically preferring members of certain racial minorities. Such a mechanistic scheme seemingly operated much like a quota and was found to violate the equal protection clause.

The civil rights movement scored a symbolic victory in the late 1980s with the establishment of the Martin Luther King Jr. holiday. Fifteen years after Dr. King's death, President Ronald Reagan signed a bill into law making the third Monday of January a national holiday celebrating the birth and life of Dr. Martin Luther King Jr. The first national celebration of the Dr. Martin Luther King Jr. holiday took place 20 January 1986. Nearly all states also have official King holidays.

Racial gerrymandering—the practice of state's drawing legislative districts to create the maximum number of majority-black districts — emerged as a contested issue in the 1990s. In 1982 Congress prohibited states from adopting laws that diluted minority political strength. After the 1990 census, the Justice Department urged southern states to increase the number of minority-black districts, advising southern lawmakers that such action was required by the Voting Rights Act. The Supreme Court has inconclusively addressed racial gerrymandering in a series of confusing cases. In *Shaw v. Reno* (1993) the justices held that the Voting Rights Act does not require states to draw unusual and oddly shaped districts just to create majority-black districts. In *Miller v. Johnson* (1995), moreover, the Supreme Court explained that a state violated the equal protection clause if race was the predominant factor in establishing district lines. Yet the gerrymandering issue is complicated because the racial composition of legislative districts is closely intertwined with partisan voting patterns. The Court has sustained legislative districts created for political advantage rather than impermissible racial reasons. Thus, the mere fact that lines were drawn to create a black-majority district does not prove that lawmakers were motivated by race. The courts and the Justice Department continue to wrestle with this thorny question.

Efforts to desegregate primary and secondary schools slowed in the 1990s following Supreme Court decisions that made it easier for school systems to be released from federal court supervision. School districts dropped busing schemes in favor of voluntary desegregation programs and began to return to neighborhood schools. Neither Congress nor the executive branch has pursued policies to foster desegregated schools. The emergence of Hispanics as the largest minority group in the United States has further complicated the desegregation process. As a result, schools in the South and across the nation are becoming more segregated. Although the *Brown* decision ended de jure school segregation, the prospects for achieving widespread racial integration remain elusive.

In the early 21st century the civil rights movement is less focused on the South and increasingly finds expression in the political arena. African American leaders are concerned with economic disparities in black neighborhoods and predominantly black schools. The issues of racial profiling, fair housing, and inadequate education are also high on the list of those concerned with civil rights. But the political climate renders uncertain the prospects for significant change.

JAMES W. ELY JR.
Vanderbilt University Law School

Catherine A. Barnes, *Journey from Jim Crow: The Desegregation of Southern Transit* (1983); Taylor Branch, *Parting the Waters: America in the King Years, 1954–1963* (1988), *Pillar of Fire: America in the King Years, 1963–1965* (1998); Charles W. Eagles, *Journal of Southern History* (2000); James W. Ely Jr., *The Crisis of Conservative Virginia: The Byrd Organization and the Politics of Massive Resistance* (1976); Adam Fairclough, *Race and Democracy: The Civil Rights Struggle in Louisiana, 1915–1972* (1995); David R. Goldfield, *Black, White, and Southern: Race Relations and Southern Culture, 1940 to the Present* (1990); Michael J. Klarman, *From Jim Crow to Civil Rights: The Supreme Court and the Struggle for Racial Equality* (2004); Richard Kluger, *Simple Justice: This History of Brown v. Board of Education and Black America's Struggle for Equality*, rev. ed. (2004); Anthony Lewis and the *New York Times, Portrait of a Decade: The Second American Revolution* (1964); Harvard Sitkoff, *A New Deal for Blacks: The Emergence of Civil Rights as a National Issue* (1978); J. Harvie Wilkinson III, *From Brown to Bakke: The Supreme Court and School Integration, 1954–1978* (1979).

Civil War

The South was once a small corner of an American Indian civilization that covered two continents. Then the South was in the middle of the western fringe of the British Empire. Next the South was one section within a union of former colonies. In that union the South became a self-conscious minority section, later a collection of "conquered provinces," and still later "Uncle Sam's other province." Whether the site of "the Nation's No. 1 economic problem" or the potential recipient of Sunbelt prosperity, the South has been a peculiar region within the American nation. And southerners have defined themselves within the context of a civilization, empire, union, or nation in which they have been a minority. The single exception to this was that four-year "moment" during which the South was itself a de facto nation, the Confederate States of America.

In theory, Confederate southerners should have been able to shape their corporate identity and define themselves as a separate people. In fact, a war for their survival as people and nation severely circumscribed the inclinations and efforts of southerners to create a recognizable Confederate culture. Some historians have even contended that the Confederate South never quite became a nation and thus never developed a national life worthy of the name. To be sure, the Confederacy lived only briefly, and then only in the midst of a devastating, modern war. But within limits, the Confederate experience led (and drove) southerners into novel cultural expressions and relationships, some of which outlived the abortive southern nation.

Lt. General John C. Pemberton, Vicksburg battlefield monument, Mississippi, 1936 (Walker Evans, photographer, Library of Congress [LC-USF342-008085-A], Washington, D.C.)

Discovering Confederate southern culture is a challenge. Examinations of some traditional forms of cultural expression—art, music, literature, and the like—are disappointing. During the war southerners sang and listened to music that was all but identical to that of their enemies. Both northern and southern armies marched to the strains of "Dixie," and soldiers on both sides sang romantic ballads like "Lorena." Paintings, such as William D. Washington's *The Burial of Latané*, enjoyed brief fame but have since served as examples of "sentimentalism," "exaggeration," and "historical anecdote" in 19th-century art. Confederate southerners produced little in the realm of belles lettres and less of any lasting value. And the trench networks at Vicksburg, Petersburg, and elsewhere were but sad architectural expressions that fortunately did not endure in southern life. None of this should be very surprising; wartime is seldom conducive to contemplative pursuits, especially when the war is going badly. Southerners, like most people at war, preferred escape and diversion to challenge and creativity in their theater, books, and songs.

Nevertheless, Confederates did make significant contributions to southern culture; the challenge in discovering these contributions lies in knowing where to look for them. Augusta Jane Evans's *Macaria; or, Altars of Sacrifice*, which was the most popular novel produced in the Confederacy, was not the best example of southern literature during the war. Southerners who responded immediately and directly to wartime experience in letters, diaries, magazines, and newspapers did, however, generate a body of literature that was lively and lasting. John M. Daniel and Edward A. Pollard in the *Richmond Examiner*, to cite only one newspaper, offered vigorous (often vicious) editorials, as well as vivid coverage, from the South's battlefields. The family papers of the Fleets in Virginia and the Joneses in Georgia have become classics a century after their composition as *Greenmount, a Virginia Plantation Family during the Civil War* and *The Children of Pride: A True Story of Georgia and the Civil War*. Likewise, the diaries of Mary Chesnut and Phoebe Pember continue, with reason, to charm readers. Confederate southerners generated a "literature of immediacy," which generally surpassed the leisured efforts of southern writers in the rest of the 19th century.

The Confederate experience affected southerners in myriad ways; the creation of an informal wartime literature is only one example. "Rebel ingenuity" is another. The agricultural southern people involved in an industrial war developed a remarkable resourcefulness. Esteemed oceanographer Matthew Fontaine Maury developed "torpedoes" (mines) for the Confederate navy, and officers in the niter and mining bureau learned how to use urine in the manufacture of gunpowder. On the home front southerners experimented with substitutes for coffee and adjusted to the scarcity of imported items.

Among Confederate institutions the church proved to be the most steadfastly patriotic. Most southerners recognized the authority of some Protestant evangelical denomination, whether or not they took an active part in organized religion, and southern churches were overwhelmingly supporters of the Cause. Quakers, Universalists, and the like who did not share the enthusiasm of their fellow Protestants were few in number compared to the evangelical majority, and other southern religious minorities, Jews and Roman Catholics, actively backed the Confederacy. In the early months of the war, sermons likened southerners to God's chosen people and northerners to Philistines. Later, when southern armies seemed to be losing, the church offered an explanation: God was testing and chastening the southern people; in renewed righteousness lay God's favor and victory. Churches not only preached national salvation, they sent chaplains, and countless tracts, into Confederate camps for the sake of individual souls. Revivals swept through the ranks of the Confederate armies, especially during 1864, and religion offered spiritual comfort to many in the midst of death and defeat. Southern churches, too, developed a stronger social consciousness in response to wartime. Congregations donated their bells to be recast as cannon, offered their buildings as hospitals, and organized knitting and sewing sessions to fashion items of clothing for the troops. As the Confederacy collapsed, southern churches offered the consolation that religion transcends temporal circumstance and that righteousness would ultimately prevail.

Certainly the Civil War contributed to the southern "cult of the soldier" — the conviction that the military was an ultimate expression of manhood. Even when the dirt, disease, and death of war's reality contradicted this conviction, many southerners clung to the fantasy. For families of those who died in camp and combat and for thousands of wounded men, the association of military service with manhood somehow justified the sacrifice.

That the administration of Jefferson Davis and the Confederate Congress should have authorized the participation of black southerners in the "cult of the soldier" is some index of the war's impact upon the South. In 1861 Confederate vice president Alexander H. Stephens proclaimed slavery to be the "cornerstone" of the southern nation. By 1864 the southern government was advocating the use of black troops in the war, and Robert E. Lee went on record as welcoming black men into his armies. When the Congress finally acted to arm the slaves, the Davis administration made sure that black soldiers would serve as free men. These efforts occurred too late to save the Cause, but their very occurrence is significant.

The idea of woman as southern belle, ornament and object, did not fare well in wartime. Women often became heads of households when men went off to fight. Confederate women also became nurses, refugees, and factory workers. The variety of experience was novel, and to the degree that it became more than an emergency irregularity in the lives of southern women, it revised roles and expectations among these women.

However much wartime influenced southern life, the most profound effect of the Civil War upon southern culture occurred only after the war was lost. It is supreme irony that southern culture since 1865 has been more the product of Lost Cause mythology than Confederate realities. The southern response to defeat, reunion, and Reconstruction inspired a myth-history that ennobled the destruction of the southern nation. The Lost Cause mythology held that the southern cause was not only undefiled by defeat but that the bloodbath of war actually sanctified the values and mores of the Old South. High priests of this message were beaten warriors. Southerners enshrined the politicians and especially those military officers who had presided over failure and defeat. The influence of the unreconstructed proved to be pervasive.

The Lost Cause inspired a romantic literature perhaps best exemplified by Margaret Mitchell's *Gone with the Wind*. If literary critics are correct, the myth helped to spawn the Southern Literary Renaissance and fueled the intellectual movement known as the Nashville Agrarians. Indeed, the Lost Cause became a civil religion south of the Potomac, and it continues in various ways and degrees to influence southern thought and action.

The Civil War offered southerners the opportunity to win their independence and mold for themselves a national, as opposed to sectional, culture. As Confederates, southerners did respond creatively to the stress of wartime. But the most significant impact of the Civil War upon southern culture lay, not in its reality, but in its memory. The memory may have been myth; but for many southerners the Lost Cause has been myth believed and acted upon.

Recent historical studies of the Civil War have reflected broader historiographical concerns in the study of the American South, including race, social class, gender, and geographical diversity within the South. "Americans and others continue to revisit the period of the Civil War because that period continues to speak to contemporary questions — questions about race, community, and identity," writes Emory Thomas. "Moreover, the Civil War as human drama continues to evoke interest and fascination." Historians have explored the social context of the war in the South and filled in details on the creation of the Confederacy's culture and how the new national identity evolved in the course of the war. They have shown continuing interest in Confederate leaders, with major new biographies of Robert E. Lee, Jefferson Davis, and Stonewall Jackson appearing, and in military strategy, with the western theater of war gaining increased attention. An interest in the home front is surely one of the most important recent trends in Civil War studies.

One point of contention among historians has been the unity — or lack of it — in the Confederacy. The title of William Freehling's book *The South vs. the South: How Anti-Confederate Southerners Shaped the Course of the War* (2001) suggests his argument that the Confederate political and military crusade did not reflect the breadth of the South's society and interests. Upcountry yeoman would seem to have had differing economic interests from plantation-district whites, and the lack of regionwide early commitment to secession suggests division. The compelling nature of events in early 1861, especially Lincoln's call to arms, may have driven commitment to the Confederacy more than a unified ideology. Many historians have seen fundamental disunity in yeoman opposition to conscription, discontent over privations, inequalities between planter and yeoman sacrifices, and women's unhappiness at men's removal from the region's farms and plantations. Some historians have argued for a lack of fundamental antebellum southern distinctiveness from the North, which became apparent during the war. Guilt over slavery and the lack of yeoman commitment to defending slavery, in some interpretations, weakened the will of southern whites to win. Other historians argue against an overemphasis on internal divisions in the Confederacy. Acknowledging that doubts and sacrifices existed, they see them leading to a renewed commitment until war's end.

The role of African Americans in the war has also been a key theme in the recent historiography of the Civil War. Studies have shown the numerical importance of southern African Americans joining Union armies and fighting for their freedom. Slaves sometimes remained on plantations but with a gradual disruption of life there because of the absence of men at war and the physical devastation in parts of the South. Clarence Mohr's study of blacks in Civil War Georgia stressed the importance of place in understanding black responses to the evolving wartime context. In coastal areas, slaves entered the Union armies as soon as possible, but in the isolated interior they were more cautious. Debates among Confederate leaders near the end of the war about arming slaves suggest how the evolving wartime context pushed the new nation toward dramatic changes in the racial status quo.

Women's changing wartime roles have been the subject of considerable work as well. Studies by George C. Rable, Drew Gilpin Faust, and LeAnn Whites show the support of women for the war effort as it began, but then their emerging doubts and opposition as suffering and privations continued. Elite women assumed larger public roles and struggled sometimes with new responsibilities in dealing with slaves and overseers. Yeoman women faced even greater challenges, having to figure ways to keep small farms operative and gain access to limited public resources. A distinctive spiritual crisis affected women, but they generally remained resilient to the end.

The study of historical memory has found fertile ground in post–Civil War efforts to remember the war. Works by William Blair, David Blight, Fitzhugh

Brundage, Alice Fahs and Joan Waugh, and John Neff have shown how memory became tangibly embodied in many cultural and political arenas, such as public monuments, parades, soldiers' memoirs, political campaigns, and textbook publishing. Commemorations in particular were resonant rituals that enacted competing ideologies among northerners, southern whites, and African Americans. Memorial Days and Emancipation Days until at least the turn of the 20th century were competing ceremonies for the presentation of alternative views of southern history. The symbolic bodies of the Civil War dead loomed large in the South's and the nation's imaginations. Issues of regional reconciliation and racial oppression hovered around those dead bodies.

Literature and popular culture portray the Civil War in dramatic ways that have refreshed in recent decades the war's centrality in southern and American culture. Shelby Foote's epic study *The Civil War: A Narrative* (1958–74) continues to grow in its impact as a magisterial telling of the war's human meanings. While professional historians find its lack of historiographical concerns limiting, the trilogy of books reaches wide popular audiences and engages readers who appreciate Foote's literary skills and his portrait of the rhythms and tragedies of the fighting. Allan Gurganus's *Oldest Living Confederate Widow Tells All* (1984) and Charles Frazier's *Cold Mountain* (1997) were popular novels that emphasized the experiences of common soldiers and women in the war. The latter book was made into a major Hollywood film, another movie that kept the war well placed in the popular imagination. *Glory* was significant in dramatizing the saga of African American soldiers and idealistic northern whites fighting for the Union.

Ken Burns's *The Civil War* (1990) deserves special recognition for using the genre of documentary film to present the Confederate, Union, and African American narratives in a compelling manner before wide audiences on public broadcasting. Burns emphasizes the suffering of the war in this nine-episode saga, using memorable black and white photographic images, written excerpts from diaries and letters, and the recurring sounds of cannons firing and period music playing to create an evocative world of war. The alternating voices and images of Shelby Foote and historian Barbara J. Fields suggested competing interpretations of the war's meanings and added to its effectiveness. Edward Ayers's *Valley of the Shadow* (http://valley.vcdh.virginia.edu) represents a new genre in the presentation of the Civil War, a Web site that gathers primary sources and interpretive perspectives for the varied audiences of the online medium.

EMORY THOMAS
University of Georgia

Edward L. Ayers, *In the Presence of Mine Enemies: War in the Heart of America, 1859–1863* (2003); Henry Putney Beers, *Guide to the Archives of the Government of the Confederate States of America* (1968); William Blair, *Contesting the Memory of the Civil War in the South, 1865–1914* (2004); David W. Blight, *Race and Reunion: The Civil War in American Memory* (2001); Jim Cullen, *The Civil War in Popular Culture: A Reusable Past* (1995); Clement Eaton, *A History of the Southern Confederacy* (1954); Alice Fahs and Joan Waugh, *The Memory of the Civil War in American Culture* (2004); Drew Gilpin Faust, *The Creation of Confederate Nationalism: Ideology and Identity in the Civil War South* (1988), *Mothers of Invention: Women of the Slaveholding South in the American Civil War* (1996); Shelby Foote, *The Civil War: A Narrative*, 3 vols. (1958–75); Douglas Southall Freeman, *The South to Posterity: An Introduction to the Writings of Confederate History* (1939); Gary W. Gallagher, *The Confederate War* (1997); David Goldfield, *Still Fighting the Civil War: The American South and Southern History* (2002); James M. McPherson and William J. Cooper, *Writing the Civil War: The Quest to Understand* (1998); Randall M. Miller, Harry S. Stout, and Charles Reagan Wilson, eds., *Religion and the American Civil War* (1998); Clarence L. Mohr, *On the Threshold of Freedom: Masters and Slaves in Civil War Georgia* (1986); John R. Neff, *Honoring the Civil War Dead: Commemoration and the Problem of Reconciliation* (2005); Allen Nevins, James I. Robertson Jr., and Bell I. Wiley, eds., *Civil War Books: A Critical Bibliography* (1967); George C. Rable, *Civil Wars: Women and the Crisis of Southern Nationalism* (1989); James G. Randall and David Donald, *The Civil War and Reconstruction* (2d rev. ed., 1969); Charles P. Roland, *The Confederacy* (1960); James W. Silver, *Confederate Morale and Church Propaganda* (1957); Emory Thomas, *Confederacy as a Revolutionary Experience* (1971), *The Confederate Nation, 1861–1865* (1979), in *Warm Ashes: Issues in Southern History at the Dawn of the 21st Century*, ed. Winfred B. Moore Jr., Kyle S. Sinisi, and David H. White Jr. (2003); Frank E. Vandiver, *Their Tattered Flags: The Epic of the Confederacy* (1970); LeAnn Whites, *The Civil War as a Crisis in Gender: Augusta, Georgia, 1860–1890* (1995); Bell I. Wiley, *Confederate Women* (1975), *The Plain People of the Confederacy* (1943).

Cold War

The Cold War was the period of nuclear-armed competition between the United States and the Soviet Union, lasting from the end of World War II until the withdrawal of Soviet military forces from Eastern Europe in 1989 and the disappearance of the Soviet Union itself in 1991. Americans considered themselves the leaders of what they called the free world, the non-Communist nations of Europe and the Americas. Much of the Cold War served as a contest between the Soviets and Americans for the friendship and alliance of the new

Third World nations of Asia and Africa, which emerged out of colonialism into independence after 1945.

U.S. policymakers believed that a key to waging the Cold War was American openness. In contrast to the secrecy and duplicity they associated with Communists and the Soviet Union, they hoped that maximum exposure to Americans' essential decency and democratic practices would convince Third World peoples of the virtues of capitalism and Western-style democracy. In this regard the South proved to be a stumbling block for the nation's Cold War purposes, particularly before 1965. Constituting a majority of the world's population, Third World peoples of color doubted that the treatment and status of African Americans south of the Mason-Dixon line made American society a model they wished to emulate. Racial discrimination abounded in the rest of the United States as well, but the South's legacy of rigid segregation and racial violence gave the region a particular prominence as Americans sought to convince others that their country was the leader of a truly free world.

Race reformers in the South used the logic of anti-Communism to promote racial equality. Civil rights workers emphasized the close attention that Africans and Asians paid to the treatment of black southerners and the ease with which the Soviets used American racial discrimination and violence to undercut U.S. claims to being the leading apostle of freedom. This argument won out, for the most part, at the level of the federal government. The administrations of Harry Truman, John Kennedy, and Lyndon Johnson—and, to a lesser extent, Dwight Eisenhower—recognized this weakness and gradually moved the nation toward eliminating legal racial distinctions. Washington's Cold War priorities abroad eventually lent support to the work of the civil rights movement.

In their resistance to racial change, most white southerners in the first two decades after 1945 used the logic of anti-Communism in a very different way. With support for civil rights outside the South growing, white supremacists in Dixie took up the slogan of anti-Communism in part as a cover for preserving racial segregation. The few American Communists enthusiastically supported racial equality, reactionaries noted, so it must be a subversive idea. Indeed, racial equality was a subversive idea in most of the South before the mid-1960s, and white supremacists worked to associate it closely with Communism. White southerners shared the genuine abhorrence of Communism of most Americans, but their concern for preserving traditional racial hierarchies gave their anti-Communism a particularly zealous and distorted cast.

The South benefited from the vast expansion of military spending that became standard during the Cold War. More than one-third of the federal funds for new military bases and defense industry contracts during World War II went to states of the former Confederacy, as warm weather and inexpensive land close to the coast made for attractive sites for training millions of new soldiers for service overseas. This was the starting point for the growth of the Sunbelt, which continued throughout the Cold War era and has done much to shape American society and politics ever since.

The South's distinctive racial mores during the first half of the Cold War engendered uncertainty about whether the region was more similar to or different from the rest of the country. Part of the uncertainty stemmed from the disproportionate influence that the region had in the nation's political life. The late 1940s and early 1950s marked the apex of southern influence in the U.S. Congress. Seniority rules and the one-party character of southern politics had elevated Dixie Democrats into the chairs of a majority of the most powerful committees in both the House and the Senate. Journalist William S. Whyte observed, "So marked and so constant is this high degree of Southern dominion . . . that the Senate might be described as the South's unending revenge upon the North for Gettysburg."

The South's influence reached into the executive branch as well. Almost all of the Cold War presidents displayed some kind of particular affection for the region. Truman, Johnson, and Jimmy Carter grew up in former slaveholding states. Eisenhower vacationed frequently in Georgia and spoke publicly of his respect for the Confederacy. Kennedy had the fewest personal ties to Dixie, but Richard Nixon ran his 1968 campaign on a "southern strategy" and remained solicitous of white southerners thereafter. Ronald Reagan campaigned for "states' rights" in Philadelphia, Miss., in 1980, and George H. W. Bush moved to Texas as a young man and considered it home thereafter. The South was a familiar and even intimate place to the men in charge of American foreign relations. From Truman to Johnson, American presidents viewed segregationist officials not as dire enemies in a struggle for control and direction of the American South, as did civil rights workers by the 1960s, but rather as a stubborn, backward-looking, but respected part of the nation's leadership. These presidents also tended to share, to varying extents, the suspicion of segregationists that the civil rights movement was at least potentially subversive, if not actually Communist influenced.

The far-reaching changes that swept through southern society in the second half of the 20th century cannot be fully understood apart from the international context of the Cold War. The American civil rights movement fit in the larger story of decolonization — the international civil rights movement — and the Cold War struggle over world leadership and the meaning of "freedom."

Despite their ties to the segregated white South, U.S. policymakers ultimately accepted the necessity and even rightness of desegregation as a Cold War imperative.

THOMAS BORSTELMANN
Cornell University

Thomas Borstelmann, *The Cold War and the Color Line: American Race Relations in the Global Arena* (2001); Pete Daniel, *Lost Revolutions: The South in the 1950s* (2000); John Egerton, *Speak Now Against the Day: The Generation before the Civil Rights Movement in the South* (1994); Joseph A. Fry, *Dixie Looks Abroad: The South and U.S. Foreign Relations, 1789–1973* (2002); David R. Goldfield, *Promised Land: The South since 1945* (1987).

Colonial Heritage

Judged by a conception of culture as the pursuit and patronage of arts and letters, the early South has conventionally been found wanting. No more in the North than in the South, however, did early American poets, painters, or philosophers achieve a golden age of the mind, the spirit, or the imagination. No more in Boston or Philadelphia than in Williamsburg or Charleston did drama or divinity, song, story, or scholarship rise above provincial consequence.

By another standard the planters of the southern colonies were, in fact, highly significant. On the ethnographic level—culture as the integrated lifeways of an entire people—students of the outposts south of the Delaware need not be defensive at all. The southern provinces prefigured the American way of life more clearly than even the Middle Atlantic did. From the sunrise of settlement, at Roanoke and Jamestown, southern colonists manifested the norms and values that ultimately mastered the continent.

The colonial South was quintessentially American. Colonists were settled on the Chesapeake for almost a quarter of a century before the *Arbella* eased into Massachusetts Bay, and the priority of the plantations of the South was more than merely chronological. The men who established England's first successful stronghold in the New World were engaged in such decidedly American enterprises as racial exploitation, representative self-government, and market-oriented economic endeavor for a decade and more before the Puritans dreamed of departing their mother country. The men and women who succeeded them consolidated their initiatives and fused them into a coherent course of life.

That course appalled the few who clung to conventional European categories. Would-be reformers condemned again and again the immoderate ac-

Payne Limner, Alexander Spotswood Payne and His Brother,
John Robert Dandridge Payne, with Their Nurse (c. 1790–1800)
(Slide and Photography Library, Virginia Museum of Fine Arts, Richmond)

quisitiveness that dispersed southerners over the countryside and the impor-
tunate self-interest that left them indifferent to the common good. But the
criticisms fell on deaf ears. Planters set out from the first to advance their own
affairs. At Roanoke they abandoned the fort for their farms. From Jamestown
they fanned out along the river rather than remain in the town. And ever after,
they continued heedless of calls to congregate for the sake of religion, the common defense, or civility itself.

Southerners simply would not subordinate their unruly ambition to any
public concern or sense of social responsibility. In the words of the 18th-century
planter Robert Beverley, "the chief design of all . . . was to fetch away the trea-
sure . . . aiming more at sudden gain than to form a regular colony." Exactly on
account of such worldly priorities, southern colonial social institutions were
always unable to control southern settlers.

Virginians and Carolinians, Marylanders and Georgians alike had crossed
the ocean as adventurers and evolved virtues appropriate to their situation.

They esteemed independence and prized personal liberty. They resented discipline, spurned spirituality, and often indulged themselves with hedonistic abandon. They cultivated a taste for proud display. As they did, they disdained civic consciousness and forfeited social cohesion. They committed little to the community. They valued their own private pursuits above all, and they measured them primarily by criteria of material accumulation.

None of this inattention to the common good was unique to the South or in any way exceptional in a wider prospect of English outposts in the New World. If there was a peculiar institution in early America, it was not southern slavery and the extravagant avarice it embodied. It was the New England town and the anachronistic restraint of greed it attempted. If southern ways were distinctive at all, they were distinctive only in their intensity. Lust for the good life—a heedless, headlong scramble after personal gratification—was already at the center of an emerging American dream. Such lust was simply less impeded in the southern provinces.

In their pell-mell pursuit of that dream southerners developed a recognizably American readiness for slavery, refusal of deference to their designated superiors, and attachment to a rough-hewn democracy of hustlers, speculators, and salesmen. In their devotion to the subtropical monocultures that afforded them their opportunities for aggrandizement, southerners enmeshed themselves more elaborately than any other mainland Americans in market relations and market values. And in doing so, southerners immediately encountered the enduring American dilemmas of labor and laziness.

When southern pioneers and publicists extolled their region, they exalted above all the indolent ease that the land allowed. In their New World as in Adam's, "everything seemed to come up by nature." Husbandmen lived "almost void of care and free from . . . fatigues." By the bounty of a benign providence, the earth brought forth "all things in abundance, as in the first creation, without toil or labor."

In every precinct colonists were content to "sponge upon the blessings of a warm sun and a fruitful soil." Domestic stock cost them "nothing to keep or feed" because animals grazed freely in winter as well as summer, sparing settlers the drudgery of fencing and the tedium of foddering. Cattle, swine, and sheep could all be left to themselves to feed on the rich and self-renewing grasses of the new continent. Fish and fowl too presented themselves for the settlers' effortless enjoyment. Marylanders met "rich bosoms" of marine creatures in their bays, all "easily taken." Carolinians could "easily gather" more oysters in a day than they could "well eat in a year." And all the planters encountered birds "so numerous . . . that you might see millions in a flock."

Everywhere men echoed the enthusiasm of the initial English endeavor in the New World, that the land lavished its largesse upon them without their exertion. The husbandman as much as the herder and the hunter lived on the "benevolent breast" of nature. Crops that others elsewhere had to cultivate with unremitting diligence simply "thrust . . . forth" in the South "as easily as the weeds." American grains were "so grateful to the planter" that they returned him "his entrusted seed" with a treble growth; and they were "so facilely planted that one man in 48 hours may prepare as much ground and set such a quantity of corn that he may be secure from want of bread all the year following." Men managed "very easily" though unwilling to work "above two or three hours a day" or more than "three days in seven." Indeed, under such circumstances, it was difficult to distinguish work from leisure. Planting presented itself as a pastime of "pleasure," hunting as an "exercise" of "delight," and fishing as a "pretty sport" for profit, in a land in which everything grew plentifully "to supply the wants or wantonness of man."

Yet such celebration of hedonic ease was a perilous ploy. Even as it stimulated real estate sales, it stirred specters of corruption, inciting castigation of the colonists as degenerate outcasts of the Old World. The exaggeration of effortlessness that enticed also offended. The emphasis on immunity from harsh labor that enthralled also appalled. Southerners uncertain of their own civility were sensitive to suggestions that they might be overwhelmed by the wilderness and lapse into self-indulgence.

Virginians therefore feared the felicity they flaunted, that so "little labor" was "required to fill their bellies." Carolinians bemoaned the blessing they boasted, that their paradise was "apt to make people incline to sloth." And Georgians trembled that their prolific province might be "deformed by its own fertility." The same settlers who proclaimed their tracts gardens of earthly delight insisted that they would not welcome people who wished to live there in a "state of idleness and dependence." They declared that men "were appointed to cultivate the earth," not to bask in its bounty.

Exactly as they careened from one extreme to the other, colonial southerners enunciated the dilemma in economic ethics that would occupy the nation ever after. Just as they gloated over their effortless indolence in one breath and gloried in their exemplary industry in the next, so they anticipated the tension between the imperative to work and the compulsion to consume that would set the shape of aspiration for centuries in America.

Suspended between those demands for exertion and those dark desires for exemption from exertion, the planters of the southern provinces were also driven to develop an incipiently American temporal horizon. Because they disdained methodical economic endeavor yet sought the splendid display that rewarded such steadiness, they could only envision attainment of their ends by sudden strokes of fortune. Because they scorned unremitting application to a calling, they could only imagine success by slipping the constraints of history itself.

The past, then, held little fascination for southerners of the 17th and 18th centuries. It provided them no notable local heroes, memorialized for them no vivifying regional myths, and engendered in them no discernible curiosity. It certainly entailed no burdens. Indeed, it was rarely invoked even to validate prevailing social arrangements or to legitimate specific institutional establishments.

Early southerners simply ceded their patrimonies. The fragility of their attachment to traditions was evident in the unraveling of the religious and familial threads that webbed men and women in the mother country. The permanence of their ties to the land on which they lived was legible in the flimsy houses in which they encamped upon the country, far into the 18th century. And the transiency of their interests was apparent in the ease with which they departed their estates and operations for others elsewhere. As George Washington noted, the great fortunes of the Tidewater were not made by a steadfast cultivation of the southern staples. They were the result of shrewd speculation in frontier lands, and they reflected the readiness of the planters to relinquish established assets for the sake of visionary futures.

Colonial New Englanders might revere ancestors and look to the past for legitimate authority. Colonial southerners were impatient of inheritance and eager for futurity. Thomas Jefferson declared their sense of time in his insistence that "the earth belongs in usufruct to the living." He articulated the logic of their lives in affirming that he liked "dreams of the future better than the history of the past." And increasingly his countrymen, north as well as south, came to concur. That early southern sensibility came to color a national culture sublimely indifferent to history and uncommonly attracted to New Freedoms, New Deals, and New Frontiers.

Ironically, as the nation came to the colonial South's sense of time, the South itself came to take history seriously. First in the declining economies of the Tidewater, then across a region ravaged by civil war, southerners created legends of cavaliers and cherished memories of gallant warriors and galling defeat. But in their initial period of settlement their experiences embodied a quite different heritage.

Recent work of interdisciplinary scholars has buttressed the theme of the southern colonies prefiguring the American way of life. The role of the environment in creating a distinctive context in southern places for cultural development, the interaction of Native Americans and settlers from Europe and Africa, the emergence of particular social relations in a slave society, and the shaping forces of the early modern Atlantic world have been among key topics in the study of the southern colonies.

The rise of environmental studies has led to research that looks specifically at the landscape and ecology of early settlement. Promoters advertised southern colonies as little Edens for the supposed ease of life. Life was, however, perilous in the 17th-century southern colonies. Mortality was high in the hot zones of the Carolina Lowcountry and the Virginia-Maryland Chesapeake, creating deadly counterimages of Eden. The environment promoted agricultural development, though, and helped set the people of the emerging South on a course of staple-crop agriculture, including tobacco, rice, sugar, and cotton.

Indians have seldom been given serious attention for their role as original creators of cultural life based around southern environments, but historians and archaeologists increasingly give credit to Indians as formative groups in southern culture. Whether in agricultural practices, naming patterns of geographical places, foodways, or folklore, Indians pioneered southern culture. Most white settlers transferred English ways to the colonies and identified with England. Africans were so prominent in South Carolina that a Swiss traveler in 1737 remarked that "Carolina looks more like a negro country than like a country settled by white people." In truth, the early South had the kind of ethnic diversity traditionally associated with the 19th-century United States, although such ethnic pluralism would decline in the South in that century. Germans, Irish, Scots-Irish, Swiss, Dutch, and other Europeans were prominent in southern colonies.

Racism and patriarchal privilege emerged out of the colonial period as defining features of southern society. The decades of the late 1600s saw passage of laws and development of new cultural practices to regulate a society increasingly reliant on slave labor and determined to legitimate the economic dominance, social authority, and political power of white male gentry. These inequalities were southern variants of national patterns. Slavery remained a legal institution throughout northern colonies, as well as southern, and gender inequalities were not unique to the South. Still, the social relations that developed in a society increasingly embracing a hierarchical order put the southern colonists on a path to different development in the 19th century from that of northern society.

Historians have traditionally measured the southern colonies against the colonies to the north, the beginning of enduring North-South contrasts that would take on increased meaning in the sectional conflict of the antebellum period. The southern colonies should also be seen as a part of other contexts in a dynamic early modern period. Most broadly, the South was a key player in the economic life of the Atlantic world. European markets promoted the South's attachment to staple-crop agriculture, and ideas and cultural fashions circulated in the South, as well as elsewhere in the Atlantic world. The islands of the Caribbean had a great influence on the South, as in the role of Barbado planters and the slaves they brought with them helping to transform South Carolina. While the English colonies have been the traditional focus for colonial southern historians, recent work explores the Gulf South as the first South, with Spanish settlements in 16th-century Florida the real beginnings of the region's European historical inheritance.

MICHAEL ZUCKERMAN
University of Pennsylvania

David Armitage and Michael J. Braddick, *The British Atlantic World, 1500–1800* (2002); Ira Berlin, *Many Thousands Gone: The First Two Centuries of Slavery in North America* (1998); David Bertelson, *The Lazy South* (1967); Timothy H. Breen, *Puritans and Adventurers: Change and Persistence in Early America* (1980); Carl Bridenbaugh, *Myths and Realities: Societies of the Colonial South* (1952); Kathleen M. Brown, *Good Wives, Nasty Wenches, and Anxious Patriarchs: Gender, Race, and Power in Colonial Virginia* (1996); Richard Beale Davis, *Intellectual Life in the Colonial South, 1585–1763* (1978); James Horn, *Adapting to a New World: English Society in the 17th-Century Chesapeake* (1994); Rhys Isaac, *The Transformation of Virginia, 1740–1790* (1982); J. W. Joseph and Martha Zierden, eds., *Another's Country: Archaeological and Historical Perspectives on Cultural Interactions in the Southern Colonies* (2002); Cynthia A. Kierner, *Beyond the Household: Women's Place in the Early South, 1700–1835* (1998); Edmund S. Morgan, *American Slavery, American Freedom: The Ordeal of Colonial Virginia* (1975); Mart A. Stewart, *"What Nature Suffers to Groe": Life, Labor, and Landscape on the Georgia Coast, 1680–1920* (1996); Peter Wood, *Black Majority: Negroes in South Carolina from 1670 through the Stono Rebellion* (1974); Bertram Wyatt-Brown, *Southern Honor: Ethics and Behavior in the Old South* (1982).

Confederate States of America

After Abraham Lincoln's election in November 1860, South Carolina called a convention, which unanimously adopted the Ordinance of Secession on 20 December 1860. A Declaration of the Immediate Causes of Secession justified the action, and the convention urged other southern states to follow this lead. Six other states promptly responded in early 1861: Mississippi on 9 January; Florida on 10 January; Alabama on 11 January; Georgia on 19 January; Louisiana on 26 January; and Texas on 1 February. There was considerable opposition to secession in many of these states. Georgia, a geographically crucial state for any southern resistance, seceded 4 March. The four border states were slow and cautious in approving secession, but after the Confederate attack on Fort Sumter, S.C., in April of 1861, Virginia (17 April), Arkansas (6 May), North Carolina (20 May), and Tennessee (8 June) left the Union. The slave states of Missouri, Kentucky, and Maryland remained in the Union, and the western counties of Virginia formed a new state, West Virginia. Divided in sentiment, the people in the border South were the source of the most frequent brother-against-brother warfare. The border South had economic and patriotic ties to the North, but slavery and social customs made it a southern area, too. Missouri was the scene of bloody fighting during the war, and 30,000 in that Unionist state fought for the Confederacy.

Delegates from the seceding states met at Montgomery, Ala., on 4 February 1861 to organize a provisional government for the Confederate States of America. The delegates saw themselves following in the steps of the American revolutionaries fighting for self-determination against a distant, oppressive government. The Confederate Constitution was modeled on the federal document and contained few innovations. It did recognize and guarantee slavery in all territory belonging to the new government, and it prohibited protective tariffs, appropriations for internal improvements, and the payment of bounties. It overtly asked for the "favor and guidance of Almighty God." The new constitution was officially adopted 11 March 1861. Jefferson Davis of Mississippi was chosen president of the new government, and Alexander H. Stephens became vice president. The Stars and Bars became the official flag. Confederate founders intentionally created a Christian slave owners' republic based on an ideal of social harmony. They did not sanction political parties, yet considerable discord developed.

In proclaiming their political independence, southern leaders seemed willing to compromise on earlier principles. Delegates to the convention created a stronger central government than secession rhetoric seemed to support. The concept of states' rights was not explicitly affirmed in the document. Leaders of the new government were generally moderates and conservatives, not the fire-eating revolutionary secessionists. The tension between centralization and localism would be a continual headache for those leaders.

At the start of the war, a serious discrepancy existed in the resources of the two combatants. The Union had a population of 22.7 million, compared to the 9 million (including 3.5 million slaves) in the Confederate states. In addition to

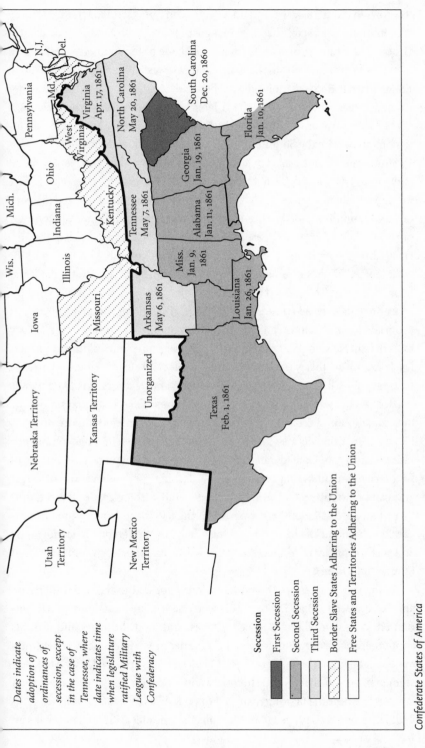

Confederate States of America

(Source: Bernard Bailyn et al., The Great Republic, 3d ed. [1985])

Dates indicate adoption of ordinances of secession, except in the case of Tennessee, where date indicates time when legislature ratified Military League with Confederacy

Secession

First Secession

Second Secession

Third Secession

Border Slave States Adhering to the Union

Free States and Territories Adhering to the Union

South Carolina
Dec. 20, 1860

Florida
Jan. 10, 1861

Georgia
Jan. 19, 1861

Alabama
Jan. 11, 1861

Miss.
Jan. 9, 1861

Louisiana
Jan. 26, 1861

Texas
Feb. 1, 1861

Arkansas
May 6, 1861

Tennessee
May 7, 1861

North Carolina
May 20, 1861

Virginia
Apr. 17, 1861

West Virginia

Kentucky

Missouri

Unorganized

Kansas Territory

Nebraska Territory

Utah Territory

New Mexico Territory

Iowa

Illinois

Indiana

Ohio

Pennsylvania

Mich.

Wis.

N.J.

Md.

Del.

its growing industrial capacity and an extended rail system for transportation, the Union had an established national government, navy, and regular army of 12,000. The Union strategy was a naval blockade of the southern coast and an invasion of the region from the North and Midwest. When Lincoln issued the Emancipation Proclamation on 23 September 1862 and declared slaves under Confederate control to be free after 1 January 1863, the goals of the Union war effort became not only nationalism but also human liberty. The North thus attempted to isolate the South economically, politically, and morally.

Southerners made war with great hopes of victory. The Confederacy raised and equipped a formidable fighting force. Josiah Gorgas, the chief of ordnance for the Confederate forces, resourcefully supplied the armies with needed weapons and munitions, and the Tredegar Iron Works produced innovative weaponry in the form of torpedoes, submarines, and plates for ironclads. Southerners had the enthusiasm of fighting for a cause, for tribal defense, and for what seemed like basic human concerns—freedom, home, family, the land, and racial solidarity. They feared fundamental change in their way of life.

Confederates faced considerable problems in defining a public culture appropriate to a new nation. This South had few publishing houses, lower literacy rates than in New England, and much of cultural expression was through a folk-level oral culture that was seemingly not a viable venue for distributing patriotic messages. Distribution of news was a problem, and a national mail system was needed. As the war went on, with the disruptions of physical destruction, the dissemination of a centralized national ideology became even more difficult. Nonetheless, Confederates created a national culture seen in songs commemorating victories in Confederate armies, a Confederate national seal, images of southern heroes on postage stamps and broadsides, and publications of magazines and newspapers that conveyed Confederate ideologies. Confederate culture highlighted the southern embrace of the ideals and heroes of the American Revolution at the beginning of the Civil War, but gradually iconography and rhetoric put forward specifically Confederate images (such as the martyred Stonewall Jackson).

As the war progressed, though, divisions appeared in the social solidarity and cultural unity. Banking resources were inadequate, inflation rose, citizens refused to submit willingly to heavy taxes, and food shortages and protests about them occurred. Conscription became necessary, and desertion became a major problem for the military. Social-class conflicts appeared, as the burdens seemed to grow heavier for the humble as time went on, while some plantation families not near the fighting managed to do well and speculators clearly profited. Jefferson Davis proved to be an uninspiring leader and could not make an eloquent case for national unity. Advocates of states' rights, such as Governor Joseph E. Brown of Georgia and Zebulon B. Vance of North Carolina, hounded him, and by war's end Davis was unpopular.

Southern institutions and people in them generally rallied around the Confederacy, and they felt the disruptions of war. Churches, schools, colleges and universities, businesses, social groups, ethnic groups — all were affected by war. Colleges contributed soldiers and civilian leaders, while businesses reoriented their facilities to war work. Religion was particularly important in supporting political and military activities. Southern ministers and religious organizations supported the Confederacy and proved to be essential in maintaining morale. Leading ministers such as James Henley Thornwell and Stephen Elliot preached on the home front that the Confederacy was a holy crusade against the atheistic North, and revivals occurred periodically within the ranks of the Confederate armies. Episcopal bishop Leonidas Polk and Baptist minister Mark P. Lowrey were only two of the many ministers who became Confederate generals. Ministers also judged the sins of the nation in a jeremiad, but while they might criticize the shortcomings of slave masters, they did not abandon the proslavery justification for the war.

The myth of the southern lady had appeared in the antebellum era, but the war challenged the image. Women were left to run the plantations and to raise the crops on small farms. They cared for the wounded under deplorable hospital conditions and found and shipped necessary supplies to men at the battlefront. The South's women experienced physical deprivation and the psychological trauma of the absence of loved ones and grief over the dead. The Confederate experience surely provided the context for new roles and expectations for women in southern culture and perhaps represented one stage in their liberation from gender stereotyping.

War also led to the more dramatic emancipation of southern slaves from the peculiar institution. Although the Emancipation Proclamation issued in 1862 did not immediately free slaves in the Confederate-controlled areas, it was a symbolic landmark for southern blacks — the Day of Jubilee. The Thirteenth Amendment to the federal Constitution became law on 18 December 1865, providing a constitutional prohibition against slavery. Most slaves stayed on the plantations during the Civil War, but evidence of slave conspiracies and plots in Virginia, Alabama, and Arkansas has been discovered. Thousands of blacks fought for the Union against slavery. The legend of the faithful wartime slave became, nonetheless, a key part of a romanticized myth of the Old South plantation.

Despite defeat in the war, the southern military made its greatest impact on the southern imagination while fighting for the Confederacy. Confederate military leaders were the true cultural heroes of the period—Robert E. Lee was the Virginia cavalier, Thomas J. "Stonewall" Jackson the holy warrior, Jeb Stuart the gallant horseman, P. G. T. Beauregard the hot-tempered Louisiana Creole, and Nathan Bedford Forrest the Tennessee guerrilla fighter. The names of battles had a lyrical, biblical ring to them: Manassas (Bull Run) in July 1861, Shiloh in April 1862, Antietam in September 1862 (the bloodiest day of the war), and the crucial Confederate defeat at Gettysburg in July 1863. There was Chancellorsville in Virginia, where Lee lost Stonewall Jackson, victim of a bullet from one of his own soldiers; Vicksburg, where the Confederates lost the West; Chickamauga and Chattanooga, which had been the key to the Confederate heartland; the fiery battle of Atlanta; Sherman's march to the sea; and the melancholic Appomattox, where Lee surrendered his 26,000 troops and refused to approve a guerrilla war against the North.

Each battle contained its own folklore and legends, gave birth to its songs, jokes, stories, heroes. Writers, singers, painters, sculptors, storytellers, and others have attested to the Confederacy's continuing cultural appeal by producing artifacts that explore the war's memory. "For every Southern boy fourteen years old," wrote William Faulkner of the memory of the decisive Gettysburg in *Intruder in the Dust* (1948), "not once but whenever he wants it, there is the instant when it's still not yet two o'clock on that July afternoon in 1863, the brigades are in position behind the rail fence, the guns are laid and ready in the woods . . . and Pickett himself with . . . his hat in one hand . . . and his sword in the other looking up the hill waiting for Longstreet to give the word and it's all in the balance, it hasn't happened yet, it hasn't even begun yet, it not only hasn't begun yet but there is still time for it not to begin."

The Confederacy lived in the social imagination of the South long after the war ended. The memory of it became enshrined in the statues, monuments, parks, and textbooks of the Lost Cause, the dominant public memory of the region. African Americans enacted a different collective memory, one that criticized the Confederacy as a defense of slavery and lauded emancipation. But Confederate heroes in granite dominated the physical and symbolic landscape of the South, and images from the Confederate battle flag continue to be the focus of controversy in the contemporary South.

CHARLES REAGAN WILSON
University of Mississippi

William A. Blair, *Cities of the Dead: Contesting the Memory of the Civil War in the South, 1865–1914* (2004); David W. Blight, *Beyond the Battlefield: Race, Memory, and* the American Civil War (2002); Robert E. Bonner, *Flag Passions of the Confederate South* (2002); Ken Burns, *The Civil War: A Film by Ken Burns* (1990); E. Merton Coulter, *The Confederate States of America, 1861–1865* (1950); William C. Davis, *The Cause Lost: Myths and Realities of the Confederacy* (1996); Paul Escott, *After Secession: Jefferson Davis and the Failure of Confederate Nationalism* (1978); Drew Gilpin Faust, *Creation of Confederate Nationalism: Ideology and Identity in the Civil War South* (1988); William Freehling, *The South vs. the South: How Anti-Confederate Southerners Shaped the Course of the War* (2001); Douglas Southall Freeman, *The South to Posterity: An Introduction to the Writing of Confederate History* (1939); Randall Miller, Harry S. Stout, and Charles Reagan Wilson, eds., *Religion and the American Civil War* (1998); George C. Rable, *The Confederate Republic: A Revolution against Politics* (1994); Charles P. Roland, *The Confederacy* (1960); Emory Thomas, *Confederacy as a Revolutionary Experience* (1971), *The Confederate Nation, 1861–1865* (1975); Frank E. Vandiver, *Their Tattered Flags: The Epic of the Confederacy* (1970); Bell I. Wiley, *Plain People of the Confederacy* (1943), *The Road to Appomattox* (1956); C. Vann Woodward, ed., *Mary Chesnut's Civil War* (1981).

Emancipation

Emancipation troubles southern culture, raising issues that make many, regardless of race, uncomfortable. Emancipation is a story of liberation and loss, of identities gained and identities shattered, a history that places conflict and domination at the center of the region's past. Representing the promise of freedom and equality on one hand and the broken dream of plantation slavery on the other, emancipation is above all else a shared history of conflict. Yet where does a revolution—one that pitted southerner against southerner—fit in the construction of a common southern identity or a shared southern culture? This dilemma so challenges the South that emancipation has been quieted and domesticated in the myths of the region.

The dominant white southern parable of emancipation transforms the moment of freedom from a political act to a personal one. Freedom, according to this story, left African Americans bereft, compelled to return home to their white folks. In *The Unvanquished*, William Faulkner recounted the tales of his youth, writing that those "who had followed the Yankees away . . . [had scattered] into the hills [to] live in caves and hollow trees like animals I suppose, not only with no one to depend on but with no one depending on them, caring whether they returned or not or lived or died or not." Noble white southerners, such as the Sartorises, took African Americans back in, both the faithful Ringo, who had never left, and the unfaithful Loosh, who had walked off declaring, "I going. I done been freed . . . ; I dont belong to John Sartoris now; I belongs to me and God." According to Faulkner and his peers, whether African Americans claimed freedom or not, the end result was the same: former slaves returned to the plantation household.

Our national narrative recognizes the political significance of emancipation, emphasizing that Abraham Lincoln waged a four-year bloody civil war to free the slaves. Yet this story elides the fact that it was not Lincoln, the U.S. military, or the federal government that freed the slaves. The push for emancipation began in the South.

Enslaved black southerners freed themselves during the Civil War, altering the course of the war and the nation. In what historian Steven Hahn writes was "the most sweeping revolution of the 19th century, [slaves] shifted the social and political course of the Atlantic world." Because of their actions, the U.S. Congress adopted the Thirteenth Amendment in 1865, abolishing slavery across the nation. Emancipation, therefore, is largely a southern story defining a region and a people.

At the outset of the Civil War, slaves identified President Abraham Lincoln and the Union army as their allies in the struggle for freedom. Yet the Lincoln administration was a reluctant partner. As Lincoln stated in 1862, "My paramount objective in this struggle is to save the Union and is *not* to either save or destroy slavery. If I could save the Union without freeing any slave I would do it, and if I could save it by freeing all the slaves I would do it; and if I could save it by freeing some and leaving others alone I would also do that. What I do about slavery, and the colored race, I do because I believe it helps to save the Union." Southern institutions, including slavery, would be respected in order to bring the South back into the nation.

As early as May 1861, African Americans declared themselves free by running away and entering Union army camps. Throughout the antebellum era, slaves kept informed about national politics. Using their positions as domestic servants, artisans, and draymen, black southerners circulated news gathered on and off the plantation. Each time the conflict over slavery entered the national debate, African Americans took notice and crafted an image of the North as a place of salvation. The Civil War brought the North into the South. The land of liberty suddenly lay within reach. As the Union army invaded Virginia, South Carolina, and the Mississippi Valley, slaves stood ready to run for freedom.

The first African Americans who ran for Union lines were similar to those who ran away before the war. They were young adults (predominantly men) without children. Making policy as they waged war, Union generals responded to the freedpeople's exodus in a number of ways. General John C. Fremont simply freed every slave who came within his lines. Outraged, Lincoln removed him from his command. General Benjamin Butler decided to keep former slaves within his lines not as free people but as "the contraband of war." Slaves, he reasoned, were valuable property—instruments of war—that could be used to assist either the Confederacy or the Union. From Butler's perspective it was better to have slaves serve the Union than the enemy. As word spread that Butler permitted black southerners to stay and work within his lines, hundreds of slaves began to make their way to Union lines across the South. In August 1861 the U.S. Congress responded by passing the First Confiscation Act, which declared that those black southerners employed directly by the Confederate military could be held as "contraband." All others should be returned to their masters. Refusing to mark such distinctions, slaves began to travel into Union lines in great numbers, with women and children joining the men. They liberated themselves. Slowly, Congress reacted, passing the Second Confiscation Act in July 1862, stating that all slaves held in rebel territory could be legally seized by the Union. Eventually over 400,000 slaves freed themselves by walking into Union lines. Laying claim to their bodies and to the right of self-determination, they denied slaveholders' rights of mastery. Subsequently, on 1 January 1863, the Emancipation Proclamation freed slaves held in the Confederacy.

For every African American who left the plantation, hundreds remained behind. One did not have to run away to claim liberty. Freedom could be won at home. In what W. E. B. Du Bois named "The General Strike," many African Americans on the plantations refused to work efficiently for the slaveholders while others refused to work for masters at all. Instead, African Americans stayed at home and went to work for themselves.

African Americans claimed freedom as southerners. Liberty, for most, rested on family, land, and the crop because each promised a kind of self-sufficiency and independence from outsiders. Black and white southerners shared these values, and this fact brought them into direct conflict.

Many, but not all, white southerners refused to share public space or political power with black southerners. Viewing emancipation as a zero-sum game, planters felt that their freedom would be sacrificed if African Americans became fully free. Many whites would not acknowledge African American claims because the land, the family, and the crop (not to mention the political and civil rights that went with them) were integral to white identity and power. To grant African Americans rights threatened an erasure of white manhood.

Emancipation exposed the fiction of white men's independence. Planter men found themselves dependent on free labor, dependent on their women for financial support, and, in the case of the wounded, literally dependent on others for mobility. More profoundly, as black southerners took up arms and asserted their claims, they challenged what the white man saw as *his* household — *his* land, *his* crops, and *his* workers. As plantation slavery dissolved, mastery, whiteness, and manhood all lost their mooring.

White southerners fought back, limiting black southerners' access to voting rights, civil rights, the public sphere, and freedom from fear. Each limitation took a toll on the public remembrance of emancipation. Immediately following the war and up to the turn of the century, black southerners celebrated Emancipation Day with parades and speeches, retelling the story of how they won their freedom. As each southern state imposed segregation (and turned a blind eye to lynching), violence disrupted and finally stopped these celebrations across much of the South. States filled the silence created in the absence of Emancipation Day ceremonies with newly minted histories that defamed Reconstruction, credited the Yankees with emancipation, and depicted black southerners as either bestial or childlike. Black southerners — Carter Woodson, Pauli Murray, Susie King Taylor, and Anna Julia Cooper, to name just a few — responded with histories of their own. The history of emancipation became a segregated history, and, in many ways, it still is. The history of emancipation tends to be written either as an African American freedom struggle (the study of "Emancipation" and "Reconstruction") or as the study of white's loss, mourning, and nostalgia for an invented past (the study of "The Lost Cause").

Yet emancipation is a shared history, one that reminds us of how brutal, contested, and revolutionary that sharing has been. If southern culture emphasizes stasis, tradition, and a common identity, then emancipation represents its opposite — the struggle between white and black, slave and free, rights and privilege. Emancipation disturbs southern myth by exposing the fact that each of these histories is dependent on the others. Far from being opposed, southern culture and emancipation are contingent upon one another. Southern culture, in large part, is the act of forgetting emancipation and its implications. Manners, congeniality, and honor work to paper over conflict and to refuse to speak of southerners' unpleasantness to southerners. Emancipation, therefore, is an unspoken referent, a hidden heart, of southern culture.

NANCY BERCAW
University of Mississippi

David W. Blight, *Race and Reunion: The Civil War in American Memory* (2001); Elsa Barkley Brown, in *The Black Public Sphere: A Public Culture Book* (1995); W. E. B. Du Bois, *Black Reconstruction in America: An Essay toward a History of the Part which Black Folk Played in the Attempt to Reconstruct Democracy in America, 1860–*

1880 (1935); Laura F. Edwards, *Gendered Strife and Confusion: The Political Culture of Reconstruction* (1997); Barbara Jeanne Fields, *Slavery and Freedom on the Middle Ground: Maryland during the Nineteenth Century* (1985); Eric Foner, *Nothing but Freedom: Emancipation and Its Legacy* (1983), *Reconstruction: America's Unfinished Revolution, 1863–1877* (1988); Joseph T. Glatthaar, *Forged in Battle: The Civil War Alliance of Black Soldiers and White Officers* (1990); Thavolia Glymph and John J. Kushma, eds., *Essays on the Postbellum Southern Economy* (1985); Steven Hahn, *A Nation under Our Feet: Black Political Struggles in the Rural South from Slavery to the Great Migration* (2003); Mitchell A. Kachun, *Festivals of Freedom: Memory and Meaning in African American Emancipation Celebrations, 1808–1915* (2003); Clarence Mohr, *On the Threshold of Freedom: Masters and Slaves in Civil War Georgia* (1986); James L. Roark, *Masters without Slaves: Southern Planters in the Civil War and Reconstruction* (1977); Armstead L. Robinson, *Bitter Fruits of Bondage: The Demise of Slavery and the Collapse of the Confederacy, 1861–1865* (2005); Leslie A. Schwalm, *A Hard Fight for We: Women's Transition from Slavery to Freedom in South Carolina* (1997).

Foodways

The first white men to come into the South ate what the American Indians ate. From the southern Indians the Europeans had much to learn about cultivated plants, wild fruits and nuts, the animals of the forest, and the fish in ocean, rivers, and lakes. They had to learn these lessons to survive and later push their way westward.

The Indian diet included much game, and Indians near the coast ate large quantities of fish and shellfish. In their fields they grew corn, beans, squash, and other vegetables. They harvested wild plums, hickory nuts, chestnuts, blackberries, and other forest foods. Indians elsewhere on the continent domesticated the turkey and had developed the potato, tomatoes, eggplant, all peppers except black pepper, probably sweet potatoes, and possibly cowpeas. Both the Indians and the European settlers drew from other cultures, too. Originating in Brazil, the peanut was carried to Africa and later, bearing the African name "goober," was brought to Virginia aboard the slave ships.

As settlers reached the frontier, they planted corn and other food plants as soon as possible but relied at first on game or fish, although fish played a large role only along the coasts of the Atlantic and the Gulf of Mexico. The pioneer in the interior was happy to have a catfish, especially a large one, but he trusted his rifle more than his rod, net, or fish trap.

Buffalo provided the best meat, but they were quickly exterminated east of the Mississippi River. The pioneer also relished the meat of the black bear; he even salted it and cured it like pork. If killed in the autumn, the bear provided fat for shortening or other uses. Some southerners ate bear more or less regularly throughout the 19th century, but in most areas the animal disappeared as settlers multiplied. That left as big game the white-tailed deer, and venison was a frequent dish on southern tables until, and in some areas long after, the Civil War. Wild turkeys were astonishingly abundant and unbelievably unwary in the pioneer South, and they played a large role in the pioneer diet. So did smaller game, especially rabbits, squirrels, raccoons, and opossums.

One should not think of the pioneer as baking a bear ham, roasting an opossum, or turning a haunch of venison on a spit. As often as not the southern frontiersman had only one cooking pot, and whatever was available went into that pot to mix with the previous day's leftovers.

The Indians lived in a feast-or-famine condition much of the year, and when food was abundant, they stuffed themselves. In the England that the earliest settlers called home, a host took as much pride in the quantity of the food he served his guests as in its quality. This background, combined with the abundance of food in the South as compared to that available to German, English, Scotch, or Scots-Irish peasants in the Old World, carried the concept of "big eating" over to the southern frontier and from the frontier forward to the Old South and eventually to the modern South.

As soon as he could, the pioneer farmer planted corn and established a herd of swine. Thus, the primary items in the diet of most southerners when the frontier had passed were cornbread and pork. Wild hogs were already in the forests, and those that the settlers brought with them were little tamer than their wild kinsmen. High in the shoulder, low in the rear, thin, with a long head and snout, and very swift of foot, they were often killed in the woods. More often, however, the owner carried out a "roundup" each fall, castrated excess boars, marked the ears of pigs born since the last roundup, and took those destined for killing home to be fattened on corn. Gradually, better-quality boars were brought in, and the quality of southern swine improved.

Hog killing usually took place during the first spell of cold weather that seemed likely to last for several days. Chitterlings (small intestines), livers, knuckles (ankles), brains, and other edible parts that could not be preserved had to be eaten quickly, and an orgy of pork eating followed hog-killing day. During those hectic days the fat was boiled in a large pot and rendered into lard. Cracklings, the crisp remnant of this process, were delicious baked into a pone of cornbread, called cracklin' bread. Scraps of leaner meat were pounded or ground into sausage.

Hams, shoulders, jowls, and sides of bacon could be cured to last indefinitely. After being trimmed, these pieces were buried in salt for four to six weeks. Then in the smokehouse they were smoked, preferably with smoke from hickory wood. Farmers differed as to the use of sugar, spices, and the like to flavor hams and shoulders, but almost all rubbed red pepper into exposed areas to prevent contamination by skipper flies, whose larvae would burrow through the meat.

So long as he had pork, the southerner ate it every day and at nearly every meal. Fried ham, shoulder, bacon, or sausage was almost an essential part of breakfast. The main meal, in the middle of the day, usually included pork and, unless it was Sunday or some special occasion, fried pork. Vegetables were normally either fried or, most often, boiled with a piece of fat-cured pork. A dish of green beans, for example, was not good unless it had enough grease in it to "wink back" when one lifted the lid and looked at it. This is the way vegetables were cooked in most southern households well into this century.

Southerners did eat meat other than fish, game, and pork from time to time. Once the frontier stage had passed and predatory animals had begun to follow the Indians into oblivion, it was possible to raise poultry; and chicken, duck, goose, and turkey became fare for Sundays and holidays. Fried chicken became the delicacy that it has remained ever since, and hen eggs and, occasionally, duck eggs became table items. Southerners sometimes ate beef, but it appeared on the table far more often in Texas and on the prairies of Louisiana than elsewhere in the South. Technically, what southerners ate was not really beef but veal, or "baby beef." Animals that had reached maturity were too tough for chewing.

Milk cows, on the other hand, were prized possessions. Compared to the dairy cows of today, they were inferior creatures that produced little milk, an important food for the antebellum southern family, as well as for families in later eras. In general, mutton was not a favorite southern meat, but Virginians seem to have been fond of it, and it was certainly not unknown in Tennessee, Kentucky, and Louisiana.

Cornbread was the primary bread of nearly all antebellum southerners. Most southern mills ground corn well but could not handle glutinous wheat, though there were flour mills in the Upper South. Moreover, rust reduced the yield of wheat in most of the South. The more prosperous did eat yeast bread; beaten biscuits were a common item on plantation tables, but this was not true of the ordinary farmer's or townsman's table.

Cornbread took many forms, from the elementary hoecake baked on a hoe blade or board in front of the fireplace to various sophisticated mixtures of cornmeal with milk, buttermilk, eggs, shortening, and even sometimes flour or sugar. Cracklin' bread has already been noted. Hushpuppies were balls of corn bread and additives, such as onion, fried in the grease where fish were, or had been, frying. Cornbread did not keep well, and this led to the expectation of hot bread with meals, a fact that delayed and infuriated many a Yankee or foreign traveler.

Corn itself was an important vegetable, and for breakfast or supper many a living southerner has eaten cornmeal mush, which in modern parlance is a cereal. Green corn, "roasting ears," could be roasted in the shuck, boiled as corn on the cob, or sliced off the ear and cooked in various ways. Ripe corn, treated with lye obtained from an ash hopper, became hominy; and hominy, dried and broken into small bits, became hominy grits. Hominy grits, next to cornbread, was the most nearly universal southern food. It was, and still is, delightfully good served with butter or gravy—or even solidified, sliced, and fried.

In one or another part of the South almost all vegetables eaten anywhere else were served. Southerners were especially fond of green beans, butter beans (a variety of lima bean), okra, eggplant, red beans, and white or navy beans. Carrots, parsnips, squash, cabbage, and even green peas (usually called English peas) were eaten, but with less enthusiasm. Southerners enjoyed Irish potatoes, but they could not be kept over the winter for seed, and the necessity for imported seed limited their popularity.

The great triumvirate of southern vegetables was made up of turnips, cowpeas, and sweet potatoes, and it would be difficult to say that one was more important than the others. Turnips were often planted in an open space near a pioneer's house site before he had built the house because they could be planted in late summer and would produce turnips and greens before a freeze ruined them. The greens were more valued than the turnips themselves, and in the spring they met the residents' almost desperate need for a green vegetable.

Cowpeas were of many varieties. Today, black-eyed peas, crowder peas, and "blue hulled peas" are almost the only variations known, but many others have flourished, including whippoorwills, britches and jackets, cuckold's increase, and tiny lady peas. Better green but good dry, peas were boiled with a piece of fat salt pork. With cornbread they provided enough calories and enough protein to sustain a hard day's work, and that was what the southern farmer needed. The liquid in which any vegetable had been cooked—the "pot liquor" —could be eaten with cornbread, but the pot liquor of cowpeas was especially delicious. Local custom and preference determined whether the cornbread was dunked or crumbled.

It would be difficult to exaggerate the role of the sweet potato. From the harvest in late summer until as long as they lasted into the winter, sweet potatoes were a major item in the antebellum southern diet. Like the turnip, they could be preserved in a "hill" of earth and decaying vegetable matter, but some farmers had a "potato house," partly or wholly underground, in which the potatoes were stored for protection. Sweet potatoes could be boiled, baked, candied, fried, or made into pudding or pie. Most often they were baked in the coals of the fireplace, and a hot sweet potato with butter was an especially delectable dish.

On the great plantations the food in the mansion's dining room was far more elaborate and abundant than in the house of the ordinary southerner. Travelers and Yankee tutors have left accounts of gargantuan meals. Turtle, venison, ham, turkey, and chicken might grace the same meal, with fruits and vegetables in equal abundance. These plantation meals were often accompanied by good wines, whereas in the farmhouse or the townsman's home, milk, coffee, or whiskey was more likely to serve as the drink. Indeed, once the Scots-Irish had learned to make whiskey from corn, tremendous quantities of that beverage were drunk on the frontier and in the antebellum South.

The food of the slaves, though sufficient, was as modest as the food of the great planter was abundant. In most of the South the basic slave ration was two to three pounds of cured pork and a peck of cornmeal a week per adult. In coastal areas fish might be substituted for pork much of the time, and in southwest Louisiana and Texas slaves got much beef, but these were exceptions. The basic ration was supplemented by vegetables in season, and especially by turnip greens, cowpeas, and sweet potatoes. On large plantations the slaves' meals might be prepared in a common kitchen, but in most instances they were cooked in the cabin. This meant primarily in a pot in the fireplace, and southern blacks became accustomed to boiled foods; until recently, and probably to this day, black people of the South tend to eat more boiled foods than do southern whites.

The Civil War left the South impoverished, and the lowest economic classes of society bore the hardest burden. The vast majority of former slaves became sharecroppers, and they were soon joined by millions of southern whites. Sharecroppers got their food and other necessities from a plantation commissary or from a general store. It was still cornmeal and pork, but the cornmeal now came from the corn belt, and in the milling much of the nutrition had been removed. The pork was no longer homegrown and killed on the plantation; it too came from the Midwest, but rather than bacon it was fatback, the layer of

Dinner after the corn shucking, Granville County, N.C., 1939 (Odum Photographic Survey, Southern Historical Collection, University of North Carolina, Chapel Hill)

meat between the skin and the ribs, containing little protein. The basic diet of cornbread and fatback was not supplemented by fruits and vegetables nearly to the extent of antebellum days. Diseases associated with malnutrition, especially pellagra, which had seldom been observed before the Civil War, began to take a heavy annual toll. Nor was malnutrition confined to sharecroppers; cotton-mill workers, poor townsmen, and the slum dwellers of the developing southern cities also suffered.

Some of the poorer yeoman farmers who managed to hold on to their land were malnourished also. In general, however, they ate pork that they had raised and killed themselves, and they took their own corn to the mill. They may have had to buy fatback from the general store part of the year, but most had milk from a scrub cow or two. Also, they planted a vegetable garden, and the old triad of turnips, cowpeas, and sweet potatoes helped them survive. Yeoman farmers were much more likely than tenants to have a fruit orchard.

Two very significant changes, one in food itself and the other in preparing food, took place during the later 19th century. As the result of increased wheat production and new milling methods, the great flour mills of the Middle West brought the price of flour down so low that even relatively poor southerners could afford it. Even the comparatively prosperous farmer or townsman had seldom eaten wheat bread before the Civil War, but by 1900 wheat-flour biscuits had become as common as cornbread. People ate huge quantities of biscuits. Many farmers bought one or more barrels of flour before the winter almost isolated them from the store. The smallest amount available for sale was twenty-four pounds in a cloth sack.

Food patterns formed on the southern frontier persisted well into the 20th century, until after World War II in many small-town and rural areas. Canned goods, commercial bread, and the refrigerator joined the cookstove and cheap flour in making a difference, albeit a small one. However, urbanization, the dislocation and travel brought on by two world wars, the ease of travel in the age of automobiles and interstate highways, and the homogenizing effect of radio and television eventually brought major changes in southern eating habits.

Probably the most basic change was the growth in "eating out," a trend spurred by the availability of reasonably good restaurants in the cities (superb ones in some cities) and, especially, by the advent of so-called fast foods. The hamburger emporium, the fried-catfish stand, and the fried-chicken establishment provide meals for a tremendous number of southerners every day. It is noteworthy that two of these foods, chicken and catfish, have been a part of the southern diet for 200 years. Furthermore, they are still fried.

American food culture is heavily regionalized. Southern foods went with southerners who were part of migrations out of the South, and barbecue and fried chicken became more Americanized than ever in the 20th century. Movements of new populations into the South similarly transform regional foodways today. Sushi restaurants are found throughout the South and certainly in small towns with Nissan or Toyota factories. Indian curry and other dishes can be found at convenience stores, as well as in restaurants. Mexican grocery stores have ceased being exotic within a few years, and Mexican restaurants are pervasive. Many of these new populations, in turn, enjoy the various regional styles of barbecue, which may be as authentic a surviving icon we have from the earlier South. Cookbooks for the southern kitchen proliferate, and national food magazines tell readers about frying Cajun turkeys or making fried pies. The meat-and-three plate lunch may be an endangered species, but good ones are still prized.

JOE GRAY TAYLOR
McNeese State University

John T. Edge, *A Gracious Plenty: Recipes and Recollections from the American South* (1999); John Egerton, *Southern Food: At Home, on the Road, in History* (1987); Damon Lee Fowler, *Damon Lee Fowler's New Southern Kitchen: Traditional Flavors for Contemporary Cooks* (2002); Jessica Harris, *The Welcome Table: African American Heritage Cooking* (1995); Sam B. Hilliard, *Hog Meat and Hoecake: Food Supply in the Old South* (1972); "Our Food, Our Common Ground," *Southern Exposure* (November–December 1983); Barbara G. Shortridge and James R. Shortridge, *The Taste of American Place: A Reader on Regional and Ethnic Foods* (1998); Stephen A. Smith, in *American Material Culture*, ed. Edith Mayo (1985); Joe Gray Taylor, *Eating, Drinking, and Visiting in the South: An Informal History* (1982); Gertrude I. Thomas, *Foods of Our Forefathers* (1941); Rupert P. Vance, *Human Geography of the South: A Study of Regional Resources and Human Adequacy* (1935); Eugene Walter, *American Cooking, Southern Style* (1971).

Foreign Policy

The southern experience in world affairs reflects variations on a set of ideas common to much of the American experience. Southerners have identified with internationalism especially through multilateral organizations focused on European matters and Anglo-American cooperation. Southerners also have shown signs of isolationism, a "nonentangling" outlook usually aimed at Europe and Britain but sometimes at Latin America, Africa, or the Pacific. Finally, a strong strain of expansionism persisted through much of the South's antebellum, as well as postbellum, experience. This belief in the justice of southerners' increasing their influence over foreign places has often appeared in conjunction with territorial growth and colonialism, but, in other instances, it has surfaced in a nonterritorial form — expansion for trade and investment, as well as for religious reasons. A review of the major episodes of the South's history in world affairs reveals internationalism, isolationism, and expansionism at work in particularly southern ways, that is, until the late 20th and early 21st centuries, and places the South's experience in world affairs within the broader context of ideals and self-interest in American history.

Like most American viewpoints, southern ideas about the world began with the activism and assertiveness spawned by the Renaissance, Reformation, and

Enlightenment. With these movements Western people increasingly perceived the improvement of their condition on earth as a matter of religious mandate. Although this concept of progress is a well-established part of New England's history, the people of the southern colonies had much the same cultural background and reflected a similar optimism and fervor. Abundant natural resources, removal from the "decadent" Old World, a Puritan zeal even in the predominant Anglican churches, a liberal belief that "property" was a matter of "right" and the key to "individual freedom"—here were cornerstones of a powerful sense of manifest destiny and progressive idealism in the developing culture of the colonial South. Southern colonials also responded to less idealistic forces. An unending frontier and brutal Indian fighting, plus more fighting and diplomatic intrigue against Spanish and French colonials, were all part of the unavoidable realities of living in a Western society and competing for empire in the New World. Because of these experiences, Anglos in the southern colonies developed a high tolerance for violence (though they rarely enjoyed, much less excelled at, soldiering) and became effective users of economic and political self-interest. By the end of the colonial era, two key ingredients of the South's future foreign policy outlook had begun to surface: a faith in its mission (idealism) and a pursuit of realpolitik (materialism and self-interest).

During the American Revolution and the early national period, most views articulated in the South reflected these two strains of expansionism in equal, balanced proportions. A powerful array of southern expansionists—George Washington, Thomas Jefferson, James Madison, James Monroe, and Henry Clay —helped guide the nation through the first and second wars with Britain and onto a course of continental and foreign expansionism seen in the acquisition of Louisiana, Florida, and Missouri and in the development of the Monroe Doctrine. The vast majority of southerners thrived in the mainstream of Jeffersonian expansionism. Sensitive to what soon would jell as "the southern interests," that is, slavery and export economics, a subsidiary group of southern congressmen dissented, however, from the goal of a neighborly reciprocity with Latin America. This sectional self-interest would soon broaden and carry considerable weight.

Indeed, the transition from the Jeffersonian to the Jacksonian era brought major changes. Those southerners uninvolved with slavery continued to reflect the old balance of ideals and self-interest. Some slave owners did too, but, for the other Jacksonian planters, ideals quickly became subordinate to self-interest as abolitionists began to attack their "peculiar" labor institution. When the West realigned with the Northeast on the tariff issue, the already defensive planters became even more fearful. A new congressional alliance might ban slavery from the territories and weaken the South's role in national affairs. Thus, in the three decades before the Civil War many planters who feared social and economic ruin showed little enthusiasm for the mission of expansionism. With a steely, defensive tone, they advocated territorial growth for their own sectional self-interest. If President James K. Polk was chiefly a commercialist with national goals, he still made good use of the South's practical and materialistic political focus—and the missionary idealism among other elements of the South—as he maneuvered the nation through its final transcontinental thrust to the Pacific. Ironically, the planters' realpolitik was a far less effective force in the policy when it was channeled by its own sectional leaders. The southern dream of a Caribbean empire remained just that, a dream. And when secession and war finally came, the southern strategy of a supposedly hard-nosed realpolitik lacked the deft diplomacy to translate this approach into the foreign negotiations essential to a Confederate victory.

Embittered by defeat at the hands of what they understood to be an imperialistic Northeast, after the Civil War many white southerners who once had been expansionists took antiexpansionist stances regarding much of the northeastern-controlled U.S. foreign policy. Southern views of the late 19th century reflected misgivings about American expansion into Hawaii, Cuba, Puerto Rico, and the Philippines. Still, by 1898 most southerners ultimately surrendered to the patriotism generated by the action against Spain, showing cautious interest in the anticipated opening of Caribbean and Pacific markets. Yet they still talked incessantly about the pain and dislocation a similar surge of Yankee imperialism had brought to their own region just half a century earlier and characterized that type of expansionism as contrary to key American principles of self-determination and autonomy. They also focused on contemporary problems spawned by the new foreign expansionism: the annexation of nonwhites could cause further conflict in their already strained race relations. Over half the southern senators voted with the anti-imperialist opposition to the treaty of Paris. In short, more than party politics was involved. Isolationism—generated out of anti-imperialist principles and racism—grew to consensual proportions in the postbellum period. Such a tormented reversal made certain southerners appear ambivalent, and many downright insular, as they reacted to America's rise to world power.

Yet a small, vocal, and powerful group within the emerging middle class showed signs of being anything but isolationists. To publicists such as Alabama politicians John Tyler Morgan and Joseph H. Wheeler, both acclaimed veterans of the Confederacy, the American mission of the late 19th century remained as justified as it had been in the days of Jefferson. But these two also represented some key differences. Morgan worried that a growing national expansionism would create a burgeoning U.S. government and military, which, unchecked, could turn on "southern autonomy" interests—the South's various components of sectional uniqueness—much as it had between 1860 and 1865. Wheeler, by contrast, after rekindling his old friendship with the greatest of all Yankee entrepreneurs, J. P. Morgan, showed little concern about northeasterners gaining control over the Philippines, as well as Birmingham, Ala., and waxed eloquent about a northeastern-controlled national government and economy being not only good for foreign policy but a key to southern modernization. Still, on racial objections to world power they were together, blithely responding that the problem could be solved with segregation. With ideals and self-interest harmonized in classic Gilded Age liberalism, these "new southerners" would simply export the emerging institutions of their own region.

In the 20th century Wheeler's, not Morgan's, views on national government and foreign expansionism gradually prevailed as the dominant view of the South. The ascendancy of Woodrow Wilson spurred southern expansionism to rapid and full recovery. Many white southerners, even some of the lower classes, perceived President Wilson's crusade for a moral and legal world order receptive to American influence as clear indication of "the return of the South" to international prominence. In fact, with the exception of a few isolated cases like Mississippi's James K. Vardaman, southerners identified with Wilson's notion of international order as something brought back to life from the presidency of another great southerner, Thomas Jefferson. That historical connection had serious flaws. Although born a southerner, Wilson derived his internationalism primarily from experiences with idealistic liberals of the Northeast, some with abolitionist roots and most with far less pragmatism than the sage of Monticello. Yet as Civil War memories dimmed and sectional reconciliation offered industry and profits, as well as psychological security, southerners grasped at Wilsonian internationalism as "a southern idea" reunited with American patriotism. Southern Wilsonians actually were motivated as much by the practicalities of New South economics and politics as by a renewed enthusiasm for the American mission. Still, they followed Wilson straight through the crusade of World War I and then down to his unpragmatic approach to the League of Nations.

The ironic and contradictory outlook—balanced, Jeffersonian expansionism advanced through the medium of relatively strong idealism—did not die with Wilson. During the 1920s and 1930s the League of Nations Association and the Carnegie Endowment for International Peace, two organizational bridges between the Wilsonianism of World War I and II, recruited far more effectively in the South than in any areas beyond a few urban centers in the Northeast where they were based. Indeed, between the wars, southern voices dissenting from Wilson's internationalism were uniquely few. And when war reopened in Europe in 1939, a regional arm of the Carnegie Endowment, the Southern Council on International Relations, worked to convert this regional sentiment into political support for President Franklin D. Roosevelt's developing war policies. After the war Southern Council members and other southerners urged the second chance at realizing the dream of Wilsonian internationalism—the United Nations. Nevertheless, in the early 1950s, shortly after the creation of the UN, most southerners turned against the organization because it seemed ineffective in achieving the Wilsonian goal of blocking the growth of socialist and communist power. They also feared Joseph McCarthy's attacks on supporters of organized internationalism. Such a waning interest in internationalism did not place southern leaders at odds with others associated with the general goals of Wilsonianism; on the contrary, it brought them closer together. The Cold War caused most Americans once committed to internationalism to move to the right and to espouse American rescue of the world through collective security agreements, economic expansionism, and interventionism. Considering this trend, the South's interventionist sentiment in the Korean War and in the initial stages of the Vietnam War appeared synchronized to late-20th-century American expansionism.

Other than the dissent from a few antiexpansionist mavericks like Florida's Claude Pepper, there have been only two major exceptions in this recent harmony between southern and national attitudes. In the 1950s and 1960s Richard B. Russell of Georgia and many other southern leaders balked at sending economic aid to the nonwhites of Africa, Latin America, and the Mideast, whereas many expansionists and the few enduring internationalists from other sections generally supported these measures. Southerners feared that competing low-technology products might be developed in these lands with the assistance of American funds. More important, southerners exhibited a racial reaction to nonwhites that was triggered by the civil rights movement at home. In some ways this attitude resembled the isolationism reflected by southerners in the years following the Civil War; in other ways, momentarily setting aside modern racial sensitivities, it bore out Senator Morgan's concern about foreign policy creating a powerful U.S. government that then attacked "southern autonomy." On the other hand, just as stabilization of southern internal affairs gradually eased southern insecurities after the turn of the century and resulted in a new interest in expansionism, so did the slackening of the civil rights movement a century later contribute to increased southern political support for numerous foreign aid projects.

At roughly the same time, the late 1960s and early 1970s, another peculiarly southern attitude emerged. At this time certain high-profile southerners in Washington — and the majority of their constituencies — followed Mississippi's James Eastland in opposing withdrawal of American troops from Vietnam long after most other Americans had accepted the limits of interventionism. At least as early as World War I, southerners had seemed excited about formal military activity abroad because of investments and jobs it provided within the generally poor southern population: economic opportunities in home-front war industries and military bases, plus "jobs" abroad through actual military service. These same considerations, coupled no doubt with the southerners' relatively high tolerance for violence and strong anti-Communist sentiments, encouraged what was characterized as a prolonged southern militarism in the Vietnam episode. In time this attitude, too, gave way to internal forces, taking down with it the presidency of Texan Lyndon Johnson.

As increased black voting power raised issues of human rights in southern politics and elevated Andrew Young and other advocates of economic aid to national prominence, the interventionist strain of southern expansionism lost out. Simultaneously, the economic development of the Sunbelt created more jobs and a slightly larger middle class of whites and blacks. These upwardly mobile businessmen and professionals lived off corporate profits and often looked to reports from the local chapter of the Council on Foreign Relations for appropriate responses to world problems. They advocated whatever moderation in American policy was necessary for American capitalism to reverse its energy shortages and trade imbalances and to establish more influential relations with developing nations.

Finally, out of this moderated expansionist consensus, in which ideals were increasingly harmonized with self-interest, there emerged Georgia's Jimmy Carter. President Carter's approach to foreign policy has been criticized for its lack of cohesiveness, its case-by-case "engineer's approach" to world problems in need of consistent U.S. policy, and a poorly planned intrusion in Iran. Yet Carter's advocacy of expanded American trade was complemented by an equal emphasis on human rights, reduction of nuclear arms, and other progressive internationalist goals. If this policy reflected little uniquely southern, more often than not it was attuned to the influence the United States might expect to have in a given area of the world, especially regarding Africa, an area in which Carter benefited from the advice of his close friend from Georgia, Andrew Young. Moreover, U.S. policy did indeed appear effective with the

Camp David talks aimed at peace in the Middle East. Still, frustrated toward the end of his term, Carter gravitated toward a post–World War II bipolarity, a military buildup against the U.S.S.R., as his chief foreign agenda. With the demise of the internal issue of race, the man in the White House did not look as much like the southerner as the American cold warrior.

Ultimately, under two distinctly nonsouthern presidents, Ronald Reagan and George H. Bush, a strong extension of Carter's focus on the U.S.S.R. figured into the demise of the Soviet empire and the end of most strains of the Cold War. Yet this did not mean an end to complexity in foreign policy; quite the contrary. With another southerner in the White House, the former Arkansas governor Bill Clinton, U.S. policy focused on encouragement of democracy abroad, with less emphasis on human rights and more on the "enlargement" of U.S. access to foreign markets. Despite his accent, Clinton seemed quite the American centrist who benefited from a strong economy at home while remaining relatively unsuccessful on foreign policy matters except those influenced by America's "hot" economy. When the former Texas governor George W. Bush succeeded Clinton, here was a third recent southerner in the White House who had little foreign policy experience. Tragically, Bush would gain that experience almost overnight as foreign-based terrorists launched devastating attacks on New York City and Washington, D.C.

Hence, in the nation's first 150 years, southerners increasingly showed relatively unique southern ideas in foreign policy and delivered certain well-experienced foreign policy leaders to deciding junctures in American history. In the late 20th century and early 21st century, however, the demise of a uniquely "southern way of life" with regard to race and economics (if not football, music, and food) produced a southern foreign policy sentiment more harmonious with the rest of America's. From another perspective, in the minds of most educated Americans, and certainly many historians, Woodrow Wilson provided a substantial ideological foundation for the predominant foreign policy sentiment of the 20th-century South. Actually, however, the viewpoint that helped most recent southerners reclaim at least some of their once-powerful role in world affairs was not so much Wilsonian internationalism but rather the more basic Jeffersonian approach, that of harnessing ideals to self-interest (minus the earlier agrarian/racial rhetoric) to pragmatically achieve national influence abroad. In the early 21st century, it is this less sectionally distinctive, but more confident, cultural prism that most southerners look through as they focus on the world.

TENNANT S. MCWILLIAMS
University of Alabama at Birmingham

Henry Blumenthal, *Journal of Southern History* (May 1966); Alexander DeConde, *Journal of Southern History* (August 1958); Joseph A. Fry, *Dixie Looks Abroad: The South and U.S. Foreign Relations, 1789–1973* (2002); George L. Grassmuck, *Sectional Biases in Congress on Foreign Policy* (1951); Alfred O. Hero Jr., *The Southerner and World Affairs* (1965); Charles O. Lerche Jr., *The Uncertain South: Its Changing Patterns of Politics in Foreign Policy* (1964); Tennant S. McWilliams, *The New South Faces the World: Foreign Affairs and the Southern Sense of Self, 1877–1950* (1988); Robert E. Osgood, *Ideals and Self-Interest in American Foreign Relations* (1953); Paul Seabury, *The Waning of Southern "Internationalism"* (1957).

Frontier Heritage

In 1893 a Wisconsin-born historian, Frederick Jackson Turner, read a paper titled "The Significance of the Frontier in American History" at the annual meeting of the American Historical Association. He launched a new hypothesis in which the American frontier was viewed as the dominant factor in the development of American civilization. "The existence of an area of free land, its continuous recession, and the advance of American settlement westward," he stated in his first paragraph, "explain American development."

Even today, more than a century after Turner read his paper, historians cannot ignore his thesis. A generation of graduate students at Wisconsin and later at Harvard studied under him. In time they wrote hundreds of monographs with Turner's thesis as their basic premise. Many of his students went on to become successful history professors. They in turn passed Turner's ideas on to more historians; they also produced a number of American history texts from elementary to college level. All of them were imbued with Turnerian ideas even if Turner was not mentioned by name. Although the frontier hypothesis has suffered considerably in the past 50 years, it must still bear consideration when American history is being interpreted.

In his essay Turner gave proper attention to the southern frontier. Land hunger, he noted, drove the Scots-Irish, Germans, and many other colonials into the transmontane South. Discovery of salt springs along the Kanawha, Holston, and Kentucky rivers freed them from dependence for that commodity on the Atlantic Coast. These men of Kentucky and Tennessee were so fiercely independent that the new nation almost lost them. They demanded free navigation of the Mississippi and initially profited most from the Louisiana Purchase. As for the institution of slavery, Turner did not consider it of prime importance in the history of American development.

Finally, for all the American people, Turner found in the frontier experience "intellectual traits of profound importance." He perceived a "coarseness and

Abandoned farmhouse in Ozark Mountains, 1940
(John Vachon, photographer, Library of Congress [LC-USF34-061051-D], Washington, D.C.)

strength combined with acuteness and inquisitiveness: that masterful grasp of material things, lacking in the artistic but powerful to effect great ends; that restless, nervous energy; that dominant individualism, working for good and for evil, and withal that buoyancy and exuberance which comes with freedom."

Davy Crockett, a southerner born along the Nolichucky River in east Tennessee in 1786, exemplifies just such a man. Restless yet ambitious, he moved first to middle Tennessee, served in military campaigns against the Creek Indians, and next settled for several years in west Tennessee. From there he was elected to the state legislature and later to Congress, where he served three terms. Still restless and not yet 50, he headed for Texas and achieved immortality by dying at the Alamo. Another exemplar was Sam Houston, who possessed those same traits of intelligence, restlessness, a practical turn of mind, a dominant individualism, and an ability to effect great ends that Turner identified as frontier attributes.

Certainly the most successful southern frontiersman was Andrew Jackson. He was a leader of the rough-and-tumble society that constituted the businessmen's and planters' world of the Tennessee frontier. He had fought duels, lost and won horse races, speculated in land, purchased slaves, married a beautiful frontier woman, and entered into the turbulent politics of his adopted state. A natural leader of men, he climbed the frontier political ladder as the representative of a people who possessed a fierce belief in a rustic democracy that left no place for Indians and accepted the institution of slavery. The spirit of the frontier spoke through him when Jackson stated in his bank veto message that the benefits of government should, "as Heaven does its rains, shower its favors alike on the high and the low, the rich and the poor."

Turner's great essay embraced all frontiers, north and south (but always west), and a chronology from colonial times until the end of the frontier as defined by the Bureau of the Census in 1890. He did not differentiate regional frontiers.

Subsequent critics did, pointing out certain frontier characteristics that were not so admirable. The frontier, they said, demonstrably fostered violence, lawbreaking, discrimination against minorities, anti-intellectualism, and individualism so fierce that it worked against the common good. Such unpleasant characteristics were self-evident in the lives of southern frontiersmen like Crockett, Houston, and Jackson.

The word "frontier" does not appear in the indexes of several of the principal texts and surveys of southern history. Emphasis has instead been placed on the antebellum South as a rural area — a dynamic but raw agrarian society advancing into a wilderness that indeed was the southern frontier, but which in the South was not always looked upon as such. A description of a southern frontier heritage may sound to some like an essay on the rural aspects of the South.

The southern frontier began with Jamestown and the beginnings of Virginia and spread northward into Maryland and southward along the coast eventually to embrace North and South Carolina, Georgia, and north Florida. Pioneers from the southern coastal colonies spilled over the Appalachians into Tennessee and Kentucky. After the War of 1812, the practical application of the cotton gin, and the rapid elimination of the Five Civilized Tribes, the Old Southwest filled in. This included the Black Belt, so named for its deep, black loam, which, with the warm, humid climate, made the cultivation of short-staple cotton economically profitable. Besides Georgia (1788) and Louisiana (1812), Alabama (1819) and Mississippi (1817) had achieved statehood by 1819. Within another generation Arkansas (1836) and Texas (1845) were added as states with a southern outlook. Florida, very much a frontier although south, not west, of the other states, entered the Union in 1845. W. J. Cash in *The Mind of the South* (1941) emphasized the persistence of frontier conditions in the South: "It is impossible to conceive the Great South as being, on the whole, more than a few steps removed from the frontier stage at the beginning of the Civil War."

In every sense the South's progression was along an advancing frontier. Crushing the Indians, buying the land, breaking it to the plow, and building cabins, outbuildings, and fences were common tasks. Roads had to be constructed leading to new villages where trade, religion, education, business, litigation, and government flourished. The steamboat, a practical conveyance by the 1820s, made water highways of the sluggish southern rivers. As with other frontiers, the southern one produced a raw, heavy-drinking, vulgar, speculative, turbulent society. Augustus Baldwin Longstreet in *Georgia Scenes* (1835) and Joseph Glover Baldwin in *Flush Times of Alabama and Mississippi* (1853) well portrayed the southern frontier society at the time of land booms and rapid settlement. In addition, there was the southern cattlemen's frontier. It included the red-clay hill regions of northern Georgia and Alabama, the pine barrens of the Carolinas, and central Florida's prairies; to a degree, the cattle industry thrived in every southern state in the antebellum period. However, the barefooted, floppy-hatted "cracker" with his long whip never struck the romantic vein of the national psyche as did his later counterpart, mounted and gazing out over the Great Plains.

All of this was a part of the frontier experience and was similar to the societies of the same period in the Old Northwest and trans-Mississippi West. Yet the South's frontier experience differed from the common frontier experience in a number of ways. One-crop agriculture, especially the raising of tobacco and cotton, both of which enervated the soil, made it absolutely necessary for southerners to advance to new lands. Soil depletion forced Virginians and Carolinians to pack up and leave their old fields for the Black Belt. Once there, they again depleted the soil. They practiced the negative frontier characteristic of waste. The land was abused because of the belief that more free land always lay to the west—even as far west as Texas's Brazos River bottoms. So too were the pine and live oak forests logged and left as wasteland to catch on fire or become a malarial morass. Such practices occurred on other frontiers, but in the South the damage was greater. This was not because the southern frontiersman was any more rapacious of the land than his northern or western fellow pioneers but because the single-crop system, the southern climate with heavy rainfall, and the nature of the southern soil resulted in greater, longer-lasting damage. Soil erosion was an early problem resulting in the end of one frontier and the beginning of another.

These differences also created or made more inevitable a social system that is usually considered harmful to southern progress. Some have called the southern social system, based upon one-crop agriculture, which was callous to the maintenance of good soil and extremely detrimental to all but the most successful of southern planter-businessmen, a "hothouse" society. A yeomanry existed that was more likely to lapse downward into "po' white" status than rise to plantation aristocracy, and once the social status was set, it was very difficult for a white person to rise out of it. Beyond attaining manumission, blacks were relegated to lowest status, of course, as slaves. This social stratification was notably a southern frontier characteristic, not a national one. Yet the system was unstable, and southern literature is filled with narrations of aristocratic families who fell upon hard times and tried desperately to retain their status. William Faulkner's fictitious Yoknapatawpha County, with its Compson family, is of this genre. Eudora Welty's stories of southern families in rustic settings likewise harken back to frontier times.

Individualism, a trait common to all frontiers, was a fine-tuned tradition on the southern frontier. It manifested itself in a dislike of government — any government — that proposed to control a man's life — how he ran his plantation or his business, how he managed his slaves, or where he fired the woods or chose to go hunting. To the proud white southern agrarian, the Bill of Rights was the most important part of the Constitution.

This individualism did not extend to religion or political opinions, where orthodoxy ruled. The frontier South worshipped God through many sects, but nearly all were fundamentalist and emotional in their attraction. Their religious spectrum did not include atheists, Deists, Unitarians, or other groups who questioned in any way the accepted emotional, fundamental appeal of religion by Bible, and Bible alone.

Slavery, as the solution to racial problems, broached no opposition, and although Turner was not bothered by slavery on the frontier, certainly it contributed to the South's distinctiveness. Similarly, on matters of the tariff, internal improvements, and interpretation of the Constitution, the white southern frontiersman accepted a common attitude and stuck to it. He was not, as men were on other frontiers, an equalitarian. He accepted the concept of class, beginning with the black slave, working upward past the free black, the poor white, the yeoman farmer, and the plantation owner; in towns, the merchant, banker, and gin operator (often one and the same person) adhered to many of the same ideas, though for a few years prior to the Civil War he may have voted Whig instead of Democratic.

The southern rural frontier allowed a white man to carry a gun, use profanity, break the Sabbath, participate in a lynching, drink heavily, or fight a duel, and have it all considered normal. Such a person, if he was capable of accepting discipline, made an excellent soldier. He served well in all the nation's wars (although he was on the Confederate side in the 1860s).

The southern frontier heritage, then, includes fundamentalist religion, perhaps the strongest rugged individualism in the modern nation, and a love of the outdoors stemming from frontier ruralism, including hunting and fishing. A strain of violence may still be discerned. For many decades into the 20th century, to be a white southerner was also to be a Democrat, for the society demanded that everyone adhere to the majority political opinion. Loyalty to family, honor, love of the land, and devotion to country, all inherited from the frontier-rural traditions of their pioneering past, remain strong among southern whites today.

Frederick Jackson Turner's frontier thesis stressed the frontier movement as a process, "a migrating region," but recent work sees the frontier as a place or places. The term "backcountry" is used increasingly to describe the frontier, at least for the 17th and 18th centuries. The study of the backcountry is an interdisciplinary project involving historians, geographers, archaeologists, anthropologists, and ethnohistorians. Issues of settlement patterns, human environment relations, evolving landscapes, ethnic diversity, and regional boundaries engage scholars across disciplines.

Geographer Donald Meinig talks of the "Southern Interior," identifying its cattle- and hog-raising economy, with a minimum of subsistence farming. He differentiates an isolated Appalachian region from a more prosperous area of the Carolina Piedmont and central Kentucky and Tennessee. He labeled this area between the Atlantic Coast and emerging plantation regions as "the border zone."

Meinig did not use the term "backcountry," but Robert D. Mitchell defines it as "an area, or at least a zone, with a reasonably distinct regional expression and set of boundaries." Wilbur Zelinsky, an influential cultural geographer, sees settlement patterns, building traditions, and ethnic-folk origins as defining features in understanding the backcountry. Geographers imagine the early southern interiors as the beginning of the Upland South of mountains and hills and the people who settled there. The exact boundaries remain unclear, though, with some scholars giving the colonial backcountry an expansive definition, from southeastern Pennsylvania down to central Florida.

Historian David Hackett Fischer traces the transmission of cultural features from the northern British borderlands region to the southern backcountry, interpreting these traditions and practices as the major determinants of the backcountry's development. He analyzes speech patterns, building forms, and foodways as examples of this British and southern backcountry connection.

Some interpretations of backcountry settlers in the colonial era overlap with Turner's assessment of frontier pioneers. Terry G. Jordan and Matti Kaups write of the "American Backwoods Frontier," seeing settlers there as individualistic, suspicious of authority, without class consciousness, bound by family ties, and mobile within a woods environment. Movement remains important to recent scholars of the backcountry, as it was to Turner, but settlement adaptation to landscape is a more central concern, along with the continuing need to define the relationship between the interior South and the coastal South in the colonial era. Ethnohistorians make an important contribution in seeing the backcountry as a contact zone between native peoples and pioneer settlers. Cultures were sometimes shattered and reformed, they interacted, and they generally remained in flux during the colonial era.

RICHARD A. BARTLETT
Florida State University

Ray Allen Billington, *America's Frontier Heritage* (1966); Joan E. Cashin, *A Family Venture: Men and Women on the Southern Frontier* (1991); Andrew R. L. Cayton and Fredrika J. Teute, eds., *Contact Points: American Frontiers from the Mohawk Valley to the Mississippi, 1750–1830* (1998); Thomas D. Clark, *The Rampaging Frontier* (1939); Avery O. Craven, *Journal of Southern History* (August 1939); David Hackett Fischer, *Albion's Seed: Four British Folkways in America* (1989); Gene M. Gressley, *Agricultural History* (October 1958); Terry G. Jordan and Matti Kaups, *The American Backwoods Frontier: An Ethnic and Ecological Interpretation* (1989); Todd M. Lieber, *Mississippi Quarterly* (Fall 1969); Donald W. Meinig, *The Shaping of America: A Geographical Perspective on Five Hundred Years of History*, vol. 1 (1986); James Merrill, *The Indians' New World: Catawbas and Their Neighbors, from European Contact through the Era of Removal* (1989); Robert D. Mitchell, in *The Southern Colonial Backcountry: Interdisciplinary Perspectives on Frontier Communities*, ed. David Colin Crass et al. (1998); Gregory H. Nobles, *William and Mary Quarterly* 46, no. 4 (1989); Frank L. Owsley, *Journal of Southern History* (May 1945); Malcolm J. Rohrbough, *The Trans-Appalachian Frontier: People, Societies, and Institutions, 1775–1850* (1978); Timothy H.

Silver, *A New Face on the Countryside: Indians, Colonists, and Slaves in the South Atlantic Forests, 1500–1800* (1990); Daniel H. Usner Jr., *Indians, Settlers, and Slaves in a Frontier Exchange Economy: The Lower Mississippi Valley before 1783* (1992); David J. Weber, *The Spanish Frontier in North America* (1992); Wilbur Zelinsky, *The Cultural Geography of the United States* (1973, 1992).

Globalization

James McBride Dabbs wrote, "Of all the Americans, the Southerner is the most at home in the world. Or at least in the South, which, because of its very at-homeness, he is apt to confuse with the world." This statement might suggest a nascent globalism — southern hospitality as humanism — though it also points to an insularity that is inward-looking rather than hospitable.

A historical perspective reveals a globalized South that preceded the southern identity, contributing to and then molded in part by the American Civil War, Reconstruction, and Jim Crow. In the 21st century, the American South is reemerging as a global player and is potentially a distinctive contributor to world culture.

As David Moltke-Hansen and other scholars show, the South, as an identifiable region, is recent, from about 1830. The southern identity was created for political, economic, and cultural reasons as people spread from the older southeastern states westward to Arkansas and Alabama. It was not always there. Literary figures such as William Gilmore Simms forged the identity, and political dispute, then war, hardened it. It was preceded by a time when the South was emerging globally as an economic force and was a culturally diverse area attracting a variety of immigrants. At least 50 languages were spoken in Charleston alone in the 18th century. Charleston's per capita income in that century was the highest in the nation. Few thought of the South as a distinct region of the emerging new nation. It is intriguing to imagine that Thomas Jefferson and John Adams, close friends whom we now imagine as southerner and northerner, respectively, might not have thought of those identities at all in the late 18th and early 19th centuries.

The 18th-century South, then, had more in common with the 21st-century South than with the late 19th- and 20th-century South in its global connections. The intervening two centuries gave birth to the burden of southern history, with slavery and defeat forging a southern identity often oppositional to the North and the nation. Now, in the 21st century, the South has emerged again as an economic force, and again it is attracting immigrants — this time Asian and Hispanic. This global epoch provides an opportunity for southern identity to move from oppositional within the nation to integrative within the world.

Commentators such as Peter Applebome, writing as recently as the late 1990s, recognized changes in the South, but primarily within a national perspective—how the South was growing in national influence, how America was becoming "Dixiefied" even as Dixie was becoming Americanized, to use the phrase of John Egerton. But the South is also, like the rest of the world, part of globalism, and has been accelerating in this role since the end of the 20th century.

What is globalism, and, more to the point, what is southern globalism? How is globalism emerging in the South? Globalism is the economical, political, and cultural integration of the world. It has local impacts in each of those areas and creates diversity as people, goods, and ideas migrate from one place to another. Globalism is not just capitalism—booming when the economy booms, disappearing when it falters, as in recent times—it is also an attitude. Recent data suggests that southerners tend toward a global attitude. Southernism is defined culturally, historically, economically, psychologically, and geographically as a concern and an identification with the South. Globalism is a concern and identity with the wider world. The two concerns and identities can clash, but they can also overlap and interweave.

Data from the 2001 Southern Focus Poll, administered by the *Atlanta Journal-Constitution*, suggest that while some southerners see themselves both as different from nonsoutherners and as connected to the world as a whole, a majority of those surveyed focused first on their global ties. When asked whether they saw themselves primarily as different from nonsoutherners or as linked to people around the world, nearly 50 percent of respondents answered that they felt "connected to people around the world." Fewer than a third of those surveyed viewed themselves initially in terms of their difference from nonsoutherners.

Aside from what the results of this poll suggest, signs of globalism are everywhere in the South, though of course with a southern accent. (This is true literally: children of migrants from China, Germany, and elsewhere speak like their native-born peers). Diversity affects everyday life: teller machines at banks ask customers: "English or Spanish?" The majority of agricultural workers in North Carolina are now Hispanic.

Not only is the world coming to the South, but the South is also going to the world. The South has a long tradition of contributing globally. Even in its dark days it led world missions, sent some of its children for education overseas, and traded its cotton on foreign markets, and now it is a leader in new global businesses.

Yet the South is a distinctive player in America's role as global leader. The

South has a connection to the Third World, for the South itself, in part, was and is a Third World in certain places. Continuing poverty and cultural isolation from the cosmopolitanism of metropolitan centers continue to characterize rural pockets of the South. Studies show how southern plantation owners were quite similar to Russian estate owners, Junkers of East Germany, and landowners in Caribbean, Latin American, and other colonial plantation-based societies. James E. Crisp at North Carolina State University defines the South as a unique overlap of a white majority and a plantation society. The South can be seen as the northernmost extension of the plantation system of South America and the Caribbean and the southernmost extension of a dominant Northern European culture. Others compare the South with South Africa, and Alistair Sparks's *The Mind of South Africa* is explicitly modeled after W. J. Cash's *The Mind of the South*. Other scholars note parallels and connections among British, Dutch, and French colonial economies and societies and the antebellum South. Slavery ended almost simultaneously in all these places, around the 1860s, and often for similar reasons as in the South. The dramatic impact that Harriet Beecher Stowe's *Uncle Tom's Cabin* had on the slavery debate in the 1850s can be compared to the impact the book *Multatuli* had in the Netherlands East Indies, later Indonesia, in the 1860s.

The South also has many modern First World, or "northern," features: Charlotte, home to Bank of America, the second largest bank in America, ranks second after New York in banking assets, and the South represents the fourth largest economy in the world. Southern products and companies can be found around the globe: Coca-Cola, cigarettes, the news organization CNN, Delta Airlines, Quintiles. Southern missionaries provide enormous services around the world. Southern Baptist missionaries, for example, have established hospitals in many areas, from Nigeria to Indonesia.

These endeavors are southern in that they originate in or are based in the American South. But the question remains: Does the South convey any distinctive ideas to the world? The South's cultural features, such as Protestantism and its general Northern European heritage, tie it just as often to the global North as to the global South.

Certain experiences and values define the South as a potential mediating force between the United States and much of the world. The South's music conveys messages — spirituals with their deep themes of oppression and "we shall overcome." The South conveys historical caveats through its burden of history, including not only war, defeat, and the experience of being colonized but also internal problems — the oppression of African Americans, of women, of poor whites, and of Native Americans. It also may impart its values, such as traditions of kinship, family, community, and the importance of a sense of place. These experiences and qualities afford the South a special role in international relations and cultural construction.

Michael O'Brien has argued that the South, as a part of the United States, resonates with Europe in a special way, that is, as apart from unrelenting American triumphalism, and his point could apply throughout the world. One of the most famous fictional southerners, Scarlett O'Hara, has much in common, for example, with women in most of the world: she is part of a patriarchal order and one that is colonized and defeated; she struggles and fails yet prevails. In Indonesian women's accounts of experiences rather similar to southern women's during wartime, one finds very similar attitudes. Perhaps this helps explain the appeal of *Gone with the Wind* globally. Scarlett has more in common with women in much of the world than has, say, Gloria Steinem or Hillary Clinton. She is more like Megawati Sukarnoputri (daughter of Indonesia's leader, Sukarno), whose name bespeaks patriarchy combined with feminine power (Megawat).

The South makes a particular contribution to globalism by buttressing the value of place. Paradoxically, transcendent ethics that ignore place have fostered the destruction of the earth: they define mission and exploit place to achieve it. Alternative ethics value the earth, including the place we inhabit, and preserving and sustaining it is itself an ultimate value. The value of place, at least in principle, can be part of this position (as Thomas Berry shows in *The Great Work*). In this sense, the agrarian ethic of Jefferson and Goethe is more communal and less destructive than the industrial ethic of Franklin. Southerners have long since claimed a special sense of place. Maybe the Agrarians were right, but their views need refinement through global ecology.

Whatever the contribution of the South to the world, the key point is that a global South differs fundamentally from a regional South. The South as region is defined as oppositional to the nation, while the South as global is defined as integrated with the world. The South did not fight the world, it fought the rest of the nation: hence it can be global without the resentment and emotional baggage that it brings when it reunites with the nation. And the South, with its kinship to other Souths, can be global with a difference—the South's can be a tempered globalism, qualified and balanced by a sense of place.

JAMES L. PEACOCK
CARRIE MATTHEWS
University of North Carolina at Chapel Hill

Peter Applebome, *Dixie Rising: How the South Is Shaping American Values, Politics, and Culture* (1996); Thomas Berry, *The Great Work: Our Way into the Future* (1999); James C. Cobb and William Stueck, eds., *Globalization and the American South* (2005); Peter A. Coclanis, *The Shadow of a Dream: Economic Life and Death in the South Carolina Low Country, 1670–1920* (1989); James E. Crisp, *History 243: The United States, 1845–1914* (1985); James McBride Dabbs, *Who Speaks for the South?* (1964); John Egerton, *The Americanization of Dixie: The Southernization of America* (1974); David Goldfield, in *Which "Global Village"? Societies, Cultures, and Political Economic Systems in a Euro-Atlantic Perspective*, ed. Valeria Gennaro (2002); Lothar Hönighaussen, Marc Frey, and James Peacock, *Regionalism in the Age of Globalism*, vols. 1 and 2 (2005); David Moltke-Hansen and Michael O'Brien, eds., *Intellectual Life in Antebellum Charleston* (1986); Michael O'Brien, *Southern Cultures* 4, no. 4 (1998); Celeste Ray, *Highland Heritage: Scottish Americans in the American South* (2001); James Peacock, *Virginia Quarterly Review* (Autumn 2002); James Peacock, Harry Watson, and Carrie Matthews, eds., *The American South in a Global World* (2005).

Great Depression

The Great Depression began with the collapse of the stock market in late 1929, and it devastated the American South more than any other region during the 1930s. The calamity's paralyzing severity and dismaying persistence enveloped the whole republic; nationwide statistics reveal that fully a third of the workforce was unemployed, and by 1933 the nation's business activity had plunged to half that of 1929. But the American South suffered even greater harm as yearly per capita income plummeted from a national low of $372 in 1929 to just $203 in 1932.

Southern agriculture, in marked decline since the end of World War I and uniquely scarred by tenancy, sank deeper into stagnation; even nature seem hostile as the 1930–31 drought, the severest on record, staggered the failing southern farm economy. Southern industry, still in its infancy, with only 15 percent of the nation's factory workers, fell even farther behind that of the North. Partners in misfortune, both rural and urban southerners shared the bitter trials of the times as the Depression exacerbated long-standing problems of poverty, race, and class.

Some southerners starved to death in the depths of the Depression. Thousands scavenged through garbage dumps; uncounted numbers of the homeless took refuge in city parks; evicted families lived in packing crates, junked automobiles, or anything else that might provide some shelter. Because a physician's fee was an easily cut expense, illnesses went untreated in a society hesitant to

conditions. And the industry's evolution had given rise to the company town where management owned or controlled housing, schools, churches, and government. Owners generally responded to the Depression with wage reductions, increases in production quotas, and work stretch-outs. Workers' resistance to these draconian measures prompted immediate discharge effected by institutionalized violence.

Resignation born of stunted expectations typified the industrial South. Even the company town's selective paternalism furnished support only so long as the worker kept his peace — and his job. Religion, family, or the close-knit society of a southern mill town provided what little enduring comfort employees gained. For the southern industrial worker the Depression was thus a lost decade; not until 1939 would the number of industrial jobs regain the 1929 level.

Southern farmers faced even worse circumstances. In the South's distinctive agricultural system, tenancy had replaced slavery as the "peculiar institution" after the Civil War. Most southern farmers, white or black, were tenants; over 60 percent plowed land they did not own in the cotton states of Arkansas, Louisiana, Mississippi, Alabama, and Georgia. For blacks the figure ballooned to over 80 percent.

Cotton served as tenancy's dynamic. Half of all southern farms produced cotton, and tenants worked three-quarters of these; production had totaled 14,096,000 bales in 1929. The landowner demanded cotton, for which a market always existed, but the Depression drove cotton prices to a record low of 4.6 cents per pound and production to only 10,613,000 bales. Beyond these developments, however, cotton neatly fitted a stringent pattern of controls over the life of the southern sharecropper, strictures the landowner tightened during the Depression.

Essential to the exploitative pattern was the country store, often owned by the landholder. Since the tenant usually began the crop year without cash, the owner guaranteed his credit at the nearby store where he was obligated to buy — at inflated prices and exorbitant interest rates. To insure steady purchases during the Depression, some landowners even forbade tenants to plant gardens or keep food animals. Although some sharecroppers did manage to flee to such comparative havens as Cleveland, Detroit, or California, many, black and white, lived on in a state of outright peonage, ensnared by the South's skewed legal system.

The domination of the whole of southern society by the white landowning class made all this possible. Political control insured complaisant lawmakers and enforcers who cowed the tenants. Denied access to public education, tenants had little comprehension of alternatives to their pattern of life. In the religious South even churches served planter interests by preaching to tenants the need for hard work and debt payment while neglecting to urge upon landowners biblical injunctions concerning masters' duties to laborers. By 1935, in the peasant society that was the South, 1,831,475 farms were tenant operated.

In the cotton country of northeastern Arkansas, hard-pressed sharecroppers finally sought relief by forming the Southern Tenant Farmers' Union (STFU). The nonviolent though racially integrated STFU called for nothing more radical than fair treatment and adherence to established laws. But a planter-led reign of terror crushed this stirring of tenant assertiveness with shootings, beatings, kidnappings, and kangaroo justice.

Black and white alike bore the weight of the malignant sharecropping system, which extracted from them the last measure of both labor and dignity, but the realities of a rigidly segregated society handicapped blacks even further. The most remarkable aspect of southern tenancy during the Depression is the striking triumph of the human spirit over the inhuman environment. Caught in an economic and cultural trap in certain respects fiercer than slavery, tenants displayed a luminous courage and an inexorable determination.

Only sweeping changes could restructure southern society after the Depression. The coming of World War II, with its military draft and insatiable demands for war industry workers, drew the next generation of potential sharecroppers from the farm; seeing a better world, they would never return.

Many landowners, envisioning greater profits in operating mechanized and larger single units safe under governmental subsidies, had begun to encourage an exodus of sharecroppers as the Depression lingered. The New Deal's Agricultural Adjustment Administration (1933) paid landowners, not the tenants who did the work, 50 percent more for plowing under cotton than for harvesting it. At the same time, improved farm machinery and the increasing availability of capital helped make mechanization more attractive; in 1930 southern farmers used only 134,000 tractors; that number had climbed to 255,000 in 1940 and 468,000 by 1945. These factors helped speed tenancy's demise, as the number of white tenants declined a remarkable 25 percent during World War II.

The South's Depression story is not, however, one of unrelieved misery. Normal work persisted to a degree; while perhaps a third of the labor force sat idle, the remainder still held jobs and often shared their meager bounty with impoverished friends, as traditional southern neighborliness proved more compassionate than Washington's geographically and racially distorted policies. Many craft workers, although finding fewer tasks, did remain relatively busy. A favorably located merchant with a long-established clientele often maintained an acceptable traffic. Not surprisingly, professionals in the legal and health fields, the planters' close allies, suffered least of all. Depression then, as always, was a matter of relative and selective decline.

Most southerners, however, struggled through these years with wounds healed only lightly by a government more interested in relief and recovery than in real reform. The impersonal numbers on unemployment lists and graphs of falling income meant empty stomachs, sinking spirits, and desolate confusion. Although despair existed, the survival of an open-hearted and optimistic spirit may be the most remarkable legacy of these impoverished southerners.

JOHN L. ROBINSON
Abilene Christian University

Roger Biles, *The South and the New Deal* (1994); James C. Cobb and Michael V. Namorato, eds., *The New Deal and the South* (1984); David E. Conrad, *The Forgotten Farmers: The Story of Sharecroppers in the New Deal* (1965); Pete Daniel, *The Shadow of Slavery: Peonage in the South, 1901–1969* (1972); Federal Writers' Project, *These Are Our Lives* (1939); Elna C. Green, ed., *The New Deal and Beyond: Social Welfare in the South since 1930* (2003); Donald H. Grubbs, *Cry from the Cotton: The Southern Tenant Farmers' Union and the New Deal* (1971); Jack Irby Hayes Jr., *South Carolina and the New Deal* (2001); James A. Hodges, *New Deal Labor Policy and the Southern Cotton Textile Industry, 1933–1941* (1986); Janet Irons, *Testing the New Deal: The General Textile Strike of 1934 in the American South* (2000); Jack Temple Kirby, *Rural Worlds Lost: The American South, 1920–1960* (1987); David E. Kyvig, *Daily Life in the United States, 1920–1940: How Americans Lived During the Roaring Twenties and the Great Depression* (2004); Robert S. McElvaine, *The Great Depression, 1929–1941* (1984); Gavin Wright, *The Political Economy of the Cotton South* (1978).

Historians

The oldest tradition of historical literature in the South is that of state descriptions and history, which commenced before the settlement of Virginia with the pamphlets and books that promoted and inflated the virtues of colonization. It continued through the studies of Robert Beverley (*History and Present State of Virginia*, 1705), William Stith (*History of the First Discovery and Settlement of Virginia*, 1747), and Thomas Jefferson (*Notes on the State of Virginia*, 1785). In the Spanish and French colonies, there were comparable works. By the 19th century a considerable body of such writings existed, among them David Ramsay's *History of South Carolina* (1808), Charles Gayarré's *Histoire de la Louisiane* (1846), and Charles Campbell's *History of the Colony and Ancient Dominion of Virginia* (1860). Such history was an amateur undertaking, local in focus and patriotic in tone, sometimes though not often allied to the foundation of state historical societies. Before 1861 such organizations existed in 10 states: Virginia (1831), North Carolina (1833), Louisiana (1836), Georgia (1839), Tennessee (1849), Alabama (1850), South Carolina (1855), Florida (1856), and Mississippi (1858).

Notable before the Civil War, however, was an absence of southwide historiography, which had to wait until the late 19th century brought a generation of southerners schooled by the experiences of war and Reconstruction. The first broader historical organization was the Southern Historical Society, founded in New Orleans in 1869 by ex-Confederates and dedicated to the vindication of the Lost Cause. Its successor, the Southern History Association, founded in Washington in 1896, was both more New South in persuasion and less bitter in tone; its publications appeared between 1896 and 1907. Insofar as professional historiography is an offshoot of urban modernity, it is no surprise that the southern historical and educational industry should have commenced outside and on the borders of the South before moving into the region later. The earliest centers of academic southern history were the Johns Hopkins University, where Herbert Baxter Adams taught Woodrow Wilson and William P. Trent; Columbia University, where William A. Dunning instructed students of Reconstruction such as Walter L. Fleming and J. G. de Roulhac Hamilton; and the University of Chicago, where William Dodd directed Frank L. Owsley's studies. The first course in southern history was taught by James C. Ballagh at Johns Hopkins in 1896, and the first within the South was taught by William K. Boyd at Trinity College (later Duke University) in 1907.

Usually under the direction of northern graduates born in the South, an infrastructure of graduate programs, journals, archives, presses, and professional organizations was fashioned indigenously after 1920. About a hundred doctorates in history were granted by southern universities between the world wars, mostly on southern topics. In 1930 the Southern Historical Collection, the largest archive of regional documents, was founded at Chapel Hill. In 1934 the Southern Historical Association was organized, and publication of its *Journal of Southern History* commenced in 1935. In the 1920s the University of North Carolina Press began to publish books on regional history and culture, and in 1937 the Louisiana State University Press began a multivolume *History of the South*.

Southern history, as both a professional and an amateur pursuit, has largely and consistently been written in the South by southerners for southerners and published by southern journals and presses. Though a wider national and international interest was sparked by the civil rights movement, there is mixed evidence that this curiosity is in decline, perhaps more slowly in Europe, where scholars sponsored in the 1980s the Southern Studies Forum as a subdivision of the European Association of American Studies, but more rapidly in the North. Nonetheless, the study of southern history forms an important and perhaps permanent subculture in American social discourse, possessed of many private symbols and rituals. There is a healthy amateur industry, flourishing as tourism, cheerfully anecdotal political journalism, and military and genealogical antiquarianism; all are characterized by a warmth of nostalgia for hoop skirts, Earl Long's penchant for striptease artists, or grandfather's exploits at Shiloh.

Professional historians in the South are notable for being an accepted part of their society, often partisan about the South, formerly bitter against the North but recently — as a function of growing relative affluence — more amiable. Their specialties are social history (particularly of slavery and race relations), biography, and political history. Military history, once popular as a function of bitterness, is now in decline, at least among professional historians. Economic history has been a weaker tradition, and intellectual history (save as literary history) has been almost nonexistent until very recently. Southern historians tend to divide by social persuasion (usually conservative, often liberal, rarely radical), by place of birth (Virginians, Tennesseans), by ancestry (yeoman, planter, Tidewater, Piedmont), by gender (male, female), and by sexual orientation (heterosexual, homosexual), rather than by theoretical persuasion (Marxist, Hegeian, postmodernist). However, the youngest generation of southern historians shows a marked, if wary, interest in theory.

Southern history is implicitly comparative, because scholars of southern history assume a distinction between southern and "northern" culture and occasionally offer formal comparisons with non-American cultures, as in the writings of Eugene D. Genovese (Japan and Sicily), Stanley Elkins (Latin America), Peter Kolchin (Russia), or C. Vann Woodward (Europe). More usually — and this is necessary to its function as social discourse — southern history is inward-looking. The old tradition of state history continues and constitutes the bulk of southern historical literature, chiefly because archives and higher education are organized largely by states. So southern history tends to be either the aggregate of state histories or, more commonly, narrative by synecdoche, in which a part is made to do service for the whole.

There is no known analysis of the social origins, recruitment patterns, or social habits of southern historians as a tribe, but there are several works that study individual historians, by way of intellectual biography or as part of an attempt to plot historiographical changes.

MICHAEL O'BRIEN
Jesus College, Cambridge

John Boles and Evelyn Thomas Nolen, eds., *Interpreting Southern History* (1987); Glenn Feldman, ed.; *Reading Southern History* (2001); Arthur S. Link and Rembert W. Patrick, eds., *Writing Southern History* (1965); Michael O'Brien, in *Rewriting the South: History and Fiction*, ed. Lothar Hönnighausen and Valeria Gennaro Lerda (1993); Wendell H. Stephenson, *Southern History in the Making: Pioneer Historians of the South* (1964).

Historic Preservation

In the South, an understanding and a respect for the past are such a part of its culture that historic preservation represents more than the perpetuation of physical resources. Historic resources serve as a link to the past; they reinforce an individual sense of identity and orientation, as well as a sense of place. Change can pose a threat to historic resources and to the culture and identity of people within a region. Given an abundance of historic sites and the degree to which the region cherished its past, it is not surprising that the South would provide fertile ground for the evolution of historic preservation. The potential threat to Mount Vernon, George Washington's home, gave Ann Pamela Cunningham the inspiration for the first national preservation campaign, creating a model for preservation efforts across the country. Virginia's Williamsburg became the nation's first outdoor museum, providing an example of restoration that focused on both buildings and the spaces between them and re-creating the character of the historic community. Threats to the historic area of Charleston were a catalyst for creation of the first local preservation ordinance in America, based on land-use control. While a few communities followed Charleston's lead, it would be the last third of the 20th century before this preservation tool was widely accepted. In the aftermath of World War II, new development driven by consumer demand for housing, automobiles, and highways was unleashed. Cities expanded into the countryside, while federal urban renewal programs threatened the historic cores of many cities, endangering and/or destroying many historic resources. Citizen concern about the loss of historic resources led Congress, in 1949, to create the National Trust for Historic Preservation to foster citizen awareness of preservation through programs of advocacy and education. Almost 20 years later, in response to continued loss of historic resources, the U.S. Conference of Mayors prepared a report, *With Heritage So Rich*, that documented the destruction resulting from federal programs and made recommendations for change. Congress reviewed the report, and its response was passage of the National Historic Preservation Act in 1966. The act incorporated most of the report recommendations and provided a program, based upon a federal/state partnership, that provided incentives for increased involvement of citizens in preservation activities. In the interim following establishment of the National Trust, citizens began to organize non-profit organizations to combat deterioration, urban-renewal programs, and an absence of municipal preservation policy. In Georgia, the Historic Savannah Foundation organized in 1955, and it established a model for citizen activism that rescued the 2.2-square-mile central area of the city as a result of a survey, created a revolving fund for the purchase and resale of endangered properties, and established covenants to protect restored properties. These efforts not only revitalized the most historic area of the city but also created a tourism industry that, today, brings in $1 billion annually. Thirteen years after this effort began, the National Trust showcased the city as the site of its 1968 annual meeting to provide lessons and inspiration to preservationists across the nation.

The National Historic Preservation Act created a comprehensive national preservation policy that established a nationwide network of state historic preservation offices with provision of federal matching funds to support their work. The act provided for determination of the historic significance of properties and listing on a National Register of Historic Places, financial benefits to those properties listed, the review of the impact of federal programs on historic properties, and incentives for federal tax credits for rehabilitation of historic buildings utilized for income-production. The impact of the National Historic Preservation Act was immediate. No longer could local governments obtain federal funds for projects destructive to historic resources without review. As intended, the act provided a stimulus to local preservation initiative and spurred surveys at local and state levels that led to National Register listings and benefits to listed properties; at the same time, it energized citizens to form community-oriented nonprofit preservation organizations that developed a slate of preservation initiatives. The increased activity prompted the National Park Service, the designated National Historic Preservation Act administrator, to issue a call to the nation's academic community to develop degree programs to prepare individuals to provide the professional guidance and expertise needed by state agencies, elected officials, citizens, and organizations. As a result of the tax-credit program, authorized in 1976 for the rehabilitation of historic buildings utilized for income-production, $23 billion in private investment was made by October 2001. The significance of the tax-credit program was the creation of financial incentives for the reuse of historic buildings and disincentives for razing them for new construction.

In 1978 the favorable decision of the U.S. Supreme Court on the constitutionality of local government regulation of historic properties encouraged states to adopt enabling legislation where needed and communities to adopt local preservation ordinances. An expansion of local government activity was encouraged by the 1980 amendment of the National Historic Preservation Act, creating the Certified Local Government program, including a special category of grants, to bring cities into the federal/state partnership. As of 2003, 1,228 certified local governments are participants with $40 million provided in grants. Increased citizen activism encouraged the creation of statewide nonprofit preservation organizations during this time, with Preservation North Carolina and the Georgia Trust for Historic Preservation leading the way in the South.

The National Trust launched its Main Street Program in 1980 to revitalize central business districts in five states. By 2002 this program had served over 1,600 communities, in 40 states, that had made an investment of $17 billion in downtown revival. Collectively, the Main Street, Certified Local Government, and tax-credit programs made historic preservation an economic reality and a positive factor in terms of jobs created, the sale/rehabilitation of buildings, sales and income tax collections, income from heritage tourism, and the growth of property values in designated local districts. These indices signaled that preservation was, or could be, a major element of a community's economic success.

Efforts to strengthen the preservation movement and to extend it more fully to all citizens in the last decade of the 20th century included the 1992 amendments to the National Historic Preservation Act. The amendments were intended to bring Native Americans and African Americans more completely into the preservation partnership through provisions for tribal historic preservation officers having the authority of state historic preservation officers on tribal lands and authorization of assistance to minority colleges and universities. In addition, in 1993, the National Trust, through its Preservation Partnerships Program, sought to help emerging and established statewide and local nonprofit preservation organizations improve their effectiveness. By 2002 the National Trust had facilitated the increase of full-time-staffed statewide organizations from 17 to 38 and created a statewide and local partnership including 32 statewide organizations in 31 states and 21 local organizations in 15 states. The National Trust's Southern Field Office reports that all 12 of the states in its area have statewide organizations with 10 having full-time staff and two having part-time staff.

The story of 20th-century historic preservation is one of expansion, especially in terms of philosophy, legislation, legal standing, economic significance, and the inclusion of diverse resources and all ethnic groups within American society. This process revised definitions of what is historic, articulated areas of significance, expanded the range of resources to reflect the broad patterns of history, and broadened understanding of what constitutes cultural heritage and the means with which to protect it. Terms such as "vernacular architecture," "cultural landscapes," "heritage areas," "rural preservation," "interior easements," "transfer-of-development rights," "smart growth," "private property rights," "cultural diversity," "property stewardship," "tear-downs," "maritime preservation," "economic benefit," and "heritage tourism" have all become a part of the lexicon of contemporary historic preservation. As preservation entered the 21st century, accomplishments included an increase in the number of resources identified and protected, an increase in the number of trained preservation professionals from a still-growing number of institutions offering preservation degrees, the development of African American and other minority initiatives on both state and regional levels, increased use of financial and legal incentives to facilitate preservation, broadened attention to a variety of resource types, recognition of landscapes as preservation resources, an increased understanding of the economic impact of preservation activities, and growing recognition of preservation opportunities as environmental and quality-of-life issues.

Concerns and challenges related to preservation, now and in the future, include our society's continuing reluctance to recognize the purpose, need, value, and potential of planning for the development and redevelopment of our environment in recognition of the values of historic preservation. Too many areas eligible for local protection have not been designated or ordinances may be weak or poorly enforced. The constant migration of new residents to the South feeds development often insensitive to historic preservation. The character of historic buildings is often destroyed by conversion to condominiums, and neighborhood character, especially in established areas, is threatened by those who want to purchase properties and make inappropriate changes or demolish them for new construction. Today, the greatest threat to historic areas is from private individuals, not the federal government. Another problem is the conflicting values of those concerned with preservation of the built and natural environments. Despite problems, preservation is a success and much has been accomplished. The continuation of that success will depend on the degree to which society can be educated to recognize and appreciate the philosophy of preservation and provide the funds necessary for its implementation.

JOHN C. WATERS
University of Georgia

Diane L. Barthel, *Historic Preservation: Collective Memory and Historical Identity* (1996); James M. Fitch, *Historic Preservation: Curatorial Management of the Built*

World (1990); Robert E. Stipe, *A Richer Heritage: Historic Preservation in the Twenty-First Century* (2003); Norman Tyler, *Historic Preservation: An Introduction to Its History, Principles, and Practice* (1999).

Historic Sites

With the founding of the Mount Vernon Ladies' Association of the Union in 1856, the South became an early leader in the historic preservation movement in the United States. The association, chartered by the Commonwealth of Virginia, was organized with the sole purpose of purchasing and preserving George Washington's home and its surrounding grounds. Also in 1856 Tennessee provided funds to purchase and preserve Andrew Jackson's estate, the Hermitage. Like so many early preservation efforts, these mansions were selected for restoration and perpetual care largely because of their association with important figures in American history. A few other sites and structures were saved because of their role in significant events.

The Civil War interrupted historic preservation efforts throughout the South and also provided scores of potential sites with which to memorialize the Lost Cause. By the end of the century several Civil War battlefields had been set aside as national military parks. Tennessee's Chickamauga and Chattanooga park, formed in 1890, was one of the first. By the early 1900s the South seemed intent on preserving almost any Civil War site of even moderate significance. Although the region was often forced to rely on federal aid to finance these preservation efforts, state and local activities continued. The Association for the Preservation of Virginia Antiquities, a private organization founded in 1888, concentrated its early efforts on preserving colonial sites in the Jamestown area. Other state and local organizations gradually emerged to tackle specific preservation projects. In Virginia, for example, Richmond's Confederate Literary Society was founded in 1890 to preserve the Confederate White House, and the Thomas Jefferson Memorial Foundation purchased Monticello in 1923. Both were typical of the local organizations that collectively have played a crucial and continuing role in southern preservation efforts.

During the 1920s John D. Rockefeller became interested in preserving and restoring Williamsburg, Va., and his interest and financial assistance in the project demonstrated the potential of private preservation efforts. Several other communities, including Charleston, S.C., and St. Augustine, Fla., drew on the experience, techniques, and spirit of the Colonial Williamsburg project to develop historic districts of their own. For the first time, historic preservation in the South began to reflect larger cultural and historic concerns. While Williamsburg and similar sites were usually related to major historic events and

The tomb of George Washington, Mount Vernon, Va. (The Mount Vernon Ladies' Association, Library of Congress [LC-USZ62-108347], Washington, D.C.)

personalities, the preservationists and historians associated with these projects also attempted to interpret patterns of everyday life. As the 1900s wore on, this impulse became ever more significant, but the portrayal of southern society at historic sites has nevertheless largely focused on the white elite.

Several major federal initiatives had enormous impact on the development of southern sites. The establishment of the National Park Service to administer federally funded sites (1916) and the Historic Preservation Act of 1935, which finally provided focus to the national preservation movement, were especially noteworthy. Although state and local organizations would continue to preserve and interpret the past throughout the region, southern reliance on federal leadership and funding for major projects, particularly in the area of military sites and parks, became increasingly important. At Civil War parks the significance of this national support has been seen in the tendency of federally funded areas to play down the Lost Cause myth in favor of a more straightforward interpretation of events. Still, southern organizations have often been able to contribute monuments and exhibits to national battlefield parks, which continue to emphasize, however subtly, the romance and glamour of the Confederacy. At other sites, particularly those related to the colonial period, federal leadership has tended to favor a portrayal of colonial life that emphasizes an emerging national character, whereas those colonial sites administered by southern organizations often seek to demonstrate the uniqueness of the southern identity.

A number of culturally significant patterns emerge from an examination of the South's preservation activities. First, the sheer number of such areas in the South suggests that the region indeed does tend to be more enamored with its history than other portions of the United States. The 11 states of the Confederacy together with Maryland, Kentucky, and Missouri account for 45 percent of eastern historic sites listed in the National Register of Historic Places and over 36 percent of all listings. State and local sites, which sometimes are not included in the register, are also a bit more common in the South than in other areas. Southern preservationists have the advantage, particularly in the Atlantic Seaboard areas, of an unusually lengthy history. Moreover, much of the Revolutionary War and virtually all of the Civil War were fought on southern battlefields. Nevertheless, the region's early leadership of the preservation movement and the continued high level of state, local, and individual enthusiasm for preserving the past have enabled the South to outstrip the level of commitment in most other regions.

The nature of the sites preserved and exhibited is also revealing. One important theme in the southern preservation movement always has been the memorializing of southern leadership during the colonial and Revolutionary periods. Numerous sites, from the reconstructed House of Burgesses at Williamsburg, to the homes of Washington and Jefferson, to the Yorktown and Jamestown areas, demonstrate the crucial role played by southerners in shaping the early history of the United States. Although Virginia tends to dominate in this category, North Carolina, South Carolina, and Georgia have also preserved significant sites.

The southern insistence on its own uniqueness of identity and aristocratic origins is suggested by the dominance of plantation architecture among historic restorations. The life of the colonial and antebellum white elite is interpreted at literally scores of sites, and from George Mason's Gunston Hall in Virginia southward to Louisiana's Oak Alley the South seems to be one great plantation. The romance of the antebellum years and the heroic struggle for the Lost Cause are clearly central themes in historic preservation in the South. This was especially true of work carried out during the period from 1890 to 1930, but even in more recent periods this impulse has carried considerable weight.

Perhaps the best example of this movement to memorialize the plantation South is found at Stone Mountain Park near Atlanta, Ga. This state-owned recreation area includes the "Ante-Bellum Plantation" exhibit, a romantic reconstruction of a "typical" 1850s plantation. This plantation never actually existed but has been assembled on the spot from period buildings that were moved to Stone Mountain from throughout the state. That the scene is drastically glamorized is confirmed by the use of the Kingston House to represent the home of the overseer and his family, for the structure was actually the main house at Allen Plantation near Kingston, Ga. Such portrayals, even those that are not so exaggerated, have played a significant role in shaping popular conceptions of southern history.

Other segments of southern society often have been slighted by this emphasis on the plantation South. Indeed, it might be argued that those elements that are missing from historic sites are as significant as those that are present. For example, many plantations have been preserved with little or no reference to slave life and culture. Although some sites have begun to exhibit slave quarters (Gunston Hall and the Stone Mountain Plantation, for example), many others have none at all. Some slave quarters that are preserved or reconstructed — for example, those at Mount Vernon — are not typical and are sometimes far more commodious and well furnished than would have been the case. The last quarter century has seen more preservation attention to African American historical sites, as at Freedmen's Village in Arlington, Va., and the William Johnson House that is part of the Natchez National Historic Park in Natchez, Miss. The southern middle class, the southern merchant, and the southern poor white are similarly slighted, at least in terms of the number of sites preserved. Even when merchants and artisans are represented, as at Williamsburg, the overall effect often suggests that this portion of society merely provided support and service for the more important planter class. Another curious weakness in the portrayal of the region's history is found in the comparatively limited number of sites related to Native Americans. In terms of numbers of sites, only in Mississippi does the interpretation of the Native American impact on the South approach realistic proportions. Native Americans in Mississippi have pressed for recognition of their forebears' contributions, and one result has been a change in many historic plaques.

The record of southern history as preserved in historic sites is, then, both an illustration of the South's desire to maintain a sense of identity and a reinforcement of popular images of the region held generally throughout the nation. That the historic South as it is preserved never existed is not the point. The preserved past is a record of regional pride and identity that seeks to highlight and help preserve southern distinctiveness in the face of forces that would "Americanize" the region. As many scholars have suggested, the use of the past, particularly the preserved past, is an ideological exercise. Nowhere is this clearer than in the South.

CHRISTOPHER D. GEIST
Bowling Green State University

Craig Evan Barton, *Sites of Memory: Perspectives on Agriculture and Race* (2001); Edward D. C. Campbell Jr., *Journal of Regional Cultures* (Fall–Winter 1982); Alvar W. Carlson, *Journal of American Culture* (Summer 1980); Beverley Da Costa, *Historic Houses of America Open to the Public* (1971); Larry Ford, *Growth and Change* (April 1974); Christopher D. Geist, in *Icons of America*, ed. Ray B. Browne and Marshall Fishwick (1978); Charles B. Hosmer Jr., *Presence of the Past: A History of the Preservation Movement in the United States before Williamsburg* (1965); U.S. Department of the Interior, National Park Service, *The National Register of Historic Places* (1974); Robert R. Weyeneth, *Historic Preservation for a Living City: Historic Charleston Foundation, 1947–1997* (2000); Walter Muir Whitehill, *Interdependent Historical Societies* (1962).

History, Central Themes

The earliest explanation of southern distinctiveness began with the climate. In 1778, when the South Carolina Assembly was debating the ratification of the Articles of Confederation, politician William Henry Drayton saw the union of the states as a threat to the plantation economy. "From the nature of the climate, soil and produce of the several states," he said, "a northern and a southern interest naturally and unavoidably arise." Meteorological conditions encouraged certain activities among the inhabitants, Drayton declared, and they in turn made possible a particular lifestyle that became characteristically southern.

One hundred fifty years later, historian U. B. Phillips agreed. "Let us begin by discussing the weather," he said, in a widely quoted statement, "for that has been the chief agency in making the South distinctive." To Phillips, as to Drayton, climate encouraged sectional interests by settlers in the American states.

Weather and soil imposed an agriculture of semitropical staple crops—from tobacco and rice to indigo and cotton and sugarcane—that yielded quick profits. The large returns induced planters to create ever larger estates, which led to a labor shortage. The availability of land and the lack of people willing to work for someone else together produced the plantation system of coerced labor. "The house that Jack built," as Phillips described it, grew inexorably from a determinative weather pattern.

Other interpreters have echoed Phillips's views. Author Clarence Cason defined the South as that part of North America where the temperature reached 90 degrees Fahrenheit in the shade at least one hundred afternoons a year. The oppressive heat compelled cooks to concoct gastronomic delights to tempt sluggish appetites, thus giving rise to the food-and-condiment school of southern analysts. Other scholars suggested that the humid heat purified and strengthened a Nordic racial strain to engender a superior type of humanity, sometimes called "cavalier."

The environmentalists thus defined the central theme of the South by the plantation and its products, themselves the result of climate and soil conditions. Staple crops, servile laborers, and lordly masters who in theory emulated Old World manorial rulers—this was the South of Phillips and his followers.

The idea of the climate-determined South was largely mythic, however, and it appeared so self-serving—an excuse for glaring inequities in the status quo—that it has been under constant attack. It was also difficult to defend in a region that extends from sea level to the forested heights of Appalachia, from humid woodlands to semiarid plains.

Even as critics questioned the climate theme, other scholars pursued the possibility that the South might be identified on the basis of behavior patterns. Charles S. Sydnor pointed the way to new paths of investigation, arguing that southern historians must define their subject before proceeding further. The plantation environment of rural farmlands and sparse population provided examples of the social patterns he used to define the region. W. J. Cash agreed, portraying the southern mind as "what happened when the tradition of aristocracy met and married with the tradition of the backwoods." John Hope Franklin identified the South in the 1950s as a violent land still under frontier conditions, with blood feuds, a dueling code, and a strong military tradition.

Earl E. Thorpe perceived a male sheikdom of erotic libertinism in a harem-like world of subjugated and complaisant women. Slavery was, in his view, as much a sexual institution as an economic or a social one. Other scholars, however, stressed the gynecocracy—the matriarchy—of the isolated estate, in the families of both masters and slaves. That same isolation and underpopulation convinced David Bertelson that the staple-crop society lacked social unity and showed little evidence of community activities, even those as important as road and bridge building. The lazy South was his version of the central theme.

The geographer Wilbur Zelinsky discussed what he called "settlement characteristics" as a way of identifying the South. In house types and urban morphology, including a lack of spatial pattern to farm buildings and a high incidence of abandoned buildings, he found a "constellation of traits" that were coterminous with the South and represented regional characteristics.

Other observers of southern society have at one time or another defined their subject in terms of such phenomena as fireworks at Christmas and a quiet Fourth of July, mockingbirds, xenophobia, a chivalric respect for the ladies, a slovenly and dialectical speech pattern, and shoeless, clay-eating poverty. Pellagra, malaria, and hookworm have also provided thematic interpretations.

Subsequent investigators saw significance in the region's religious expression. Known colloquially as the Bible Belt, the Southeast comprised the largest block of Protestant Christian evangelicals to be found anywhere, and at times that faith impelled people to attack the alluring temptations of flesh and mind. Publicity surrounding the 1925 Dayton, Tenn., trial of John T. Scopes, who had been charged with the crime of teaching evolution, dramatized the religious attitudes of southerners and made these beliefs an easy explanation for regional distinctiveness.

One-party politics and a preference for a confederated league of semi-independent member states ("states' rights") gave rise to another theme that took its cue from political platforms and voting patterns. Many political observers in more recent times have discussed the Sunbelt South and its implications for government policies.

The presence of black Americans, of course, has been a major guidepost to a definition of southern distinctiveness. The negative side of the region's racial and social relationships—slavery, segregation, violence, and disfranchisement—has provided interpretive themes. An exception came from historian-folklorist Charles Joyner, who wrote that "the transformation of African culture into African-American culture has been one of the major themes of American history, with innumerable implications for every aspect of American life."

Twentieth-century efforts by the national government to eradicate racial practices spurred irreconcilable white historians to pursue still another central theme. The South, they declared, came into existence only under attack from outsiders. Egocentric sectionalism, or the 100-year effort to reconstruct the South along northern dimensions, required otherwise divided southerners to unite in defense of their interests.

More recent analysts, such as C. Vann Woodward, have found the central theme of southern history to be southern history itself. Prosperity, optimism, and unvarying triumph, said to be the content of the national past, did not describe the aberrant record of southern history. That, went the argument, made the South, and southerners, different. Other students, such as George B. Tindall, sought the essence of the southern character in a preference for myth, the unreal, and the romantic, because reality was too unpleasant.

The most recent expression of a search for a central theme for the South focuses on the idea that "the South" was socially constructed and served the self-interests of its promoters. Among others, Edward Ayers, James Cobb, and Richard Gray have written from this view. Sociologist John Shelton Reed draws much from history in his influential, related argument that a southern regional self-consciousness has survived the sweeping changes in the South since World War II.

No single attribute, or collection of conditions, has succeeded in explaining satisfactorily the continuing awareness of a separate South. It may indeed be necessary to conclude that aside from the idea or belief, the South has no definite existence. That conclusion does not detract from the South's reality or its impact, for ideas are a powerful force in human affairs. The search for the American South is a chapter in the intellectual history of the country, and the idea of the South is one of the most significant facts in making the present what it is.

DAVID L. SMILEY
Wake Forest University

Peter Applebome, *Dixie Rising: How the South Is Shaping American Values, Politics, and Culture* (1996); Edward Ayers, *The Promise of a New South, 1920–1941* (1977); David Bertelson, *The Lazy South* (1967); W. J. Cash, *The Mind of the South* (1941); Clarence Cason, *90° in the Shade* (1935); James C. Cobb, *Redefining Southern Culture: Mind and Identity in the Modern South* (1999); Robert S. Cotterill, *The Old South: The Geographic, Economic, Social, Political, and Cultural Expansion, Institutions, and Nationalism of the Ante-bellum South* (1936); W. T. Couch, ed., *Culture in the South* (1934); Carl N. Degler, *The Other South: Southern Dissenters in the Nineteenth Century* (1974); John Hope Franklin, *The Militant South* (1956); David Goldfield, *Still Fighting the Civil War: The American South and Southern History* (2004); Richard Gray, *Southern Aberrations: Writers of the American South and the Problems of Regionalism* (2000); Charles Joyner, *Down by the Riverside: A South Carolina Slave Community* (1984), *Shared Traditions: Southern History and Folk Culture* (1999); Michael O'Brien, *The Idea of the American South, 1920–1941* (1979); Nell Irvin Painter, *Southern History across the Color Line* (2002); U. B. Phillips, *Ameri-*

can Historical Review (October 1928); David Potter, *The South and the Sectional Conflict* (1968); John Shelton Reed, *The Enduring South: Subcultural Persistence in Mass Society* (1986); Charles S. Sydnor, *Journal of Southern History* (February 1940); William R. Taylor, *Cavalier and Yankee: The Old South and American National Character* (1957); Earl E. Thorpe, *Eros and Freedom in Southern Life and Thought* (1967); Frank E. Vandiver, ed., *The Idea of the South: Pursuit of a Central Theme* (1964); Charles Reagan Wilson, *Baptized in Blood* (1980); C. Vann Woodward, *The Burden of Southern History* (1961); Wilbur Zelinsky, *Social Forces* (December 1951).

Indian Eras, Paleoindian Period
12,000–10,000 B.P. (10,000–8000 B.C.)

The first people who came into what would become the American South, dubbed the Paleoindians by archaeologists, came to this continent around 12,000 B.P. to 14,000 B.P. This was the Late Pleistocene, an era commonly known as the Ice Age. It was considerably colder than today, and large ice sheets, or glaciers, covered much of the globe. The giant Ice Age glaciers were formed when frigid temperatures froze sea water into ice sheets. In North America, the Laurentide and Cordilleran glaciers, at their maximum size, covered all of present-day Canada and part of the United States, with the Laurentide extending into eastern North America to about latitude 37° north, or to about present-day northern Virginia and central Ohio and Illinois. Much of the global sea waters were frozen into ice sheets, lowering the sea levels across the world approximately 400 feet. The lowered sea levels exposed a "land bridge" at the Bering Strait connecting Siberia to Alaska. Since the Bering Strait sea shelf is less than 300 feet deep, when the sea levels were low, the sea shelf was exposed, thus forming a land bridge connecting the two continents. Actually, this land bridge was more of a continent, since at its maximum width it measured about 1,000 miles. Geologists call this continent Beringia, and the first people who came to the Americas simply walked across it or traveled along its coast in simple skin-covered boats, hunting and fishing in the fjords and inlets of the coast. The first southerners, then, were part of a long-term migration of people who over a few thousand years traveled from Siberia to Alaska across Beringia.

The plant life in the South during the Ice Age resembled that of today's more northerly climes. The Appalachians, for instance, were covered by a spruce forest. In the Coastal Plain, Piedmont, and Interior Highlands and Lowlands the vegetation system was a temperate, broadleaf forest with maple, hickory, ash, and beech trees. Some species found in the Ice Age broadleaf forest are still here, most notably the southern magnolia and the flowering dogwood. The peninsula of Florida was covered with a forest dominated by cypress and gum trees. The animal life during the Ice Age was also quite different. The most striking animals were large mammals (or megafauna) such as the American mastodon and the woolly mammoth. But there were also horses, bison, giant land tortoises, ground sloths, giant moose, giant beaver, musk ox, peccaries, dire wolves, saber-toothed cats, the American lion, and in Florida the giant armadillo. Many species of the period, are still around today, such as white-tailed deer, rabbits, rodents, muskrats, peccaries, bears, and, of course, cockroaches.

The Paleoindians had no system of writing and therefore left no written documents describing their lives; hence what is known about them comes from archaeologists examining their material remains (or artifacts). Southern Paleoindians were hunter-gatherers whose lives revolved around the environment and the Ice Age resources available. Paleoindians used animal and plant resources to make tools and everyday items such as clothing, baskets, fishhooks, and so on. But, because this was so long ago and because southern soils are so acidic, artifacts made out of perishable materials usually are not preserved. Fortunately, Paleoindians made many of their tools out of fine-grade stone, which preserves well. Stone tools, then, are an important piece of evidence of Paleo life.

Stone projectile points known as Clovis and Folsom points are the most common kind of stone tool associated with Paleoindians throughout the Americas. Paleoindian hunters attached these points to the end of spears and used them to hunt large mammals. In the South, such megafauna as mastodons and mammals traveled in small groups or singly to navigate the forests. Southern Paleoindians assuredly hunted the megafauna, and Clovis and Folsom points are found throughout the South, but southern Paleoindians also had to rely on a larger array of animals than did their counterparts in the American West. Archaeologists at southern Paleo sites have also recovered the remains of white-tailed deer, rabbit, and other smaller animals.

In the South, on sites with good preservation, archaeologists have also recovered the remains of nuts, roots, berries, and other wild vegetable foods, as well as the stone tools used to prepare them. Paleo men and women plaited and wove plant fibers into clothing, and they used bone, as well as stone, in making many kinds of tools. On the sites in the coastal areas, archaeologists understand the Paleoindians to have relied more heavily on marine resources, especially fish and shellfish. In those areas of the South where there are caves, Paleoindians chose to live in these natural shelters. In other areas, they lived in what archaeologists call "open-air" sites, meaning that they built their huts, usually made out of saplings and hides or thatch, under the open sky.

Being hunter-gatherers, Paleoindians chose to live near critical resources, specifically fresh water, stone, usable wild plants, and wild animals. In the South, Paleoindians would settle seasonal base camps near a fresh water source and then go on foraging expeditions for food and stone. When the season changed, they would move their camp to another location for that particular season. Paleo and later people regularly returned, for example, to live in northern Alabama's Dust Cave, which suggests it was a favorite place for prehistoric southerners.

Material remains can tell much about a prehistoric people's subsistence and economy but cannot speak to the more intangible aspects of life such as social and political systems, religion, kinship, and so on. These aspects of Paleo life, then, are not well known. However, by combining archaeological information with what is known about contemporary hunter-gatherers, archaeologists can make some inferences about Paleo social life. Generally, archaeologists believe that southern Paleoindians lived in bands, or small groups of about a dozen or so families, all connected through kinship. Contemporary band-level societies are egalitarian, meaning that all adults have equal say in group decisions and no one has more possessions than anyone else. In fact, given that hunter-gatherers have to be able to move with the seasons, they do not acquire a lot of material goods. Paleoindians, then, probably had a scant material life, and they more than likely were not interested in acquiring more items. Looking at the regional distribution of artifacts, archaeologists believe that southern Paleoindian bands had defined territories. In other words, a band's base camps and procurement camps were established in certain areas, and foraging and hunting expeditions were carried out within certain areas.

The Paleoindians migrated into the Americas during the last 2,000 years of the Ice Age, and as the climate began to change, so did the Paleo way of life. Around 14,000 B.P. the climate across the globe began to get warmer. The large ice sheets began to melt, eventually reaching their current positions at the North and South poles, and the vegetation and animal life also changed to become more like it is today. In the South, the Appalachian spruce forest was replaced by a temperate broadleaf forest dominated by oak, hickory, and chestnut. The temperate broadleaf forest of the interior South was replaced by an oak, hickory, and pine forest, known today as the southern mixed forest. And the temperate broadleaf forest in the Coastal Plain and the Florida Panhandle's cypress and gum forest were replaced by the longleaf pine forest. The rising sea levels also moved the edge of the coastline inland.

Over 30 genera of American megafauna became extinct at the end of the Ice Age. Archaeologists look on this mass extinction as deriving from the complex interactions between humans and a changing environment. The Paleoindians contributed to the extinctions through their nonselective and sometimes excessive hunting techniques, which, combined with the dramatic climatic changes and the subsequent loss of habitat, reduced the Ice Age megafauna populations to a point where they were not able to rebound. With the end of the Ice Age came the end of the Paleo way of life. The people, however, did not go away; they adapted to their changing environments and began an extraordinarily successful way of life that proved sustainable for over 7,000 years, a way of life known today as the Archaic.

ROBBIE ETHRIDGE
University of Mississippi

VICTOR THOMPSON
MAUREEN MEYERS
University of Kentucky

David G. Anderson and Kenneth E. Sassaman, eds., *The Paleoindian and Early Archaic Southeast* (1996); Brian M. Fagan, *The Great Journey: The Peopling of Ancient America*, (2003).

Indian Eras, Archaic Period
10,000–3000 B.P. (8000–1000 B.C.)

With the end of the Ice Age, the first settlers of the Americas had to adjust to a changing environment. Geologists call this time of environmental change the Holocene. During this time, global temperatures increased and many of the glaciers melted. Much of the water melting off the largest North American ice sheet, the Laurentide, ran off in drainages that went through the South to the seas. In time, the braided, shallow, trench streams of the Ice Age gave way to the large alluvial river systems typical of the South today. These alluvial river systems provided both rich aquatic resources, such as freshwater fish and mussels, and lush plant resources because of the fertile soils in the alluvial floodplains. In the South, archaeologists refer to this time period as the Archaic period (10,000–3000 B.P.) and to the people, as well as their way of life, during this time as the Archaic cultural tradition. Archaeologists typically divide this era into three time periods — the Early Archaic (10,000–8000 B.P.), the Middle Archaic (8000–5000 B.P.), and the Late Archaic (5000–3000 B.P.). Like their Ice Age ancestors, the Paleoindians, Archaic people were hunter-gatherers; however, their way of life had changed dramatically. Over the course of the Archaic, about 7,000 years, population grew, technology changed, aquatic resources became more important, settlements became denser and were occupied longer, and people began the process of domesticating the first plants in the South.

The cultural achievements of Archaic peoples laid the foundations for the more complex prehistoric societies that would later inhabit the region.

During the Early Archaic, life was very much like it was for the Paleoindians, with people living in small, mobile, family groups moving from camp to camp. However, archaeologists find many more Early Archaic than Paleoindian sites, indicating a gradual increase in population. By the beginning of the Holocene the Ice Age animals were extinct, forcing people to adapt to more localized game. Archaic people now hunted the smaller animals found throughout the South, especially wild turkey, black bear, and white-tailed deer; they also foraged for nuts from upland groves of trees. Early Archaic people also invented the "atlatl," or spear-thrower, which is a stick with a hook carved at one end for attaching a spear and a handle carved at the other end for throwing. By using an atlatl, a hunter could increase the range and velocity of a thrown spear. Archaeologists have also noted that Early Archaic people made many different types of spear points, which they understand to indicate the emergence of regionally distinct cultures in different parts of the South at this time. One reason for the emergence of these distinct cultures may be that people began to depend more on locally available resources. The focus on localized resources and the increasing population may have led to restrictions in the amount of contact between different groups, resulting in the development of local styles and attitudes.

During the Middle Archaic, prehistoric people once again experienced a shift in environmental conditions. Between 9000 B.P. and 5000 B.P. the climate gradually became warmer and drier. This climatic shift is often referred to as the "Hypsithermal climatic interval." One result of the Hypsithermal is that certain wild food resources became restricted to certain areas. Although regionally distinct cultures emerged during the Early Archaic, this trend was intensified as Middle and Late Archaic peoples began using specific areas of the landscape more intensively, particularly those areas that were near swamps and river bottoms. While aquatic animals had always been part of the Archaic diet, they became much more important during this time. As a result of these changes, people lived in larger base camps in huts made of wood and plant materials such as thatch or bark, and the huts were built on the higher grounds, or terraces, of river bottoms. In many southern river bottoms, these sites are marked by large accumulations of mussel shells or "shell middens." A midden is a gradual accumulation of domestic debris and food remains and usually indicates long-term use or reoccupation of a particular site. In these shell middens, people left behind not only heaps of discarded freshwater mussel shells and other aquatic foods such as fish and turtle but also fishing tools and other artifacts associated with daily life. Today, these mussel shell middens are still visible and can cover several acres in some river bottoms, testifying to the extent to which some Archaic people relied on these resources. Despite the heavy reliance on aquatic resources, Archaic people continued to hunt and gather terrestrial plants and animals.

Many of the Middle and Late Archaic sites in alluvial floodplains are "stratified sites," where Archaic people lived for much of the year. People would go on short hunting or foraging expeditions into the upland not far from the river bottom, but most of life took place in base camps. The importance of these places is also reflected in the number of individuals that were buried at these riverine sites. Hundreds of burials are associated with these sites, likely marking a particular band's claim to an area of the landscape. The number and the intensive reoccupation of these floodplain sites suggest that there was a slow increase in population over the Archaic period and that this population increase may have caused band territories to become smaller and more tightly packed. Furthermore, with the shrinking of territories, people became more protective of their resources and territories. Many of the burials at these sites exhibit evidence of violent trauma, which may reflect intergroup conflict.

While evidence suggests conflict during the Middle and Late Archaic, there is also evidence that some groups cooperated and shared resources. For instance, many middens contain an array of nonlocal materials, including stone, copper, mica, and finely crafted pins made out of bone that were probably worn by individuals from visiting groups. "Bannerstones" are an example of stone tools made of imported stone. These functioned as counterweights on atlatls, they come in a variety of geometric shapes, and most are polished to a beautiful smoothness. Most bannerstones are made of stone found only in specific areas of the South, yet they have been discovered throughout the region. The wide distribution of bannerstones and other finely crafted stone objects likely indicates that Archaic peoples were engaged in a wide exchange network of relatively hard to get stone and well-made goods that helped to underwrite alliances between bands, thus ensuring cooperation, encouraging sharing of resources and territory, and alleviating conflict. Given that increased population density and decreased foraging ranges could increase the potential for competitive relationships between Archaic bands, this gift-giving would have been a strategy to ensure cooperative and friendly relationships between neighboring groups.

Middle and Late Archaic people who lived along the southern coasts had a slightly different lifestyle than their riverine neighbors. The seas rose rapidly during the Early and Middle Holocene, because of the melting of Ice Age glaciers, reaching their present levels during the late Holocene. As a result, many Early and Middle Archaic sites along the coast are now under water, and archaeologists mostly find the remains of Late Archaic villages. These sites contain the remains of most every kind of fish, shellfish, and other marine resource that would have been available, as well as plant resources like acorns and land animals such as white-tailed deer. In other words, these coastal Archaic people were supreme fisher folk, but they also continued to hunt and gather other resources. Like their riverine counterparts, coastal Archaic people discarded shells, mostly oyster but also clam and other kinds, which formed impressive middens four to five meters high that one can still see today. Some of these middens are circular with large, central clean areas that archaeologists believe functioned as town plazas. These "shell rings" represent some of the earliest year-round settled villages in the South. With this new "settled" life came new technologies such as pottery. The Archaic people living along the south Atlantic coast were among the first Americans to make ceramic wares. Their pottery, called "fiber-tempered pottery" because of the vegetable fibers used as a tempering agent, appeared around 4,500 years ago and quickly spread throughout much of the Deep South — the south Atlantic coast, southern Florida, Alabama, middle Tennessee, and into the lower Mississippi River valley.

Middle and Late Archaic people set another process in motion that would come to dominate much of later prehistory — monumental construction, better known as mound building. Mound building is the intentional construction of an earthen or shell monument. This practice should not be confused with the gradual accumulations of shell and debris described earlier. While intentional mound building began in the Middle Archaic in the lower Mississippi Valley and in Florida, no mounds come close to the size, scale, and complexity of those found at the Poverty Point site in northeast Louisiana. Built around 3300 B.P., Poverty Point is certainly one of the most impressive achievements of Archaic southerners. It is a large village with six mounds — three small platform mounds, one large conical mound, and two massive mounds thought to be shaped like birds — and six concentric elliptical ridges around an open area. Who lived at Poverty Point and why they did so are still not entirely clear. The large amount of debris from everyday life found on the elliptical ridges suggests that Poverty Point had a large resident population. However, the giant bird-effigy mounds indicate that the town also had some sort of political, social, or religious import. The size and complexity of the town, the mounds, and the other earthen structures suggest that the Archaic people living at Poverty Point were quite sophisticated and had an eye toward community planning and beauty. The artifacts found at Poverty Point are made of stone found in other parts of the Southeast and the Midwest — quartz, magnetite, chert, galena, flint, schist, soapstone, green stone, copper, even obsidian. At Poverty Point, artesans crafted this fine stone material into exquisite tools and art pieces. Whatever else it may have been, Poverty Point was certainly the Archaic trade center in the eastern woodlands.

The Archaic, while one of the most successful periods in the South in terms of its inhabitants' way of life, was also a time of important changes. Over 7,000 years, Archaic people saw an increase in population throughout the South. They invented sophisticated tool kits for exploiting a broad variety of natural resources. More and more of them stayed in villages for longer and longer periods of time. And they forged wide trade networks, exchanging raw materials and finished products, while also increasing their social, economic, political, and religious ties. During the Archaic period the foundations were laid for cultural traditions that would dominate southern prehistory until European contact.

ROBBIE ETHRIDGE
University of Mississippi

VICTOR THOMPSON
MAUREEN MEYERS
University of Kentucky

Jon L. Gibson, *The Ancient Mounds of Poverty Point: Place of Rings* (2001); Kenneth E. Sassaman and David G. Anderson, eds., *Archaeology of the Mid-Holocene Southeast* (1996).

Indian Eras, Late Archaic Domestication of Plants and the Woodland Period
3000–1000 B.P. (1000 B.C.–A.D. 1000)

At the end of the Late Archaic period, people in the South began to grow their own food, which would forever change their lives. Archaeologists initially separated the Woodland period from the Archaic period because of this achievement; however, recent evidence indicates that the transition to food production most likely began during the Late Archaic. The prehistoric transition to agriculture poses the question: why did humans become farmers? Whereas hunter-gatherers live off the natural resources at hand, farmers utilize the landscape intensively and create a local environment that suits their needs. Farming is very labor intensive and time consuming and a high-risk endeavor because of the possibility of crop failure. In other words, farming is not necessarily an obviously better way to get along. Yet food production began in many different areas of the world between 8000 B.P. and 3000 B.P. in several clear cases of independent invention. In each case, however, the process unfolded according to local environments and the social organizations of local people.

In the South, the transition to agriculture began in the Late Archaic and developed further during the Woodland. (The Woodland lasted from 3000 B.P. to 1000 B.P., and archaeologists divide it into three distinct periods, the Early Woodland, 3000–2500 B.P., the Middle Woodland, 2500–1500 B.P., and the Late Woodland, 1500–1000 B.P.). Archaic people returned regularly to favored river floodplains, and such reoccupations altered local conditions around these sites, opening up forest for sunlight and enriching the soil through waste disposal. This process created favorable environments for several disturbance-driven weedy species that are quite prolific, in particular chenopod, marsh elder or sumpweed, wild gourds, and sunflower. This ecological succession would not have been lost on Archaic peoples, who were probably the preeminent botanists and wildlife biologists of all time. Thus it makes sense that they would start intentionally weeding, watering, and otherwise working to increase the production of these plants. The next logical step would be to begin harvesting and storing seeds and intentionally sowing them during their next seasonal stay. The selective harvesting, storing, and success rate of the stored seeds would lead to changes in genotype and physical characteristics, and hence to domestication, of these plants.

Once gardening got started, it became quite popular and spread throughout the Southeast. Woodland people also invented new tools such as stone hoes, pestles and mortars, and grooved axes for farming and food processing tasks. People assuredly still hunted wild game and gathered wild plant foods, but during the Early Woodland, they added more and more domesticated plants to their diet. By the Middle Woodland, corn and tobacco made their first appearances in the South. By the Late Woodland, people were relying more on their gardens than on their foraging activities. Although they cannot do so definitively, most archaeologists assign either a Southwest or a Mesoamerican origin for both corn and tobacco. Corn would eventually become the staple crop for the southeastern Indians, but for most of the Woodland period, corn was but one of several starchy seed plants being grown.

With farming, people become invested in their agricultural activities and tend to stay near their gardens throughout the growing and harvesting season. The Woodland period saw an increase in what archaeologists call "residential stability," or the amount of time people stayed at in one location. In the Early Woodland, people still inhabited a place and moved with the change in seasons. But by the Middle Woodland, as their reliance on grown foodstuffs increased, people began living in permanent villages with multiple structures, trash pits or middens, and plazas. Residential stability meant that people could store foodstuffs, and Woodland villagers typically built large, bell-shaped pits next to their houses in which to store their surpluses, along with such wild foods as hickory nuts. Most Woodland villages were typically small farming communities, with about 20 to 40 families; however, as discussed below, a few urban centers emerged during the Middle Woodland. Like their Archaic ancestors, though, Woodland peoples still preferred to live on the terraces in river floodplains, where they had access to freshwater, as well as fish and shellfish and the usual wild game, such as deer, turkey, raccoon, rabbit, bear, and squirrel. Given the Woodland peoples' new interest in gardening, the rich alluvial soils would have been especially attractive.

Many technological changes occurred during the Woodland. Since they still depended on wild game and fishing for their animal proteins, Woodland peoples continued to make fishing gear and to use spears and atlatls. In the Late Woodland period, they invented the bow and arrow, and they also began to make smaller, triangular points for their arrows, or true "arrowheads." White-tailed deer and turkey were favored game animals, but Woodland hunters also brought home many other types of wild game, such as rabbit, opossum, duck, squirrel, and raccoon. The most important technological achievement, however, was the refinement and elaboration of ceramic technology. Woodland potters moved from the relatively crude, fiber-tempered wares to experimentations in paste, temper, form, firing techniques, and decoration. They began to make a variety of storage and cooking wares in assorted shapes, all designed with distinctive rims and body decoration. Woodland potters used one decorating technique known today as "stamping," in which they would carve a paddle with a certain design and then impress this design into the pot before firing. In fact, as pottery became more advanced technologically, regional ceramic styles began to appear, and archaeologists oftentimes differentiate between different "cultures" based on particular stamped designs on ceramics. Such designs changed over time, but they also differed across regions. Charting these changes over time and space allows archaeologists to see differences in groups both across regions and across time. The development of ceramics occurred as people practiced more horticulture and settled in more permanent villages. Ceramic technology allowed seeds to be stored for short- and long-term uses. However, pottery would have been difficult to move around with, so its presence was amenable to a sedentary lifestyle.

During the Early Woodland, in the Ohio River drainage, people known today as the Adena people elaborated on some Archaic period customs by burying their dead in earthen mounds, often with elaborate grave goods. Adena burial mounds vary in size, ranging from a few feet to nearly 70 feet high. The larger mounds typically have log tombs in them that usually contain the remains of a single individual, but sometimes they contain the remains of more than one person. Clearly the people buried in these mounds were important to the group, given their elaborate burials. Adena people also built large animal effigy mounds, such as the famous Serpent Mound in Ohio—a long, sinuous earthen mound that resembles a giant snake.

By the beginning of the Middle Woodland, the Adena people had elaborated their mortuary customs and spread their influence throughout much of the eastern United States. What archaeologists call the Hopewell culture emerged from this change, and its center had shifted slightly south, to the south-central Ohio River valley. Like their Adena forebears, the people of Hopewell also built elaborate ceremonial earthworks that were the graves of important people. They also buried these people with exotic and finely crafted gifts, many of which were made out of materials obtained through an extensive trade network that covered much of the South and most of the Midwest. People from Hopewell also spread their mortuary customs, and apparently the ideas of commemoration behind them, throughout much of the same area. Archaeologists sometimes refer to this region of trade networks and similar mortuary practices as the "Hopewellian Interaction Sphere." Within this sphere, Middle Woodland people of the Southeast built burial mounds and traded such things as mica, quartz crystals, marine shells, and shark and alligator teeth for items such as galena from Missouri, flint from Illinois, grizzly bear teeth, obsidian, and chalcedony from the Rockies, and copper from the Great Lakes. This kind of interaction and the adoption of Hopewellian burial practices, however, did not occur uniformly throughout the South.

One of the most spectacular Middle Woodland sites in the South fell just within the southernmost periphery of the Hopewell Interaction Sphere. Today the site is known as the Kolomoki Mounds, and it is a historic park in present-day Early County, Ga. Between 1650 B.P. and 1250 B.P. (A.D. 350 and A.D. 750), the people at Kolomoki built at least seven earthen mounds, including a 56-foot-high, flat-topped mound, two burial mounds, and four smaller ceremonial mounds. Kolomoki was also a large urban center, which, at its height around 1650 B.P. to 1400 B.P. (A.D. 350–600), may have been the largest such center north of Mexico.

Around 1500 B.P. (the Late Woodland), the archaeological record reveals a sharp decline in the construction of Middle Woodland burial mounds in the Hopewellian core area of the Ohio River drainage. The decline in the construction of burial mounds was accompanied by a disruption of the long-distance trade in exotic materials. Traditionally, archaeologists have viewed the Late Woodland as a time of cultural decline. Late Woodland settlements, with the exception of sites along the Florida Gulf Coast, tended to be small in comparison to those of the Middle Woodland, and few outstanding works of art or architecture can be attributed to this time period. Archaeologists view the Late Woodland as a very dynamic period, however. Bow-and-arrow technology, allowing for increased hunting efficiency, became widespread. New varieties of maize, beans, and squash gained economic importance at this time, and although settlement size was small, the number of Late Woodland sites increased markedly over the number of Middle Woodland sites, indicating a population increase. These factors suggest that the Late Woodland period was an expansive period, not one of a cultural collapse.

ROBBIE ETHRIDGE
University of Mississippi

VICTOR THOMPSON

MAUREEN MEYERS
University of Kentucky

David G. Anderson and Robert C. Mainfort Jr., eds., *The Woodland Southeast* (2002); Thomas J. Pluckhahn, *Kolomoki: Settlement, Ceremony, and Status in the Deep South, A.D. 350 to 750* (2003); Mark Williams and Daniel T. Elliott, eds., *A World Engraved: Archaeology of the Swift Creek Culture* (1998).

Indian Eras, Mississippian Period
1000–300 B.P. (A.D. 1000–1700)

Around 1,000 years ago, prehistoric southerners went through a qualitative change in life, especially political life. This era of the ancient chiefdoms of the American South is called the Mississippian period. Like the other prehistoric periods, archaeologists divide the Mississippian into the Early Mississippian (1000–800 B.P. or A.D. 900–1200), the Middle Mississippian (800–500 B.P. or A.D. 1200–1500), and the Late Mississippian (500–300 B.P. or A.D. 1500–1700). The Mississippian people built the flat-topped, pyramidal, earthen temple mounds famous throughout the South, and they have come to epitomize the southeastern Indians. Anthropologists call the particular political organization that characterized the Mississippian period a "chiefdom." Chiefdoms had a centralized political authority and were ruled by leaders (usually called "micos") who were permanent officials with high rank and authority. They had the authority to settle disputes, punish wrongdoers, make judgments, and so on. A mico, considered the earthly representation of the sun, the Mississippian people's principal deity, was typically born into a chiefly lineage, the members of which were considered related to supernatural beings. Such supernatural connections sanctioned the chiefly elite's status and prestige, as well as its religious and political authority.

The mico and his or her lineage ruled over a well-defined territory, which typically extended along the length of a river valley, which, in addition to providing good transportation routes and water supplies, had good bottomland soils for agriculture. The economy of Mississippian chiefdoms was based on trade in exotic goods and intensive corn agriculture, supplemented by beans, squash, pumpkins, gourds, and sunflowers. The chiefly elite usually did not engage in agriculture, but they received tribute from the citizens in the form of foodstuffs, exotic goods, animal skins, stone, and other raw and finished materials. Chiefs would then use these goods to settle disputes, garner allies, aid villages that were low on resources, or otherwise maintain control and order over all the towns and villages under their domain. Most people lived in farming villages, and some were protected by palisades, or tall walls, made out of tree trunks — clear evidence that chiefdoms were usually under some sort of outside threat. In fact, one of the characteristics of the Mississippian geopolitical landscape was incessant low-level warfare as indicated not only by the palisaded villages but also by the warrior iconography in much of the artwork of Mississippian peoples.

The center of a chiefdom was the large ceremonial and political center where the mico and many of those in the chiefly lineage lived. Archaeologists now call these centers "temple mound complexes" because they were large towns with several earthen mounds and large open plazas and several homesteads. But the dominant architectural feature most certainly would have been the temple mound, a large, pyramidal earthen structure with a flat top. The mico's temple was built on top of this mound, thus symbolically separating him or her from the common folk and emphasizing his or her prestige, power, and sacredness. Temple mounds vary in size throughout the Southeast, but the most impressive are around 70 feet high. The mounds were built in increments and over several generations. When a mico died, priests burned the temple, and the citizens then covered the mound with another earthen mantle. Every time a mico died, the temple mound was enlarged, thus also symbolically increasing the chief's power. The mico was buried in the temple mound with much pomp and ceremony and usually with a rich assortment of grave goods. In some cases, vassals accompanied micos into the afterlife. These "retainer burials" indicate the extent of a chief's power, for in many cases, the vassals' hands were bound, indicating that he or she did not go voluntarily.

In addition to temple mounds, smaller flat-topped pyramid mounds were often situated throughout a chiefdom center, but within sight of the temple mound. Large houses were built on top of these mounds, and archaeologists believe them to be the homes of members of the elite lineage, who probably also served in some political or religious office. The conical burial mounds located next to these smaller mounds likely contain the remains of the elite caste who lived on the flat-topped mounds. Temple mound complexes are some of the most spectacular archaeological sites in the world. Many of these mound complexes today are preserved as state or national parks, such as Cahokia in Missouri, Moundville in Alabama, Etowah in Georgia, and Winterville in Mississippi.

Most of the temple mound complexes of the Early Mississippian were not very impressive, with one exception. The largest of all Mississippian mound complexes was occupied during this time—a site and park in St. Louis known today as Cahokia. At its height, around 900 B.P. to 800 B.P., Cahokia was a sprawling urban center comprising over 100 mounds of various sizes and covering six square miles, with a population of around 20,000. Cahokia also has the largest earthen monument in North America. The temple mound at Cahokia is known today as Monks Mound. Archaeologists estimate Monks Mound to measure about 955 feet by 774 feet at its base and a little over 92 feet tall. The total area covered by the stones it is made of and how deep they reach is unknown. Cahokia undoubtedly dominated the Early Mississippian landscape, but by the Middle Mississippian, the Mississippian way of life was firmly established across most of the South. The most famous Middle Mississippian sites are Moundville and Etowah, but impressive Middle Mississippian mound complexes are located throughout the central Mississippi River valley, the lower Ohio River valley, and most of the mid-South, including western and central Kentucky, western Tennessee, and northern Alabama and Mississippi. This region appears to be the core of the classic Mississippian culture area.

Artifacts from this period are quite stunning, and clearly artistry and craftsmanship were highly valued and craftspeople labored over their crafts whether they were used ritually or in everyday life. Craftspeople used stone for tools, fashioning not only small projectile points for use on arrows and larger ones for use on spears but also large blades and well-polished celts and chisels. People usually made their stone tools out of locally available stone, but they also used imported raw materials such as chalcedony and jasper. Soapstone ear spools (a kind of earring), shell gorgets and beads, stone pipes, and other personal-use items can be attributed to artisans of this period. They also fashioned awls, needles, and fishhooks out of bone, and Mississippian potters also made finely crafted ceramics in a variety of forms featuring a variety of decorations.

The objects crafted for ritual and political purposes during the Mississippian period constitute some of the most important artwork from the South. Here, specialized craftspeople lavished their artistic sensibilities on an assortment of mediums — stone, clay, mica, copper, shell, talc, feathers, fabric, and so on — to fashion an amazing array of ceremonial items such as headdresses, earspools, beads, cups, masks, statues, ceramic effigies and wares, ceremonial weaponry, and breastplates, among other things. Many of these ritual items were decorated with a specific repertoire of motifs such as the hand-and-eye motif, the falcon warrior, bilobed arrows, severed heads, spiders, rattlesnakes, mythical beings, and others. Archaeologists call this array of ceremonial objects the Southeastern Ceremonial Complex, and they once postulated that the many ritual and ceremonial objects that are decorated with similar motifs meant that Mississippian peoples across chiefdoms, despite their mutual antagonism, shared a common belief system. Today, archaeologists, while not abandoning this idea altogether, also believe that the common motifs may represent the large exchange network of prestige items in which the elite of the chiefdoms were engaged.

Mississippian farmers were capable of producing substantial agricultural harvests, yet they continued gathering wild plant foods, which added necessary nutrients and mineral supplements to their diets and undoubtedly provided some variety and spices. They especially liked hickory oil. Likewise, people still depended on wild animals for their meat proteins. Among other things, they hunted deer, bear, turkey, and small mammals and took turtles, fish, and mollusks from the rivers and streams.

But the chiefdoms were not uniform across space and time. Archaeologists understand the classic Mississippian chiefdoms such as Cahokia and Moundville to have been quite large, and they call them "complex chiefdoms." A complex chiefdom was a political organization in which one large chiefdom, say, for example, Cahokia, exercised some sort of control or influence over smaller chiefdoms within a defined area. The smaller chiefdom would have been a "simple chiefdom," that is, one in which the elite controlled only the villages connected to it, and a simple chiefdom may or may not have fallen under the influence of a complex chiefdom. By the Late Mississippian, complex and simple chiefdoms existed side by side, and, in a few cases, a single, especially charismatic leader forged an alliance of several complex and simple chiefdoms into a "paramount chiefdom." Coosa, which Hernando de Soto visited in the sixteenth century in northwest Georgia/northeast Alabama, is probably the most famous paramount chiefdom in the South.

In addition, archaeologists describe the "cycling" of chiefdoms — a sort of rise and fall through time of various chiefdoms in various locations. For example, in the Savannah River area in present-day Georgia there were a number of chiefdoms that rose and fell between 900 B.P. and 400 B.P. (A.D. 1100 and A.D. 1600), after which the area was abandoned until around 320 B.P. (A.D. 1680). In other words, the many mound sites in the South were not all occupied at the same time.

The Mississippian period is perhaps the best-known prehistoric era in the South not only because much archaeological work has focused on this period, but also because the Mississippian way of life was described by some of the first Europeans to visit the South. Therefore, written documents supplement the archaeological record. However, the invasion of Europeans also brought the end of the Mississippian way of life.

ROBBIE ETHRIDGE
University of Mississippi

MAUREEN MEYERS
University of Kentucky

David G. Anderson, *The Savannah River Chiefdoms: Political Change in the Late Prehistoric Southeast* (1994); David J. Hally, ed., *Ocmulgee Archaeology, 1936–1986* (1994); Adam King, *Etowah: The Political History of a Chiefdom Capital* (2002); Vernon James Knight Jr. and Vincas P. Steponaitis, eds., *Archaeology of the Moundville Chiefdom* (1998); Timothy K. Perttula, *The Caddo Nation: Archaeological and Ethnohistoric Perspectives* (1992); Marvin T. Smith, *Coosa: The Rise and Fall of a Southeastern Mississippian Chiefdom* (2000); Biloine Whiting Young and Melvin L. Fowler, *Cahokia: The Great Native American Metropolis* (1999).

Indian Eras, Contact to 1700

The meeting of the Old and New Worlds was one of the most profound transforming events in human existence. Around 12,000 B.P. the land bridge connecting Siberia to Alaska disappeared and effectively sealed off the New World from the Old. Certainly there were some minor encounters between Native Americans and others, such as the Norse colonists in Canada and perhaps some eastern sailors en route to South and Central America. But none of these contacts established viable, long-term colonies or sustained relations. Nor did any of the Indians cross into Europe in any appreciable numbers. Rather, the most dramatic meeting of the two worlds occurred in the 15th and 16th centuries with the European expansion and invasion into the New World.

In the late 15th and early 16th centuries European sailors explored portions of the Atlantic coastline; however, the European colonization of North America did not begin until about 30 years after the invasion of Central and South America, around 1500. For the most part, the same Spanish conquistadors who had conquered the Southern Hemisphere led these first attempts. One of the first places they explored was the part of the continent closest to them—the American South. Spanish conquistadors such as Juan Ponce de Leon and Lucas Vázquez de Ayllón made contact with native southerners, and their expeditions, although ending in failure, provided invaluable information for Hernando de Soto, who would launch his expedition in 1539. Landing in present-day Tampa, Fla., and moving north, Hernando de Soto was one of the first Europeans to explore the southern heartland. Although his expedition, too, failed in its objective to settle a colony in North America, De Soto's visit had a profound impact on native people.

Spanish exploration occurred during the last hundred or so years of the Mississippian period. De Soto and his army saw several important chiefdoms in the South. In northwest Georgia, De Soto encountered a powerful mico named Coosa, who had built an alliance of several chiefdoms into what archaeologists now call a paramount chiefdom. When De Soto and his army of 600-plus men trekked through the interior South, they lived off the supplies of the native people. They also came as a conquering army, and their relationships with local people were usually hostile. Consequently, De Soto's expedition had a major impact on native lives, especially in those chiefdoms that saw intense military action. This was the case at the chiefdom of Napituca in northern Florida, at Chicaza in Mississippi, at Anlico in Arkansas, and especially at Mauvila in Alabama, where the Indians suffered heavy losses in a battle that was fought on 18 October 1540. In addition, it is thought that the presence of invading foreign powers in the Southeast—both the 16th-century explorers and the colonizers in later times—had a destabilizing effect on the chiefdoms. That is, the means by which Mississippian peoples conducted warfare must have changed, and this may have made the Southeast, for a time, a more hazardous place in which to live.

But the destruction caused by these destabilizing events pales in comparison to the loss of life as a consequence of Old World disease introduced among New World populations. In the 14,000 years before contact, the people of the New World had adapted to an entirely different disease environment than that of the people in the Old World. European colonizers and their domesticated animals thus brought Old World germs into a "virgin soil population," or a population that had never been exposed to these diseases and therefore had no natural or acquired immunity to them. The latest estimates for loss of native life stand at around 90 to 95 percent over a few generations. Anthropologist Russell Thornton has called it the "American Indian holocaust." We still are not sure which specific diseases impacted the Southeast and when the epidemics first occurred.

Nor do we have a commonly accepted measure of the total population in the Southeast before the diseases struck, nor of the precise nature of the loss of life. Also to be determined is whether the native population all across the Southeast collapsed in a relatively brief period of time or whether, as has been proposed, the loss of life occurred over two or three generations with successive waves of disease epidemics.

The consequences of this population collapse are evident in the archaeological record. Some populations declined sharply, and some areas were abandoned altogether. The people ceased building mounds and ceremonial centers, and the level of ritual and artistic production declined sharply. The elaborate status goods seen in late prehistoric graves disappeared from the archaeological record in later times, suggesting a leveling of social status. The populations of the chiefdoms had dropped to a fraction of their original number. The people suffered an incalculable loss of knowledge and tradition, since in epidemics the old are among the first to die, and in an oral society, the elderly are the repositories of knowledge. Traditional ways of minimizing the level of violence between chiefdoms and within chiefdoms undoubtedly broke down. Consequently, life in the Southeast likely became less predictable and palpably more hazardous, and the survivors of the epidemics—a small percentage of the total population—likely found themselves faced by unprecedented challenges.

On the heels of disease epidemics, native southerners found themselves face-to-face with Spanish, French, and English colonists, all vying for southern territories and Indian allies. In Spanish Florida and French Louisiana, Catholic missionaries devoted their lives to trying to win the Indians over to a new religion, to new languages, and to new ways of thinking and doing. An even more severe disruption, however, was posed by the English, who came on the cutting edge of a new way of organizing and running the world economy. The English came to trade and to make money, but to trade and make money in a way that steadily eroded the economic and social institutions of native people.

In the 17th and 18th centuries the southeastern Indians had to organize new societies in which they could cope with the new world in which they found themselves. Quite naturally, some of them tried to reorganize themselves in terms of their old beliefs and social arrangements. Traditional ways were most tenacious in places where the Spanish and the French were dominant. The principal examples of such "traditionalist" societies were the Apalachees of present-day northern Florida, the Caddos of present-day western Louisiana and eastern Texas, and the Natchez of present-day Mississippi. None of these traditionalist societies had much staying power, however. The Apalachee were crushed in 1704 by English-sponsored Creek slaving raids. The Natchez were extirpated by 1730, after having revolted against the French colonists. The Caddoans, who lay far to the west of the English sphere of influence, were somewhat insulated, but as the 18th century wore on, they gradually gave up their old-time ways. The traditionalist societies faded from history. The survivors dispersed, forming "coalescent" societies of people from different cultures and speaking different languages. The coalescent societies formed in areas where the English influence was the strongest, and, in large part, they adapted to the new economic system ushered in by the English and Dutch—the global market system.

The new economic system was a capitalist market system, and it was ushered in by a trade in dressed deerskins, but, more important, by a trade in enslaved Indians that affected virtually all of the natives in the Southeast. Slavery was not unknown to the indigenous peoples of the eastern woodlands, and they practiced a version of it at the time of contact. Once slaves became a commodity, however, a powerful new dynamic began shaping the lives of the southeastern Indians: European traders would give guns to a group of Indians on credit and ask to be paid in Indian slaves. The armed group would then raid an unarmed rival Indian group for slaves. The unarmed group, now vulnerable to Indian slave raiders, would then need guns and ammunition for protection, because Indians equipped only with bows and arrows were at a military disadvantage to slave raiders armed with English-made guns. The Indians could not make their own guns, and they depended on the European trade for flint-lock guns, as well as for shot and powder. At this point, anyone needing guns had to become a slave raider. In this way, a cycle emerged that ensnared all native peoples who came into contact with it. The process snowballed until virtually all of the Indian groups in the Southeast both possessed firearms and owed enormous debts to English traders.

Indian slave raiders captured Indian slaves by the thousands, mostly women and children, and sold them to English, French, and Dutch slavers who shipped them to the sugar plantations in the Caribbean, although some certainly went to the new coastal plantations in Virginia, South Carolina, and French Louisiana. For most Indian groups, already seriously diminished by losses from disease, slaving was a serious blow. Wherever slaving penetrated, the same processes unfolded: many Indian groups moved to get away from slave raiders; some groups joined others in an effort to bolster their numbers and present a stronger defense; some groups became extinct when their numbers dwindled to nothing because of disease and slave raiding; and all those left became engaged in the slave trade. The result was the creation of a shatter zone of instability that covered the eastern woodlands. Slaving unleashed chaos and panic, because Indian groups could not be sure that their neighbor would not turn on them as slave catchers. Some groups moved closer to the English and French colonies, where they became known as "settlement Indians" and "petite nations," respectively. Others joined together in alliance as slave catchers, forming coalescent societies. The Creeks, Cherokees, Chickasaws, Choctaws, and Catawbas, among others, are the coalescent societies that have left the greatest mark on American and southern history. These societies, comprised of the descendants of the great Mississippian chiefdoms, kept some Mississippian ways such as their farming techniques, matrilineal kinship, and perhaps their town governing structures, among other things, but they also forged new political, social, and economic institutions to deal with the new circumstances of their life after contact.

ROBBIE ETHRIDGE
University of Mississippi

Robbie Ethridge and Charles Hudson, in *Cultural Diversity in the U.S. South: Anthropological Contributions to a Region in Transition*, ed. Carole E. Hill and Patricia D. Beaver (1998); Robbie Ethridge and Charles Hudson, eds., *The Transformation of the Southeastern Indians, 1540–1760* (2002); Alan Gallay, *The Indian Slave Trade: The Rise of the English Empire in the American South, 1670–1717* (2002); Charles Hudson, *Knights of Spain, Warriors of the Sun: Hernando de Soto and the South's Ancient Chiefdoms* (1998); Charles Hudson and Carmen Chaves Tesser, eds., *Forgotten Centuries: Indians and Europeans in the American South, 1521–1704* (1994); Jerald T. Milanich, *Laboring in the Fields of the Lord: Spanish Missions and Southeastern Indians* (1999); Russell Thornton, *American Indian Holocaust and Survival: A Population History Since 1492–1991* (1987).

Indian Eras, Deerskin Trade, 1700–1800

The white-tailed deerskin trade was the primary source of interaction between American Indians and Europeans in the 18th-century South. More than any other economic activity, the deerskin trade maintained alliances, built fortunes, furthered the cause of empire, altered Indian cultures, caused strife, and impacted the natural environment. According to anthropologist Shepard Krech, Europeans in the South desired deerskins "above all else save land and slaves" and "deerskins and slaves were the supreme commodities in the 18th-century South."

Starting in the 1640s English traders from Virginia and Spanish traders from St. Augustine and the Indian mission town of San Marcos de Apalachee penetrated the southern interior in search of Indians to trade deerskins. European demand for southern deerskins soared, however, after the establishment of Charles Town and Carolina by the English in 1670 brought numerous profit-seeking traders deep into Indian country. European need for deerskins also increased markedly in the early 18th century because of diseased and decimated cattle herds in Europe. In Europe, especially England and France, deerskins were used to make pants, gloves, workers' aprons, harnesses, saddles, and book bindings. Carolinians also made the floppy "South Carolina hat" out of deerskins.

The number of deerskins exported from the South in the 18th century is staggering. In the late 17th and early 18th century, around 85,000 deerskins went to Europe annually via Virginia and Charles Town. By about 1760, annual exports from Charles Town averaged 178,000 deerskins; from Savannah, 100,000–150,000 deerskins; and tens of thousands of skins from French New Orleans. Mobile and Pensacola contributed still more thousands of deerskins, especially after the towns had been acquired by the British in 1763, and St. Augustine also contributed to the skin export trade. In the middle of the 18th century, as many as 500,000 deerskins left the South each year, with the numbers dropping slowly in the late 18th century to around 100,000 annually by 1800. Deerskins literally served as currency and may be the source of the American monetary term "buck," as all types of goods could be bought in the South with deerskins and commodity prices were often expressed per number of deerskins, with the larger buckskins being the standard of measurement.

Indian suppliers participated in the deerskin trade for a variety of reasons. Southeastern Indians had always hunted white-tailed deer for an essential source of food, clothing, and tools, but the new use of deerskins as an item of exchange for European merchandise meant that hunting deer assumed greater importance. Southeastern Indians traded their deerskins for a variety of utilitarian items, including metal goods, such as knives, hoes, axe heads, and fishhooks, and for manufactured cotton and wool cloth used in blankets and various types of clothing, especially shirts, leggings, and overcoats. Indians also traded for a variety of novelty items such as Jew's harps, coffee, jewelry, silk handkerchiefs, and paint. Among the most sought after and expensive items were guns and the gunpowder and ammunition that made them functional. Even at the height of the deerskin trade in the mid-18th century, one smoothbore musket cost at least 16 deerskins, representing a significant portion of a successful hunter's yearly effort, with only the best hunters killing around 100 deer per year. Indians sought items that bolstered their social status in addition to making their work easier. Acquisition of European manufactured goods became a major mark of status among southeastern Indians in the 18th century, and maintenance or attainment of high status drove Indian demand for European trade items. Southeastern Indians considered European goods and the makers of such goods to be spiritually powerful, at least in the early years of the trade, as the technological expertise demonstrated by the objects lay beyond Indian abilities to reproduce. Trade also required diplomacy; southeastern Indians conducted trade only with relatives, and nonrelated peoples were considered enemies. Diplomatic meetings enabled Indians, typically Indian women who controlled access to the matrilineal families, to turn European representatives into metaphoric kin and then engage in trade. Whether for utilitarian purposes, for status, or for other reasons, growing Indian need for merchandise meant that more deer had to die.

The lucrative deerskin trade produced the benefits of profit but also had negative impacts on people and nature in the South. Conducting business in a largely unregulated atmosphere, British traders in particular were prone to trading watered-down rum to Indians in exchange for deerskins. Alcohol and traders' assaults on Indian women caused tremendous social strife within native villages. Generational and political disputes also arose over which European country could better supply Indian trade needs, sometimes leading to civil wars within Indian groups or to wars between different peoples. As the deer population in the South declined over the course of the 18th century, from many millions to near extinction in some local areas, Indian groups came into more frequent conflict with one another over lands that still held deer. By 1800 European and American demand for deerskins tapered off significantly, leaving all Indian groups and many individuals with large debts owed to trading companies. Land became the primary resource available to pay those trade debts, and southeastern Indians quickly adopted other profit-generating activities, such as cattle ranching, cotton farming, and slave ownership, in order to raise the financial resources necessary to continue to acquire the manufactured goods on which they had come to depend.

GREG O'BRIEN
University of Southern Mississippi

Kathryn E. Holland Braund, *Deerskins and Duffels: Creek Indian Trade with Anglo-America, 1685–1815* (1993); Verner W. Crane, *The Southern Frontier, 1670–1732* (1929); Tom Hatley, *The Dividing Paths: Cherokees and South Carolinians through the Revolutionary Era* (1995); Shepard Krech, *The Ecological Indian: Myth and History* (1999); Joel W. Martin, in *The Forgotten Centuries: Indians and Europeans in the American South, 1521–1704*, ed. Charles Hudson and Carmen Chaves Tesser (1994); James H. Merrell, *The Indians' New World: Catawbas and Their Neighbors from European*

Contact through the Era of Removal (1989); Jerald T. Milanich, *Florida Indians and the Invasion from Europe* (1995); Greg O'Brien, *Choctaws in a Revolutionary Age, 1750–1830* (2002); Claudio Saunt, *A New Order of Things: Property, Power, and the Transformation of the Creek Indians, 1733–1816* (1999); Timothy Silver, *A New Face on the Countryside: Indians, Colonists, and Slaves in South Atlantic Forests, 1500–1800* (1990); Daniel H. Usner Jr., in *Handbook of North American Indians*, vol. 4, *History of Indian-White Relations*, ed. Wilcomb E. Washburn (1988), *Indians, Settlers, and Slaves in a Frontier Exchange Economy: The Lower Mississippi Valley before 1783* (1992); Richard White, *The Roots of Dependency: Subsistence, Environment, and Social Change among the Choctaw, the Pawnee, and the Navajo* (1983).

Indian Eras, Indian Removal, 1800–1840

When the invention of the cotton gin made upland cotton a viable cash crop for thousands of Upcountry settlers, Georgia and the territory that became the states of Mississippi and Alabama were home to 32,800 first people, 53,400 free people, and 30,000 enslaved people. By 1840, when the first postremoval censuses were taken, the same region was home to 922,000 free people and 737,000 enslaved people. Census takers failed to note any remaining Cherokees, Creeks, Choctaws, and Chickasaws because nearly all of them had been expelled from the region during the previous decade.

Why would state and federal governments forcibly expel people whose ancestors had inhabited the land for millennia? President Andrew Jackson had advocated removal since his days as the commander of the Tennessee militia in the Creek Civil War and cited the threat that Indians posed to settler society, as well as the incompatibility of the two cultures. Rather than await what everyone expected to be their inevitable extinction, Jackson believed that the federal government had to remove the indigenous people to the West, where they could perpetuate their "race." Despite considerable opposition to the proposal in both houses, Jackson garnered enough congressional support to see the measure pass, and he signed the Indian Removal Act on 29 May 1830.

Choctaws were the first to experience removal under the auspices of the Indian Removal Act, and subsequent treaties with the Creeks in 1832, the Chickasaws in 1834, and the Cherokees in 1835 secured the removal of those nations and the cession of their land. All told, the federal and state governments expelled just more than 50,000 people from their homelands, some in chains, others at gunpoint, and acquired almost 30 million acres of land for settlement, taxation, and development. In the ongoing construction of a society whose citizens saw the world in terms of white freedom and black slavery, there was simply no place for Indians.

The federal government kept no systematic records of the removals, so it is difficult to ascertain how many people died. Perhaps a third of removed Choctaws perished, while the tally of 4,000 Cherokee deaths on the Trail of Tears, one-quarter of the total number of Cherokees removed, is a likely estimate. Perhaps 10,000 Cherokees who would have lived or been born had removal not occurred were wiped from the face of the earth. Such death tolls must also be understood in the context of the loss of land. Indeed, for Choctaws, separation from their homeland meant death, and Choctaw conceptions of the West as a place where spirits were lost only compounded their misery, sense of loss, and despair for the future. One of their leaders, a man named George Washington Harkins, understood all of this. As he departed his homeland, his mother earth, on a steamer bound for Fort Smith, Ark., he mourned the total destruction of his people's world. "We found ourselves," he wrote from the ship's deck, "like a benighted stranger, following false guides until surrounded by fire and water — the fire is certain destruction, and a feeble hope was left of escaping by water."

For the Mississippi House Indian Committee, however, the removals, the deaths, and the despair augured a new beginning, "the dawn of an era . . . when . . . this state would emerge from obscurity, and justifiably assume an equal character with her sister states of the Union." Indeed, to the United States, the removals were a triumph. Land had been opened for settlement, the Indians had been saved, and the unrelenting expansion into the West could continue unabated. But what did the South lose with the removals? Were the removals acts of ethnic cleansing akin to what happened in the Balkans in the late 20th century? And why are not Indians remembered in the same way that the slaves and planters of the early 19th century South are? Is it because they were removed from our memories as well? Such questions suggest that even today we have failed to come to grips with what removal meant to the South then and what it means to the South today.

JAMES TAYLOR CARSON
Queens University

Donna Akers, *American Indian Culture and Research Journal* (1999); James Taylor Carson, *Searching for the Bright Path: The Mississippi Choctaws from Prehistory to Removal* (1999); Michael D. Green, *Politics of Indian Removal: Creek Government and Society in Crisis* (1982); Lucy Maddox, *Removals: Nineteenth Century American Literature and the Politics of Indian Affairs* (1991); Ronald Satz, *American Indian Policy in the Jacksonian Era* (1975); Russell Thornton, in *Cherokee Removal: Before and After*, ed. William L. Anderson (1991).

Indian Eras, Since 1840

Because the majority of Native Americans were forcibly removed from the Southeast in the 1830s, southern Indians have been split geographically. The removal treaties set up Indian Territory (modern-day Oklahoma) as their permanent homeland, with federal guarantees of full ownership of lands and internal self-government. The Cherokees, Chickasaws, Choctaws, Creeks, and Seminoles were each granted a separate area. Though they were bitterly factionalized on the removal question (especially the Cherokees), the transplanted nations made remarkable progress in reestablishing themselves in the new lands during the 1840s and 1850s.

The Civil War tragically reopened factional disputes as those families who had cooperated with removal (led by "mixed blood" slave owners) favored allying with the South. The withdrawal of U.S. troops, continual delays in federal treaty payments, and more favorable treaty terms from the Confederate government strengthened the pro-South Indians. Treaties of friendship were signed in 1861, and Confederate Indian regiments were organized. Along with Texas troops they terrorized pro-Union and neutral Indians, who fled to Kansas. Death and destruction occurred in the Indian Territory's severe guerrilla warfare, which laid waste to the countryside.

In 1865 the United States ignored the Unionist Indians but imposed new treaties that punished southern Indians even more than the Confederates. Slavery ended and blacks were made citizens of the nations, but the Indians lost half their lands (the western half of Indian Territory was taken for settlement of Plains Indians), and the federal government imposed more restrictions on tribal governments. Indian governments were deeply divided because of wartime loyalties and new questions concerning white and black squatters on their remaining lands. These internal divisions weakened the Indian nations precisely at the time when the United States was putting most pressure on them. Congress and the courts set policies in the 1870s and 1880s that abrogated past treaty guarantees, forced the tribal governments to accept railroad land grants, and transferred legal matters from native to federal courts.

By the 1890s Congress had abolished communal landholdings and substituted individual allotments, and then it abolished the tribal governments altogether. In 1907 Oklahoma was admitted as a state. Although some acculturated Indians did well financially, many traditionalists lost control over their lands through legal proceedings declaring them "incompetent" or through illegal graft and intimidation. Traditional Indians isolated themselves in rural communities on economically marginal lands, while their government "guardians" or white settlers reaped bonanzas from oil discoveries. The 1936 Oklahoma

Indian Welfare Act attempted to reestablish tribal governments, but with only mixed success. By the 1970s these governments had become more active in attempting to deal with continuing impoverishment among Oklahoma Indians.

Meanwhile, native peoples remaining in the Southeast suffered other problems. Some of these groups (North Carolina Cherokees, Florida Seminoles, Mississippi Choctaws, Alabama Creeks) represented only small portions of the removed nations who managed to escape removal by settling on isolated, economically marginal lands; others, who had never been pressured to remove, continued to reside in long-settled areas of Virginia (Chickahominy, Mattaponi, Pamunkey, Rappahannock), the Carolinas (Catawba, Lumbee, Haliwa, Coharie, Waccamaw), and Louisiana (Houma, Chitimacha, Tunica, Coushatta).

Whatever their origin, each native community isolated itself and survived by developing a localized subsistence economy. If whites became interested in Indian lands, they tried to dispossess the natives by lowering them to the status of landless blacks. This process culminated in guerrilla resistance during the 1860s by the Lumbees, the largest southeastern remnant. By the late 19th and early 20th centuries, as agriculture and timbering expanded in the South, more Indians lost their lands and were forced to become sharecroppers or wage laborers. Their local subsistence economies were destroyed, and their living standard declined as they entered the cash economy.

Up to this time southeastern Indians had continued to follow their traditional lifestyles, with many aboriginal activities predominating among the removal escapees and a mixed Indian-European-African folk culture thriving among the nonremoved groups. Once they lost their independent economy, acculturation to modern white-dominated society occurred. Indians suddenly expressed great interest in Christianity and education, as they struggled to control their own institutions (mainly the church and the school) as an ethnic group within the larger society. Several federally unrecognized groups attempted to gain treaty status as a means to protect their landholdings and legitimize their Indian status. Federal reservation Indians, especially the Cherokees, had to deal with a more diverse population because of white intermarriage and government-forced acculturation policies.

The 20th century saw a steady increase in acculturation, due partly to intermarriage and government policy but more significantly because of outside employment. Especially since World War II more Indians have migrated to take jobs off the reservation, and some of them have abandoned a distinct tribal identity to merge into the larger urban society. Ease of automobile travel has encouraged this migration, as well as a reverse migration of white tourists to visit Indians. On the Cherokee and Seminole reservations in particular, much of the economy has become dependent on tourism. Television has also encouraged acculturation.

Yet even as Indians' lifestyles have become more like those of other southerners, their identity as Indians persists. The majority of them are not disappearing into the larger society as assimilated individuals. Instead, both reservation and unrecognized Indians are emphasizing their distinctiveness through revitalization of cultural traits (language, music, mythology, clothing, crafts) and a sense of a shared past in their kinship relations.

Better education has promoted more community organization and political-legal activism. This has also exposed southern Indians to other Indians outside the South and has promoted a Pan-Indian identity. By ending their isolation and attaching themselves to the larger Indian movement of the past several decades, they have preserved their Native American identity. If an Indian community has managed to retain at least some landholdings, and a sense of general community and kinship, its ethnic survival seems assured. The South will continue to be, as it has in the past, an area of three cultural and racial groups.

WALTER L. WILLIAMS
University of Cincinnati

Jesse Burt and Robert Ferguson, *Indians of the Southeast, Then and Now* (1973); Angie Debo, *And Still the Waters Run: The Betrayal of the Five Civilized Tribes* (1972); W. McKee Evans, *To Die Game: The Story of the Lowry Band, Indian Guerrillas of Reconstruction* (1971); John R. Finger, *Cherokee Americans: The Eastern Band of Cherokees in the Twentieth Century* (1991); H. Craig Miner, *The Corporation and the Indian: Tribal Sovereignty and Industrial Civilization in Indian Territory* (1976); Theda Purdue, ed., *Nations Remembered: An Oral History of the Five Civilized Tribes, 1865–1907* (1980); Daniel H. Usner, *American Indians in the Lower Mississippi Valley: Social and Economic Histories* (1998); Walter L. Williams, ed., *Southeastern Indians since the Removal Era* (1979).

Jacksonian Democracy

The source of the political division of antebellum America into Jacksonian and Whig parties lay in the expansion of the market economy in the years between the War of 1812 and the Civil War. Acceptance of the values of the marketplace and resistance to those values each implied a conception of the meaning of freedom. For Jacksonians—dedicated to defending the ideal of economic and social self-sufficiency and fearful of being exploited by centers of power in the society—freedom was something the citizenry had by right, although evil, anti-democratic forces were attempting to take it away. A man was free when he was dependent on no one else for his livelihood and welfare. Movements and institutions whose success would diminish the existing autonomy of the individual were thus by definition aristocratic and inimical to the American experiment. For Whigs, freedom was not something Americans already had but something for which they perpetually strived. A man became free by fulfilling his potential, by becoming all that he could be. The shackles of ignorance and poverty were his greatest enemies; the expansion of knowledge and opportunity was his principal security. Morality and justice required that citizens cooperate in order to build a better social order for all.

These differing definitions of freedom carried with them differing notions of the proper role of government. Whigs sought the enactment of programs intended to break the bonds that they felt held the mass of Americans in economic, social, or moral bondage: governmental aid for the construction of railroads, roads, and canals; protective tariffs; central regulation of the currency supply and the banking system; the establishment of public schools; the prohibition of the sale of liquor; and the creation of hospitals to cure the insane, institutions to train the deaf and blind, and penitentiaries to redeem criminals. Jacksonians generally regarded all such programs as the products of paternalistic elitism. They thought it intolerable that the ordinary citizen should be taxed to benefit railroads, factories, and banks; that his private conduct should be regulated; that his children should be forcibly indoctrinated with alien, urban ideals.

The Jacksonians campaigned for the abolition of all property qualifications for voting and officeholding, hoping that a broadened electorate could use the government not to assist the growth of corporations but to restrict and ultimately to destroy them. But beyond such activities, which they considered defensive, Jacksonians sought limited government, states' rights, and strict construction of federal and state constitutions. They viewed their political party as a trade union of the electorate through which ordinary citizens, individually weak, could band together and use their numbers to counterbalance the power of the wealthy. Whigs, on the other hand, were often doubtful that poverty-stricken, ill-educated citizens were capable of appreciating what was actually in their own best interest. Whigs conceived of their party as a sort of religious denomination, an organization of believers seeking to convert and to save the society at large. Though practical political considerations quickly led Whig politicians to abandon their early defense of restrictions on voting and officeholding, the Whigs continued to insist upon examinations for admission to such professions as law and medicine — examinations that Jacksonians frequently opposed.

In the Lower South the origins of Whiggery lay in the use of nullificationist doctrines to insist upon the right of each state to expel the Indians within its

boundaries. The ease with which these nullifiers embraced the broad-construc-
tionist program of the national Whig Party in the later 1830s is an index of the
degree to which ideology in the region was an extension of interest. Those merchants and planters who had eagerly sought the opening of Indian lands for
speculation and commercial exploitation also eagerly awaited roads, railroads,
and the easy credit promised by a national banking system. Although the majority of planters supported the Whigs, planters were not the cutting edge of
the party; the intellectual leaders of Whiggery were the urban merchants and
factors, whom the planters envied and emulated. The strength of the Jacksonians, in contrast, was usually to be found concentrated in those areas of the
region most isolated from large-scale market agriculture.

In the Jacksonian period the attitudes and programs at issue between the
parties in the South were essentially the same as those at issue throughout the
nation. The expansion of the market economy and its values was a national
phenomenon, and the response to it was national, embodying fears and hopes
as real in the South as in the North. However, states' views toward one institution—slavery—differed. Slavery was an integral assumption in the ideology of
each party. Jacksonians conceived of it protecting communities of self-reliant
small farmers from the marketplace; as they saw it, with slaves to supply plantation labor, the white, independent yeomanry could not be converted into
a proletariat, subservient to planters and capitalists. Whigs thought slavery a
mechanism of social mobility, another of the many happy institutions facilitat-
ing the efforts of the industrious to achieve economic success. Both regarded
it as essentially American, a bulwark of the freedom and democracy that were
the Republic's distinguishing characteristics. Therefore, when proposals to exclude slavery from the western territories gained popularity in the North, both
Jacksonians and Whigs in the South concluded that the absence of slavery from
the territories would lead to the establishment in them of a hierarchical, un-
American society, on the northern model.

Just before the advent of the party period in the early 1830s, Lower South
factions that would become Jacksonians and Whigs were united in desiring
the expulsion of the Indians—the Jacksonians so that settlers could establish
independent farms on the Indians' lands and the Whigs so that the territory
could be brought into the expanding American economy. The end of the party
period in the mid-1850s found Jacksonians and Whigs throughout most of the
region equally united in desiring slavery in the West—the Jacksonians because
it would permit the yeomanry to be secure from the exploitation of the rich
and the Whigs because it would promote the settlers' material advancement. In
the intervening decades, however, the issues dominant on the national scene—

banking, tariffs, and aid to internal improvements—revealed the sharply differing conceptions of freedom held by the more upwardly mobile and by those less willing to take risks in both the South and the nation at large. The salience for a time of this set of issues permitted the definition of the two parties in the southern states.

With the collapse of the Whig Party in the 1850s the Democrats lost their social and ideological coherence. A group of ambitious younger Democratic politicians, who generally accepted the label "Young America," began to use aspects of Jacksonianism, especially its devotion to laissez-faire and strict-constructionist doctrines, in ways that defended rather than attacked commercial and industrial interests. Adopted in most instances as well by the leaders of the Republican Party during the 1850s, these ideas became the ideology of American's dominant culture after the Civil War; they have often been called, though misleadingly, "social Darwinism."

Reconstruction in the southern states led to virtually all whites in the region becoming Democrats and had the effect in the later 19th century of depriving the yeoman constituencies—to which southern Jacksonianism had most strongly appealed—of a political party dedicated to defending them from rival sectors of society. And the heretical "social Darwinist" formulation of the Jacksonian creed deprived them, in some measure, of their familiar ideology upon which to ground a protest against their evident marginalization, in the South as elsewhere. The elimination of the public domain, and with it the squatter who had lived upon it, as well as the end of the open range for the grazing of livestock with the passage of fencing laws, left the yeomanry's economic and social position increasingly precarious. Yet important elements of the Jacksonian tradition persisted, particularly in the most isolated, small-farming areas of the South. Its influence is to be seen in the Independent movement of the late 1870s, in the Farmers' Alliance of the 1880s, in the Populist movement of the early and mid-1890s, and, indeed, in the appeals of popular political leaders well into the 20th century.

J. MILLS THORNTON III
University of Michigan, Ann Arbor

J. L. Blau, *Social Theories of Jacksonian Democracy, 1825–1850* (2000); Richard E. Ellis, *The Union at Risk: Jacksonian Democracy, States' Rights, and Nullification Crisis* (1990); Lacy K. Ford Jr., "Social Origins of a New South Carolina: The Upcountry in the Nineteenth Century" (Ph.D. dissertation, University of South Carolina, 1983); Steven Hahn, *The Roots of Southern Populism: Yeoman Farmers and the Transformation of the Georgia Upcountry, 1850–1890* (1983); Lawrence F. Kohl, "The Politics of

Individualism: Social Character and Political Parties in the Age of Jackson" (Ph.D. dissertation, University of Michigan, 1980); J. Mills Thornton III, *Politics and Power in a Slave Society: Alabama, 1800–1860* (1978); Harry L. Watson, *Jacksonian Politics and Community Conflict: The Emergence of the Second American Party System in Cumberland County, North Carolina* (1981); Rush Welter, *The Mind of America, 1820–1860* (1975).

Jeffersonian Tradition

Thomas Jefferson is invariably linked in the American mind with such concepts as liberty, freedom, and democracy. Indeed, the Jeffersonian tradition, as a general pattern of recognizable beliefs and behavior, provides much of the basis for America's liberal tradition. Through Jefferson, Charles M. Wiltse writes in *The Jeffersonian Tradition in American Democracy* (1960), "the political liberalism of accumulated centuries passed into the American democratic tradition, where it helped to mold the American way of life." To basic liberal tenets Jefferson added his own strain of agrarian thought, which praised the superiority of a self-sufficient, agricultural lifestyle. The independent yeoman farmer became a symbol for American democracy, and the image persisted, particularly in the South, into the 20th century.

Southerners have invoked Jefferson's precepts on numerous occasions in the 160 years since his death. For much of America's history the South has served as "a kind of sanctuary of the American democratic tradition," according to David M. Potter. Until comparatively recently the region was still a bastion of Jeffersonian ideals, at least for liberal critics of American society. There, Jefferson's agrarian descendants carried on resistance to the crass commercialism and capitalism of the Northeast and Midwest.

Following themes elaborated by Frederick Jackson Turner in the late 19th century, Americans easily linked the frontier with the development of democratic institutions and economic opportunity. Turner's "frontier thesis" exalted the role of the West, yet agrarian democracy and frontier democracy share obvious similarities, as William E. Dodd later noted in *Statesmen of the Old South* (1911). One of the first historians to realize the implications of agrarian democracy, Dodd asserted that the "real South" was precisely the South of Thomas Jefferson. Any conservative, hierarchical developments, as opposed to progress along democratic, equalitarian lines, were mere aberrations from true southernism. Dodd subjected his thesis to little critical evaluation, and later writers have disputed his findings. But his version was not entirely lacking in historical foundation. Jefferson and the Jeffersonian tradition originated in the South,

Monticello, Thomas Jefferson's home (John Collier, photographer, Library of Congress [LC-USW-34-46448-D], Washington, D.C.)

and for much of American political history the region has supported men who shared such ideas.

Southerners have invoked, in addition to Jefferson's agrarian philosophy, a number of other principles that can be traced to the intellectual and political heritage of the third president. His name is often associated with arguments sustaining states' rights, and southerners cite his authorship of the Kentucky Resolution of 1799 as evidence of his opposition to the extension of federal power. Inhabitants of the region recall his arguments against Alexander Hamilton's plans for industrialization, national banks, and tariffs, and much of America's anti-urban tradition can be traced to Jeffersonian origins as well. Ironically, for all his praise of yeoman farmers as God's "Chosen People," Jefferson eventually admitted the need for commerce and manufacturing, and his immediate successors in the White House acquiesced in the chartering of a Second Bank of the United States and the development of a tariff policy. Slavery also received considerable attention in Jefferson's writings, but his recommendations for abolition did not endear him in the South. Few southerners would admit that such ideas represented Jefferson's settled policy.

Jefferson's commitment to liberalism, grounded in the 18th-century Enlightenment, provided the intellectual foundation for his writings on agrarianism, states' rights, and restricted governmental power, as well as his opposition to slavery. The most widely known examples of his ideas on liberal political theory appear in the Declaration of Independence and in other sources, including his *Notes on the State of Virginia*. His liberalism contributed to the practical reforms that connected his administration with those of Andrew Jackson, Woodrow Wilson, and Franklin D. Roosevelt. Both Jeffersonian agrarianism and idealism surfaced in the programs advocated by the Populists in the 1890s and in the writings of the Nashville Agrarians in the 1930s.

Jefferson's influence in the South remains difficult to assess precisely. The region unquestionably cherished his agrarianism and his defense of states' rights, but his more liberal, equalitarian doctrines languished there in the years after independence. By the "era of good feelings" Jefferson was viewed as the defender of states' rights in his native Virginia, where his principles coincided with powerful economic and political interests. The nullification movement in South Carolina contributed to the transformation of his image in the South. The patriot who was eulogized in 1826 as the "Apostle of Liberty" in 1826 became the "Father of States' Rights."

Jefferson's Kentucky Resolution enhanced his position among nullifiers, because his words in that document implied that nullification of an unconstitutional federal law was a legitimate procedure. Nullification, Merrill D. Peterson asserts in *The Jefferson Image in the American Mind* (1960), "was the pivot upon which many state rights Jeffersonians swung toward the policies of sectionalism, slavery, and secession." At the very least, the Jeffersonian tradition was linked to the South's cause, and the episode also demonstrated that Jefferson's ideas could be appropriated for purposes alien to the original intent.

The nullifiers were not the only faction in Jacksonian society to rely on the Jeffersonian tradition. Jacksonian democracy itself revived essential Jeffersonian themes that were modified and strengthened by new influences in the 1830s and 1840s. In the *Age of Jackson* (1945) Arthur M. Schlesinger Jr. defines Jacksonian democracy as a "more hard-headed and determined version of Jeffersonian democracy," adding that democrats had to accept that new era's industrialism, factories, mills, labor, banks, and capital—all distasteful to orthodox Jeffersonians. The latter's view of independent yeomen as the nation's unique class of producers had to be enlarged to accommodate urban wage earners.

In the meantime, defenders of slavery still invoked Jefferson, noting that the Virginian had owned extensive property in slaves throughout his life. At the same time, the Wilmot Proviso linked the Jeffersonian heritage with the growing opposition to the extension of slavery into the western territories. The proviso revived the language and intent of the old Northwest Ordinance of 1787, which banned slavery in the states of the Old Northwest. Jefferson made no contribution to that legislation, although he had proposed a similar ban on slavery in Congress's 1784 land ordinance. Congress had rejected that restriction, only to add its own to the Northwest Ordinance. Southerners viewed Jefferson's alleged authorship of the antislavery provision as one of his "fatal legacies," but most doubted that he ever favored outright abolition. Later, southerners advocated the concept of popular sovereignty in Jefferson's name, for it implied frontier individualism, self-government, and local control. Even Stephen A. Douglas described his brainchild, popular sovereignty, as "the Jeffersonian plan for government in the territories."

As the South's leaders gradually retreated from the democratic idealism of the Jeffersonian tradition, the Democratic Party lost a degree of its identity, and its spokesmen seemed opposed to the doctrines that many Americans typically defined as being Jeffersonian or liberal. In the 1850s the new Republican Party easily incorporated the Jeffersonian commitment to human rights, antislavery, and agrarian democracy. The powerful rhetoric of free men and free soil composed an idealistic image for the new Republican Party. And in the political upheaval that flowed logically from the compromises of 1850, the Republican platform corresponded to what most Americans imagined to be Jeffersonian and "in essentials," Merrill D. Peterson adds, "with what had in fact been Jeffersonian."

After the Civil War, Democratic leaders called for a return to Jeffersonian principles, but Jefferson's influence in the party remained limited until the 1880s and 1890s. Only in 1892, for example, did the party's platform openly reaffirm allegiance to the principles formulated by the third president. As for the New South of the postwar era, its dynamic leaders preached industry, business, and progress. By the 1880s such tendencies in the region stimulated the rise of a vocal group of Jeffersonian critics. The oratory of such men as Robert L. Dabney and Charles C. Jones conjured up the polemics of John Taylor of Caroline and reflected more clearly the influence of Thomas Jefferson than Jefferson Davis. These critics saw the growing cities of the South much as Jefferson and John Taylor had earlier described urban centers — "sores on the body politic."

By the 1890s some southern Jeffersonians had drifted toward the Populist Party, and in that era of agrarian revolt they emphasized the radical side of the Jeffersonian tradition. Although men like George G. Vest of Missouri and John Sharp Williams of Mississippi remained within the Democratic Party, Tom Watson's disillusionment led him to the Populist Party, where he worked to revive the agrarian alliance of earlier years. The Populist-Democratic fusion and the ensuing defeat of William Jennings Bryan in 1896 destroyed Watson's hopes and those of most agrarians in the South.

When Populists invoked Jefferson's philosophy in the 1890s, they harked back to the lost world of independent cultivators, doing so at a time when the South yearned to advertise its new, modern outlook. At the same time, agriculture had become more of a business and less of a way of life. Still, Populists evaded their critics by appealing to the body of native southern tradition and doctrine that dated back to the writings of the Revolutionary period. Moreover, southerners recalled the ideas upon which their ancestors relied when they provided the leadership against Hamilton's Federalists and later against the Whigs. The Texas Populist "Cyclone" Davis campaigned with volumes of Jefferson's collected works tucked under his arm, and in response to questions answered: "We will now look through the volumes of Jefferson's works and see what Mr. Jefferson said on this matter." Professor Dodd is likely correct in his contention that Jefferson would have been a Populist in 1892.

With the Populist defeat the Jeffersonian tradition entered a period of quiescence, although Woodrow Wilson invoked his name and praised his philosophy in the years before World War I. By the 1920s the Jeffersonian tradition was of limited value in America; clearly its agrarianism was of little worth in the Jazz Age, and liberal reform found few successful advocates. Yet in the next decade, Franklin D. Roosevelt's administration was keenly aware of its intellectual and political roots in the liberal tradition of Jefferson, and such measures as the Civilian Conservation Corps reflected the president's personal commitment to the land. Roosevelt, too, shared a Jeffersonian suspicion of the crowded atmosphere of large cities and feared their detrimental impact on people. As a result of the New Deal's response to the Great Depression, the Democratic Party of Thomas Jefferson became the Democratic Party of Franklin D. Roosevelt.

Jeffersonian ideals flourished in the 1930s, according to a newspaper columnist who declared, "Everyone has a kind word for him. Nearly everyone writes a book about him." Jeffersonian agrarianism enjoyed a special resurgence in some parts of the South, following publication of *I'll Take My Stand: The South and the Agrarian Tradition* (1930). The essays by the Twelve Southerners, or Nashville Agrarians, praised the agrarian way of life while damning the modern, industrial New South. The book stimulated a vigorous debate in southern intellectual circles, but this last agrarian revival ran its course before the end of the decade. Still, the movement testified to the tenacity and vitality of the Jeffersonian tradition. For southerners, Jefferson's writings served as a bulwark against unwanted change and as a defense for the southern way of life. If the Jeffersonian heritage could not exclude the forces of progress or defuse the power of an ever-expanding federal government, those concepts always offered a calm, self-sufficient alternative to the exigencies of modern life.

More recently, controversies over Thomas Jefferson's relationship with his slave Sally Hemings have brought attention to the centrality of race to American identity, going back to Jefferson's ambivalent views of slavery.

GEORGE M. LUBICK
Northern Arizona University

R. B. Bernstein, *Thomas Jefferson* (2003); Daniel J. Boorstin, *The Lost World of Thomas Jefferson* (1981); Jan Ellen Lewis and Peter S. Onuf, *Sally Hemings and Thomas Jefferson: History, Memory, and Civic Culture* (1999); Peter S. Onuf, ed., *Jeffersonian Legacies* (1993); Merrill D. Peterson, *The Jefferson Image in the American Mind* (1998), ed., *Thomas Jefferson: A Profile* (1968); David M. Potter, in *Myth and Southern History*, ed. Patrick Gerster and Nicholas Cords (1974); Twelve Southerners, *I'll Take My Stand: The South and the Agrarian Tradition* (1930); Clyde N. Wilson, *From Union to Empire: Essays in the Jeffersonian Tradition* (2003); Charles M. Wiltse, *The Jeffersonian Tradition in American Democracy* (1960); C. Vann Woodward, *Origins of the New South, 1877–1913* (1951).

Korean War

Historians have found few distinctively regional aspects to the Korean War. In fact, neither southern historians nor American military historians have even sought systematically to explore either the role the South played in the war or the role the war played in the South.

The economic effect of the Korean War was similar in the South and the rest of the nation. Inflation appeared in 1950, leading to rising prices, including the historic end of the nickel Coca-Cola. The position of the region's farmers did not improve, despite the rising demand for food; costs of production rose to offset rising farm prices. The federal government's freeze on wages and prices in January 1951 helped control inflation in the South, and increased prosperity and lowered unemployment marked the final two years of the war. Defense spending for the Cold War, as well as the Korean War, was especially important in promoting southern economic improvement in the early 1950s. As in World War II, southern bases were key mobilization points for American soldiers.

A few prominent southerners symbolized various aspects of southern attitudes toward the war. Georgian Dean Rusk was one of Secretary of State Dean Acheson's closest advisers; Senator Tom Connally of Texas, chairman of the Senate Foreign Relations Committee, was an unquestioning supporter of President Harry Truman's policies; Congressmen L. Mendel Rivers of South Carolina endorsed Douglas MacArthur's request to use atomic weapons during the war against North Korea and China; Lieutenant General Walton H. Walker of Texas, Commander of the Eighth Army, was a high-ranking military figure; Virginia Durr opposed the war and her husband, Clifford, lost his job with the Farmers Union after she signed a petition opposing American involvement. The Korean War was the first occasion testing Truman's policy, established by executive order in July 1948, of desegregating the military.

Southern public opinion generally supported the Korean War enthusiastically. Americans were convinced the conflict was a just one, caused at the height of the Cold War by Communist aggression. When Herbert Hoover suggested in December 1950 a new isolationist policy and abandonment of Korea, Ralph McGill of the *Atlanta Constitution* wrote that this would be national suicide, and he seemed to reflect regional attitudes. Conservative southerners were uncomfortable with a national policy aimed not at total military victory but at limited war for strategic purposes.

CHARLES REAGAN WILSON
University of Mississippi

Clay Blair Jr., *The Forgotten War: America in Korea, 1950–1953* (2003); Bernard C. Nalty, *Strength for the Fight: A History of Black Americans in the Military* (1986); John Edward Wiltz, in *The Korean War: A Twenty-five Year Perspective* (1977).

Maritime Tradition

American experience began on the water and steadily moved inland. The various peoples who discovered, explored, and settled this country depended on bodies and arteries of water. Of necessity they were conscious of matters marine and riverine. The writings of the colonists who settled along the Atlantic Seaboard, the Gulf region, and even the interior abound with references to the importance of the waters and their existence. This was equally true of both southerners and those who lived north of the Chesapeake Bay. Yet few historians, including southerners, recognize that the southern states have a maritime heritage. For example, in 1954 Clement Eaton characterized southerners as "agricultural and unskilled in the ways of ships."

This was certainly not true in the colonial period. In 1769 exports from the southern colonies to Great Britain were four times more valuable than the products sent there from the colonies above Chesapeake Bay. In the English colonies, Norfolk and Savannah, along with a number of small ports such as Edenton and New Bern, N.C., and Georgetown, S.C., were established by the crown as official ports. Charles Town (Charleston) was the most important port of the colonial South. In 1769 two hundred vessels carried Charleston's exports to market in Europe, the West Indies, and the other American colonies. In that year more ships entered Virginia and Maryland ports than those of all other colonies combined.

The majority of ships engaged in maritime trade with the southern colonies were built outside of those provinces. Nevertheless, a substantial shipbuilding industry did develop in the South. This was inevitable considering the section's dependence upon water transportation, as well as the availability of abundant timber. Between 1740 and 1773 there were at least five shipyards in South Carolina that built a total of 24 square-rigged ships, as well as a large number of sloops and schooners. During the decades preceding the Revolutionary War, nearly a hundred ships engaged in the coastal and foreign trade were built in North Carolina.

Fishing was primarily for subsistence in the colonial period. Salted fish in barrels were sold to ships trading with the southern colonies, and occasional cargoes were carried to the West Indies. Weirs and fishpots were employed, and large seines were introduced in the 1760s. Fishing was not done in the ocean but rather in the rivers and sounds.

The American Revolutionary War was as much a maritime as a land war in the southern colonies. The British blockade extended as far south as Savannah, and privateers from Charleston, New Bern, Norfolk, and other ports along the South Atlantic Seaboard ranged as far as the West Indies seeking prizes. Lord Cornwallis's surrender at Yorktown in October 1781 was at least partially a result of naval action in the Chesapeake Bay and the subsequent siege of British forces on land and water.

The War of 1812 was primarily a maritime war in the southern states, occasioned by blockade and privateering, and concluded by the British combined attack against New Orleans in January 1815.

The early decades of the 19th century witnessed the expansion of the United States to include the Gulf region from Florida to Texas. The rapid growth of sugar and cotton production, along with exports from the Midwest, made New Orleans by 1820 the second most important port in the country. New Orleans had been founded as a port by the French early in the 18th century, but it was the development of steam transportation on the Mississippi River and its tributaries that crystallized the port's rapid rise in importance. Mobile, another Gulf port with French origins, also developed rapidly and by the Civil War was the third largest exporting city in the country.

The first half of the 19th century saw the appearance of dozens of small ports throughout the region. The expansion of steam navigation on inland waters along the seaboard and the interior states was a major factor in the development of the southern economy. Steamboats became feeders, carrying cargoes to coastal ports and later to rail centers.

Shipbuilding expanded as shipping expanded. In the United States as a whole, over 8,000 vessels of wood or iron were constructed between 1849 and 1858. Of this number, southern shipyards built approximately 1,600. One writer in 1850 estimated that the South, including Maryland and Kentucky, had 145 shipyards.

In the middle of the 19th century, commercial fishing began to emerge as an industry of importance in the South. This was partly a result of improved transportation, which enabled fish and shellfish to reach inland markets, and partly the result of seasonal trips to southern waters by New England fishermen. In the 1830s Connecticut fishermen were using gill nets off Savannah and smack fishermen were reaching as far south as Florida. By 1860 North Carolina had 33 commercial fisheries and its herring fishery concentrated in the Albemarle Sound area was among the largest in the world.

The Civil War was devastating to southern fishermen, as it was to others engaged in maritime activities. The Union blockade, although never totally effective, was tight enough to severely limit maritime trade. Union combined operations gradually gained control of the navigable waters in the Confederacy. Maritime activities in the southern states, however, achieved some success. Several hundred vessels ran the blockade, bringing into southern ports badly needed supplies and other goods. An impressive number of warships, including more than 20 armored vessels, were built for the Confederate navy. Many of these ships contributed to the defense of southern ports, including Mobile, Savannah, Charleston, and Richmond.

The postwar years saw a revival and expansion of maritime activities in the South. Shipping along the coast, linking the Gulf and south Atlantic ports with the Northeast, revived but with some important changes. Wooden schooners continued to carry certain low-grade cargoes, particularly lumber and naval stores. With the expansion of railroads into coastal areas, steamship traffic declined. Local river steamers prospered, however, carrying passengers and cargo to railheads.

While the construction of wooden vessels declined nationwide after the Civil War, it gradually revived in the South late in the 19th century. Nearly 3,000 wooden vessels were built in the southern states in the period between 1865 and 1900. Various factors contributed to this: local needs, the development of a wooden barge-building industry for inland waterways, and the rapidly expanding commercial fishing industry in the South.

Improved rail transportation resulted in the introduction of the iced-fish trade in the mid-1870s. First introduced in North Carolina, it spread farther south in the 1880s. By 1880 Charleston had an important offshore fishery with the catch of blackfish, flounder, and red snapper being shipped to northern markets. Of the 17 schooners and 49 sloops built in Charleston from 1870 to 1880, two-thirds were engaged in commercial fishing. In the 1880s the oyster industry became important in the North Carolina sounds, but it was not until the 20th century that shrimp would become commercially important.

Although the fishing industry would continue to expand in the 20th century, only in the shellfisheries (oyster, crab, shrimp), particularly shrimp, did the southern states gain a position of prominence. Louisiana would take the lead in shrimp harvesting, followed by Texas and Florida. The introduction of the outboard motor and the otter trawl early in the century, the development of refrigeration in the 1920s, and the continued improvement in transportation in the coastal areas were the major factors that stimulated the shrimp industry. By the middle of the century, southern shrimping had overtaken in value all rival shrimp or shellfish catches from Maine to Alaska. In 1956 the national shrimp catch (more than 90 percent from southern waters) paid fishermen $70 million, followed in order by salmon ($46 million), tuna ($43 million), and oysters ($30 million). In 1950 the New England states had approximately 10,500 fishermen while the southern states claimed more than 23,000. By the 1980s nearly 38 percent of the total poundage of fish and shellfish caught in the United States came from the southern states.

The shipping industry in the southern states went through a transition in the latter years of the 19th and early years of the 20th centuries. Developments in road and rail transportation resulted in a significant decline in river and coastwise traffic. This in turn gradually ended the maritime commerce for most of the small southern ports. Only the ports with deep-water harbors capable of holding the large ocean-going vessels survived and actually expanded. New Orleans continued to lead southern ports and remains the third largest port in the United States. The Hampton Roads area, comprising the ports of Norfolk, Newport News, and Hampton, Va., grew into the largest exporter (in volume) in the country and once handled 90 percent of coal exports. Charleston is 13th, and Houston and Galveston, Tex.; Wilmington, N.C.; Savannah, Ga.; and Tampa and Jacksonville, Fla., also rank among the country's important ports.

Shipbuilding has also gone through a transition. The decline in inland and coastwise shipping resulted in a parallel decline in shipbuilding in the southern states. At the turn of the century only a few southern yards had built iron or steel ships; the overwhelming majority concentrated on wooden ship construction. Only Newport News Shipyard in Virginia was building metal vessels on a large scale. World War I witnessed a revival of the shipbuilding industry in the South with the construction of steel, concrete, and wooden vessels. This boom ended shortly after the war was over. The pattern recurred in World War II. A large number of shipyards in addition to Newport News build steel merchant and naval vessels in the South.

Wooden vessels continued to be built in southern yards, but by the second decade of the 20th century nearly all of them were small fishing vessels. Since the 1970s, steel and fiberglass fishing vessels have challenged the wooden boat–building industry.

Finally, the U.S. Navy has long been a major presence in the coastal South. Southern naval bases have been the training and embarkation points for soldiers and sailors in overseas conflicts since the Spanish-American War. Pensacola's Naval Air Station has been the home of the navy's air training program since 1914. Bases such as the Norfolk Navy Yard and the Charleston Navy Yard have been major economic forces in their communities and beyond. Although it has closed in the last decade, the Charleston base once had been a Polaris submarine base, a Sixth Fleet supply and ammunition depot, and the host of a mine warfare program, as well as facilities for nearby air force and marine bases. Maritime activities of many sorts, then, continue to be important in the region's economic life.

WILLIAM N. STILL JR.
East Carolina University

Charles C. Crittenden, *The Commerce of North Carolina, 1763–1789* (1936); Rusty Fleetwood, *Tidecraft: The Boats of Lower South Carolina and Georgia* (1982); Joseph A. Goldenberg, *Shipbuilding in Colonial America* (1976); Herbert Ryals Padgett, "The Marine Shellfisheries of Louisiana" (Ph.D. dissertation, Louisiana State University, 1960); William N. Still Jr., *Confederate Shipbuilding* (1969); George

Rogers Taylor, *The Transportation Revolution, 1815–1860* (1951); Emory Thomas, *Georgia Historical Quarterly* (Summer 1983).

Massive Resistance

On 25 February 1956 U.S. senator Harry F. Byrd of Virginia urged a program of "massive resistance" to oppose southern school desegregation. The term became shorthand for the broad array of recalcitrant efforts aimed to block the campaign for civil rights waged by southern African Americans and their liberal allies. Given the initial intensity and fervor of massive resistance in the mid-1950s, it proved to be a relatively short-lived, and decidedly unsuccessful, phenomenon. But the movement contained the seeds of a popular rejection of liberal social and political change that would linger in southern politics for many decades to come.

Well before the tumult of the 1950s, southern conservative forces had already shown their strength. Southern Democrats bolted the Democratic Party in 1948 following the party's adoption of a strong civil rights plank. Dixiecrat presidential candidate Strom Thurmond carried four Deep South states but was unable to sustain a larger political following beyond the southern Black Belt.

The spark that set forth a broader-based resistance movement came on 17 May 1954 with the Supreme Court's decision in *Brown v. Board of Education*. Initial reaction to *Brown* was mixed. Editorials in newspapers of the Upper South urged moderation and peaceful compliance, but whites in the Deep South were defiant. By 1956 the Supreme Court had issued its implementation orders and resistance leaders had galvanized a fierce opposition. Several southern states passed interposition resolutions in February and March 1956, an echo of southern resistance movements of the 1830s. At the federal level, all but three southern senators and congressmen signed the "Southern Manifesto," a declaration of defiance against the *Brown* decision.

Despite the bluster of massive resistance, opposition leaders faced a difficult task in uniting white southerners. A majority of southern whites wanted to keep segregated institutions, but they were divided over just where segregation needed to be preserved and how to go about preserving it. In Virginia, massive resistance leaders who attempted to pass pupil placement laws or tuition grant programs for private schools met a determined white opposition committed to preserving and protecting public education. Even in the Deep South, the segregationist governor of Mississippi, J. P. Coleman, called his state's interposition resolution "legal poppycock" and warned against insurgent resistance groups replaying wars that they could not win.

The resistance movement spawned a variety of new organizations, none more important than the Citizens' Councils. In the summer of 1954 in the small Mississippi Delta town of Indianola a group of influential white citizens met to discuss how they could resist school desegregation. The meeting led to the first chapter of the Citizens' Councils, an organization that spread like wildfire across the Lower South. By October 1956 the Association of Citizens' Councils claimed a membership of 80,000 in Mississippi alone. Council membership boomed not just in the Black Belt but wherever the local African American community aggressively challenged existing segregation laws.

The Citizens' Councils styled themselves as a modern political interest group, replete with a monthly publication and a series of television programs featuring interviews with policy makers. Citizens' Council leaders denounced violence publicly, but in private they were more cavalier. Citizens' Council leaders rarely perpetrated acts of violence, but they condoned and subtly encouraged them. In 1955 four African Americans were murdered in Mississippi. No arrests were made, and nothing was heard from the councils. When a Citizens' Council chapter in Alabama debated how best to handle threatened integration of the local public swimming pool, one of the town's respected leaders summed up the sentiments of many: "I figure any time one of them gets near the pool, we can let some redneck take care of him for us."

Other more extreme groups were also on the rise in the 1950s and 1960s. Klan resurgence was not particularly widespread in the years immediately following *Brown*, but as civil rights activities expanded in the late 1950s and early 1960s, white extremists followed suit. A 1966 report by the House Un-American Activities Committee reported 192 klaverns of the United Klans of America (UKA) in North Carolina with an estimated membership of 7,500. Georgia had 57 UKA klaverns, not counting splinter Klan groups that often evaded public scrutiny. Other extremist groups like Americans for the Preservation of the White Race also formed during these years. The rise of extremist groups reflected class tensions within the resistance movement. In Alabama, for example, the Citizens' Councils divided between small-town Black Belt leadership and the urbanized, working-class following of Asa Carter, a Klan stalwart and, later, a speechwriter for George Wallace. Carter's group eventually broke with the councils to form a Klan organization that carried out numerous acts of racial violence against African Americans in the Birmingham area.

The leaders of massive resistance often framed their struggle as part of the larger struggle against the global Communist menace. U.S. senator James Eastland of Mississippi used his chairmanship of the Senate Subcommittee on Internal Security to hold hearings on a variety of civil rights organizations. Many southern states formed select committees that investigated or in some cases even outlawed civil rights organizations. Prominent anti-Communist speakers such as Billy Joe Hargis, Myers G. Lowman, Robert Welch, and General Edwin Walker regularly toured the South, denouncing social progressives who, they maintained, were either dupes or outright agents of the broader Communist conspiracy.

The first major showdown between the forces of massive resistance and the federal government came in Little Rock, Ark., in 1957. A reluctant President Eisenhower sent National Guard troops to force the enrollment of nine African American students at Central High School. Arkansas governor Orville Faubus's defiance showed the strength of resentment. Faubus had made his career as an economic liberal in a hardscrabble state known for its relative moderation on racial matters. But in 1957 Faubus was cornered and he threw his chances in with rearguard forces.

Other prominent confrontations between defiant state leaders, African Americans, and federal officials would follow. As many moderate whites were eager to point out, segregationists who counseled outright defiance to civil rights demands were often their own worst enemies. African American civil rights activists targeted areas where protests were likely to provoke white reaction and, in the process, win public support for the civil rights movement outside of the South. The best example came in 1963 when the Southern Christian Leadership Conference led demonstrations in Birmingham. Police commissioner Eugene "Bull" Conner used police dogs and high-powered fire hoses against nonviolent African American demonstrators. The images appeared on the front pages of newspapers around the world and played an important role in leading the Kennedy administration to send civil rights legislation to Congress.

White southern business leaders played an important role in ending the standoff in Birmingham in 1963. All across the South, white businessmen concerned about the economic costs of defiance checked the spread of massive resistance policies. Business leaders in Atlanta, eager to avoid costly boycotts and to project an image of tolerance, dubbed their city "too busy to hate." The "pocketbook ethics" of these business leaders often led to tokenism that effectively usurped the momentum of civil rights protest. From the perspective of business leaders themselves, however, their moderation staunched more radical movements on both the Right and the Left. By the mid-1960s business moderation had emerged in even the most defiant pockets of the South.

The passage of the 1964 Civil Rights Act dealt the most serious blow to massive resistance. Many white business owners who had remained passive in the face of massive resistance for fear of losing business desegregated their enterprises, claiming that they were simply following the law. Federal legislation also played a critical role in school desegregation, which remained the most contentious issue for white southerners for the remainder of the 1960s. A decade after the *Brown* decision, massive resistance leaders could claim an impressive record. Only 1.4 percent of African American children in North Carolina were in school with whites. In Florida, Louisiana, and Arkansas the percentages were 2.6, 1.12, and .81, respectively. But Title VI of the 1964 Civil Rights Act tied the power of the federal purse to southern compliance. Along with legislation such as the Elementary and Secondary Education Act, which dramatically increased the amount of federal education dollars, the federal government transformed the fight against southern schools and greatly undermined the resistance forces. Freedom-of-choice desegregation plans immediately became the most common method for southern school districts to resist meaningful desegregation. But in 1968 the Supreme Court declared that freedom-of-choice plans were allowable only if they provided substantial changes in schooling patterns. The following year the Court ordered immediate integration in some of the most recalcitrant school districts of the Deep South.

As efforts to preserve segregated public schooling failed, resistance leaders increasingly turned their attention to private schooling. By the mid-1960s the Citizens' Councils had fully embraced this campaign. The organization's monthly publication *The Citizen* regularly published articles with titles such as "How to Start a Private School" and "A Parent Compares Private and Public Schools." The 1966 annual convention was devoted expressly to the issue of private schooling. For a time in the mid- to late 1960s, it looked as though white flight to private academies might seriously impair southern public schooling. The Southern Regional Council estimated that by 1970 some 400,000 white students had enrolled in new southern private schools. Southern states passed tuition-grant and textbook-loan programs for private schools, and southern politicians actively promoted private alternatives to public education. But fears of a mass exodus from the public schools never materialized. The federal courts struck down state-level supports for private education, and in 1970 the Nixon administration established a policy to deny tax exemptions for racially discriminatory private schools. By the early 1970s, despite movements toward private academies, public schools in the Deep South were among the most integrated schools in the country.

Historians continue to debate the legacy of massive resistance politics. White resistance to civil rights dovetailed with a renascent post–World War II American conservatism, and southern leaders struggled to identify their own efforts as part of this larger cause. James J. Kilpatrick, editor of the Richmond *News*

Leader and the architect of Virginia's massive resistance program, was the most prominent massive resistance leader in the national conservative movement. Throughout the 1960s he was the point person on all matters southern for the *National Review*. Some prominent leaders of massive resistance would go on to play an important role in the conservative wing of the emerging southern GOP, most notably South Carolina senator Strom Thurmond and the journalist-turned-politician Jesse Helms of North Carolina.

No one played a more important role in bringing the concerns of white southerners to the nation's attention than George Wallace. Wallace's relative success in several midwestern and border states in the 1964 Democratic Primary campaign first exposed the "white backlash" against civil rights outside of the South. In 1968 his populist campaign denounced a panoply of liberal caricatures—pencil-necked bureaucrats, northern suburban do-gooders, and long-haired antiwar protesters—and in the process effectively shifted the terms of the national debate to the right.

But some historians dispute the notion that massive resistance was the forerunner to an emerging southern Republican majority. The modern Republican Party first took hold in the Upper South and in urban and suburban areas that were among the first places to reject what was seen as the ungainly path of massive resistance. Numerous historians of the Nixon administration have concluded that accusations of a Republican "southern strategy" to exploit the white backlash against civil rights have been overstated. Regardless of how literal the connections were between massive resistance and the modern southern Right, the movement coincided with and contributed to a broader popular confrontation with mid-20th-century liberalism that was hardly confined to the American South.

JOSEPH CRESPINO
Emory University

Numan V. Bartley, *The Rise of Massive Resistance: Race and Politics in the South during the 1950's* (1999); Jack Bass, *The Transformation of Southern Politics: Social Change and Political Consequence since 1945* (1995); Earl Black, *Southern Governors and Civil Rights: Racial Segregation As a Campaign Issue in the Second Reconstruction* (1976); Merle Black and Earl Black, *The Rise of the Southern Republicans* (2002); Dan Carter, *The Politics of Rage: George Wallace, the Origins of the New Conservatism, and the Transformation of American Politics* (1995), *From George Wallace to Newt Gingrich: Race in the Conservative Counterrevolution, 1963–1994* (1996); Hodding Carter III, *The South Strikes Back* (1959); David Chappell, *Inside Agitators: White Southerners in the Civil Rights Movement* (1994); Yasuhiro Katagiri, *The Mississippi State Sovereignty*

Commission: Civil Rights and States' Rights (2001); Michael J. Klarman, *From Jim Crow to Civil Rights: The Supreme Court and the Struggle for Racial Equality* (2004); Matthew Lassiter and Andrew Lewis, eds., *The Moderates' Dilemma: Massive Resistance to School Desegregation in Virginia* (1998); Alexander Leidholdt, *Standing before the Shouting Mob: Lenoir Chambers and Virginia's Massive Resistance to Public-School Integration* (1997); Jeff Roche, *Restructured Resistance: The Sibley Commission and the Politics of Desegregation in Georgia* (1998); Jeff Wood, *Black Struggle, Red Scare: Segregation and Anti-Communism in the South, 1948–1968* (2003).

Mexican War

The war with Mexico (1846–48) was a significant episode in the cultural life of mid-19th-century America. Widely perceived as the country's first foreign war, the conflict embodied many elements of romanticism. Fought in a strange and exotic land against an unfamiliar foe at a time when Americans were reaching out to distant places, the war provided a window on a civilization and a people that differed markedly from their own. At the same time, it assumed all the rhetorical trappings of a romantic nationalism that preached a unique mission and destiny for the Republic. The war was viewed as an opportunity to recall Americans to the idealism of the American Revolution at a time when the Revolutionary generation was passing from the scene and to advance the republican form of government the Revolution had sired. Stung by the taunts of Europeans against their "experiment in democracy," many Americans saw the war as a test of republican vitality. In fighting against a country dominated by military leadership, Americans regarded the war as a measure of the ability of a republic, lacking a strong professional military force and relying on untrained citizen-soldiers, to fight a successful foreign conflict. The Mexican War was an exercise in national self-identity, as Americans looked more closely at themselves and their place in the sweep of history.

Although the imaginative response of the South to the war did not differ significantly from the national norm in its general manifestation, southerners did perhaps react to the war with greater homogeneity and less equivocation. The tension between republican simplicity and the rise of what was called the "commercial spirit," with which northerners were grappling, was largely absent in the agrarian South. The elements of romanticism, fostered by a concern for the past, a reverence for heroes, and an allegiance to a code that emphasized honor, had a stronger grip on the southern than on the northern mind. Opposition to the war, seated in the North in such reform activities as the abolition and peace movements, as well as in certain constituencies of the Whig Party, was less evident in the southern states. And, finally, the militant tradition, so widely identified with the South, made southerners more receptive to the romance of the war. There is, however, danger in exaggerating the difference between the South and the rest of the United States, for Americans in all parts of the nation shared essentially the same imaginative outlook.

When President James K. Polk issued his first call for volunteers following the outbreak of the war, southerners were among the first to enlist. In some states, like Tennessee, the numbers so far exceeded the quotas levied by the president that large numbers had to be turned away. Many of the volunteers were motivated by a spirit of adventure and a curiosity to visit a land they had only read about in storybooks. Mexico, with its ruins of a destroyed civilization and its stirring tales of the heroic struggle between Montezuma and Cortez, held the aura of romance for which so many Americans yearned. To a generation nurtured on Sir Walter Scott, the Mexican War seemed to be a step into a romantic past. Volunteers were likened to young knights, and there was much talk of chivalry. Many were the soldiers who fancied themselves marching off to meet the foe on some medieval field. The mountains and villages of Mexico and the Mexican soldiers themselves, especially the colorful, armor-clad mounted lancers, seemed straight out of a book. To the *Southern Quarterly Review*, an "age of chivalry" had returned, every soldier fighting "as if he were striving to pluck from the 'dangerous precipice,' the glittering flowers of immortality."

Because of its geographic proximity to the Mexican battlefields, the South played an important part in the logistics of the war. New Orleans became the principal supply depot and embarkation point for the army in Mexico. Volunteers from the western states traveled down the Ohio and Mississippi rivers to a staging area on the site of Jackson's triumph over the British south of the city. New Orleans newspapers dispatched the first war correspondents to the scenes of action; their reports, first printed in the New Orleans press, were speeded to newspapers throughout the country. The first perceptions of the conflict to be circulated were those of southern newspapermen. When the volunteers returned to the United States, they sailed to New Orleans (and, to a lesser extent, Mobile), where they were accorded their first triumphant homecoming celebrations. Southern orators, poets, and politicians vied with one another in their colorful rhetoric as they welcomed the returning heroes. The veterans were compared with the "sainted fathers of our land," carrying on the analogy between the Mexican War and the American Revolution that was so large a part of the imaginative response. Lighting anew the "fires of freedom," they had unfurled the "standard of the stars above those lofty palaces where once floated the golden gonfalon of Cortez." Jefferson Davis's Mississippi Rifles, fresh from their triumph on the field at Buena Vista, were received with a wild enthusiasm;

their feats, it was said, would live on in the "enduring records" of the Republic. Future Civil War heroes such as Davis and Robert E. Lee first made their military reputations in Mexico.

The war penetrated the American (and hence, the southern) imagination in many different ways, in literature, poetry, art, music, and drama. Soldiers kept diaries and journals and published accounts of their campaigns soon after their return home. Historians began writing histories of the war almost as soon as the war began. New Orleans newspaperman Thomas Bangs Thorpe, with a reputation already established as a writer of southwestern humor, not only followed the army as a correspondent but wrote the first accounts of the campaigns on the Rio Grande and against Monterrey. Albert Pike, an Arkansas volunteer, wrote a poetic description of the battle of Buena Vista on the field before the guns had hardly cooled, and his work was widely reprinted throughout the country. In South Carolina, Marcus Claudius Marcellus Hammond, younger brother of the prominent planter-politician, penned the first complete analysis of the war's military operations, serialized in the *Southern Quarterly Review*.

In a class by himself was William C. Falkner, of Ripley, Miss., great-grandfather of the 20th-century novelist, who was turned back at the first call for volunteers. He later served in Mississippi's Second Regiment but to his disappointment was too late to take part in any of the fighting. Nonetheless, Falkner commemorated his service in a 493-stanza, 4,000-line poem, "The Siege of Monterey," in which he portrayed the war's leaders as Homeric heroes. Undaunted by the failure of his poem, Falkner turned to fiction in *The Spanish Heroine: A Tale of War and Love*, a stock romance dealing in part with the battle of Buena Vista.

The South's greatest antebellum literary figure, William Gilmore Simms of South Carolina, was among those American writers who helped create the mood in which the war was viewed. From his early poem "The Vision of Cortes" (1829) to his biography of the Chevalier Bayard, published during the war, Simms wove a romantic net that captured the southern responses to the conflict. His work on Bayard held up to the wartime generation the ideal of a soldier in whom heroic valor was blended with the gentle virtues of knightly honor and chivalry. When South Carolina's Palmetto Regiment returned home after winning distinction in the battles around Mexico City, Simms celebrated the event with a collection of verses, *Lays of the Palmetto: A Tribute to the South Carolina Regiment, in the War with Mexico*, the "outpourings of a full heart, exulting in the valor and worth, and lamenting the misfortunes and losses, of the gallant regiment."

The Mexican War was marked by bitter conflict between North and South over the explosive question of the expansion of slavery into the western territories. The clash of northern and southern interests seemed to polarize popular sentiment. At the same time, however, there were those in the South who perceived the war as a force for national unity, symbolized by the volunteers from both North and South who marched, camped, and fought side by side. It was symbolic, for example, that a New York regiment and South Carolina's Palmetto Regiment fought together in the Valley of Mexico in a brigade commanded by an Illinoisan.

Southerners (and northerners) saw something in the war that transcended sectional conflict. It was put into words by President James K. Polk, North Carolina born and Tennessee reared. The war gave meaning to the American Republic. "Who can calculate the value of our glorious Union?" Polk asked. "It is a model and example of free government to all the world, and is the star of hope and haven of rest to the oppressed of every clime." The war, in the imaginations of countless Americans, had demonstrated the strength of the Republic and had legitimized its mission. "We may congratulate ourselves," said Polk, "that we are the most favored people on the face of the earth."

ROBERT W. JOHANNSEN
University of Illinois at Urbana-Champaign

K. Jack Bauer, *The Mexican War, 1846–1848* (1992 ed.); Marcus Cunliffe, *Soldiers and Civilians: The Martial Spirit in America, 1775–1865* (1973); Clement Eaton, *The Mind of the Old South* (rev. ed., 1967); John S. D. Eisenhower, *So Far from God: The U.S. War with Mexico, 1846–1848* (1989); William Jay Jacobs, *War with Mexico* (1993); Robert W. Johannsen, *To the Halls of the Montezumas: The Mexican War in the American Imagination* (1985); Ernest M. Lander Jr., *Reluctant Imperialists: Calhoun, the South Carolinians, and the Mexican War* (1980); Rollin G. Osterweis, *Romanticism and Nationalism in the Old South* (1949); Fred Somkin, *Unquiet Eagle: Memory and Desire in the Idea of American Freedom, 1815–1860* (1967); Ronnie C. Tyler, *The Mexican War: A Lithographic Record* (1973); Richard Bruce Winders, *Mr. Polk's Army: The American Military Experience in the Mexican War* (1997).

Migration, Black

To black southerners, migration has symbolized both the limitations and the opportunities of American life. As slaves, many suffered forced migrations with the attendant heartbreaks of separation from family and community. As freedmen and freedwomen they seized upon spatial mobility as one of the most meaningful manifestations of their newly won emancipation. Subsequently, black southerners sought to better their conditions by moving within the rural

South, to southern cities, and finally to northern cities in a frustrating quest for equality and opportunity. Simultaneously, white southerners acted to restrict such movement, because until the mechanization of cotton culture, black geographic mobility—like black social and economic mobility—threatened the racial assumptions and labor relations upon which the southern economy and society rested.

The first significant migration of black southerners followed the American Revolution and the subsequent opening of the trans-Appalachian West to settlement by slaveholders. The enormous expansion of cotton cultivation in the early 19th century, combined with the closing of the foreign slave trade (1808), soon transformed a forced migration dominated by planters carrying their own slaves westward to one increasingly characterized by the professional slave trader. Although the Chesapeake remained the major source for the interstate slave trade, after 1830 North and South Carolina, Kentucky, Tennessee, Missouri, and eventually Georgia also became "exporters" of slaves. The plantations of Alabama, Mississippi, Louisiana, Florida, Arkansas, and Texas were worked largely by these early black "migrants" and their children. Although it is difficult to determine the volume of the domestic slave trade, one historian has estimated that over 1 million black southerners were forcibly relocated between 1790 and 1860.

The forced migrations of the antebellum South were complemented by barriers against voluntary movement. Although each year hundreds of slaves escaped, they represented but a fraction of the southern black population. Even free black southerners were hemmed in, and by the 1830s their movement across state lines was either restricted or prohibited.

During the Civil War white fears and black hopes generated opposing migration streams. Many slave owners responded to the approach of Union troops by taking their slaves west, either to the western, Upcountry areas of the eastern states, or from the Deep South to Texas and Arkansas. Thousands of slaves, on the other hand, fled toward the advancing army.

Ex-slaves continued to move away from plantations after the war ended. For many, like Ernest J. Gaines's fictional Miss Jane Pittman, the act of moving constituted a test of the meaning of emancipation. Others sought to reunite with family separated by antebellum forced migration. Much of the movement grew out of a search for favorable social, political, and economic conditions, especially the chance for "independence," which was closely associated with landownership. The flurry of migration generally involved short distances, often merely to the next plantation or a nearby town or city.

Southern cities offered ex-slaves the protection of the Freedmen's Bureau and the Union army, higher wages, black institutions, political activity, and freedmen's schools. But under pressure from whites — and often faced with the prospect of starvation — many of the thousands who moved cityward soon returned to the plantations. Urban whites considered the black city dweller a threat to social order, and planters sought to stabilize and reassert dominance over their labor force. Vagrancy laws provided a temporary mechanism, and even after the legislative reforms during Reconstruction, the economic structure of the cities limited the urbanization of the black population. Few jobs outside the service sector were available to blacks, and black men especially found that survival was easier in the countryside. Black southerners continued to migrate to cities in modest numbers; by 1910 fewer than one-fourth lived in communities larger than 2,500. Some people moved back and forth, mainly between farm and small town, following seasonal labor patterns. This kind of mobility also characterized rural nonfarm labor and established what one historian has called a "migration dynamic," which later facilitated movement to northern cities.

Most black southerners who migrated longer distances in the 19th century headed for rural destinations, generally toward the south and west. During the 1870s and 1880s rumors and labor agents drew blacks living in the Carolinas and Georgia to the Mississippi Delta and other areas in the Gulf states with promises of higher wages and better living conditions. Usually, migrants found social and economic relations similar to what they had left behind. The search for "independence" continued, with black southerners trying Kansas in the 1870s and then Arkansas and Oklahoma between 1890 and 1910. Movement became as central to southern black life as it has been to the American experience in general. Because blacks for so long had been unable to move freely, however, it acquired a special mystique manifested as a major theme in black music and symbolized by the recurrent image of the railroad as a symbol of the freedom to move and start life anew. By the 1890s one black southerner in twelve would cross state lines during the decade in search of the still-unfulfilled promise of emancipation. Local moves remained even more frequent.

The direction and historical impact of black migration shifted dramatically during World War I. Northern industrialists, previously reluctant to hire blacks when they could draw upon the continuing influx of white immigrants, turned their attention southward as immigration ceased and production orders began pouring in. Some sent labor agents into the South, but news about opportunities and conditions in the North traveled more often via an emerging black communications network comprising letters from earlier migrants, northern newspapers (especially the *Chicago Defender*), and railroad workers. Observers and subsequent scholars offered various catalogs of "economic" and "social" factors that "pushed" migrants from the South and "pulled" them toward the North. Floods, boll weevil infestations, and credit contractions contributed to the urge to move to northern cities offering higher wages than those available to black southerners. Jim Crow, lynching, disfranchisement, and discrimination in the legal and educational systems contrasted with seemingly more equitable and flexible race relations in the North. Most migrants left because of a combination of motivations, which they often summarized as "bettering my condition." For the first time, however, thousands of black southerners looked to industrial work, rather than landownership, in their hopes to enjoy the prerogatives of American citizenship.

Nearly one-half million black southerners headed north between 1916 and 1920, setting off a long-term demographic shift, which would leave only 53 percent of black Americans in the South by 1970, compared with 89 percent in 1910. Nearly all of these migrants went to cities, first in the Northeast and Midwest, and later in the West. Most followed the longitudinal routes of the major railroads, although by World War II, California was drawing thousands of migrants from Texas, Oklahoma, Arkansas, and Louisiana. At the same time, black southerners moved to southern cities, which by 1970 contained two-thirds of the region's black population. Even the massive urban unemployment of the Great Depression only moderately slowed the continuing flow northward, and movement accelerated to unprecedented levels during World War II and the following decades.

Many white southerners initially responded to this "Great Migration" by continuing the tradition of constructing barriers in the paths of black migrants. As always, landlords and employers feared the diminution of their labor supply, a threat that in the 19th century had stimulated the enactment of a corpus of legislation designed to limit labor mobility. As a social movement and a series of individual decisions, however, the Great Migration also constituted a direct —although unacknowledged—threat to the fiber of social and economic relations in the South. The system rested upon the assumption that blacks were by nature docile, dependent, and unambitious. The decision to migrate and the evolution of a "movement" suggested dissatisfaction, ambition, and aggressive action. As they had in the past, white southerners tended to blame the movement on "outside forces" (in this case, labor agents), and localities ineffectively sought to stem the tide by tightening "enticement" laws and forcibly preventing blacks from leaving.

The Great Migration transformed both American urban and African American society, as migrants adapted to urban life while retaining much of their southern and rural culture. It was not unusual for southern communities to re-constitute themselves and their institutions in northern cities. Frequent visiting between relatives in the South and North has contributed to this interchange between regional cultures, and the South is still "down home" to some north-ern black urbanites.

As a historical process, black migration within and from the South suggests some important continuities suffusing much of southern history: the coercive implications of white dependence on black labor; the refusal of blacks to accept their "place" as defined by whites; and the search for identity and opportunity articulated by black writer Richard Wright, whose personal migration experi-ence began with the hope that "I might learn who I was, what I might be."

Since the 1970s African Americans have increasingly moved to the South, part of a "reverse migration." In the 1970s, 1.9 million blacks came to the re-gion, and in the 1980s 1.7 million blacks moved to both rural and urban areas in the South. The 1990s witnessed a dramatic increase in this migration, with 3.5 million African Americans moving south. The 2000 census showed that 55 percent of the African Americans in the United States lived outside the South, but that percentage was lower than in previous decades.

JAMES GROSSMAN
University of Chicago

William H. Frey, *Census Shows Large Black Return to the South, Reinforcing the Re-gion's "White-Black" Demographic Profile*, Research Report 01-473, University of Michigan Population Studies Center (2001), *Population Today* (May/June 2001); Florette Henri, *Black Migration: Movement North, 1900–1920* (1975); Allan Kulikoff, in *Slavery and Freedom in the Age of the American Revolution*, ed. Ira Berlin and Ronald Hoffman (1983); Nell Irvin Painter, *Exodusters: Black Migration to Kansas after Reconstruction* (1976); Arvarh Strickland, *Missouri Historical Review* (July 1975); Carter G. Woodson, *A Century of Negro Migration* (1918).

Military Bases

Observers of the southern scene have long remarked upon Dixie's distinctively martial spirit. Highly visible evidence of this is the presence of so many mili-tary, naval, and air installations in the South. They range in time from the Cas-tillo de San Marcos in the South's oldest city, St. Augustine, to the futuristic George C. Marshall Space Flight Center in Huntsville, Ala. They range in size from Williamsburg's restored Powder Magazine, which supplied Virginia Fron-tier Rangers, to the 465,000 acres of sprawling Eglin Air Force Base in Florida, where both the Tokyo raiders of 1942 and the Son Tay raiders of 1970 secretly trained. They range in climate and terrain from the green live oaks and mani-cured lawns of Fort Myer in humid Tidewater Virginia to the sunbaked parade-ground plaza of Fort Bliss in the desert of El Paso, Tex.

During the colonial wars three European powers—Spain, France, and En-gland—established forts in the South. Spanish soldiers and monks were prob-ing northward from Spanish Florida, cavaliers and voyageurs established French Louisiana on the Gulf Coast and were moving up the Alabama River, while English traders and trappers were pressing inland from Charles Towne in Carolina down around the tag end of the Appalachians. There were military posts at Saint Elena, on the site of today's Parris Island Marine Corps Base; at Fort Frederica, near the former Glynco Naval Air Station near Brunswick, Ga.; and at Fort Maurepas on Biloxi Bay, close to the present-day Keesler Air Force Base. Within 80 miles of the site of Montgomery, later considered the Cradle of the Confederacy, were the short-lived Spanish Fort Apalachicola on the Chattahoochee, the French Fort Toulouse commanding the Alabama, and the British post at Okfuski on the Tallapoosa. The key to the strategy of all the contenders was control of southern coasts and rivers.

The British eventually won the prize of North American hegemony, only to be displaced in turn by their American colonial cousins in the War of Indepen-dence, the outcome of which was finally decided at the fortifications around Yorktown, Va. Then the infant United States had to fortify its seaboard against foreign invasion and to garrison inland posts against the perceived threats posed by American Indians, the British still in Canada, and the Spanish still in the Floridas. One southern stronghold—Fort McHenry in Baltimore Harbor—gave us our national anthem during the War of 1812. Defense of two other forts created rallying cries for war—the Alamo in 1836 in the Texas war for indepen-dence and Fort Sumter in 1861, site of the opening battle of the Civil War.

As the United States became a world power in the 20th century, climate in-fluenced the choice of the South for military installations. To raise mass armies to fight abroad in two world wars, America needed good weather to train its forces, especially its new air arm. In World War I, 13 out of the total of 16 Na-tional Guard cantonments were in the South, as were 6 of the 15 national army camps. There arose Camps (later Forts) Lee, Gordon, and Benning, not to men-tion Camps McClellan and Sheridan in Alabama, while aviation cadets learned to fly at Langley, Carlstrom, Brooks, and Kelly Fields.

Surviving military posts represent a history of military architecture. There are the wooden stockades from the colonial wars, restored at James Towne and Fort Toulouse. Brick coastal defense forts built after the British seaboard inva-sions during the War of 1812 are strung around the southeastern littoral. Among hese are Fortress Monroe, Va., where Confederate president Jefferson Davis was later held by Union authorities, and Fort Massachusetts on Ship Island in Mississippi Sound, site of "Beast" Butler's advance in occupying New Orleans. Rifled artillery rendered all these masonry forts obsolete before they were finished. Some of these forts were overlaid with the low-level concrete-and-steel coast artillery batteries of the Spanish-American War period, batteries that never fired a shot in anger, much like the twin Forts Washington and Hunt guarding the Potomac River approach to Washington, D.C., and Forts Morgan and Gaines protecting Mobile Bay, past which, earlier in 1864, Admiral Farragut had damned the torpedoes and ordered full speed ahead.

After World War I, some of the sprawling temporary cantonments were kept. Tar-paper and fiberboard huts were replaced by brick, stucco, and tile barracks, many of Spanish-inspired architecture, at such bases as Quantico, Pensacola, Maxwell, and Randolph Fields and Forts Knox and Sam Houston. Then during World War II they were swamped with inducted men and women. "Tent cities" mushroomed alongside well-groomed peacetime garrisons. New temporary installations arose, only to be activated again for the Korean War, made permanent in the Cold War, and used again to train men for the Vietnam War. The first special warfare groups to go to Vietnam in 1961 were the army's Green Berets from Fort Bragg, the navy's SEAL teams from Little Creek, Va., and the Air Commandos from Hurlburt Field, Fla.

Local citizens were both attracted to and repelled by military bases. On the one hand, they appreciated the dollars the bases brought to local economies, not just as extra monies during wartime booms but as cushions against depressions and recessions. On the other hand, the honky-tonk atmosphere surrounding many bases repelled local citizens — never mind that local businessmen often foisted land "on the wrong side of town" on the services. One recalls Jacksonville, N.C., in 1944. Southern townspeople often disliked northern servicemen, whom they viewed as loud-talking Yankees with brusque manners; some northern servicemen felt a reciprocal dislike. Nevertheless, many nonsoutherners fell in love with the South, met and married southern women, and stayed. Many nonsouthern servicemen who experienced the discomforts of preparing for war at Camps Lejeune, Blanding, Shelby, or Polk were glad to get home to Waukegan or Walla Walla. If the servicemen were black, and especially if they were from the North, assignment to a post in the still rigidly segregated South was painful. There was racial trouble, for instance, at Camp Van Dorn, Miss. At Tuskegee Army Air Field, however, black men proved they could fly and became combat pilots over Europe in the thrice-decorated 99th Fighter Squadron.

Military bases are the centers for a distinctive sense of community among active and former service personnel. Today, many retired military officers and noncommissioned officers live in Norfolk, Charleston, Southern Pines, Montgomery, and San Antonio. Military amenities abound because senior southern congressmen such as Georgia's Carl Vinson, South Carolina's L. Mendel Rivers and Mississippi's John Stennis had so packed military installations into their districts that they had been accused of sinking their states under the weight.

The military tradition continues to attract southerners. Sociologist Morris Janowitz found in 1950 and 1971 that officers with southern affiliations by birth schooling, or marriage continued to be represented disproportionately in America's military. During the Vietnam War, when there was a national backlash against the military, ROTC continued to thrive on southern college campuses, and the Virginia Military Institute and South Carolina's Citadel maintained their traditions of military service. The 101st Airborne Division easily meets its recruiting quotas in the area around its Kentucky home, Alabama's National Guard is one of the largest in the nation, and southern small-town armories and American Legion posts remain social clubs for good old boys.

JOHN HAWKINS NAPIER III
Montgomery, Alabama

Army-Navy-Air Force Times Magazine (28 June 1978); Irvin Hass, *Citadels, Ramparts and Stockades: America's Historic Forts* (1979); Morris Janowitz, *The Professional Soldier* (1960, 1971); Theo Lippmann Jr., *Baltimore Sun* (20 April 1969); David McFarland, *Montgomery Advertiser and Alabama Journal* (20 June 1982); John H. Napier III, *Alabama Review* (October 1980); Duncan Spencer, *Washington Star-News* (1 May 1974).

Military Tradition

For a century and a half commentators have written about the bellicosity and martial spirit of the southerner. Other observers have analyzed Dixie's military proclivities to determine the reasons for their enduring tenacity. More recently, some writers have sought to deny the existence of a peculiarly southern military tradition.

Back in 1835 Alexis de Tocqueville reported that the white southerner was "passionately fond of hunting and war." During World War II, D. W. Brogan, in explaining to his fellow Britons their wartime American Allies, stated that "in the South, the heroes were nearly all soldiers." In 1943 Alabama editor John Temple Graves II published the book *The Fighting South*. Later, the distinguished black historian John Hope Franklin examined the antebellum South nd saw there a distinctive military spirit, as did fellow historian Avery O. Craven and political scientist Samuel P. Huntington.

However, the British historian Marcus Cunliffe has denied that before the Civil War the South was any more martial than the North. He held that Dixie's martial prowess was a post-Appomattox myth fostered for the benefit of northerners to rationalize why it took them four bloody years to win the Civil War, despite the overwhelming odds in their favor, and as solace to southerners for their crushing defeat. The South's earlier enthusiasm for fighting the War of 1812 and the Mexican War, in contrast to northern tepidity and even civil disobedience in both conflicts, has been explained away as a drive to extend chattel slavery into new lands. Yet the South did rally behind the national war effort in 1812 and 1846 and went down fighting to the last in 1865.

Some writers think that the South's enthusiasm for the military ethos was even more marked after Appomattox than before Fort Sumter, and much evidence supports this idea. Military schools and colleges continued to attract public support and students. After Reconstruction volunteer military companies proliferated in the South. For instance, in 1885, Montgomery, with a population of less than 25,000, had five military companies, and later a black unit appeared. W. J. Cash noted in *The Mind of the South* (1941) that in 1898 young southerners rushed to don blue uniforms for the Spanish-American War. They had also been drawn back to West Point and Annapolis, so that by 1910, 93 percent of U.S. Army general officers had southern affiliations—by birth, family, residence, schooling, or marriage. In World War I two of the three top commanders in the American Expeditionary Force (AEF) in France were General John J. Pershing from the border state of Missouri and Lieutenant General Robert E. Lee Bullard from Alabama. All four commanders of the first outfit to fight on the western front, the 1st Division ("The Big Red One"), were southerners.

Before Pearl Harbor, Texans bragged that the federal government introduced the draft to keep them from filling up the ranks of the armed forces. Professor Brogan explained that southerners early favored American intervention on the Allied side in World War II more than other citizens because from experience they "knew that war could settle a lot." When the Korean War broke out, 46 percent of the American military elite still had southern affiliations, although the South's population was then only 27 percent of the country's total. When the U.S. armed forces intervened in Vietnam, the top army and air force commanders were southerners, and later antiwar activism was almost nonexistent on the campuses of Dixie.

More recently, indications are that southern overrepresentation in the officer

Texan Audie Murphy, World War II battlefield hero and movie star, a modern embodiment of the military tradition (Audie Murphy Collection, Baylor University, Waco, Tex.)

corps may have ended, perhaps because of declining southern distinctiveness, along with increasing urbanization and affluence. Other factors may include changes in the military profession itself, with the military manager nearly replacing the heroic warrior, and a lingering racist perception that the services are filling up with blacks. The democratization of the career military force has resulted in a decline in participation by the southern upper and upper-middle classes, following the pattern set earlier by their northern peers.

Various explanations have been offered for the traditional military bent of the white southerner. One was southern upper-class affinity for the ideal of the English country gentleman, with its concept of noblesse oblige and the pattern of the oldest son's farming and the others' choosing the church, the law, and the army. More recently F. N. Boney has denied the reality of this ideal and asserted that the plain folk, the "rednecks," were the uniquely belligerent warriors of the South. However, he also denies the reality of a distinctive planter elite, holding that most of them were "at heart rednecks on the make." Grady McWhiney and Forrest McDonald claim, despite the demographic evidence to the contrary, that southerners were of Celtic descent and more ferocious than northerners, who, they argue, were all Anglo-Saxon.

Contradictory explanations would have it that Johnny Reb was particularly amenable to hierarchy and discipline, coming as he did from a deferential society, or, on the contrary, that he was an unregenerate individualist standing up for his rights. A favorite explanation is that he was rural, an outdoorsman expert at camp life, hunting, and shooting, but today's largely urbanized South still provides more than its share of recruits for the forces. Preoccupation with honor supposedly predisposed the young of the past to the profession of arms, but that concept is virtually extinct today with the "me generation," and probably was 30 years ago with the "silent generation." Yet another construal is that the southerner is militant because he is a violent white racist, Cash's "proto-Dorian," who just lives to shoot "gooks," but the southern black man also has made a fine soldier. During the Civil War 186,000 blacks served in the Union army and 29,000 were in the Union navy, while others served in Confederate forces. The Department of War created four African American units after the war, and many black southerners served in them in the western Indian wars. Blacks fought in World War I and II, although in segregated outfits. President Harry Truman opened new opportunities for black southerners in 1948 when his executive order ended military segregation.

The southern martial spirit has been conspicuous in the five wars that the United States has waged since 1990—in Kuwait, Bosnia, Kosovo, Afghanistan, and Iraq. Southerners served in all five conflicts in disproportionate numbers. Exemplars are three officers from Alabama. The first, a lieutenant, directed his antiaircraft battery in downing the first Iraqi Scud missile in the 1991 Gulf War. A second, a former marine and a CIA agent, was the first American killed in Afghanistan, and the third, a captain, helped capture Saddam Hussein. In 2003, 40 percent of the U.S. Army recruits came from the South. A Texan is eight times more likely to serve than is a New Yorker. Half of them from Texas, Dixie supplies 45 percent of the army's officer corps.

The southern military tradition may have become self-reinforcing, as with other elements of southern distinctiveness, persisting in an age that threatens to smother and level differences. The South struggles to maintain its own gemein schaft against homogenization, and the rest of the nation will not allow the idea of the South to perish. "The consensus remains that a separate quality of myth, tradition, and values characterizes the South despite the compelling forces of modernization," write Thomas L. Connelly and Barbara L. Bellows. A key element of this lingering regional quality is the tradition of "the Fighting South."

JOHN HAWKINS NAPIER III
Montgomery, Alabama

F. N. Boney, *Midwest Quarterly* (1980), *Southerners All* (1984); D. W. Brogan, *The American Character* (1944); Thomas L. Connelly and Barbara L. Bellows, *God and General Longstreet: The Lost Cause and the Southern Mind* (1982); Avery O. Craven, *The Growth of Southern Nationalism, 1848–1861* (1953); Marcus Cunliffe, *Soldiers and Civilians: The Martial Spirit in America, 1775–1865* (1968); James Sanders Day, *Alabama Review* (April 2003); John Hope Franklin, *The Militant South, 1800–1861* (1956); John Temple Graves II, *The Fighting South* (1943); Samuel P. Huntington, *The Soldier and the State: The Theory and Politics of Civil-Military Relations* (1957); Morris Janowitz, *The Professional Soldier* (1960, 1971); John Hawkins Napier III, *Alabama Review* (October 1980); Bertram Wyatt-Brown, *Southern Honor: Ethics and Behavior in the Old South* (1982).

New Deal

Agriculture in the 1930s was the South's major economic activity; and New Deal farm programs—such as the Agricultural Adjustment Act (1933), the Re settlement Administration (1935), and the Bankhead-Jones Farm Tenant Act (1937)—by cutting production, raising farm income, and pushing southerners from farm poverty to southern and nonsouthern cities created the basis for the sweeping change soon to come to the largely rural South. Along with the agri cultural revolution the New Deal infusion of federal money disrupted the cycle of poverty, and the region's economy began to merge with that of the nation. New Deal labor legislation such as the National Labor Relations Act (1933), the Social Security Act (1935), and the Fair Labor Standards Act (1935) helped to spur the first significant unionization of the country (one of every four workers was a member of a union by the end of the 1940s). The South, with its major industry, textiles, overwhelmingly nonunionized, was the most underunion ized region of the country, with all the attendant cultural and economic im pact of nonunionization. In the nation's poorest region, the Federal Emergency

Relief Administration provided limited but badly needed amounts of money to fund welfare programs; and the Public Works Administration (1933), the Civilian Conservation Corps (1933), and the Works Progress Administration (1935) offered public service work to the unemployed.

At first the personal popularity of Franklin D. Roosevelt and his Depression-fighting New Deal programs meant solid support among southern politicians and southern voters. But New Deal politics and programs threatened white supremacy and lessened the power of local oligarchies. The centralizing tendencies of the New Deal menaced the basic institutions of southern life. The subsequent slow defection of southern Democrats from the New Deal created a new conservative southern political culture.

The role of the New Deal in creating the modern political economy of southern society remains controversial. Statistical study indicates that the Dixie economic miracle dates from the 1940s. Ambiguity surrounds the New Deal years in the South. In many ways the New Deal nationalized southern culture, and the South became by the 1940s not the nation's number one economic problem but its ever-growing, ever-Americanizing region. The persistence, however, of such cultural patterns as racial segregation, dire poverty, and rural and small-town control kept the South looking more old than new. The New Deal, with its host of centralizing agencies and its nationalized political ideology, changed the Old South but did not destroy it. Only the war years, the racial revolution of the 1950s and 1960s, emigration, and the postwar prosperity of industrialization and urbanization would do that.

JAMES A. HODGES
College of Wooster

Roger Biles, *The South and the New Deal* (1994); James C. Cobb and Michael V. Namorato, eds., *The New Deal and the South* (1984); Pete Daniel, *Agricultural History* (July 1981), *Breaking the Land: The Transformation of Cotton, Tobacco, and Rice Cultures since 1880* (1985); Gary Fink and Merl Reed, eds., *Essays in Southern Labor History: Selected Papers, Southern Labor History Conference, 1976* (1976); Frank Freidel, *FDR and the South* (1965); Elna C. Green, ed., *The New Deal and Beyond: Social Welfare in the South since 1930* (2003); Donald H. Grubbs, *Cry from the Cotton: The Southern Tenant Farmers' Union and the New Deal* (1971); Jack Irby Hayes Jr., *South Carolina and the New Deal* (2001); Michael Holmes, *The New Deal in Georgia: An Administrative History* (1975); Janet Irons, *Testing the New Deal: The General Textile Strike of 1934 in the American South* (2000); John B. Kirby, *Black Americans in the Roosevelt Era: Liberalism and Race* (1980); William E. Leuchtenberg, *The White House Looks South: Franklin D. Roosevelt, Harry S. Truman, Lyndon B. John-*

son (2005); Robert S. McElvaine, *The Great Depression, 1929–1941* (1984); Paul E. Mertz, *New Deal Policy and Southern Rural Poverty* (1978); John Dean Minton, *The New Deal in Tennessee, 1932–38* (1959); Harvard Sitkoff, *A New Deal for Blacks: The Emergence of Civil Rights as a National Issue*, vol. 1 (1978); George B. Tindall, *The Emergence of the New South, 1913–1945* (1967).

New Deal Agencies

Whether perched in Washington, D.C., office buildings or in less swank head quarters located in every southern capitol city, New Dealers approached the South as the nation's most devastated region in the Great Depression. The re formers perceived southern needs as many; they perceived the region's re sources as pitifully few. Thus, within a decade, the South received thousand of miles of new roads, huge swaths of reclaimed land and forests, new lakes recreational parks, historical sites and museums, thousands of modern schools modern airports, public utilities galore, steel bridges, modernist-styled county courthouses, quaint Colonial Revival–styled post offices, expanded military facilities, and even new towns such as Lake Dick Cooperative Farms in Ar kansas and Cumberland Homesteads in Tennessee. For the New Dealers, all o these varied projects fit within a larger strategy of creating a new foundation for a modern South that suddenly had a rebuilt economic infrastructure but also new credit mechanisms, better-educated citizens, and a reinvigorated commu nity spirit.

Building better communities was an undertone of many New Deal efforts and New Deal–sponsored schools, like Port Allen High School in Louisiana symbolized this reform agenda best. Those new buildings often had electricity a library, a lunch room for hot meals, sanitary restrooms, and physical educa tion facilities. The building was a demonstration of the amenities required, and the necessity of modern technology, for a productive life. Reformers assumed that his new public infrastructure would almost automatically produce better-educated, more worldly consumer participants in an expanded regional and national economy. Southerners might, in time, become Americans and join the mainstream.

Reformers used programs and funding from multiple agencies. The Civilian Conservation Corps (CCC) built a public infrastructure for tourism and recre ation as it reclaimed hundreds of thousands of devastated, marginal south ern land. Popular parks such as the Great Smoky Mountains National Park in Tennessee and North Carolina and the Shenandoah National Park in Virginia were why the CCC became the best-liked of the New Deal alphabet agencies The Public Works Administration (PWA) typically funded the construction of large-scale, well-designed projects of long-term benefit, from the highway to the Florida Keys to the waterfront facilities of Gulfport, Miss., to the Mitchell County Courthouse in Camilla, Ga. The Resettlement Administration (RA) and the Farm Security Administration (FSA) reclaimed land and built model communities but also displaced tens of thousands of southerners. FSA photographers left a stunning legacy of southern life through thousands of images of everyday activities and commonplace bends in the road. The Soil Conservation Service (SCS) planted 73 million seedlings of kudzu as a barrier to further soil erosion, and the mighty vine did its job, and then some, giving several southern regions today (northern Mississippi and southwestern Tennessee, for example) virtual kudzu zoos of a vine that grows up and over everything in its path.

Compared to most of the alphabet agencies, the Works Progress Administration (WPA) reached much further into almost every southern town and village. Its Women's and Professional Projects division sponsored canning, sewing, and quilting gatherings and carried out most rural school hot-lunch programs. The WPA's Federal Art Project funded all types of visual arts, as well as performance arts. In a limited way, its projects were even color-blind; African American sculptor William Edmondson of Nashville received WPA grants in 1937 and 1939. The Federal Music Project supported musicians and the creation of classical music institutions; the agency also hired African American musicians but afforded them much more limited, stereotypical opportunities. The WPA even underwrote multiple important archaeological investigations of the region's deep prehistoric past in Kentucky, Georgia, and Louisiana. Other projects assisted historic sites and museums, such as the Hermitage, Andrew Jackson's home in Nashville, to improve their collections, buildings, and visitor services.

As a regional development project of unprecedented scope and imagination, the Tennessee Valley Authority (TVA) certainly was the most recognized, discussed, cussed, and lionized agency of them all. Its goals included flood control, improved river navigation, increased fertilizer production, better agricultural practices, natural resource conservation, industrial promotion, town design, and the generation of public electrical power through all seven states directly impacted by the agency. TVA built model towns, sponsored craftsmen workshops, and established its own demonstration farms. To New Dealers, TVA reflected what their entire program of change was all about: to bring rural southerners a better life through better soil, roads, and economic opportunities. TVA represented coordinated planning by outsiders on a massive scale not experienced since Reconstruction, and its legacy still shapes the region. But big change also meant big dislocation, which also remains felt today. TVA dams and reservoirs did more than destroy home places; they destroyed the fabric of community by demolishing or relocating local churches, cemeteries, and community landmarks. Those dispossessed of their land often struggle to sustain a sense of family and community in their new homes, no matter how modern and improved the dwellings appeared to outsiders. The importance of a sense of place to the people of the Tennessee Valley was rarely understood or appreciated by the New Dealers.

The limits of change also help to define what New Deal agencies meant for African Americans. The New Deal rarely challenged the ethos of Jim Crow segregation. Urban blacks got modern housing projects, but they were placed on smaller lots, with fewer extras, than those projects built for whites. New Deal public buildings sometimes had separate entrances for blacks; they always had separate and decidedly unequal public restrooms for African Americans. Public utilities, sidewalks, and paved roads were built but never extended into black neighborhoods. The New Deal provided some benefits to African Americans, but in general it left southern blacks with a raw deal.

The New Deal and its alphabet agencies transformed the southern public landscape but left southerners still very much southerners and still a good distance away from the American mainstream. Changes that would close that distance were left for later generations.

CARROLL VAN WEST
Middle Tennessee State University

Roger Biles, *The South and the New Deal* (1994); Kenneth J. Bindas, *All of this Music Belongs to the Nation* (1995); Phoebe Cutler, *The Public Landscape of the New Deal* (1985); Edwin A. Lyon, *A New Deal for Southeastern Archaeology* (1996); Carroll Van West, *Tennessee's New Deal Landscape* (2001).

New Deal Cultural Programs

The Great Depression had a substantial impact on many parts of southern life. The region's economy, its relationship with the federal government and the Democratic Party, and social relations between the races were all profoundly and lastingly changed by the New Deal. Franklin D. Roosevelt's policies also had repercussions on the culture of the South. The New Deal legacy may be less apparent here than in other areas, but that legacy continues to have perceptible consequences for modern southern culture.

FDR and his relief administrator, Harry Hopkins, shared a desire to use the opportunity provided by the Depression to begin an experiment in federal patronage of the arts. Attempts were made to give "appropriate" employment to writers and artists during the short-lived Civil Works Administration in the winter of 1933 to 1934, and the Treasury Department's Section of Painting and Sculpture began commissioning works of art (usually murals) for public buildings (most often post offices) in 1934. The principal effort of the New Deal to encourage culture through providing suitable work relief for people involved in the arts began with the launching of the Works Progress Administration in 1935.

Included under WPA Federal Project One were the Federal Writers' Project, the Federal Music Project, the Federal Theater Project, the Federal Art Project, and the Historical Records Survey. The dream behind the WPA arts projects was nothing less than the democratization of American culture. Stimulated by the Depression era's revival of interest in uncovering and building a distinctively American culture, the Federal One projects set out with great expectations. One of the basic problems that they confronted from the start was that the national culture they sought to shape had distinctive demarcations. Regionalism was a major movement in the 1930s, and it was strongest in the South, where it was inspired by such intellectuals as the Nashville Agrarians who published *I'll Take My Stand* in 1930 and, in a quite different way, by University of North Carolina sociologist Howard W. Odum. The regional traits peculiar to the South led to the development of unique characteristics in the New Deal arts projects in that region. At the same time, the federal supervision of its projects carried forward a slow process of homogenization of the South with the rest of the nation.

The Federal Writers' Project had a greater impact upon the South than did any of the other WPA arts projects. The FWP's most publicized accomplishment was the publication of a guidebook for each state. Their quality varied, of course, but on the whole they were a remarkable achievement. The compilers of guides in the southern states faced considerable difficulty in their treatment of blacks. Many of the white writers employed by the FWP shared the white South's stereotypical perceptions of blacks and wrote those views into the state guides. The Louisiana guide portrayed "the Negro" as "imitative." FWP editors strove to reduce such references, but sometimes they failed. They did manage to delete from the Mississippi guide the statement that "the passing of public hanging was, in the eyes of the Negro, a sad mistake," but the published version took what has been described as a tone of "amused condescension" toward blacks. For example, the authors claimed that "the Mississippi folk Negro" is "credulous," yet "he has never been known to take anyone's advice about anything."

One of the Writers' Project's most important contributions was the conducting of more than 2,000 interviews with former slaves. These slave narratives constitute an invaluable historical resource, although most of the interviewers were white and thus may have elicited less than complete candor on the part of some of the former slaves. FWP writers employed these slave narratives in writing the path-breaking *The Negro in Virginia*, published in 1940. This book and the treatment of blacks in several other FWP publications played a small role in the building of a more realistic picture of black life, history, and values. Accordingly, the FWP was one of the New Deal agencies that helped sow the seeds for the later civil rights movement.

Another important FWP contribution to southern culture was the collection of "life histories" of southern workers and farmers. These interviews, some of which were edited by W. T. Couch and published in 1939 under the title *These Are Our Lives*, marked a truly pioneering effort in social history at the same time that they turned the stories of "ordinary" people into a genuine literature. Under the direction of Benjamin F. Botkin, the FWP also collected folklore in the South. Many of these tales reached print under such names as *Bundle of Troubles, and Other Tales, God Bless the Devil! Liar's Bench Tales*, and *Gumbo Ya-ya: A Collection of Louisiana Folk Tales*.

The Federal Writers' Project's single most significant contribution to modern southern culture was the nurturing of several leading writers in the region whose talents might never have been developed had it not been for their FWP employment. Notable among these was Richard Wright, who won a $500 prize for four stories he wrote in 1939 while employed on the project. They were published as *Uncle Tom's Children*, and Wright applied the prize money toward completion of his masterpiece, *Native Son*. Eudora Welty traveled and wrote for the project in Mississippi. Her photographs are included in the Mississippi guidebook.

The Federal Music Project sought to bring first-class orchestral music to a wider audience while providing work for unemployed musicians. Its major impact on the culture of the South, however, fell into a quite different realm. It was a collaborative effort by Charles Seeger of the FMP and Alan Lomax of the FWP to collect the region's folk songs. This effort made a lasting contribution by helping to preserve a most important aspect of regional life.

The Federal Theater Project was the largest and most controversial of the WPA arts projects, but its activities in the South were not as extensive as they were in some other parts of the nation. The FTP did have some notable success stories in the region, particularly in North Carolina, where its actors put on the historical pageant *The Lost Colony*. Also, FTP directors assisted amateur groups throughout North Carolina and in Jacksonville, Fla., which became the center of a small drama revival in northern Florida.

The Theater Project in the South was not free from the political controversy that swirled about it elsewhere. FTP companies in Birmingham, Tampa, and Miami were among 22 nationwide that produced Sinclair Lewis's *It Can't Hap-*

pen Here in the fall of 1936, but officials in Louisiana refused to allow the play about the potential for dictatorship in America to be performed in New Orleans a year after the assassination of Huey Long. Thomas Hall-Rogers's *Altars of Steel*, which portrayed labor-management strife in the southern steel industry, set off an uproar when it premiered in Atlanta.

The FTP's success in bringing live theater and new ideas to the South was limited. Black FTP units were set up in Atlanta and Birmingham. The latter produced *Great Day*, a musical depicting early African history. Traveling companies existed briefly in the region, but by the fall of 1937 the FTP was operational in only three states in the South.

The contribution of the Federal Art Project in the South was principally through its sponsorship in six states in the region of Community Art Centers, some of which became permanent museums, as in Mobile in conjunction with its art education programs. More persuasive were the murals of the Treasury Department's Section of Painting and Sculpture. This was not a relief program but one with the sole aim of public beautification. Post office murals were painted in many cities and towns across the region. They offer a revealing view of southern culture in the 1930s and early 1940s, because the artists were, at least in theory, required to consult local public opinion in determining what to paint. Most southern communities seemed to prefer historical themes — themes that provided a sense of stability in the midst of the uncertainty of the Depression.

One other aspect of the New Deal played an important part in southern culture. The photography project begun under the Resettlement Administration and carried forward by the Farm Security Administration brought together many of the nation's leading photographers. Most of them spent some time working in the South. The FSA photographers, especially Walker Evans, left indelible images of southern life in the Depression years.

ROBERT S. MCELVAINE
Millsaps College

Jerrold Hirsch, *Portrait of America: A Cultural History of the Federal Writers' Project* (2003); F. Jack Hurley, *Portrait of a Decade: Roy Stryker and the Development of Documentary Photography in the Thirties* (1972); Alan Lomax, Woodie Guthrie, and Pete Seeger, eds., *Hard-Hitting Songs for Hard-Hit People* (1967); Jerre Mangione, *The Dream and the Deal: The Federal Writers' Project, 1935–1943* (1972); Karal Ann Marling, *Wall-to-Wall America: A Cultural History of Post-Office Murals in the Great Depression* (1982); Jane DeHart Mathews, *The Federal Theatre, 1935–1939* (1967); Robert S. McElvaine, *The Great Depression, 1929–1941* (1984); Richard D. McKinzie, *The New Deal for Artists* (1973); Monty Noam Penkower, *The Federal Writers' Project:*

A Study in Government Patronage of the Arts (1977); William Stott, *Documentary Expression and Thirties America* (1973).

Philanthropy, Northern

Northern philanthropy emerged as a significant social, economic, and political force in the South following the Civil War. At a time when the region was suffering from the effects of defeat, desolation, and social confusion, northerners, as individuals and through corporate bodies, sought by means of philanthropic gifts to influence the current and future direction of southern life. Generally, the philanthropists were attempting in a variety of ways to assist in "bringing racial order, political stability, and material prosperity to the American South." These goals were perceived as supportive of two crucial ends: insuring that the South's restoration enhanced rather than weakened the United States and promoting the "reformation and elevation" of the southern people, their institutions, and their politics by bringing them into greater conformity with the North.

Between the closing years of the Civil War and the middle decades of the 20th century, northerners of means invested millions of philanthropic dollars in the South. Although this giving had several phases, most donations fell into a number of clearly identifiable categories: (1) support of segregated public and private education for southern blacks and whites; (2) aid to individuals, programs, and governmental agencies endeavoring to increase the skills and productivity of southern farmers; (3) creation and support of programs designed to raise the quality of southern rural life through educational and medical programs to eliminate social diseases, increase public knowledge in regard to hygiene and health, and provide adequate medical services; (4) direct grants and matching funds to southern schools, colleges, and universities to build endowments, raise salaries, and erect new buildings; (5) studies and grants to assess and upgrade medical education and incorporate it into the major universities of the region; (6) improvement of library services and the erection of new libraries; and (7) aid to theological education.

Beginning in the 1920s some philanthropic agencies also began to support programs designed to facilitate the exchange of ideas and information between black and white leaders of the South. Although all of these programs made contributions to southern life, some had a widespread positive effect throughout the region, particularly those that sought to develop an adequate system of public and private education for whites, to increase southern farmers' productivity and improve the quality of rural life, and to professionalize and elevate the quality of medical education.

The earliest group of northern philanthropists to have an impact on the South was the Protestant missionary societies, which began during the Civil War to send money and workers into the region. Although a significant number of large and small church-related organizations engaged in this activity, the most important, in terms of money expended, schools and other institutions established, as well as constancy of interest, were the American Missionary Association (nominally nonsectarian but primarily Congregational), the Freedmen's Aid Society of the Methodist Episcopal Church, the American Baptist Home Missionary Society, and the Presbyterian Church's Board of Missions for the Freedmen. Fueled by missionary energy and the abolitionist desire to uplift the freedmen, these organizations increased their efforts after the Civil War and, in conjunction with the federal government's Bureau of Refugees, Freedmen, and Abandoned Lands, became the major forces for "uplift" and education among blacks.

When the Freedmen's Bureau went out of existence in 1870, these organizations remained actively involved in this work, becoming even more important to blacks and more controversial among southern whites. Whites accurately perceived them as subverters of traditional southern racial mores because of their support of black education based on northern models, espousal of character reform that sought to transform African Americans into black Yankees, and support of black political rights. The northern missionary societies strengthened the hostility of white southerners by an almost exclusive interest in the southern black community and its welfare. From the post–Civil War period to the first decade of the 20th century, the northern church agencies, as the largest contributors to black education, were a major philanthropic force in the South. Although the denominations that supported these groups would maintain an interest in southern blacks throughout the first half of the 20th century, after 1900 the secular philanthropic agencies began to make a greater impact.

Between 1867 and 1902 a small number of secular philanthropic foundations established by wealthy white northerners joined the missionary societies in the work of reforming and elevating the South. By 1910 these foundations, because of their focused goals and numerous connections with white business and political leaders in both the North and the South, were more visible and influential than the missionary societies. The most important of the foundations active in the South were the General Education Board of the Rockefeller Foundation, the Southern Education Board, the Julius Rosenwald Fund, the Phelps-Stokes Fund, and the Carnegie Foundation. All these agencies were established between 1866 and 1918 in direct response to two parallel developments in U.S. history—the growth of large personal fortunes derived from business and the presence of a powerful movement to promote more efficient philanthropy through organization.

The intersection of these two movements with the interest of secular philanthropists in the South is reflected in the individual histories of these foundations. Often considered the first modern American foundation, the Peabody Fund was established in 1867 by George Peabody, a wealthy banker who lived in England. This fund, using its $2 million endowment, promoted public and private black and white education in the South until it was liquidated in 1914. In 1881 a Connecticut merchant named John F. Slater, impelled by his belief that the education of the former slaves would promote black welfare and ensure "the safety of our common country," placed $1 million in the hands of a board of trustees for this purpose.

John D. Rockefeller's lifelong concern to distribute a portion of his earnings to charity led to the creation of the General Education Board in 1902. Because of its immense resources, creative programs, and capable administrators and trustees, it would become the most important of the foundations involved in southern life. Organized as a discretionary perpetuity with an endowment of over $153 million, it sought, according to its stated goals, to promote "education within the United States, without discrimination of race, sex, or creed."

Between 1885 and 1920 public concern about America's educational, medical, and social problems increased. The South, burdened with poverty, low standards of public education, health problems, and peculiar racial problems, was a special focus of these concerns. The philanthropic possibilities created by the multiplication of great private fortunes and by Andrew Carnegie's influential argument that the rich were obligated to serve others increased public esteem for the agencies established by Peabody, Slater, and Rockefeller. At the same time, they caused many wealthy Americans to view the foundation as an excellent means for stimulating efforts to solve a wide variety of problems. This belief was reflected in the increasing rate with which foundations were established after 1900. To the Progressive Era, such organizations seemed the embodiment of the new "scientific philanthropy," which sought not simply to concern itself with the symptoms of social disorder but, through research and careful application of insights, to eliminate the root causes of social problems.

During the second decade of the 20th century the Phelps-Stokes Fund and the Julius Rosenwald Fund were established. Before her death in 1910, Caroline Phelps-Stokes of New York City made provision in her will for a charitable endowment to support the efforts of black Americans to improve their conditions, especially through education. Accordingly, a foundation bearing her name was established and incorporated in 1911. This fund provided occasional direct grants to individual black schools and colleges, but its major support of black education was through a series of surveys and studies for which it provided money and other forms of assistance.

As early as 1910 Julius Rosenwald had begun a regular program of gifts to support educational and social-service institutions in the South and to provide direct aid to "talented individuals." In all instances, southern blacks were beneficiaries of his largesse. After 1917 Rosenwald's giving was institutionalized in the Julius Rosenwald Fund. Disliking the restrictive nature of perpetual endowments, Rosenwald included provisions for the termination of the fund within 25 years of his death. Sixteen years after his death in 1932 it was liquidated, having provided roughly $63 million to improve rural education, racial relations, and black health education.

The wealth of these northern philanthropic agencies gave them the power to influence greatly the lives and futures of black and white southerners. In their dealings with whites the agencies pursued specific goals but in most cases exercised a cautious and diplomatic approach designed to secure the cooperation and support of white southern leaders. By 1910 this had produced strong and, in some quarters, enthusiastic white southern endorsement of the foundations as "friends."

Initially, though, white southerners greeted the secular philanthropic agencies with the same suspicion and distrust the missionary societies received. Their public and financial support of black education and character reform at first seemed another variant on the familiar Yankee reformer, plotting to elevate blacks at the expense of southern whites. However, after 1902, as the General Education Board began to dominate the field of southern philanthropy, directly influencing the work of most other northern secular philanthropies and much of what was done by the missionary societies, the policies and programs of the secular philanthropic agencies began to convince white southerners that their welfare was uppermost in the minds of the individuals directing these organizations. This was an accurate assessment, because from 1902 to the early 1920s the major programs of the secular northern philanthropists included (1) the development of a comprehensive educational system for southern whites justified by the belief that the southern white community would neither tolerate nor fund a comprehensive educational system for blacks until they first had a good system of public and private schools for themselves; (2) a commitment to the development and maintenance of a working relationship between northern philanthropy and the dominant forces in southern society; and (3) a strong espousal of industrial rather than collegiate and professional training for blacks, based on the judgment that they needed basic skills and training that inculcated the dignity and worth of labor.

To promote racial order, political stability, and material prosperity in the South, the secular philanthropic agencies, the most important forces in northern philanthropy, accepted and made their peace with white supremacy in the South. Consequently, from 1902 to 1960, when the General Education Board exhausted its funds, the bulk of the monies expended by northern secular agencies in the South went for programs that benefited southern whites solely. Frequently, the relations of the philanthropic agencies with blacks contrasted sharply with the treatment accorded their white counterparts. With blacks, these organizations were often more directive and far less flexible in pursuing policies and programs they saw as suitable. At times, some foundation officials deemed it part of their work to directly influence the conduct of black institutions, in some instances effecting removal of persons heading them and the selection of others considered more suitable.

From the mid-1920s until the U.S. Supreme Court's 1954 decision in *Brown v. Board of Education* outlawing segregation, the major northern philanthropic agencies manifested a growing concern over the weakness of black institutions and a disenchantment with industrial education as the major tool for black development. This led to an increase in the number and amount of their grants to southern black institutions of higher education, efforts to make southern governments less discriminatory toward blacks in their distribution of public funds, and support of interracial conferences. Little was done directly, however, to attack or publicize black poverty, segregation, and political powerlessness — the root causes of the problems that plagued the southern black community. Instead, northern philanthropic agencies sought to aid blacks primarily by grants and programs designed to create a strong separate southern black community, an impossible goal given the foundations' limited resources, the size of the black community, the impact of black poverty, and the scant interest of powerful southern whites in supporting such a goal. After 1954, with the emergence of the civil rights movement, northern philanthropists began to reevaluate their programs and goals. However, the increased involvement of the federal government in all aspects of southern life steadily reduced the importance of these organizations.

Although southern blacks were the major direct beneficiaries of the northern missionary societies, the investments and programs of these groups, by providing blacks with skills and education, as well as by strengthening their will to work for a genuinely democratic and biracial society, benefited all southerners. In contrast, the second phase of northern philanthropic activity in the

South, signaled by the dominance of the secular philanthropic agencies, was more conservative. These organizations gave lip service to the missionary societies' goals with regard to black education, development, and political rights, but the chief beneficiaries of their money and programs were southern whites, with whom they collaborated until 1954 in the subordination and segregation of the southern black community.

Over the last half century the Ford Foundation, the Rockefeller Foundation, the Kettering Foundation, and others have continued to fund projects in the South, but with fewer special programs targeted at the region. Funding typically has supported education and economic development, with some projects aimed at particularly underdeveloped areas of the South, such as Appalachia and the Mississippi Delta.

ALFRED MOSS
University of Maryland–College Park

Henry A. Bullock, *A History of Negro Education in the South* (1967); Edwin R. Embree and Julian Waxman, *Investment in the People: The Story of the Julius Rosenwald Fund* (1949); Abraham Flexner, *Funds and Foundations: Their Policies, Past and Present* (1952); Louis R. Harlan, *Separate and Unequal: Public School Campaigns and Racism in the Southern Seaboard States, 1901–1915* (1968); Joyce Hollyday, *On the Heels of Freedom: The American Missionary Association's Bold Campaign to Educate Minds, Open Hearts, and Heal the Soul of a Divided Nation* (2005); Elizabeth Jacoway, *Yankee Missionaries in the South: The Penn School Experiment* (1980); Jacqueline Jones, *Soldiers of Light and Love: Northern Teachers and Georgia Blacks, 1865–1873* (1980); James M. McPherson, *The Abolitionist Legacy: From Reconstruction to the* NAACP (1976); Joe M. Richardson, *Christian Reconstruction: The American Missionary Association and Southern Blacks, 1861–1890* (1985); Morris R. Werner, *Julius Rosenwald: The Life of a Practical Humanitarian* (1939).

Philanthropy, Southern

The final 30 years of the 19th century saw several northern philanthropies aiding the South in its postwar reconstruction. Those efforts reveal that wealth in the North far exceeded the depleted fortunes of southerners and that northern philanthropy had reached a relatively sophisticated stage indicated by its interest in and ability to reach out beyond its locale and region to a distant South. It was many years before southern philanthropy even approached such a level of size and scope.

From the earliest years the people of the South had been philanthropic as individuals, supporting schools and religious institutions with generous and loyal regularity. However, indigenous organized philanthropies did not begin to appear in the South until well into the 20th century. After all, philanthropic institutions, foundations, are expressions not only of the altruistic spirit but also of accumulated capital. The postwar South had much of the former but little of the latter. Fortunes in the South had been relatively few in the decades before the Civil War, and the war drained most of those away.

In the last decades of the 19th century and the first ones of the 20th, prior to the establishment of significant numbers of foundations in the South, the major vehicle for a southern individual's philanthropy was the church or other religious institutions. Much of the care for children and the aged and even some of the available health care were sponsored by religious groups. Southerners were generous with their religious giving, and the benefit of that giving extended beyond the needs of the particular congregation to needs of the general community. The use of religious institutions for personal philanthropy was generally prevalent, but more so in the black church. Deprived of wealth-forming opportunities until recent decades, black individuals in the South supported community-service agencies through their churches.

In 1914 in Cleveland, Ohio, a new kind of philanthropic institution was born. It was called a "community foundation." Whereas the older private foundation structure, as the name implies, is a nongovernmental, nonprofit organization, funded and controlled by an individual, family, or company, the name and concept of community foundations imply that the community builds and controls them. Community foundations provide a charitable vehicle for persons who do not have major wealth and who do not wish to manage an institution in order to express his or her charitable giving interests. Community foundations allow a donor to establish a named fund within the larger community foundation and to recommend the charitable uses for the investment income from that fund, leaving the management tasks to a cooperatively employed staff. The right to recommend grant recipients can be passed on to children or others.

These kinds of foundations, which gained wide acceptance throughout America, represented the first indigenous organized philanthropy in the South. The Louisville (Kentucky) Community Foundation was chartered in 1916. The Winston-Salem Foundation (North Carolina) was formed in 1919. Others followed in subsequent decades, so that in 2001 there were 119 such institutions. Another hallmark of community foundations is the requirement that the local community be the predominant beneficiary of charitable grants by the foundation. By law, and by bent, early southern philanthropy was almost totally localized. That emphasis on local giving continues to the present.

The question of which private foundation in the South is the earliest is subject to some debate. By actual date the earliest is the Duke Endowment of North and South Carolina. Founded in 1924 by North Carolina industrialist James Buchanan Duke, this is also the first southern foundation effort to have a regional impact. The foundation supports four kinds of charitable efforts only in North and South Carolina: (1) four named educational institutions; (2) health care institutions; (3) residential children's programs and adoption placement agencies; and (4) rural Methodist churches.

It is also possible to claim that the Southern Education Foundation (Georgia) was the region's earliest private foundation. Although not incorporated under that name until 1937, this foundation has its roots in four funds, three from outside the region and one indigenous fund: (1) the Peabody Education Fund (Massachusetts), founded in 1867 by a British banker named George Peabody, to assist in the education of the South's "children of common people" in the aftermath of the Civil War; (2) the John F. Slater Fund, founded in 1882 by John Slater, and the first philanthropy in the United States devoted to the education of African Americans; (3) the Negro Rural School Fund (Pennsylvania), created in 1907 by Philadelphia Quaker Anna T. Jeanes to support African American teachers working in southern schools; and (4) the Virginia Randolph Fund (Georgia), formed in 1937 in the name of the first "Jeanes Teacher" with monies raised by the Jeanes teachers in the South. These four funds were combined in 1937 and chartered as the Southern Education Foundation. This new institution continues the aim of each of its historic parts in seeking to foster equity in education for all the South and its people. (Although its aim and work have not changed, in 1983 the Southern Education Foundation changed its charter to become a public charity funded by grants from foundations, corporations, and individuals.)

Plotting the locations of foundations in the South is a lesson in the South's economic history. Focused in urban areas, they reflect the wealth generated by the textile industry (even though much of the early ownership in that industry was located outside the South), banking, utilities, soft drinks, real estate development, agriculture, and other enterprises. For various reasons, including climate, several northern foundations have been transferred to the southern region.

The economic growth in the South following World War II is impressive. The resulting formation of organized philanthropies in the South in those postwar years is also impressive. The economic boom of the 1980s and 1990s resulted in foundation growth in the South that outstrips the foundation growth in the entire country. For example, in 1975 the combined assets of southern foundations was $2.2 billion. In 1997 those assets had grown to $39.1 billion. During the same period the assets of all foundations in America increased from $30.1 billion to $342.5 billion, those in the South representing roughly half of the increase. Between 1990 and 2000 there was a 35 percent increase in the number of foundations in America. In the South during that same period there was an increase of 91 percent (4,670 to 8,925). This growth does not imply that southern foundations were surpassing northern foundations in size or number but that some substantial progress was made in closing the long-standing gap.

Education has always been the largest consumer of foundation dollars in the South. In the early years of the 20th century this emphasis was largely expressed in gifts to colleges and universities, usually the alma mater of the donor. Private secondary schools were also supported and, again, were usually the schools of the donors. Not until the last decades of the 20th century did foundations in the South become supporters of public primary and secondary schools. This support was not in lieu of local governmental funding but for supplemental programs. Enrichment efforts, tutorial programs, supplemental equipment grants, teacher supplemental training, and similar undertakings became almost common among southern foundations.

Health programs have always followed as second in importance to southern foundations. In the early years this interest was expressed by support of local hospitals. As the years passed, grants moved beyond mere core support of the hospital to outreach efforts, access-equity efforts, supplemental training for health staff, and similar programs.

The remaining funds available to southern foundations were divided among religious causes, local rescue efforts for the poor, and the like. Only in the last third of the 20th century did southern foundations begin to broaden their grant interests. Slowly the environment captured some interest among southern foundations. Human services, including legal services, food and nutrition, housing and shelter, safety and recreation, also began to draw the attention of southern foundations. During the 1960s, when individuals and organizations were engaged in a life-and-death struggle in the South to challenge the denial of civil rights to a large segment of the southern population, many northern and midwestern foundations provided the financial fuel for these efforts. With a few exceptions, southern foundations stood on the sidelines and watched the revolution take place.

The broadening of southern foundation grant interests can be traced to two related events: an act of Congress and the reaction of the foundation community to it. In 1969 the U.S. Congress passed the Tax Reform Act, which provided new regulations for the formation and operation of foundations in America. Many foundation donors, trustees, and managers thought that the new rules were too stringent and that compliance would be too difficult. Many liquidated their foundations and distributed the assets among charitable organizations. Others threatened to follow suit. To combat this movement, to learn the compliance requirements together, and to collectively keep the Congress informed of the value of foundations to the society, an association of southern foundations was formed in 1971. It was named the Southeastern Council of Foundations and reflected similar efforts in various parts of the country. The shock of the Tax Reform Act of 1969 also brought about a revitalization of a national association, the Council on Foundations. These associations not only held the bulk of existing foundations together, they also began to share grant interests with each other, to share economies of scale, and to gain a greater understanding of regional issues and the need for foundation involvement in them. As a result, there has been a marked broadening of the grant interests of southern foundations. It is the opinion of many southern foundation leaders that if a civil rights revolution were to take place in the early 21st century, even many foundations in the South would take an active part in support of it.

ROBERT H. HULL
President, Southeastern Council of Foundations, 1978–97

Emmett D. Carson, *The Evolution of Black Philanthropy: Patterns of Giving and Volunteerism in Philanthropic Giving: Studies in Varieties and Goals*, ed. Richard Magat (1989); Martin Lehfeldt, *Philanthropy in the South: 2001, a Regional Overview* (2001); Loren Renz, *Southern Foundations II: A Profile of the Region's Grantmaking Community* (1999), *Giving Trends: Update on Funding Priorities* (2001).

Populism

Adherents of the People's Party, launched formally in 1892, were commonly known as Populists. The nucleus of the third party was the combined strength of the southern and northern branches of the Farmers' Alliance. The Alliance had grown from a local protective association of Texas cattlemen and farmers, formed in 1875 as a protective association against cattle and horse thieves, into a formidable national body. Local, county, state, and national alliances developed coordinated programs designed to achieve economic reform and benefit the agricultural classes. Southern Alliance warehouses, exchanges, and stores engaged in numerous ventures in cooperative buying and selling. As its lecturers and newspapers denounced the impoverished condition of the agrarians, the Farmers' Alliance promoted social and educational activities for farmers and their families.

The South produced a number of national leaders, such as Leonidas L. Polk of North Carolina. Dr. Charles W. Macune, an itinerant reformer, edited the *National Economist* from the Alliance's headquarters in Washington, D.C. Macune championed the subtreasury plan, which would enable farmers to store perishable products in local warehouses and receive loans on their goods while waiting for better prices. Its principles were later adapted by the New Freedom and the New Deal administrations of Woodrow Wilson and Franklin D. Roosevelt, respectively. In the 1890s the subtreasury plan became the basic economic demand of the Southern Alliance. It was denounced as dangerous socialistic heresy by the ruling Democrats, a group of conservative politicians often called Redeemers, or Bourbons, after the conservative ruling house of France that was returned to power following the overthrow of Napoleon. The Alliance was both specific and general in its program that decried the results of the convict-lease system, low farm prices, one-crop agriculture, the crop-lien system, and tenant farming. As the spokesman for the agrarians, the Alliance denounced high land taxes, exorbitant freight rates by largely unregulated railroads, and fertilizer producers who sold spurious brands at inflated prices. The Alliance launched a successful campaign against the jute manufacturers who held a monopoly on the bagging used to wrap cotton. Bankers who charged unreasonable interest rates were condemned as enemies of the indebted farmers.

In the South the Alliance worked to restore a diminishing sense of worth and dignity among farmers. The Alliance was one of the first national orders to admit women to membership. Although unable to aid the party as voters, women contributed to its social and educational programs. Later, some of the women became editors of Alliance and Populist newspapers. Ministers of the gospel, primarily evangelical Protestants, assumed leadership roles in the order from the first.

The first African American Alliance, known as the Colored Farmers' Alliance, was organized in Houston County, Tex., in 1886, and later that year a state organization was formed. Black Alliances were set up in other states, and in March 1888 a national convention was held at Lovelady, Tex. Black Alliances had their separate national, state, and local organizations, although white orders accepted them and often Alliances held joint meetings and cooperated in their objectives. Scholars have debated whether Populists advocated benefits for African Americans, but the evidence is strong that they did.

At first the Southern Alliance backed Bourbon Democrats who pledged themselves to enact the subtreasury plan and other reform measures. The Alliance strategy was to gain control of the Democratic Party and pursue its program from within the power structure. Alliance leaders anticipated success because farmers represented a majority of the population and of the ruling party.

Things went awry when the Bourbons reneged on campaign promises, and it seemed probable that the southern Alliance would copy their counterparts in the Midwest, break away, and form a third party. Yet an immediate and similar southern defection proved difficult because the Democrats had controlled the states politically since the end of Reconstruction. Their strength was based on honesty in government, fiscal conservatism, and white supremacy. Any divisive issue threatened a return to the horrors (more imagined than real) of Reconstruction and Republican rule. Certainly the relationship of black and white Alliance men alone was cause for alarm. Most white southerners wanted to maintain white supremacy and looked to the Democratic Party as the sacrosanct instrument of its preservation.

As the Alliance program faltered, desperate white farmers turned finally to a third national party: the People's Party, also called the Populist Party. Their sense of despair led them to abandon the "party of the fathers," which they considered no longer sensitive to their needs. Populism had many facets and was not confined to farmers, but when viewed as the sum of its parts, it was a class movement. The southern experience was distinct and unique. Southern Populism drew its foot soldiers from the ranks of farmers, many of whom were bedrock Alliancemen. That was so even though some Alliance leaders— Benjamin R. Tillman in South Carolina and James S. Hogg in Texas, for example—refused to leave the Bourbon Democrats and branded the Populists as dangerous radicals.

Realizing the need for additional support, southern agrarians broadened their party's appeal. The Populists were as concerned about political democracy as they were about any other reforms and adopted as party shibboleths a "free ballot" and a "fair count." In 1892 the Populists ran a national ticket, as well as candidates for local, state, and congressional offices, and in 1896 made their climactic effort, again at every level. That year southern Populists were undergirded, as usual, by their farmer ranks (some planters were Populists, but most large landowners lived in Black Belt counties where they controlled the black vote by various means of economic and even physical coercion and had long since made political deals with the other power bases: urban industrialists, businessmen, lumbering interests, textile owners, and mine operators). The agrarians reached out to and succeeded in securing support in small towns and cities from labor unions, immigrants, and nonunion workers in textile mills and mines. Blacks in counties where they could vote without intimidation gave the Populists powerful support. In North Carolina and Alabama many Republicans fused with the Populists, and, despite their obvious philosophical and political differences, made common cause in the effort to defeat the Democrats.

Particularly conspicuous were individual Populist leaders in individual southern states and a solid phalanx of newspaper editors who, despite being outnumbered by Bourbon editors, formed the reform press and fought the Democratic journalists with powerful resolve.

The 1896 Populist national ticket was doomed to failure despite the appeal of its "free silver" platform (a plan to promote inflation and ease the debt burden by having the nation coin silver at an increased ratio to gold). The reasons for defeat were many but came primarily because the Democrats also adopted free silver and because William Jennings Bryan was nominated for president by both Populists and Democrats, thereby splitting the reform vote. Other factors, including race, a lack of campaign funds, traditional loyalties, and poor organization, contributed to the Populists' defeat. At the state level, southern Populist candidates stood small chance of victory against massive fraud and intimidation. There were widespread examples of stolen ballots, stuffing of ballot boxes, voting dead people and voters long since moved away, threats, and physical intimidation. Illegal electioneering tactics (much of it defiantly and proudly admitted later) by Bourbon Democrats defeated the Populists in many local, state, and congressional races in 1896. After 1896 the Populists maintained their party apparatus but were never again a major player at the national level.

Populists openly sought black support in most southern states. Their appeals fell short of promoting social equality, but such a program was not credible in the 1890s, and many Populists declared that skin color bore no relation to political freedom and economic opportunity. Even if part of the Populists' courtship of African Americans was based on political expediency, their commitment to improved race relations was significantly greater than that of the Democrats or Republicans. The reality of the Populist threat in 1896 was seen in the reaction of southern white conservatives. New state constitutions and state laws simply eliminated African Americans as voters on grounds other than race. The devices used included direct primary elections, poll taxes, and literacy and property requirements for voting that legalized disfranchisement of blacks and a large number of poor whites.

Yet, in the long run, Populist principles prevailed, and almost without exception Populist demands were adopted later by both major parties. Monetary reform, encompassing a mass of regulatory laws affecting American society and the nation's economy, was implemented. At their best, men like Reuben F. Kolb and Joseph C. Manning in Alabama, Thomas E. Watson in Georgia, Hardy Brian in Louisiana, and a host of political philosophers, editors, and other politicians viewed Populism correctly as a movement. It was an upheaval, a native radicalism whose power base was largely rural but also contained other reform elements aimed to change national and state inequities. The Populists insisted that all citizens should share in the bounty of America, and the principles of the People's Party still resonate in the rhetoric of contemporary politicians. Populism is deeply embedded in America, and, conceding the movement's imperfections, what the Populists stood for remains timeless.

WILLIAM WARREN ROGERS
Florida State University

Robert F. Durden, *The Climax of Populism: The Election of 1896* (1965); Helen G. Edmonds, *The Negro and Fusion Politics in North Carolina, 1894–1901* (1951); Lawrence Goodwyn, *Democratic Promise: The Populist Moment in America* (1976); Steve Hahn, *The Roots of Southern Populism: Yeoman Farmers and the Transformation of the Georgia Upcountry, 1850–1890* (1982); Richard Hofstadter, *The Age of Reform: From Bryan to FDR* (1955); Robert C. McMath Jr., *American Populism: A Social History* (1992), *Southern Vanguard: A History of the Southern Farmers' Alliance* (1975). For different evaluations of Populism in one state see Sheldon Hackney, *Populism to Progressivism in Alabama* (1969), and William Warren Rogers, *The One Gallused Rebellion: Agrarianism in Alabama, 1865–1896* (1970).

Progressivism

A far-flung series of movements encompassing diverse aspects of early-20th-century public life rather than a single phenomenon, progressivism profoundly affected the modern South. Occurring across the United States, this social movement arose in response to industrialism, urbanism, and a new sense of nationhood; it also embraced the post–Civil War economy of railroads and an internationalized market economy. Viewing industrialism positively, members of the middle classes of the newly emerging towns and cities dominated progressive movements. Rejecting the localism of 19th-century rural America and accepting the realities of the industrialized world, these urban reformers sought to restructure politics and public institutions in areas such as education, moral habits, public health, and child welfare.

Although many progressives were male, a notable number were female. New roles for women shaped the course of reform, as middle-class women immersed themselves in social uplift and in efforts to recast institutions related to children. White and African American women led efforts to modernize the curricula and facilities of public schools, to regulate the use of children in mills and factories, and to institute new measures of child welfare. Southern women's efforts as foot soldiers and leaders in social reform moved them toward a single political reform: obtaining the vote. Although by 1910 the primary objective of progressive southern women had become suffrage, the opposition of antisuf-frage groups (the "antis") frustrated these state-level campaigns, and suffragists sought a national constitutional amendment. The Nineteenth Amendment was submitted to the states on June 1919, and it achieved ratification after Tennessee, on 18 August 1920, became the 36th and final state to endorse the amendment.

A strong moral fervor drove the reformers' enthusiasm. Overwhelmingly Protestant, progressives were informed by an evangelical zeal to perfect human society. They wanted to purify southern society by rooting out vice and prosti-tution, and their most determined efforts focused on eliminating the manufac-ture and distribution of alcohol. Prohibitionism occupied a prominent posi-tion in Progressive Era social reform; attempts to destroy the liquor traffic represented the most successful social reform in the South. The Anti-Saloon League, an organization originating in Ohio in the 1890s, organized state chap-ters across the South and, by the early 1900s, succeeded in persuading legis-latures to enact local-option ordinances banning breweries, distilleries, and saloons. Southern prohibitionists participated in efforts to ratify the Eighteenth Amendment, which was adopted in 1919.

Progressives in the South resembled their counterparts elsewhere in the United States. But at least two considerations made southern progressivism distinctive. The first reflected how matters of race and white supremacy domi-nated the reform agenda; the second was the ways in which southern poverty shaped the goals, objectives, and methods of reformers. Among their most im-portant objectives was to change the practice of politics, public policy, and gov-ernance. Hostile to mass democratic politics, which they saw as an obstacle to efficient government, they took various measures to regulate the ballot, refash-ion voting practices, introduce political primaries (which, though democratic, also replaced parties' traditional means of nominating candidates), institute anticorruption measures (which limited parties' access to funds), and inaugu-rate civil service reforms (which limited the patronage powers). But these re-forms occurred within the construct of white supremacy: while introducing political reform, southern states also barred African Americans from voting through methods such as the poll tax and literacy test. In truth, most south-ern progressives were white supremacists who believed that black voting mis-takenly arose during Reconstruction; ridding the system of African American participation, they believed, would be the most effective way to "reform" poli-tics. But without black political power the public policy revolution that reform-ers sought and partially accomplished in education, social welfare, and pub-lic health inordinately benefited white southerners at the expense of African Americans.

The poverty of the South also shaped a distinctive agenda. Much of that poverty was rural. In general, reformers favored the reorganization of southern farming through the introduction of modern business methods: the system of county agricultural extension agents, which became established as a national, federally run program in 1914, first started in the South. County agents pioneered new methods in farming; female home demonstration agents, working for the extension service, preached the new gospel of the modern household to southern women. At the same time, southern progressives sought to expand, modernize, and consolidate the isolated, community-controlled one-room schools that dotted the southern landscape. Other reformers began efforts to refashion the health practices of black and white southerners, focusing on the host of parasites, nutritional deficiencies, and diseases that plagued the countryside.

In the end, progressivism left a mixed legacy in the South. Progressives' reforms promised change, progress, and expanded opportunities, especially for women, for new forms of public involvement. Seeking far-reaching changes, in many instances progressives encountered resistance from a powerful tradition of community control and localism. Indeed, by the 1920s, competing traditions of modernization and traditionalism squared off in the South, and a sort of dialogue between these forces continued throughout the 20th century.

WILLIAM A. LINK
University of North Carolina at Greensboro

Hugh Bailey, *Liberalism in the New South: Southern Social Reformers and the Progressive Movement* (1969); Glenda Gilmore, *Gender and Jim Crow: Women and the Politics of White Supremacy in North Carolina, 1896–1920* (1996); Dewey W. Grantham, *Southern Progressivism: The Reconciliation of Progress and Tradition* (1984); Jack Temple Kirby, *Darkness at the Dawning: Race and Reform in the Progressive South* (1972); William A. Link, *The Paradox of Southern Progressivism, 1880–1930* (1992).

Railroads

Even before the steam engine arrived in America, southerners considered the possibility of rail travel. In the late 1820s the Charleston & Hamburg tried sailcars (which overturned or knocked the passengers out of their seats as the winds shifted) and cars drawn by a brace of dogs. For all their deficiencies—the sparks they showered on passengers, the jolting ride given by the stagecoaches used as cars, the high rate of accidents—the early steam engines worked much better. By 1830 the Baltimore & Ohio had introduced steam power to the South. That same year, Kentucky chartered the Lexington & Ohio, and Louisiana approved the Pontchartrain line from New Orleans to its nearby lake. As late as 1840 Georgia had only 185 miles of track and South Carolina had 137 — and they were better provided than most other southern states.

But in the next two decades railroads spread. During the 1850s mileage increased 244 percent in Virginia, 158 percent in North Carolina, and 1,062 percent in Mississippi. Visionaries of the Confederacy could not have wished them to grow faster. Until the late 1850s New Orleans had no rail link to Richmond; on the eve of the Civil War Arkansas had a mere 38 miles of track. During the conflict the North could depend on railroads to bring in supplies far more than could the South; and while the former expanded its network in wartime, the latter diminished it. War brought havoc, worst of all in South Carolina, where Union troops lifted rails from the roadbed, heated them, and twisted them around trees as "Sherman's hairpins." With American military aid in 1865 and public aid thereafter, a new railroad boom began. By 1900, 10 southern states had some 35,000 miles of track and Arkansas had over 3,000.

Not all southerners appreciated railroads. Many suspected them as an alien invader of the plantation world they cherished. Thus, in eastern Kentucky the Louisville & Nashville found locals so unhelpful where one station was being planned that it finally named the place Uz, after the land in which Job had suffered. Two generations earlier, the same railroad's president was so offended by rudeness and squalor in Danville, Ky., that he ordered surveyors to build the track beyond earshot of the town; from then on, townsfolk could catch the train only by chartering taxis for a three-mile trip outside the city limits. In the 1830s a leading Barnwell landholder forced a projected railroad to pass through a town 10 miles distant by refusing a right-of-way across his land. To such folk, the railroad was, as a farmer once called it, "hell in harness."

But to most southerners railroads were welcome. Believers in a New South in the 1870s saw the lines as an essential beginning: without them, no immigrants could be brought in, mineral resources exploited, or factories built. Atlanta owed its growth to railroads, just as Milledgeville owed its decline and the loss of the state capital to its refusal to fund lines in the 1850s. Where Birmingham stood in 1900 there had been only farms in 1865; the crossing of two railroads made a city known for its coal and steel production. Those who wanted a South economically independent of the North pressed for a transcontinental line from the Gulf to southern California and sought federal subsidies for it; so eager were they that a few Republican politicians in 1877 hoped to resolve the disputed presidential election by promises of aid. Southern Democrats denounced national aid to railroads, but they backed bills helping southern railroads, took

Railroad depot, Nashville, Tenn., 1864 (Brady Civil War Photograph Collection,
Library of Congress [LC-B811-2652], Washington, D.C.)

land grants for the Mobile & Ohio and the Cairo & Fulton, and used state legislatures to provide still more aid.

Few doubted that railroads would make any town prosper. In the 1890s the Missouri & Northern Arkansas showed its influence, as construction created 33 new towns. The line fostered zinc mining and turned Harrison into a major Ozark trading center whose population increased by 117 percent in the second decade of the 20th century. Bypassing Carrollton, Duff, and Old Mount Pisgah, the road doomed them all. But for this reason, competition for railroads set southern state against state, town against town, as each tried to obtain special connections and prevent any rival from sharing in the benefits. Irritated by the lack of rail connections, Florida's Panhandle threatened secession; annoyed by central Alabama's relationship with Pensacola, Mobile merchants hinted that they would join their city to Mississippi unless railroad aid was forthcoming. Louisville directors dreamed of an empire reaching the Gulf; Gilded Age Atlanta businessmen strove to dominate the Atlantic Seaboard and vied with Richmond interlopers. Often, fights dubbed "the Railroads against the People" turned out to be no more than the fight of one southern railroad's backers against another. Thus, the South became less united through railroad quarrels.

It also became less southern. From 1870 on, northern capital was crucial to southern lines, and with its money, northern control intruded. Of 311 directors on southern major roads (those with 100 or more miles of track) in 1900, 193 were northerners, including 121 New Yorkers. Northern railroads, eager to exploit Appalachian coal and timber, set the pace of development there, denuded the hillsides, and left slag and stumps where forests had been. Nor did railroads end the cash-crop economy. Rather, railroads opened new lands to cotton growers. Thus, Raymond, Miss., shipped 1,100 bales in 1851 and 7,000 bales in 1853.

Even so, railroads were welcomed with subsidies, land grants, and liberal charters. A line's completion became a holiday. When the Baltimore & Ohio commenced building, its ceremonies featured national politicians, Baltimore's mayor and city council, and surviving veterans of the American Revolution. To break ground, the company chose Charles Carroll of Carrollton, the last surviving signer of the Declaration of Independence. In 1896 the railroad even made a catastrophe an occasion by inviting visitors to Crush, Tex., to watch a railroad collision—which, when a boiler exploded, killed two onlookers and injured several more.

The railroads also took on a special, if dubious, mystique in popular culture. They became a part of the landscape, described by writers such as William

Faulkner, Eudora Welty, and Thomas Wolfe. They symbolized mobility, escape from the confinements of rural life. Southern musicians frequently sang of the rails, partly because so many of them had personal connections to railroad life. Bluesman Sleepy John Estes was a caller on track gangs in west Tennessee; Jimmie Rodgers ("the Singing Brakeman") grew up the son of a section foreman for the Gulf, Mobile & Ohio Railroad; A. P. Carter worked on a railroad crew; and Peg Leg Sam lost a leg while riding a freight train.

Two of the most popular railroad songs enshrined southern figures. As an engineer on the Illinois Central, Casey Jones saved his passengers at the cost of his own life in 1900; in 1950 the postal service issued a special stamp with the Missourian's likeness on it. John Henry, the black steel driver, who probably worked on the Big Bend Tunnel in West Virginia around 1870, actually did challenge the steam drill and win, and he may actually have driven a 14-foot hole when his rival could only do a 9-foot one. Other southern railroad ballads have a tragic flavor: classics like "The Wreck of Old 97," based on a 1903 Virginia smash-up, and "The Wreck of the C & O," based on a catastrophe some years later. Other blues and country songs take a melancholy tone from their recollection of that "lonesome whistle" sound.

Other expressions of popular culture humorously noted the inefficiency of southern lines. Playing on initials, observers christened the Georgia & Florida the God-Forgotten; the Carolina & Northwestern was the Can't and Never-Will; and the Houston, East & West Texas was the Hell Either Way You Take It. In 1903 Thomas W. Jackson published a best-selling joke book, *On a Slow Train through Arkansas*, mocking that state's transportation. One story told how a train halted. "There are some cattle on the track," the conductor explained. Soon the train was moving again, but not for long. "We have caught up with those cattle again," passengers were told. The lines' unprofitability may even have made the roads safer from robbery, though in the 1880s Rube Barrow robbed at least seven trains in the Old Southwest and even held up the same train three days apart, once on the northbound and once on the southbound journey. After the Civil War a bandit stopped the Cotton Belt, and the company president got off to chide him. "Aren't you ashamed of yourself to . . . try to rob a road as poor as this one?" he is said to have complained. "Why don't you go over and hold up the Iron Mountain?" The bandit slunk away—and took the advice.

But such joking never concealed the real need the railroads answered, nor the petty favors they could do. Southbound trains entering Florida would toot to warn farmers of a coming freeze; the branch line into Lebanon, Tenn., would blast its whistle to announce an important news story or spread the fire alarm. In Kentucky a thoughtful engineer reportedly broke into church services to play "Oh, How I Love Jesus" on his whistle, but he blasted his reputation with the ministers the next week by playing "How Dry I Am." In the early 1900s railroads ran special trains to bring city folks to lynchings in outlying counties. More substantially, the Illinois Central encouraged Mississippians to go into commercial vegetable farming by sponsoring practical demonstrations of new methods and carrying in agricultural exhibits. Thanks to railroad encouragement, Lebanon, Tenn., cedar served in the building of Pittsburgh and adorned the lounge of Chicago's Palmer House.

Southern railroads continued to grow until the 1920s. Then, under increasing competition with automobiles and trucks, the rail lines cut back service, merged, or closed down operations altogether. Between 1916 and 1960 mileage fell over 20 percent in Arkansas, Louisiana, and North Carolina. After the Depression the roads never fully recovered. The Pontchartrain was sold, and its roadbed became a boulevard, Elysian Fields Avenue. The Middle Tennessee & Alabama shared a similar ignominious fate. With the railroads' decline the towns that had been built around them either adapted to highways or died out. As engines switched to diesel power, towns that had provided coal, wood, and water vanished as quickly as they had come. Today most southern towns have at best a boarded-up depot, a mute monument to the New South that was.

Passenger trains still provide service to parts of the South through Amtrak. In 1970 Congress passed the Rail Passenger Act, creating a private company that manages the nationwide rail passenger system. Seven routes serve the Southeast providing connections among major cities and select towns.

MARK W. SUMMERS
University of Kentucky

Eugene Alvarez, *Travel on Southern Antebellum Railroads, 1828–1860* (1974); Benjamin F. Botkin and Alvin F. Harlow, eds., *A Treasury of Railroad Folklore: The Stories, Tall Tales, Traditions, Ballads, and Songs of the American Railroad Man* (1953); Norm Cohen, *Long Steel Rail: The Railroad in American Folksong* (1980); Rudolph Daniels, *Trains across the Continent: North American Railroad History* (2000); Lee A. Dew, *Arkansas Historical Quarterly* (November 1970); Lawrence R. Handley, *Arkansas Historical Quarterly* (Winter 1974); Steve Hoffus, *Southern Exposure* (Spring 1977); Richard D. Lawlor, *Tennessee Historical Quarterly* (Winter 1972); James L. McCorkle Jr., *Journal of Mississippi History* (May 1977); Joseph R. Millichap, *Dixie Limited: Railroads, Culture, and the Southern Renaissance* (2002); John Hebron Moore, *Journal of Mississippi History* (February 1979); Michael Rhodes, *North American Railroads* (2003); John F. Stover, *The Railroads of the South, 1865–1900: A Study of Finance and Control* (1955); Mark W. Summers, *Railroads, Reconstruction, and the Gospel of Prosperity: Aid under the Radical Republicans, 1865–1877* (1984).

Reconstruction

Reconstruction was the period from 1865 to 1877, when national efforts were concentrated after the Civil War on incorporating the South back into the Union. The period involved important constitutional and political issues, but from the viewpoint of cultural history Reconstruction's underlying significance was its effort to remake southern culture. Neither before nor since have Americans had the opportunity to refashion a peculiar region within a nation. Some northerners approached this in a spirit of vengeance, seeking to punish southerners for the war; others had political motives for wanting to reduce southern influence and insure Republican Party dominance and patronage for themselves; others were adventurers out to earn their fortune; still others were idealistic reformers hoping to aid freedmen adjust to their new status. Organizations such as the Freedmen's Bureau, the American Missionary Association, the northern Protestant denominations, the Republican Party, and the Union League represented the forces of the North. The image of the Yankee schoolmarm in the South was a prime example of this effort at cultural transformation. The Union soldier was another symbol of the effort: under the Reconstruction Act of 1867 the South was divided into five military districts and troops enforced government decisions. The cast of characters also included rapacious carpetbaggers, traitorous native scalawags, and ignorant freedmen.

This at least was the mythic view of Reconstruction. According to the myth of Reconstruction, for a decade after 1867 carpetbaggers, scalawags, and freedmen ran the governments of the southern states, looting their financial resources, passing high taxes, denying whites a role in government, and spreading terror throughout the region. Only with the withdrawal of federal troops in 1877 did the terror end. Historian William Dunning and his students produced numerous state studies of Reconstruction that codified this interpretation in the early 20th century. Claude Bowers spoke for a generation of historians when he called Reconstruction "the tragic era."

Beginning in the 1950s modern historians such as Kenneth Stampp, C. Vann Woodward, and others challenged and revised this mythic view. They built on W. E. B. Du Bois's earlier work, *Black Reconstruction* (1935). Reconstruction, for example, did not last as long in most states as the myth suggests. Southern conservative, white-dominated governments took power in Virginia and North Carolina in 1870, in Georgia in 1871, in Arkansas, Texas, and Alabama in 1874, and in Mississippi in 1876. Federal troops were not withdrawn in South Carolina, Louisiana, and Florida until 1877. Moreover, actual military rule ended in 1868 in all the states except Virginia, Mississippi, and Texas, where in each case it ended in either 1869 or 1870. Civil state governments were in charge after that, except for brief periods of reliance on the militia or federal troops. No more than 20,000 federal troops were involved in the process.

Fraud surely occurred in elections, but the same was true of elections elsewhere in that period and under the conservative regimes that followed the Reconstruction governments. Only 150,000 whites were disfranchised under the initial military phase of Reconstruction, out of an 1868 white registration of approximately 630,000. Few whites voted and many blacks did, and more than disfranchisement, this explains the character of the participants in the governments. Blacks held offices during Reconstruction, mostly at the local level, but only in South Carolina was there a black on the Supreme Court and only the South Carolina and Louisiana legislatures had a majority of blacks. And no black served as a southern governor.

"The tragedy of Reconstruction is that it failed," wrote Carl N. Degler in *Out of Our Past: Forces that Made Modern America* (1970). Degler points out that modern historical scholarship rejects the idea of Reconstruction as a unique period of bad government and oppression, but one should remember that generations of southerners believed the myth, which nurtured in them the belief in regional differences and a consciousness of past abuse at the hands of northerners and their own former slaves. At the end of the war southern whites had accepted the end of slavery, but Reconstruction showed their real commitment to a racial color line. This, not slavery, was a life-and-death matter. The thought of black social and political equality was unacceptable to whites. Southern whites united in the 1870s in resisting northern-imposed radical change designed to end white supremacy. After the war, in fact, the defense of white supremacy became more clearly a southern position than before. In the proslavery argument the defense of white supremacy was couched in the broader defense of slavery, but race itself became the key issue in the postbellum era.

Reconstruction was a struggle fought on many fronts. The same conflicts and issues seen in political life were also present in other areas of the culture. The Protestant denominations, for example, experienced troubles between blacks and whites, northerners and southerners. The spirit of Christian brotherhood did temper religious disputes more often than political conflicts. The northern missionary was an important symbol of Reconstruction. Missionaries came south to convert the freedmen and succeeded as blacks joined several northern-based, predominantly black denominations. They also came expecting that southern whites would reunite with the northern churches, but southern whites exercised their spiritual self-determination during Reconstruction by preserving their regionally organized churches — the Southern Baptist Convention, the Protestant Methodist Episcopal Church, South, and the Presbyterian Church in the United States of America.

Education also reflected issues of Reconstruction. Northern teachers believed education would end the ignorance and brutality that abolitionists said existed in the South. Schools would promote democracy and class equality in good American idealistic fashion. Blacks responded enthusiastically to the opportunities but faced the opposition of southern whites, who ostracized the northern teachers. Sometimes blacks also faced condescension of northern teachers who had their own racist preconceptions about southern blacks. Ultimately, though, the Radical Reconstruction program for public education was accepted. The southern white-controlled governments that came after Reconstruction did not reject black education, although insisting on racially segregated systems of instruction.

In the development of southern black culture, the Reconstruction period should not be seen as a failure. Much progress occurred in the development of vital institutions: in education and landowning, in particular, and in community development. New leadership was tested for the future. Scholars have shown that the family survived slavery and in Reconstruction became a typically southern focus for individual endeavors. There was, to be sure, a debate on approaches toward the future. Was the best strategy racial self-help or interracial cooperation? Some black leaders worked for civil and political rights, while others — and probably the majority of the freedmen themselves — favored land and education.

Efforts by southern whites to end Reconstruction began almost as soon as the radical state governments took power. Not until northern weariness with enforcing Reconstruction took hold could much be done. Virginia was the first state "redeemed," a term southern whites used. Redemption was the process of replacing the radical governments with conservative southern white governments. It was a well-organized political effort that also involved economic intimidation, community ostracism, political fraud, and violence. The Ku Klux Klan was the most common group involved in the violence. The Klan was a terrorist group that used violence against blacks and white Republicans in the name of preserving the morality and virtue of white civilization. Conservative whites eventually favored disbanding the Klan, which Nathan Bedford Forrest, its grand wizard, did in 1869, charging that outlaws had diverted it from its once high mission. Groups such as the Knights of the White Camellia and the

White Brotherhood carried on the Klan's tradition, and Congress passed three Enforcement Acts in 1870–71 to deal with their violence. Nonetheless, the use of violence and other tactics led to the election of white southern conservatives, who maintained power thereafter, ending the threat to white supremacy. These methods of regaining power were called the Mississippi plan, because they were perfected in that state in 1875–76. The Compromise of 1877, an informal, extralegal arrangement between southern Democrats and northern Republicans, brought the removal of federal troops from the South and the official end of Reconstruction.

Reconstruction had a positive legacy for the South. New state constitutions were written, many of which are still in effect as the basic documents of the states. It brought reforms in judicial systems, in codes of government procedure, in operation of county governments, in procedures for taxation, and in methods of electing governmental officials. Education was advanced, laying the basis for free public education. And constitutional amendments passed in that era supported the 20th-century civil rights movement's use of federal force to change the South's system of legal segregation.

Recent work on Reconstruction builds on the postsecessionist historians of the 1980s, who focused on shortcomings of Reconstruction state governments, including corruption, disastrous tax policies, and black disunity. They also criticized the limitations of northern reform efforts, seeing the supposed "radicalism" of the federal government as essentially conservative, with the U.S. army and the Freemen's Bureau working too closely with southern whites to cushion reform efforts.

Reconstruction scholarship, which traditionally focused on political issues, has incorporated more social and cultural perspectives, broadening the understanding of the political. Eric Foner identifies class conflicts as being as important as racial conflicts in interpreting Reconstruction. A key constituency in postwar Reconstruction politics, the Upcountry white yeomanry, was undergoing economic transformation that coincided with Reconstruction, leaving them without their former independence rooted in their local, subsistence economies. Class issues and economic concerns would weaken the yeomanry's long-term commitment to biracial politics. Foner points out that for a moment in time, "despite racism, a significant number of southern whites were willing to link their political futures on those of blacks."

Gender has also become a central concern in Reconstruction historiography, with women a newly acknowledged actor in the Reconstruction drama. The postwar redefinition of the household shaped Reconstruction politics, with such matters as legal marriage and control over women and children's labor becoming political issues.

CHARLES REAGAN WILSON
University of Mississippi

Dan T. Carter, *When the War Was Over: The Failure of Self-Reconstruction in the South, 1865–67* (1984); LaWanda Cox and J. H. Cox, *Reconstruction, the Negro, and the New South* (1973); Robert Cruden, *The Negro in Reconstruction* (1969); Laura F. Edwards, *Gendered Strife and Confusion: The Political Culture of Reconstruction* (1997); Eric Foner, *Reconstruction: America's Unfinished Revolution, 1863–1877* (2001), *A Short History of Reconstruction* (1990); John Hope Franklin, *Reconstruction: After the Civil War* (1961); Thomas Holt, *Black over White: Negro Political Leadership in South Carolina during Reconstruction* (1977); James M. McPherson, *Ordeal by Fire: The Civil War and Reconstruction* (1991); Michael Perman, *The Road to Redemption: Southern Politics, 1869–1879* (1984); Howard N. Rabinowitz, ed., *Southern Black Leaders of the Reconstruction Era* (1982); George C. Rable, *The Role of Violence in the Politics of Reconstruction* (1984); James G. Randall and David Donald, *The Civil War and Reconstruction* (1961); Heather Cox Richardson, *The Death of Reconstruction: Race, Labor, and Politics in the Post–Civil War North, 1865–1901* (2001); Kenneth M. Stampp, *Era of Reconstruction, 1865–1877* (1965); Daniel Stowell, *Rebuilding Zion: The Religious Reconstruction of the South, 1863–1877* (1998); Mark W. Summers, *Railroads, Reconstruction, and the Gospel of Prosperity: Aid under the Radical Republicans, 1865–1877* (1984); C. Vann Woodward, *Reunion and Reaction: The Compromise of 1877 and the End of Reconstruction* (1951).

Redemption

Over the past half century, the term "Redemption" has gained currency among historians of the South. When a historical term appears frequently in the literature, it usually means that it is becoming accepted as the most accurate or appropriate way of describing a particular historical period, episode, event, development, or trend. In this way, terms like the "Progressive Era," the "Civil War," and the "Early Republic" become orthodox terminology for the thing they refer to. In the case of Redemption, however, the term is now employed generally, but the episode it categorizes is not agreed upon. Redemption can allude to two different occurrences. It can refer either to the overthrow of Reconstruction between 1870 and 1876 or to the era after Reconstruction ended, from 1877 to the turn of the century. Thus, Redemption may be either a brief episode in the 1870s or a period, an era, of much longer duration.

The publication in 1951 of C. Vann Woodward's *Origins of the New South, 1877–1913* marked the beginning of historians' encounter with the notion of Redemption, because Woodward alluded to the men who came to power after the end of Reconstruction as "the Redeemers." By this, he meant to imply that these were new men, not the same elite that had formed the Confederacy and dominated it during the war. Historians before Woodward had designated these leaders "Bourbons," suggesting that, like the French royal family of that same name who returned to the throne after Napoleon, they had "learned nothing and forgotten nothing." They were therefore conservatives, even traditionalists. By introducing the new term "Redeemers," Woodward was arguing that this leadership cadre looked to the future and intended to redirect the southern economy toward manufacturing and railroads and usher in an urban, industrial society, in effect, moving it toward a "New South." The end of Reconstruction marked, therefore, something of a break with the past, a discontinuity in the course of southern history.

Since the Redeemers were in power in the decades after Reconstruction, many historians began to refer to this era as the "Redemption," sometimes using the term "the Redeemed South." All the same, the idea of these years as "the era of Redemption" or "the Redemption period" has never really been suggested in so many words. And, indeed, Woodward himself never proposed it. The term "Redemption" has been used to describe this period, but it has not really become accepted as, or attained the status of, a historical period.

More frequently, the word has alluded to the overthrow of Reconstruction in the 1870s. A collection of essays covering each reconstructed southern state was edited by Otto H. Olsen in 1980 and called *Reconstruction and Redemption in the South*, while Michael Perman's *The Road to Redemption: Southern Politics, 1869–1879* (1984) employed the term both in the book title and in the title of its part 2. The problem with the terms "Redemption" and "Redeemers" is that they were first coined by the opponents of Reconstruction and applied to themselves. In fact, the phrase "the road to redemption" was introduced as early as 1870 by John Forsyth, editor of the Mobile *Register*, who was a virulent opponent of Reconstruction. These former Confederates conceived their task to be the redemption of the white South from "Radical rule," that is, to save the South, or perhaps reclaim it, from the evils of Republican government. By calling their efforts "Redemption," they were sanitizing and justifying their overthrow, often by violent means, of duly elected governments.

On the other hand, Redemption does provide a name for the active and organized campaign undertaken by Reconstruction's opponents that lasted a number of years, ultimately toppling every one of the Republican-controlled governments, and thereby ending Reconstruction. Historians have often attributed the failure of Reconstruction to shortcomings among the southern Republicans themselves, such as internal rivalries, public corruption, poor political judgment, racial discrimination, and the like. Too often underemphasized, however, has been the ruthlessness and tenacity of Reconstruction's Democratic opponents and the massive onslaught they mounted against the Republican governments they considered illegitimate and alien.

Although it might not be the most appropriate term, Redemption therefore refers to this campaign by the Democrats, the party of the South's economic and social elite, to eliminate the Reconstruction government, state by state. The process took place in three stages. The first occurred between 1868 and 1870. As the new governments created by Congress's Reconstruction Act of 1867 were being formed in the defeated South and a new electorate of black voters was being created, the opposition's strategy was noncooperation and abstention. They refused to cooperate with the federal authorities, and they tried to defeat the new constitutions by abstaining from voting on them, thereby preventing the new governments from forming (a majority of the eligible voters had been required to participate under the terms of the Reconstruction Act of 1867, but Congress then changed the requirement). Once the governments were able to take office, the Democrats intimidated the newly enfranchised voters through violence carried out by the Ku Klux Klan, and they also acquiesced in the assassination of many of the leaders of the new Republican Party.

The second phase, from 1870 to 1873, involved public acceptance by the Democrats of the new Reconstruction governments and engagement in normal electoral competition with the Republicans who controlled them. At the same time, this overt accommodation to the reality of the new party and its new voters was accompanied by a less benign tactic. The Democrats began to subvert the Republican Party by encouraging dissension within its ranks by various means, both fair and foul. Then, whenever a division occurred and a bolt ensued, they threw their support to the bolting independents at election time, a tactic that was called fusion. By 1873 this two-pronged strategy of apparent acceptance but actual destabilization of the Republican Party had resulted in the defeat of the Republicans in Georgia, North Carolina, Virginia, Arkansas, and Texas.

In the final phase, from 1874 to 1877, Reconstruction's opponents abandoned their tacit collaboration and campaigned instead as out-and-out Democrats determined to destroy the remaining Reconstruction governments, which were located in those states with large proportions of African American voters — Alabama, Mississippi, South Carolina, Louisiana, and Florida. They played the race card vigorously so as to force whites to identify with and vote for the party of white supremacy, while they also unleashed violence and intimidation against the Republicans' black voters. Riots were instigated against blacks just before the elections in villages like Clinton, Miss., in 1875 and Hamburg, S.C., in 1876. Meanwhile, armed Confederate veterans on horseback, such as Wade Hampton's Red Shirts in South Carolina, paraded through black neighborhoods threatening likely Republican voters and sowing fear. As a result, the remaining Reconstruction governments fell to the Democrats.

This was how the South was "redeemed from Negro rule," as the instigators of these tactics described their movement. While it is useful to have a term to describe this aggressive and successful campaign by the Democrats to overthrow Reconstruction, "Redemption" is nonetheless an unfortunate epithet. Even though a historically authentic word, it is essentially a euphemism coined by its perpetrators to justify and sugarcoat their subversive and illegal actions. And therefore it is a problematic and pejorative term, rather like "carpetbagger" and "scalawag," which were coined by their detractors, the very same Democrats who overthrew Reconstruction and called it Redemption.

MICHAEL PERMAN
University of Illinois at Chicago

Edward Ayers, *The Promise of the New South* (1992); Eric Foner, *Reconstruction: America's Unfinished Revolution, 1863–1877* (1988); Glenda Elizabeth Gilmore, ed., *Who Were the Progressives?* (2002), *Gender and Jim Crow: Women and the Politics of White Supremacy in North Carolina, 1896–1920* (1996); J. Morgan Kousser, *The Shaping of One-Party Politics: Suffrage Restriction and the Establishment of the One-Party South, 1880–1910* (1974); James Tice Moore, *Journal of Southern History* (August 1978); Otto H. Olsen, ed., *Reconstruction to Redemption in the South* (1980); Michael Perman, *The Road to Redemption: Southern Politics, 1869–1879* (1984), *The Struggle for Mastery: Disfranchisement in the South, 1888–1908* (2001); W. Scott Poole, *Never Surrender: Confederate Memory and Conservatism in the South Carolina Upcountry* (2004); George C. Rable, *But There Was No Peace: The Role of Violence in the Politics of Reconstruction* (1984); C. Vann Woodward, *Origins of the New South, 1877–1913* (1951); Richard Zuczek, *State of Rebellion: Reconstruction in South Carolina* (1996).

Revolutionary Era

The Revolutionary era did not create the southern states, but it did help to create the South as a section. The efforts of national leaders during the period failed to bring the region fully and comfortably into the new national framework at the same time that events turned the South into a more distinct, uniform region. The resulting conflicts marked and marred the antebellum period and ultimately led to civil war.

Prior to 1774 southerners unquestionably thought of themselves as distinct from "eastern" or northern residents, but they thought in provincial rather than in sectional terms. When Patrick Henry in 1774 told the members of the First Continental Congress that he was "not a Virginian, but an American," the alternatives he chose were state and nation, not North and South. Fifteen years later he had changed both his outlook and his choice of terms. Fighting adoption of the Constitution, he was to argue that "southern" interests would be overpowered by the demands of "northern" states.

This is not, of course, to suggest that there was no thought of regional characteristics before the American Revolution. George Washington, arriving in Boston to take command of the Continental army, found New Englanders impossibly democratic. Abigail Adams blamed the institution of slavery for the cruelty and selfishness she found in southerners. Thomas Jefferson had clearly given some thought to sectional characteristics long before 1785, when he reported to the Marquis de Chastellux that northerners were hypocritical in religion, cool, sober, independent, and conniving, while southerners were fiery, voluptuary, indolent, generous, candid, and unsteady. Even after the adoption of the Constitution some South Carolina leaders found New York City a more acceptable location for the national capital than Annapolis because the former was more accessible.

At the beginning of the Revolutionary era at least three distinct regions existed within the South. The Chesapeake, with its tobacco culture, differed significantly from the South Carolina Lowcountry, with its rice, indigo, and majority-slave population. Even more distinct was a third region, the vast southern Upcountry, which stretched from Virginia into Georgia and was characterized by the absence of a full-scale slavery system, smaller landholdings, and a significant population of Native Americans. The Revolutionary era helped to erase many of the distinctions between these regions and contributed to a sense of sectional solidarity.

The South was ultimately defined, though, by slavery and the plantation system. The rise of the great planter families, the reduced flow of emigration from Europe, the fear of slave revolts, the desperate efforts to replicate English society, and the failure to develop a strong commercial or industrial economy were all tied to the institution of slavery. Edmund S. Morgan has suggested that even the commitment of Virginians to freedom during the Revolution was made possible by the establishment of an enslaved, and therefore powerless, working class.

The Revolution and the creation of a new nation intensified the distinction between North and South. At first the contradiction between fighting for freedom and holding slaves bothered many prominent southerners, just as it did leaders in the northern states. Pauline Maier, in a provocative essay on Richard Henry Lee, has argued that for at least one prominent Virginian, slavery was only one in a series of problems that made the South feel inferior, at least in theory, to New England. Virginia's colonial government had been inferior, the College of William and Mary was unsuitable, the economy was backward, and the climate was unhealthy. It seems unlikely that many prominent southerners gazed enviously at the "New England Way," but certainly many considered the effects of slavery unhealthy for both the enslaved and the enslavers.

With the formation of the new nation and the elimination of slavery in the colonies north of Maryland, the sense of southern isolation intensified. The Constitution marked the effort of a group of major leaders from Virginia and South Carolina to bring their states fully into the new national framework on acceptable terms. Compromises on slavery and restrictions on regulating trade marked that effort. Both northerners and southerners gave ground in a sincere attempt, temporarily successful, to bring the diverse interests of the two sections into harmony. In the long run this effort would fail, in large part because slavery became more firmly entrenched in the South.

The development of political parties in the new nation illustrates the growing sense of common economic and political interests among the southern states. Men like Madison and Jefferson opposed the Federalists not simply because the Washington administration was increasing the power of the new central government but, more important, because they feared the influences that seemed to dominate the policies of the Federalists. Alexander Hamilton's financial plans regarding the nation's and the states' debts and the Bank of the United States seemed to favor commercial interests, and the South appeared destined to remain agricultural and rural. The French Revolution and the ensuing conflict between England and France further divided the nation along sectional lines. The importance of trade brought the northern states to the support of England, while southerners were moved by the struggle of the French revolutionaries. Along with this hardening of sectional lines, the development of the cotton gin in 1791 was to reduce further the differences between the coastal areas and the backcountry, as the extension of slaveholding and the rise of an Upcountry planter class in South Carolina would illustrate.

By the time John Adams took office, the so-called Virginia-Massachusetts alliance, which had so often dominated the Revolutionary movement, was clearly broken, and at least some Federalists seemed determined to crush the

,outhern dissidents once and for all. The Alien and Sedition Acts and the machi-
nations of Alexander Hamilton drove the new nation close to disruption, and
he refusal of Adams and Jefferson to communicate for years after the election
of 1800 further illustrates the divisions between the two sections.

The Virginia presidents after 1800 seemed to unite the nation again and
bring the South not only back into the mainstream but into a position of dominance. Benjamine W. Labaree, among others, has noted that it was the merchants of the North who screamed for disunion by the second decade of the
19th century. Below the surface, however, the peculiar needs of the South, which
had presumably been guaranteed by constitutional compromises—the three-
fifths clause, the prohibition of export duties, the limits on restricting the slave
trade—were still at odds with the rest of the nation. The tendency of southerners to look to England and Europe for culture was to continue, and regional
dialects flourished.

Although it is important to remember that the South was not monolithic—
the area that produced John C. Calhoun also brought forth Andrew Jackson—
the dominant influences binding the South made it distinct from the North and,
ultimately, from the West. South Carolinians from the Charleston area who for
a time supported the Federalist Party and even the protective tariff were to be
disappointed in their hopes of creating a commercial center. In the end they
would lead the movement to secession and become the most rabid southerners of all.

Many contradictions existed in the Revolutionary South. Those who accused
New Englanders of being levelers became the firm supporters of the French
Revolution; southerners who cherished their English heritage gave up their
established church, while New Englanders clung to theirs; plantation owners
who condemned slavery and constantly worried over the issue in their private
correspondence refused to free their own slaves. Southerners were open, hospitable advocates of the ideals of freedom and virtue, fiercely loyal to their region, and confused by the seemingly insoluble problems of slavery.

The enthusiasms of the Revolutionary movement of 1774 to 1776, which
bound the colonists together and brought Patrick Henry to declare himself "an
American," soon faded as a variety of sections—and individuals—began to
pursue their own interests. The South was different, and that difference could
not be masked. In agriculture, in political institutions, in culture, and—most
important—in the development of slavery and the plantation system, there
were differences that set the region solidly apart from the rest of the nation.
The Revolution did not create those differences, and, for a time, the development of a new nation seemed to reduce their importance. But for good or for

bad the South was a distinct region in 1776 and despite many variations on the theme has remained so.

DAVID AMMERMAN
Florida State University

John R. Alden, *The First South* (1961), *The South in the Revolution, 1763–1789* (1957); Carl Bridenbaugh, *Myths and Realities: Societies of the Colonial South* (1952); Jack P. Greene, *The Quest for Power: The Lower Houses of Assembly in the Southern Royal Colonies, 1689–1776* (1963); Ronald Hoffman, Thad W. Tate, and Peter Albert, eds., *An Uncivil War: The Southern Backcountry during the American Revolution* (1985); Rhys Isaac, *The Transformation of Virginia, 1740–1790* (1982); Rachel N. Klein, *Unification of a Slave State: The Rise of the Planter Class in the South Carolina Backcountry, 1760–1808* (1990); Benjamin W. Labaree, *Patriots and Partisans: The Merchants of Newburyport, 1764–1815* (1975); Pauline Maier, *The Old Revolutionaries: Political Lives in the Age of Samuel Adams* (1980); Edmund S. Morgan, *American Slavery, American Freedom: The Ordeal of Colonial Virginia* (1975); Bruce A. Ragsdale, *A Planter's Republic: The Search for Economic Independence in Revolutionary Virginia* (1996); Charles Royster, *A Revolutionary People at War: The Continental Army and American Character, 1775–1783* (1979); Robert M. Weir, *The Last of American Freemen: Studies in the Political Culture of the Colonial and Revolutionary South* (1986).

Secession

The politics of secession consisted of the separate actions of individual southern states in late 1860 and early 1861 and did not represent a unified South acting as a concerted whole. Secession was triggered in November 1860 by the election of Lincoln to the presidency, at the head of a sectionalized Republican Party that was publicly committed to prohibiting the expansion of slavery into the federal territories and pledged—though recognizing slavery in the states where it already existed—to the ultimate extinction of slavery. Secession itself occurred in two distinct waves; in each it generally received its strongest support from those areas with the heaviest concentrations of slaves.

After a series of hastily called, highly localized, and often closely contested elections, delegates chosen on a countywide basis attended state conventions convened to decide the question of secession. Seven states had left the Union by 1 February 1861. This first wave—South Carolina, Mississippi, Florida, Alabama, Georgia, Louisiana, and Texas—comprised the original Confederate States of America, the provisional constitution for which was adopted in Montgomery, Ala., on 7 February 1861.

In the meantime Unionist sentiment remained dominant in the states of the

Upper South. Here the proportion of slaves to the total population was but half that of the Lower South (25 as opposed to 50 percent), fears of slave uprisings were less intense, economic and cultural ties with the free states were deeper, and the prosecessionist wing of the Democratic Party did not control local politics. Secession was temporarily halted. Nonetheless, virtually all political factions in the Upper South conceded the legal right of secession and agreed that any effort to coerce a seceded state back into the Union should be resisted.

Lincoln was inaugurated in early March, and any lingering opportunity for reunion floundered over the issue of the expansion of slavery. The second wave of secession was unleashed when Fort Sumter fell to the Confederacy in April and Lincoln called for state militia to put down what the North believed was a rebellion. Four additional slave states from the Upper South — Arkansas, North Carolina, Virginia, and Tennessee — joined the Confederacy rather than bear arms against fellow southern whites.

The secessionists had appealed successfully to values of individual autonomy, freedom from arbitrary power, and political self-determination. Embedded within America's 19th-century political culture and most often applied to whites only, these values could be used either for or against the Union and either to attack or to defend slavery. The politics of secession ensured that this debate would be settled only by a civil war.

WILLIAM L. BARNEY
University of North Carolina at Chapel Hill

Maury Klein, *Days of Defiance: Sumter, Secession, and the Coming of the Civil War* (1997); David M. Potter, *The Impending Crisis, 1848–1861,* ed. Don E. Fehrenbacher (1976); Ralph A. Wooster, *The Secession Conventions of the South* (1962).

Sharecropping and Tenancy

Since the post–Civil War years the plantation landlord and the tenant farmer have been among the most prominent figures in the nation's perception of the South. They have been graphic symbols of the region's ruralism, poverty, and cultural backwardness, and have exemplified the paternalism, exploitation, and social class dimensions of southern agriculture. And, indeed, until the mid-20th century these images reflected the reality of several million southerners whose lives were blighted by crop-lien tenancy.

Tenancy was a response to the disorganization and poverty of southern agriculture following the Civil War, becoming widely established by about 1880. Former slaves and landless whites needed access to land and compensation as laborers, but landlords lacked money for wages. To organize production, land-

owners allowed these workers to farm plots of 20 to 40 acres on a crop-shar
basis. They also undertook the support of their tenants during the crop seas
by extending credit for food and living necessities, secured by liens on their p
tions of the crop. Often this credit was arranged through rural store owners
furnish merchants, who were also general suppliers of feed, fertilizer, and i
plements. Planter-landlords with many tenants, however, frequently furnish
them directly, through plantation commissaries. This crop-sharing and lie
financing system was necessitated by the South's dearth of farm producti
credit. It reflected the limitations of agricultural technology; this system s
tained the large force of unskilled labor that was needed as long as cotton a
tobacco farming remained unmechanized.

Relatively few of the South's landless farmers were independent cash rente
most were share tenants and sharecroppers. The latter two levels of tenan
were defined by the farmers' contributions to production, their need for subs
tence credit, and how closely they were supervised by landlords. Share tena
often owned mules or equipment and might be able to supply some seed
fertilizer. Their furnishing needs varied, as did their supervision. According
their portions of the crop could be as much as two-thirds or three-fourths, le
of course, advances and interest. Sharecroppers, on the other hand, usually p
sessed no work stock or tools and contributed only labor. Dependent on li
credit for nearly all living necessities, and working under much supervisi
they ordinarily received no more than half the crop, from which furnishing a
interest were deducted.

In the chronically depressed southern agriculture of the late 19th and ea
20th centuries, tenancy increased steadily as many farmers lost their land
reached its peak in 1930, when the census counted 228,598 cash renters, 772,
sharecroppers, and 795,527 other tenants (mostly share tenants) in 13 southe
and border states. Tenancy was the dominant pattern in staple-crop produ
tion. In 1937 the President's Committee on Farm Tenancy estimated that te
ants and croppers represented 65 percent of all farmers in the Cotton Belt a
48 percent in tobacco regions. Approximately two-thirds of southern tenan
were white, although among croppers, the lowest tenure group, the numb
of whites and blacks were about equal. Share tenants and croppers and th
families easily comprised nearly half the 1930 southern farm population of 1
million.

Southern tenancy was the context for a culture of rural poverty. Tenants a
croppers received some of the lowest incomes in America, rarely clearing mc
than a few hundred dollars per year. Their more common experience, esp
cially in years of low crop prices, was to receive no net income at all becau

their shares of crops could not cover high-interest furnishing debts. These scant earnings kept rural southerners living right at the bottom of the national scale. Cotton and tobacco tenants lived in the fields they worked in pine-board cabins that lacked window glass, screens, electricity, plumbing, and even wells and privies. Thousands of families were without common household furnishings, stoves, mattresses, or adequate clothing and shoes. The poorest croppers subsisted on a furnish-store diet that relied heavily on salt pork, flour, and meal. Owning no cows or poultry and tending no gardens, they seldom consumed milk, eggs, or fresh vegetables. Malnutrition compounded wretched living conditions to make chronic illness a major feature of rural life, as malaria, pellagra, and hookworm infection stunted the development of children, shortened lives, and lowered the economic productivity of the poor.

Crop-lien tenancy was both exploitative and paternalistic. One of the familiar figures of southern rural lore was the tightfisted landlord who kept all accounts, charged exorbitant interest on advances, and took over his tenants' cotton for debts. As part of the local power structure, planters were in a position to make whatever settlements they wished, without challenge from illiterate tenants. Perhaps the greatest tragedy of this system was that exploitation was built into it. A landlord who was hard-pressed by mortgage and tax obligations, production costs, and low crop prices often could not profit without cutting as deeply as possible into his tenants' shares. Moreover, as planters extended credit, they also supervised tenants' farming, leaving the least skilled, especially, with little opportunity to develop competence and self-direction. Tenancy thus bred dependency among the poor.

Tenants had little security on the land. They worked under year-to-year verbal agreements that left landlords free to dispense with their services at settling time. With a great surplus of unskilled labor at hand, planters usually felt little need to hold dissatisfied or unwanted tenants. Most landless farmers were highly mobile, moving as often as every year or two. This transience was socially and economically wasteful; it deprived tenants of any role in their communities and reinforced illiteracy by preventing regular schooling of their children. It destroyed incentives to maintain farm property and contributed greatly to soil erosion.

The southern public's perception of tenancy conformed to traditional American views of poverty, which have been highly judgmental toward the poor. Rural poverty was so pervasive as to be the expected condition of landless farmers. Moreover, tenants and croppers were often seen as unworthy and shiftless people who had neither the ability nor the desire for self-improvement. Yet, at the same time, the assumption frequently expressed in the 1930s was that any ambitious, industrious farmer could work his way up an agricultural ladder, progressing from sharecropping to securer levels of tenancy, and then to small landownership. These persistent views were a major impediment to efforts to reduce rural poverty.

The Great Depression focused national attention on southern tenancy. Ironically, this public notice came as the system was beginning to break down. As hard times intensified, many landlords cut their own expenses by abandoning crop sharing, discontinuing furnishing, and converting to wage labor. This trend grew during the New Deal. Under the Agricultural Adjustment Administration (AAA) acreage-reduction contracts decreased labor needs and, in effect, encouraged landlords to dispense with tenants to avoid sharing government payments with them. This impact of the AAA was brought forcefully to public attention after 1935 by the protests of the Southern Tenant Farmers' Union. Tenancy continued as a national issue as the New Deal attempted to alleviate rural poverty through federal relief, the Bankhead-Jones Farm Tenant Act of 1937, and the Farm Security Administration.

Sharecropping declined significantly in the 1930s, and in the following decades southern agriculture underwent massive changes that swept away crop-lien tenancy. Mechanization was the most revolutionary development. From the 1930s onward the number of tractors on southern farms increased dramatically, and after World War II the cotton picker came into general use. Landlords employed wage workers to meet their more limited labor needs and discarded outmoded crop-sharing arrangements. Crop and livestock diversification and chemical weed control made farming still less labor-intensive. This transformation of southern agriculture was accompanied by a great exodus of the rural poor from the land and, in many cases, from the region.

PAUL E. MERTZ
University of Wisconsin–Stevens Point

James C. Cobb, *The Most Southern Place on Earth: The Mississippi Delta and the Roots of Regional Identity* (1992); David E. Conrad, *The Forgotten Farmers: The Story of Sharecroppers in the New Deal* (1965); Pete Daniel, *Breaking the Land: The Transformation of Cotton, Tobacco, and Rice Cultures since 1880* (1985); Gilbert C. Fite, *Cotton Fields No More: Southern Agriculture, 1865–1980* (1984); Charles S. Johnson, Edwin R. Embree, and Will W. Alexander, *The Collapse of Cotton Tenancy: A Summary of Field Studies and Statistical Surveys* (1935); Paul E. Mertz, *New Deal Policy and Southern Rural Poverty* (1978); Arthur F. Raper, *Preface to Peasantry: A Tale of Two Black Belt Counties* (1936); U.S. National Resources Committee, *Farm Tenancy: Report of the President's Committee* (1937); Rupert B. Vance, *Human Factors in Cotton Culture:*

A *Study in the Social Geography of the American South* (1929); Jeannie Whayne, *A New Plantation South: Land, Labor, and Federal Favor in Twentieth-Century Arkansas* (1996); Thomas Jackson Woofter Jr., *Landlord and Tenant on the Cotton Plantation* (1936).

Slave Culture

Torn from their native land and cast into the caldron of New World slavery, 11 million Africans were brought to the Americas during the four centuries of the Atlantic slave trade. The vast majority of those who survived the squalor and degradation of the "middle passage" and the early years of captivity — what Europeans called "the seasoning process" — suffered physical pain, psychological despair, and mental anguish. Many clung to their traditional languages, values, beliefs, and religions, but everywhere in the New World blacks found that in order to survive they would have to adjust to a new and alien environment.

In the southern colonies (later, states) the cultural transformation among slaves was relatively rapid. A majority of those who arrived in the colonies during the 17th century came from the West Indies and had already spent several years or more in the New World. During the 18th century those who came directly from Africa — called "outlandish" by the colonists — were either separated from the more "assimilated" slaves until they had accommodated themselves to the work routine or, as was the case in Virginia, sold to small slaveholders who worked alongside their bondsmen. Even as the proportion of Africans rose and the number of blacks spiraled upward — from 28,000 in 1700 (11 percent of the total colonial population) to 91,000 in 1730 (14 percent) — slave owners established procedures to reward those who learned English, acquired new skills, and embraced Christianity. Those who most readily accepted new values, called "New Negroes," and those born on American soil, called creoles, could expect preferential treatment, special privileges, and more prestigious jobs. After the closing of the Atlantic slave trade to the United States in 1808, an increasingly smaller proportion of the total slave population could claim any direct connection with West Africa.

Despite these demographic changes, many aspects of slave culture reflected the influence of Africa. In their family relationships slaves developed broad kinship patterns reminiscent of the familial patterns among various ethnic groups in their ancestral homeland. Even when families were broken by sale, blacks quickly reestablished kin networks whenever possible. Although most children lived with two parents and most adults lived in long-lasting marriages, slaves developed their own, unique family mores. They rarely, if ever, married first cousins; they engaged in sex prior to "marriage," usually with a future partner; they frequently gave their children names of blood kin outside the immediate family; and they had a much broader concept of "family" than most white southerners. "It was months before I learned their family relations," a teacher in South Carolina among the Sea Island slaves observed. "The terms 'bubber' for brother and 'titty' for sister, with 'nanna' for mother and 'mother' for grandmother, and 'father' for all the leaders in church and society, were so generally used I was forced to believe that they all belonged to one immense family."

If most slave owners showed little interest in slave families, other than encouraging childbearing, they similarly allowed blacks to practice their own brand of Christianity. One of the most distinctive cultural transformations among blacks was their adaptation of various African beliefs and rites to American Protestantism. Slaves dwelt on the Old Testament, not only because they identified with the children, but, as Nathan Huggins points out, "because those books conformed more to their own instincts for tribal and clan deities." In their use of the New Testament they focused on the story of Jesus, the parables, and the Crucifixion. Moreover, slaves ignored the doctrinal disputes between various Protestant sects, believed evil was a force of the universe rather than man's natural condition, and accepted Christianity as fundamentally collective and social rather than individualistic. Revealing their ancestral heritage, slave preachers filled their messages with cosmic imagery and played on the feelings and emotions of the congregation; and, unlike whites (except in a few evangelical sects), slaves actively participated in each religious service, shouting ecstatic prayers, singing deeply felt spirituals, clapping their hands, and fervently entreating, "Come Jesus, Come Lord. Be among us now."

Language, music, and folktales were also important in slave culture. These were, as Lawrence W. Levine indicates, "instruments of life, of sanity, of health, and of self-respect." In communicating with one another slaves sometimes retained elements of speech acquired in West Africa. Along the Sea Island Coast of South Carolina and Georgia blacks spoke Gullah (sometimes known as Geechee), a black dialect that blended various African words, names, and sounds with English. African equivalents were substituted for "tooth," "pregnancy," "alcohol," and "sweet potato"; other nouns, as well as adverbs, verbs, and adjectives, were frequently changed by using groups of words in the African style: "day clean" meant "dawn"; to "sweet mouth" meant to flatter. Blacks also used various forms of ironic or sardonic humor when discussing whites. At the same time, a number of slave words crept into the English language—"tote," "banjo," "cooter," "chigger," "yam," "okra," and "juke."

Slave music was an especially distinctive cultural form. Blacks did not draw a clear line between secular and sacred music and, like many of their ancestors in West Africa, sang a great variety of work songs and spirituals. Their lyrics, intonations, and singing style were marked by poetic beauty, emotional intensity, and rich imagery:

> Breddren, don' git weary,
> Breddren, don' git weary,
> Breddren, don' git weary,
> Fo d work is most done.
> De ship is in de harbor, harbor, harbor,
> De ship is in de harbor,
> To wait upon de Lord. . . .
> 'E got 'e ca'go raidy, raidy, raidy,
> 'E got 'e ca'go raidy,
> Fo' to wait upon de Lord.

Passed down from parents to children or from conjurers to other slaves, folktales and folk beliefs were important vehicles for transmitting social values and attitudes. Some stories came directly from Africa; others evolved out of circumstances in the New World; still others were a blending of the two. Almost all the tales involved a lesson of one type or another, lessons about mercy, prestige, patience, greed, wealth, strength, success, honor, and sexual prowess. In most instances slaves used an animal trickster to convey a portrait or to teach a lesson. In the famous Brer Rabbit and the Wolf tale, Rabbit discovers a tar baby at the side of the road (placed there by Wolf). When Rabbit's curiosity gets the better of him, he strikes the tar baby and becomes covered in the tar. Wolf comes to claim his prize. Realizing that Wolf will do exactly what he thinks Rabbit desires least, Rabbit begs not to be thrown into the briar patch, which is, of course, exactly what Wolf does, and wily Rabbit gains his freedom. Such tales were greatly enhanced by the manner of their delivery and the response of the audience. During the telling of a tale slaves chanted, mimicked, acted, and sang. "I don't know how they do it," one observer wrote, "but they will say 'lipity clipity, lipity clipity,' so you can almost hear a rabbit coming through the woods."

Although a distinct slave culture developed in America, relying on extended kinship networks, a different form of Christianity, and a rich folk heritage, many slaves rejected aspects of this culture. Overt resistance to slavery came primarily in two forms—individual acts of violence and running away. A close study of black rebelliousness in Virginia points to how African-born slaves typically ran away in groups and attempted to establish villages on the frontier whereas American-born slaves, who tried to escape in far greater numbers, ran away alone and tried to pass as free persons in the most settled areas of the state. The small number of large-scale revolts—compared to the numerous major revolutions in the Caribbean and South America—reveals the breakdown of West African communalism. Slaves who sought to improve their situation on the plantation and slaves who lived in towns and cities often sought to cast off the manners and attitudes of field hands. They dressed differently, learned to speak and act comfortably around whites, and whenever possible saved money and acquired personal possessions. In addition, as the doors to legal emancipation slowly closed during the antebellum decades, an increasing number of slaves, by one means or another, moved into what contemporaries called "quasifreedom"—halfway between bondage and liberty. While legally enslaved, these blacks lived independent, sometimes completely autonomous lives, securing their own employment, maintaining their own families, and moving about from place to place. At the same time, slaves who lived on small plantations or farms, along the frontier, or on plantations owned by French Creoles in Louisiana developed cultural mores and attitudes peculiar to their unique circumstances. In St. Landry Parish, for example, many slaves spoke French. The Civil War and general emancipation did not destroy slave culture, but more and more blacks saw the folkways of the past as a legacy of bondage and sought different values as a symbol of the future and freedom.

LOREN SCHWENINGER
University of North Carolina at Greensboro

John W. Blassingame, *The Slave Community: Plantation Life in the Antebellum South* (1972); Paul Finkelman, *Women and the Family in a Slave Society* (1989); Eugene D. Genovese, *Roll, Jordan, Roll: The World the Slaves Made* (1974); Herbert G. Gutman, *The Black Family in Slavery and Freedom, 1750–1925* (1976); Charles Joyner, *Down By the Riverside: A South Carolina Slave Community* (1984), *Shared Traditions: Southern History and Folk Culture* (1999); Lawrence W. Levine, *Black Culture and Black Consciousness: Afro-American Folk Thought from Slavery to Freedom* (1977); Roderick McDonald, *The Economy and Material Culture of Slaves: Goods and Chattels on the Sugar Plantations of Jamaica and Louisiana* (1993); Ted Ownby, ed., *Black and White Cultural Interaction in the Antebellum South* (1993); Dylan C. Penningroth, *The Claims of Kinfolk: African American Property and Community in the Nineteenth-Century South* (2003); Albert J. Raboteau, *Slave Religion: The "Invisible Institution" in the Antebellum South* (1978); George Rawick, *From Sundown to Sunup: The Making of the Black Community* (1972); Sterling Stuckey, *Massachusetts Review* (Summer

1968), *Slave Culture: Nationalist Theory and the Foundations of Black America* (1987); Thomas Webber, *Deep Like the Rivers: Education in the Slave Quarter Community, 1831–1865* (1978); Peter Wood, *Black Majority: Negroes in Colonial South Carolina from 1670 through the Stono Rebellion* (1974).

Slave Revolts

Few slaves in the antebellum South readily accepted their fate, yet large-scale slave revolts were fairly uncommon. Since the inception of slavery in colonial America, small-scale slave revolts had been frequently attempted, some even carried through to bloodshed. But perhaps due to fear and the lack of any substantial prior success, slaves primarily, and more effectively, used other day-to-day methods to anonymously protest their bondage. They participated in work slowdowns, broke tools, stole from their masters, set fire to barns and haystacks, and implemented other methods of impeding or sabotaging the efficiency of the farm or plantation upon which they worked. Nevertheless, the occasional large-scale revolt did occur—with dire and violent consequences.

One of the first effective mass slave revolts in colonial America was recorded in South Carolina on 9 September 1739. With the English and Spanish at war, the Spanish looked to disrupt English colonies by granting freedom to any slave who successfully deserted to St. Augustine. On the morning of the ninth, approximately 20 slaves gathered near the Stono River in St. Paul's Parish, which lay less than 20 miles from Charlestown (Charleston). The slaves fell upon a shop that sold firearms and ammunition, killed the two proprietors, armed themselves, and headed south toward St. Augustine. By 11 o'clock that morning the band of slaves was about 50 strong. Within a few hours, between 20 and 25 whites had been murdered. That evening a growing army of whites found the slaves resting in a field, killed half them, capturing and executing all but one—who eluded capture for three years—within the next three months. A Negro Act that was quickly finalized thereafter severely limited the autonomy of black slaves by restricting their freedom to learn to read, grow their own crops, and assemble in groups.

An aftereffect of Stono was an increasingly heightened southern awareness of the unrest of slaves and the instability of the institution. Escapes and runaways became common, and unexplained burning barns and haystacks were often blamed on malcontented slaves. As a result, southern whites meted out brutal and vicious penalties to keep any form of revolt to a minimum. After the 1790s, when the French island of Santo Domingo (also known as Saint Domingue) was rocked by a savage slave insurrection that cost some 60,000 lives and established an independent Haiti, both slave-owning and non-slave-owning whites lived in constant fear of slave uprisings. Until then, the vast majority of rebellion in colonial and postcolonial America had taken the form of escape and vandalism (notwithstanding isolated incidents such as Stono), but once word of the Santo Domingo revolt reached the American South, fear of rebellion spread like wildfire.

Three large-scale insurrections epitomize the virulent anger present within slaves in postcolonial America. Each of the three revolts was inspired in part by religion, the former two in particular by the Old Testament accounts of Moses' delivery of the children of Israel from bondage in Egypt and the Israelite invasion of the land of Canaan. Of primary influence for the latter was the New Testament's story of Christ in Jerusalem and the apocalyptic promise of a New Jerusalem. There is none more infamous than any one of the three, and none did more to show the country what a potential powder keg slavery was.

The first recorded large-scale postcolonial conspiracy was conceived in 1800 in Richmond, Va., by a 24-year-old slave named Gabriel Prosser. At the time, slavery was under attack by abolitionists across Virginia. Thomas Jefferson's antislave tract *Notes on Virginia* had been through seven editions by then, and Judge St. George Tucker, a law professor at William and Mary College, had recently published "A Dissertation on Slavery, with a Proposal for the Gradual Abolition of It in the State of Virginia." Antislavery pamphlets circulated freely. Much talk concerned liberty and equality because of the recent American and ongoing French revolutions. But there was no liberty or equality for those who wore black skin, and the antislavery chatter added up to little more than political rhetoric. Prosser, an articulate blacksmith, and his revolutionary conspirators were enraged at the hypocrisy. If they were not to be freed of their bonds by enlightened politicians, they would take their freedom by force, arguing that "we have as much right to fight for our liberty as any men."

Prosser and his conspirators plotted to march their more than 1,000 recruits into Richmond—then a town of 8,000 inhabitants—and set it ablaze, taking hostages such as Gov. James Monroe. Afterward slaves were to rise up together and fight for their freedom, as did those on Santo Domingo. But the conspiracy was doomed by infighting, confusion, floods, and, ultimately, slave informants. Whites alerted to Prosser's plan mobilized the Richmond militia, and Prosser was arrested before the first shot was fired. He and 34 of his collaborators went to the gallows.

The next large-scale insurrection came in 1822 Charleston, S.C., when Denmark Vesey was inspired by the congressional debates on slavery that resulted in the 1820 Missouri Compromise. A literate free slave, Vesey still had wives and children in bondage and was outraged by their condition and the institution of slavery itself. Soon Vesey plotted a revolt that would include city and country slaves alike. The plot was simple. At midnight six battle units would fall upon Charleston, capture the guardhouse and arsenal, seize major roads, and kill any who attempted resistance. From there Vesey intended to sail his now-free army to Haiti, but one lieutenant wanted the army to remain and hold Charleston indefinitely. Again infighting, communication breakdowns, and informants thwarted the plan. Five of the six battle units did invade Charleston, throwing the city into sheer terror, but the unorganized units were quickly suppressed by authorities. Vesey and 34 of his conspirators were hanged. Between Prosser's and Vesey's revolts not a single white person lost his life, but 70 insurgents were hanged.

Nine years later, rebels finally proved that they could pull off revolt, albeit just shy of success. In 1831 an intellectually gifted and religiously inspired field hand by the name of Nat Turner formed an insurrectionist plot in Southampton County, Va. "Nat the Prophet," as he was known, believed he had been called by God to lead a slave insurrection and had seen visions instructing him on his mission. Practically none was to be spared. Every man, woman, and child between Turner's master's plantation and Jerusalem, Va., some 12 miles away, was to be destroyed. Keeping the plan to himself until he had received the final sign, Turner recruited seven other slaves to march across the countryside killing every white person they came across en route to destroying Jerusalem.

Just after midnight, Monday morning, 22 August, Turner and four of his seven soldiers marched on the home of Turner's master, Joseph Travis. Soon all five white inhabitants, including two teenagers and an infant, were savagely executed. Turner and his band marched farm to farm massacring with bloodthirsty vengeance nearly every white person they came across, enlisting as many slaves and gathering as many weapons as they could along the way. By Monday, unorganized and now drunk on apple brandy, the army was repelled at Jerusalem, and Turner fled into the swamp. The majority of the insurrectionists, along with other innocent blacks, were captured and killed or jailed during a white counterfrenzy.

Turner remained at large for two months while all of Virginia and neighboring North Carolina waited, paralyzed with fear. Eventually he was caught and hanged, but not before at least 55 whites and nearly 200 blacks had lost their lives. From that point on, no white slaveholder lived comfortably with slavery. He now fully understood the fury and rage that lay beneath its burden.

JAMES G. THOMAS JR.
University of Mississippi

John B. Duff and Peter M. Mitchell, *The Nat Turner Rebellion: The Historical Event and the Modern Controversy* (1971); John Hope Franklin, *Runaway Slaves: Rebels on the Plantation* (2000); Thomas Wentworth Higginson, *Black Rebellion: Five Slave Revolts* (1998); Winthrop Jordan, *Tumult and Silence at Second Creek: An Inquiry into a Civil War Slave Conspiracy* (1993); Stephen B. Oates, *The Fires of Jubilee: Nat Turner's Fierce Rebellion* (1975); William Styron, *The Confessions of Nat Turner* (1967); Henry L. Tragle, *The Southampton Slave Revolt of 1831* (1971).

Slavery, Antebellum

Slavery permeated almost every aspect of antebellum southern life and culture. As an institution, slavery helped to define the South as a region, but it also intertwined the lives of white and black southerners in complicated ways. While the majority of slaves were housed on plantations in the so-called Black Belt, producing staple crops such as cotton, rice, tobacco, and sugar, a sizable minority experienced other forms of enslavement. Urban slaves were used for almost any form of work, ranging from the unskilled manual labor required at most ports, to highly skilled work in cotton factories and iron foundries. Recent historiography has shown that some urban slaves were permitted to hire themselves out for work, paying their master a weekly fee for doing so. This arrangement shifted onto the slave the burden of finding sufficient work and wages that would cover the master's demands, but it also gave some of them the independence to determine what work to accept and for whom to work. It was this flexibility that made slavery such a viable institution in the South.

The antebellum era saw a gradual shift in the attitudes that slave owners took toward their slaves. In response to abolitionist attacks about the cruelties of slavery, slave owners extolled the cradle-to-grave welfare provided for slaves and argued their labor force was better treated, and happier, than the factory workers of New England. This paternalist self-perception should be interpreted as an idealized view of race relations between masters and slaves. In reality, many masters reveled in the power they held over the enslaved and perpetrated horrific violence upon the bodies of those they claimed to protect. The docility and subservience of some slaves was therefore more a shrewd recognition that they were more likely to gain privileges from their master by adopting such a pose than proof that slaves meekly accepted their fate. In fact, the vibrancy of cultural life in the slave quarters demonstrates that masters' control over the lives of their slaves only went so far.

On most plantations the slave huts were grouped together in a "village," usually some distance from the main plantation house. This arrangement suited both parties since masters did not have their view spoiled by the hustle and

Five generations on Smith's Plantation, Beaufort, S.C., 1862
(Timothy H. O'Sullivan, photographer, Library of Congress [LC-B8171-152-A], Washington, D.C.)

bustle of the slave quarters, and slaves gained an important space where they could form communities without the usual degree of white interference in their lives. It was in the slave quarters where romantic attachments between slaves were formed, where children were born and raised, and where the elderly were cared for. Usually this space was the focus for communal singing and dancing and where stories and oral histories were repeated and learned. The larger the plantation the more important this community became in the lives of slaves.

On some of the largest plantations in coastal South Carolina and Georgia some slaves would have seen white people only rarely, since their work would have been directed by black "drivers," who in turn were instructed by a white overseer. It is no coincidence that these plantations saw the greatest retention of African culture into the antebellum era, with hybrid languages such as Gullah (or Geechee) flourishing among the slaves throughout this period.

The slave quarters were also the hub of informal economic activity among the enslaved. All slaves had time when their labor was not directed by the master or overseer, whether at the end of the working day or on Sunday, traditionally a day of rest. While some used this time for rest and socializing, many tended gardens of vegetables or nurtured chickens or other livestock for personal consumption or for trade. Other slaves made items such as baskets and sold them at local markets, and a thriving economic environment gradually emerged with slaves at the heart of it. At its most sophisticated, in coastal areas of South Carolina and Georgia where some slaves had considerable amounts of free time because of the nature of task labor, slaves operated Sunday markets in Savannah and Charleston and monopolized the supply of fresh vegetables, eggs, and milk to the urban population. In all areas slaves traded not only with each other but also with whites. Some masters bought produce from their slaves, but nonslaveholding white shopkeepers became increasingly important to the functioning of this economy. Not all the goods traded were legitimately grown or made by slaves; some items, especially tools and staple crops, were stolen from the plantation and sold for a fraction of their true value. White shopkeepers were complicit in this illegal trade since the potential profits were great while the risks of prosecution was small because the testimony of slaves would not be permitted against them in court. Although slave owners tried to suppress illegal trade, they never entirely succeeded.

Slave quarters were also at the heart of family life for the enslaved. Many slaves lived in family groups, and masters positively encouraged cohabitation among their slaves in the hopes that children would be the result. The union of a particular slave couple did not prevent the master, or other white men, from taking sexual liberties with enslaved women. Rape had terrible physical and psychological effects both on the women who endured it and the enslaved men who were powerless to prevent it. The mixed-race children resulting from such events were brought up among the enslaved community and could either be favored slaves because of their lighter complexion or prime candidates for sale since their very features reminded a mistress of her husband's infidelity. While many masters spoke of their desire to keep family groups together, most sold children away from their parents, or vice versa, when finances demanded

t. Given the stresses and strains on family life among the enslaved, it is remarkable that any form of family structure survived, but by adopting extended family networks, and by absorbing nonfamily members into a fictive kinship group, the family remained a crucial part of plantation life for most slaves.

While Anglican missionaries had tried to Christianize slaves during the early 18th century, Christianity did not really take hold among the enslaved until the post-Revolutionary era. Baptist and Methodist denominations were generally the most popular among slaves since all members, regardless of color or status, were regarded as equal before God. Moreover, the informality of evangelical services allowed for singing and dancing that had always been part of African worship but was normally frowned on by Anglicans. In some areas, separate black churches were founded with black preachers preaching to large black congregations who traveled from a large surrounding area to worship as a community. Where no such church existed, services were sometimes led by black preachers on plantations, but gradually whites became suspicious that preachers were using the cover of religious meetings to spread dissent and discontent among the slaves. In the 1830s planters sponsored a plantation mission system whereby white preachers were invited onto plantations to preach to the slaves, provided that they stressed biblical exhortations to loyalty and hard work rather than promising freedom and equality. These missions were not particularly successful since most slaves continued to be familiar with biblical stories, such as Moses leading the children of Israel out of bondage in Egypt, that were more analogous to their situation.

While many slaves accepted the teachings of Christianity, and were grateful for the solace and hope that it brought them, others continued to believe in traditional African magic. On many plantations there were particular individuals with knowledge of African medicine and magic. Herbal remedies were popular among slaves and were probably more effective than many Western medical techniques in the antebellum era. Other uses for herbs included potions and poisons, which could be used against the master, his family, his livestock, or another slave. Some slaves believed that the use of magic could give them superhuman strength or protection from harm or could inflict illness or death upon their enemies.

The use of magic by slaves is an example of how many resisted the institution of racial slavery and the power of white masters. Far from meekly accepting their fate, most slaves engaged in acts of passive or active resistance. In the most extreme cases, slaves rose up in revolt against their masters, killing and maiming whites until captured or killed. The most famous slave revolt in antebellum America was led by Nat Turner in Southampton County, Va., in

1831. Turner saw himself as a messianic figure who had received messages from heaven exhorting rebellion, and he subsequently led a killing spree that saw at least 55 white men, women, and children indiscriminately murdered. The response of local whites was swift and lethal. Most of the rebels were killed, but some, including Turner, were captured, put on trial, and duly executed. The well-organized nature of white militias, and their numerical majority in most regions of the South, meant that most slave rebellions were doomed to fail from the outset. Slaves knew what the consequences of outright rebellion would be and few were willing to engage in what would effectively be a suicide mission. Although there are many reports of slaves striking out with lethal force against a particular master or overseer and meeting the same fate as Turner as a result, such episodes were normally sparked by specific grievances and limited to specific individuals, rather than being organized plots.

The ineffectiveness of violence as a means of resistance led many slaves to prefer passive resistance to rebellion. One of the most popular forms of resistance was running away. Most commonly runaways fled the plantation for a short period of time, thereby denying their labor to their master, and returned home after a few days. Returning runaways were nearly always whipped, but the point had been made that slaves retained some agency over their labor and that specific examples of mistreatment would lead to such acts of resistance. Women were less likely than men to run away since they more commonly had family ties that bound them to the plantation. Some runaways genuinely sought their freedom, and the published narratives of some successful runaways are testimony to the incredible ingenuity of those who fled. Henry "Box" Brown had himself packed into a crate and shipped to a free state; Frederick Douglass borrowed free papers from a free black sailor and took a train to freedom; Ellen Craft used her light skin to pretend to be a white slave owner so that she and her husband could escape slavery. Some runaways were assisted by sympathetic whites, or by friendly free blacks, but most had to rely on their own ingenuity and resources.

Running away was only one form of resistance popular among slaves. Some feigned illness to avoid work; some women claimed to be pregnant when they were not; tools and machinery were mysteriously broken; supplies were stolen; and instructions were deliberately misunderstood. The plantation therefore resembled something of battleground between masters, who wanted as much work from their slaves as possible, and slaves, who generally sought to do as little work as they could get away with. The behavior of slaves to some degree conformed to the stereotypes that masters believed. Most masters saw their slaves as both lazy and stupid, and by living up to this stereotype by not understanding instructions or working slowly, slaves actually did less work. Of course, there was always a fine line between getting away with passive resistance and receiving a beating from the master or overseer, and judging just how far this behavior could be pushed relied on long experience of the system of slavery and of the attitudes of a particular slave owner.

Although many slaves resisted bondage, their actions were never sufficient to endanger the actual system of slavery. Whites were well organized militarily, and the slave-owning elite expended significant effort to ensure that nonslave-holders supported the status quo rather than siding with slaves. Elites stressed the privileges of race that bound all whites together, and they employed poorer whites as overseers and patrollers, effectively making them part of the regime of slavery. Ultimately it would take a bloody Civil War to achieve the freedom long desired by the enslaved.

TIM LOCKLEY
University of Warwick

John W. Blassingame, *The Slave Community: Plantation Life in the Antebellum South* (1979); William Dusinberre, *Them Dark Days: Slavery in the American Rice Swamps* (1996); Eugene D. Genovese, *Roll, Jordan, Roll: The World the Slaves Made* (1975); Walter Johnson, *Soul by Soul: Life Inside the Antebellum Slave Market* (1999); Jacqueline Jones, *Labor of Love, Labor of Sorrow: Black Women, Work, and the Family from Slavery to the Present* (1995); Albert J. Raboteau, *Slave Religion: The Invisible Institution in the Antebellum South* (1978); Betty Wood, *"Women's Work, Men's Work": The Informal Slave Economies of Lowcountry Georgia, 1750–1830* (1995).

Slavery, Colonial

Labor was the key to wealth in the colonial South, as it was throughout the colonial world. Planters sought inexpensive labor to produce staple commodities for export to Europe and other colonies. Virginia, the first English southern colony, initially relied on indentured servants (mostly young males from England) to fulfill their labor needs, but for a variety of reasons the colony slowly but steadily shifted to Africans.

European colonies in Brazil and the West Indies had established an extensive slave trade with Africa in the 16th century, but it was Dutch traders who brought the first Africans to Virginia via the West Indies (in 1619). Some Africans were treated as indentured servants in early Virginia and eventually received freedom, but by the mid-17th century, slavery had become ensconced as a central form of labor and social control over African workers.

Planters turned to African slave labor for a variety of reasons. As England developed more American colonies, there were relatively fewer available indentured servants to perform plantation labor. Moreover, English merchants invested their capital in the slave trade, establishing direct links with the African continent. English planters also learned that they could work their Africans harder than their European workers, as England permitted the employment of brutal punishments to discipline Africans. As the mortality rate for all Virginians declined, planters recognized that keeping more expensive slaves for a lifetime of labor was more profitable than purchasing cheaper indentured servants who would receive freedom after three to seven years. Finally, planters could increase their capital investment through possession of their slaves' offspring.

When South Carolina was settled in 1670, there was no question that Africans would provide a key source of labor. Unlike Virginia, where slavery evolved before legislation defined it, the Lords Proprietors, the owners of Carolina, provided for the institution in the Fundamental Constitution that governed the colony. Many of Carolina's planters emigrated from the plantation colonies of the West Indies, particularly Barbados, and transferred their laborers with them. Africans played a seminal role in the establishment and development of Carolina by performing numerous tasks, including cattle ranching, construction, fishing, soldiering, piloting of boats, scouting, hunting, and introducing methods for cultivating rice, which became the colony's main crop. By the end of the first decade of the 18th century, Africans comprised the majority of South Carolina's population and were increasingly confined to rice production.

Both Virginia and South Carolina restricted their slave population through a variety of legal measures designed to curtail mobility and individual freedom. Slave patrols were created to police the slaves, manumission was restricted, and marriages between Africans and Europeans were outlawed. Africans, slave and free, were barred from testifying against whites. Masters were permitted to maim and kill their slaves in order to retain control over an often recalcitrant workforce. Growing discontent among the slaves and increasing fear among the planters led to a dangerous situation in South Carolina, where slaves rebelled in 1739 in the Stono Rebellion. The slave-based society survived the tumult, and by the middle of the 18th century, slavery as an institution stabilized in the entire South, as the planter elite both strengthened their methods of social control and began to transform the institution through a paternalistic ideology by which slaves gained privileges, such as freedom from Sunday labor, access to personal plots of land, the opportunity to live in family units, and the enjoyment of sundry economic rewards.

White southerners, particularly in the Carolinas, also engaged in an extensive Indian slave trade that extended from the Florida Keys west to the Mississippi Valley. The peak period for this trade was from 1670 through the second decade of the 18th century, when more Native Americans were exported from Charles Town (Charleston) than Africans were imported. The Carolinians employed Native Americans to capture other Native Americans, most of whom were shipped to other colonies, and by this trade earned the capital with which they purchased Africans and built their plantations.

The only English colony to prohibit slavery was Georgia (founded 1733) during the first two decades of that colony's existence. Among the many reasons slavery was barred by the Trustees of Georgia, the colony's owners, was their belief that slavery degraded free labor. Georgia's inability to flourish led the "Malcontents" to lobby Parliament for slavery's legalization, and when it did occur, in 1755, planters from South Carolina and the West Indies flocked to the colony with their slaves to develop plantations. The peak years for importation of Africans to the South was in this same period (1725–50), and the profits to be made by slave labor were too great for the free people of Georgia and other colonies to resist. By the mid-18th century southern planters could see no alternative to slave labor, which had allowed them to develop a flourishing plantation economy. Racist ideas of the peculiar suitability of Africans to labor in hot countries, and of the difficulty of Europeans performing labor in the same, fueled the drive for more Africans. By the end of the colonial period Africans comprised approximately 40 percent of the population of the southern British colonies.

The ideology of racism was used to justify cruel treatment and the draconian measures employed to keep Africans enslaved. Nevertheless, many planters came to believe that their slaves possessed souls and cultivated their bondpeoples' conversion to Christianity. Whatever conversion did to assuage a slave owner's conscience, it also resulted in the large-scale Christianization of their laborers. Despite the brutality and exploitation of slavery, both slaves and slave owners came to interact in numerous positive ways, as Christianity became one of the many means by which slaves and masters communicated their interests, exchanged culture, and learned to live with the slave system. By the end of the colonial period, many colonists condemned the international slave trade for its cruelty and advocated improved treatment for their slaves, but very few opposed the institution of slavery on moral grounds until the American Revolution. Simultaneously, the African slaves became African Americans, as the cultural distinctions that divided slaves one from the other in the colonial period gave way to the development of a strong sense of community and place. Many bondpeople learned that, although they could not overthrow the institution of slavery, they could resist it in subtle ways while building lives for themselves within it.

ALAN GALLAY
Western Washington University

Alan Gallay, *The Indian Slave Trade: The Rise of the English Empire in the American South, 1670–1717* (2002); Winthrop D. Jordan, *White over Black: American Attitudes Toward the Negro, 1550–1812* (1968); Edmund S. Morgan, *American Slavery, American Freedom: The Ordeal of Colonial Virginia* (1975); Philip D. Morgan, *Slave Counterpoint: Black Culture in the Eighteenth-Century Chesapeake and Lowcountry* (1998); Peter H. Wood, *Black Majority: Negroes in Colonial South Carolina through the Stono Rebellion* (1974).

Spanish-American War

Congress declared war against Spain on 11 April 1898. The conflict grew out of the general imperialist sentiment of the age, the desire of the American business community for overseas trade, the frustrations accompanying economic depression in the early 1890s, the growth in American military power, and humanitarian interest in the supposed Spanish repression of the Cuban people. The war was short and decisive, lasting 113 days, costing 5,500 American lives (most of those died from disease or accident rather than in battle), and resulting in American control of Cuba, Puerto Rico, Guam, and the Philippines.

Southerners supported the war enthusiastically, reflecting longtime regional interests in the Caribbean. Southerners had dreamed of controlling Cuba — the "Pearl of the Antilles" — before the Civil War. Mississippian John Quitman had helped plan a filibustering expedition to seize the island in the mid-1850s. Southerners saw Cuba as the target for sectional Manifest Destiny, which would extend plantation slavery to Cuba and promote southern political strength. This hope for a southern empire in the Caribbean was the "purple dream" immortalized by Stephen Vincent Benét in *John Brown's Body*.

In the 1890s the Spanish-American War brought prosperity to parts of the South. New South boosters saw the war as a boon to regional economic growth. Chickamauga, Tenn., Mobile, Ala., and New Orleans were assembly points for American troops, while Tampa, Fla., was the chief training and embarkation site for the invasion of Cuba. South Florida had become before the war the center of Cuban settlement in the United States, as refugees from the island worked in cigar factories and planned the overthrow of Spanish rule. José Martí, the chief Cuban revolutionary figure, had visited in Tampa in 1891.

Racial attitudes were important in creating southern reactions to the war. The nation had accepted the "white man's burden" in this era of Anglo-Saxon racism. Southerners saw this national attitude as a confirmation of regional segregation. Over 10,000 black troops — known as "smoked Yankees" — served in the volunteer army that waged war. The four regular-army regiments of black troops, who had served in Indian campaigns in the West, moved to the South in reparation for a Cuban invasion. They endured segregated restaurants, hotels, waiting rooms, saloons, and other public facilities, and violence resulted. About ,000 black soldiers were stationed in Tampa and Lakeland, Fla., and tensions there led to rioting between white and black soldiers and civilians. Shortly after the rioting, black troops played a key role in the Cuban invasion, especially at San Juan Hill.

The Spanish-American War was a landmark of North-South, post–Civil War reconciliation. Young men from Dixie eagerly volunteered for the fighting. Methodist bishop Warren Candler spoke for many other southerners when he said that the military tradition, the memory of the Confederate past, and belief in fighting for principle had inspired the patriotism of 1898 in the South. "Visions of heroic sires inflamed the courage of gallant sons," he said in a speech. Southern newspapers pronounced the Spanish-American War the real end of the Civil War. Some of the unreconstructed, to be sure, proposed that southern troops be allowed to wear gray uniforms while fighting for the Union, but that was not taken seriously. Two veterans of the Confederate cause, Fitzhugh Lee and "Fighting Joe" Wheeler, were appointed as major generals, and Wheeler was credited with the best line of the war. As the Spaniards retreated during the battle, Wheeler yelled, "We've got the damn Yankees on the run." The saying was widely retold, and the humorous appreciation of it by all sides contributed to the feeling of reconciliation. The spilling of northern and southern blood in a common cause, fighting for liberty, represented a new national bond. Southerners now honored young heroes of nationalism. "These dead, at least, belong to us all," said a Confederate veteran's meeting in 1899. President William McKinley promoted this spirit, pledging in Atlanta in 1898 that the national government would now care for Confederate graves. The memory of the Spanish-American War was preserved in the stories of, and tributes to, the veterans of the struggle and by the regional folk songs such as "Manila Bay."

CHARLES REAGAN WILSON
University of Mississippi

Paul Buck, *The Road to Reunion, 1865–1900* (1938); Frank Freidel, *The Splendid Little War* (1958); Willard B. Gatewood Jr., *"Smoked Yankees" and the Struggle for Empire:*

Letters from Negro Soldiers, 1898–1902 (1971); Gerald Linderman, *The Mirror of War: American Society and the Spanish-American War* (1974); H. Wayne Morgan, *America Road to Empire: The War with Spain and Overseas Expansion* (1965); Ivan Musicant, *Empire by Default: The Spanish-American War and the Dawn of the American Century* (1998); G. J. A. O'Toole, *The Spanish War: An American Epic, 1898* (1984); Nina Silber, *The Romance of Reunion: Northerners and the South: 1865–1900* (1993); David F. Trask, *The War with Spain in 1898* (1981).

Vietnam War

The American South, whose people were the only group of Americans to suf fer a military defeat prior to the Vietnam conflict, assumed an important rol in leading the United States out of the malaise that followed the collapse o American efforts in South Vietnam. The southern way of handling defeat ha been to persist in the idea that the cause is never lost, that defeat is beyond be lief, so deeply are the roots of honor sunk into a land dearly loved.

The key to understanding the South's regional contribution to the Vietnan War is its rhetoric of belligerence, rhetoric backed by action—out of neces sity—to serve a cause with honor. To a southerner, all of this follows naturall from an ingrained sense of duty. As the Vietnam War ground to its perplexin conclusion, people in many parts of the nation wavered in their sense of pur pose, but the South's fundamental conservatism held fast. Every president sinc Richard Nixon has needed a "southern" strategy, and the core of that strateg rests in an appeal to patriotism—to a reverence for American ideals, whicl for southerners includes a readiness to defend democracy aggressively and th essential right of self-determination, no matter how cloudy and uncertain th specific case may be. Such an attitude is clearly central to the policy position and actions of George W. Bush's presidency early in the 21st century.

Texan Lyndon Johnson believed in the power of this rhetoric, but he los faith in it with the sweep of nightmarish television images and week-by-weel statistics of American casualties, which led to his surrender of the presidency Beginning with the 1968 election and continuing through the 1970s, George C Wallace—operating sometimes as a nominee of the American Independen Party and sometimes as a Democratic Party candidate—championed the rhe toric of belligerence, thus giving Richard Nixon, Jimmy Carter, Ronald Reagan George H. W. Bush, Bill Clinton, and George W. Bush a clear signal on how t win the heart of the South in the post-Vietnam era. Ironically, the southerne Carter did not catch the signal; he became the next president after Johnsor to see his ambitions fall to ruin in the wake of perceived American militar weakness during the Iranian hostage crisis. Carter's pardon of Vietnam draf esisters—his first major act as president—had led southerners much earlier to onclude that he was not zealous enough on the matter of patriotism. Clinton, who was careful to keep himself out of involvement in the Vietnam War, used military force occasionally, but he did not foreground patriotism in ways that might well be expected of someone from the South.

In the Iraq war of 2003, quite a large number of political leaders from the South who either avoided military service through various deferments or found safe military service options that would not involve time in Vietnam wound up igorously promoting war. Their detractors, keying on the disparity between personal practice in the past and present rhetorical stance, regularly refer to his collection of leaders as "Southern Chicken Hawks," a group that includes George W. Bush (Texas), Dick Armey (Texas), Bob Barr (Georgia), Tom Delay (Texas), Trent Lott (Mississippi), and Saxby Chambliss (Georgia), who won his 002 election to the Senate with campaign tactics that included challenging the patriotism of incumbent senator Max Cleland, a Vietnam veteran severely wounded in combat.

During the major escalation of an American military presence in Vietnam, the war had distinctly southern overtones. A Texan's administration sent the marines ashore. Bill Moyers, another Texan, had to field the early hard questions about combat activity involving U.S. troops, although when the questions loomed larger than the answers, Moyers departed, a foreshadowing of what would happen later to Lyndon Johnson.

For Dean Rusk, a native of Cherokee County, Ga., Vietnam became the dark center of his tenure as secretary of state. And heading the order of battle in Vietnam was William C. Westmoreland, of Beaufort County, S.C. When Westmoreland first left the South for West Point at the outset of his military career, he was reminded by his great-uncle (a veteran of Gettysburg who had also been with Lee at Appomattox) that Lee and Jackson, not just Grant and Sherman, had gone off to the academy in their time. Westmoreland brought to the Vietnam War a clear image of the honorable warrior, an image inherited directly from Robert E. Lee. The image, of course, was not sufficient to win the war.

The southern quality of the war reached far beyond Westmoreland himself. n the early 1970s, four out of five army generals were from southern towns. The disproportionate overrepresentation of southerners in the army and marines reached all the way down to the lowest ranks; many southern blacks were brought into the army through Robert McNamara's three-year Project 100,000. This infamous scheme opened up military service to "marginally qualified" youths as an escape from impoverished backgrounds. All too frequently, however, the exit led only to Vietnam—or to desertion. Largely because of the southerners placed in the service through Project 100,000 (which eventuall involved more than 240,000 men), the South is overrepresented in the cases c military desertion.

Another blemish on the honor of southerners came through the court martial of William Calley, a Floridian. Nevertheless, many southerners wer quick to defend Calley, angrily denouncing the hypocrisy of those who woul punish Calley while at the same time forgiving draft resisters. Senator Stror Thurmond of South Carolina made this point frequently, though he was hard pressed to reconcile his harsh views on Vietnam protesters with the historica precedent in the pardon extended to southerners in the aftermath of the Civi War.

The South had only 22 percent of the nation's population, but it produce 29 percent of the Medal of Honor recipients for Vietnam service, reaffirmin its claim to honor. These figures confirm the enduring nature of an outlandisl rage to valor in the region, sometimes manifesting itself in nonsensical way: which have been well documented in war scenes from William Faulkner's fic tion of an earlier time. Moreover, on the home front the protest movemen against the war never reached the cataclysmic proportions in the South tha it did in the North and far West. Despite a few major incidents on souther campuses — particularly the shooting death of two blacks by policemen durin, the 1970 confrontation at Jackson State — and student-led marches and demon strations throughout the South, protest activities tended to be more moderat there than elsewhere.

Nevertheless, some voices of protest sounded. An important protest move ment within the military developed at Fort Bliss in El Paso, Tex., where th GI's for Peace staged public rallies and published a newsletter, *Gigline*. Alsc at the University of North Carolina at Chapel Hill, drama teacher Paul Green best known for writing a series of outdoor historical plays, including *The Los Colony*, became an early, outspoken critic of the Vietnam War. In Chapel Hill after a series of student-administration standoffs in the late 1960s, the war re sistance movement evolved to a weekly silent vigil in front of the post office o East Franklin Street. Yet even as quiet as this protest was, it drew the ire and con tempt of Jesse Helms, then a radio commentator for WRAL in Raleigh. At on point, when the North Carolina legislature was considering creation of a stat zoo, Helms responded that there was no need to create a zoo — all the legisla tors needed to do was put a fence around the university in Chapel Hill. Such response typified the stance taken by southern practitioners of the rhetoric o belligerence. L. Mendel Rivers of South Carolina, chairman of the Armed Ser vices Committee, asserted during the war that Americans protesting the gov

rnment's war policy were "filthy buzzards and vermin," a viewpoint revived
nd invigorated through the 1980s and 1990s by Senator Helms of North Caro-
na to denounce anyone who questioned the use of American military capa-
ilities wherever and whenever the need might arise.

Backing for such a determined position on the American role in Vietnam
ame readily and regularly from the churches in the South, particularly those
epresented at the Southern Baptist General Convention. The military itself had
formidable presence in the South as well. In 1967, a typical war year, 42 per-
ent of the stateside payroll for military personnel went to the 11 former states
f the Confederacy. Two outcomes merit special attention. First, this particu-
ar infusion of federal dollars resulted in dependence on the military by an
xtended network of people and proliferation of sprawling ghettos of seamy
ightclubs and other clip joints around military bases. These situations con-
nued after the Vietnam conflict ended; thus, the South's economic status was
ed closely to war. Second, large numbers of soldiers who went to Vietnam
assed through training at southern bases: Fort Benning and Fort Gordon in
eorgia, Fort Bragg in North Carolina, Parris Island in South Carolina, and
ort Polk in Louisiana.

Many southern bases built mock Vietnamese bases for training soldiers in
ne ways of war, Vietnam style. In this endeavor the climate of the South con-
ributed significantly, giving trainees a feel for the heat, humidity, and other
iscomforts to be encountered in combat. Anyone entering the main gate at
ort Polk, La., was greeted by an unabashed declaration of southern pride in
reparing soldiers for battle in Vietnam: "Welcome to Ft. Polk, Birthplace of
ombat Infantrymen for Vietnam."

Occasionally, people of southern origin found themselves at odds with the
American role in Vietnam—and hence at odds with their own background.
'hree such southerners, Dan Rather (Texas) and Tom Wicker and David Brink-
y (both of North Carolina), often seemed to be in the vanguard of critics of
ne war in the national press; Wicker eventually landed on President Nixon's
enemies list" for his denunciation of several military strategies in Vietnam.
Vhile the peace talks dragged on, Brinkley took sharp issue with the account-
ng of American dead each week in terms of numbers only. As their broadcast
areers developed, Rather, Wicker, and Brinkley all left the South, and perhaps
nis distance, coupled with their journalistic preoccupation with facts instead
f rhetoric, contributed to their individual variation from the southern norm.

The case of the southern veteran after the war also shows some cracks in the
hetoric of belligerence. The proportion of Vietnam veterans to total popula-
ion in the 1980 census is the same for the South as for the nation generally,

about 22 percent. The South was disproportionately represented in enlistees, so it appears that many southern soldiers chose to remain in the military rather than return to civilian life. For the veterans who returned ravaged by the horrors of their combat experience, coping with the mood at home has not always been easy. John Givhan's life story, *Rice and Cotton: South Vietnam and South Alabama* (2000), accounts for one man's remarkable efforts to maintain spiritual integrity and solidarity with his culture of origin after the loss of a leg in Vietnam. James R. Wilson's *Landing Zones: Combat Vets from America's Proud Fighting South, Remember Vietnam* contains stories in a similar vein. Southern veterans interviewed in Myra McPherson's earlier *Long Time Passing: Vietnam and the Haunted Generation* had reflected some of the same sense of dislocation suffered by veterans across the nation. As elsewhere, many veterans in the South suffer quietly.

One distinguished exception to this pattern is James Webb, a decorated marine veteran and author of *Fields of Fire* (1978), perhaps the most widely read novel of the Vietnam War, with over a million copies in print. Webb's southern heritage is reflected in one of the novel's main characters, a lieutenant named Robert E. Lee Hodges. Three members of the Hodges family died at Gettysburg, all full of the glory of fields of fire; his grandfather died in battle under Pershing; and his father fell in the Battle of the Bulge. Hodges himself dies in Vietnam, yet the express purpose of Webb's fiction is to reassert the honor of fighting for one's country.

Anxieties about the possibility of another Vietnam quagmire peaked in the aggressive rhetoric of belligerence during the Reagan and Bush presidencies, fueled in part by the Iran-Contra enthusiasms of marine Lt. Col. Oliver L. North, a native of Texas and a Vietnam veteran, who took a warlike face and hawkish language to every international scene he ever encountered. In this era of saber-rattling, a new generation of writers from the South produced a large number of imaginative texts exploring the Vietnam War, frequently with a distinctive effort to contextualize or interrogate the Vietnam experience within the context of the South's deep history, often against a Civil War backdrop. Strong poetry dealing with Vietnam emerged from Yusef Komunyaka of Louisiana, Walter McDonald of Texas, and David Huddle of Virginia. A representative sampling of southern novelists who engaged the Vietnam War to reconcile the experience in regional terms includes the following works of fiction: Barry Hannah's *Ray* (1980), Jayne Anne Phillips's *Machine Dreams* (1984), Clyde Edgerton's *Raney* (1985) and *The Floatplane Notebooks* (1988), Bobbie Ann Mason's *In Country* (1985), Pat Conroy's *The Prince of Tides* (1986), Win ton Groom's *Forrest Gump* (1986), Madison Smartt Bell's *Soldier's Joy* (1989), Larry Brown's *Dirty Work* (1989), Harry Crews's *Body* (1990), and James Lee Burke's *In the Electric Mist with Confederate Dead* (1993).

Thus do fiction and fact converge, with the South seemingly less traumatized than other regions and undaunted by the failure to preserve some semblance of democracy in Southeast Asia. In an ironic twist of fate, the Vietnamese refugees who have found Gulf Coast weather to their liking are living proof of an American military defeat. Still, the South is undaunted, destined to keep repeating the rhetoric of belligerence and dwelling in it with determined purpose. After sending the 82nd Airborne from Fort Bragg, N.C., to the tiny island of Grenada, Ronald Reagan gained a good measure of southern allegiance in his 1984 reelection campaign. No matter how the future of Iraq turns out, southern support for President George W. Bush's war initiative in 2003 will stay remarkably strong, a pattern in the South carried forward out of Vietnam. An understanding of presidential politics from the 1970s into the first decade of the 21st century must thus include recognition of the South's steadfast role in the Vietnam War.

OWEN W. GILMAN JR.
St. Joseph's University

Kent B. Blevins, *Foundations* (July–September 1980); Marion A. Bressler and Leo A. Bressler, *Country, Conscience, and Conscription: Can They Be Reconciled?* (1970); G. David Curry, *Sunshine Patriots: Punishment and the Vietnam Offender* (1985); Owen W. Gilman Jr., *Vietnam and the Southern Imagination* (1992); James Givhan, *Rice and Cotton: South Vietnam and South Alabama* (2000); Melton A. McLaurin, in *Perspectives on the American South*, vol. 3, ed. James C. Cobb and Charles Reagan Wilson (1985); Myra McPherson, *Long Time Passing: Vietnam and the Haunted Generation* (1984); James Reston Jr., *Sherman's March and Vietnam* (1985); Charles P. Roland, *The Improbable Era: The South since World War II* (1976); James Webb, *Fields of Fire* (1978); William C. Westmoreland, *A Soldier Reports* (1976).

War of 1812

The people in the southern states generally supported the War of 1812, reflecting the strong spirit of American nationalism in the region in that era. Southern presidents Jefferson and Madison steered the nation's course in the events leading to war, and southern congressmen endorsed efforts to gain respect for American neutral rights — the main cause of war. A majority of congressmen representing the farming areas of the South and West voted for war, whereas the members from the maritime regions of the Northeast voted against the declaration of war. British interference with American trade had damaged south ern farm exports in cotton and tobacco, hurting the region economically and making it eager to stand up to the British.

In addition, Americans on the frontier, in both the South and the Northwest saw war with the British as a way to end Indian attacks on pioneer settlers and gain land in Canada and Florida. The "war hawks" were congressmen eager for war, and many of them were southerners — Henry Clay from Kentucky, John C Calhoun and William Lowndes from South Carolina, and Felix Grundy from Tennessee. Virginian John Randolph tagged them "war hawks" because of thei belligerent nationalism that sought a fight.

The nation was unprepared for war, though, when it came. The earliest fight ing in the South included a Native American uprising on the frontier. The Creeks won a victory at Fort Mims, north of Mobile, in August 1813, but Andrew Jackson then led a volunteer militia campaign that crushed Indian resistance The key battle was at Horseshoe Bend, on the Tallapoosa River, in March 1814 The Creeks surrendered about 60 percent of their territory as a result of the Treaty of Fort Jackson in August of that year. The British campaign in the South concentrated on blockading the coastline and raiding coastal settlements. The Chesapeake Bay area was especially hard hit, including the invasion of Wash ington, D.C., on 24 August 1814. The British moved on to Baltimore but did not launch a major attack on the well-fortified U.S. forces.

The battle of New Orleans was the culminating event of the War of 1812 and a major contribution to both the national and regional imaginations. The British hoped to seize the port city and gain control of the Mississippi River. Andrew Jackson organized efforts to strengthen the Gulf Coast defenses in the fall of 1814 and led an unauthorized raid into Pensacola, in Spanish Florida, where the British had been planning attacks. In November, Americans put up new fortifications on various approaches to New Orleans. The Treaty of Ghent was signed in Europe on 24 December 1814, officially ending the war, but this news did not reach the combatants in North America until after the battle of New Orleans. On 8 January 1815 British commander Sir Edwin Pakenham, who was contemptuous of the Americans, launched a frontal attack on Jackson's forces who included an eclectic combination of frontier riflemen, upper-class Creole volunteers, free blacks, and pirates. Pakenham and about 2,000 British died in the assault.

The peace treaty ending the war settled few of the trade problems that had led to war, but the conflict itself became a major symbol of early American nationalism. The South was particularly proud of the victory over the British at New Orleans. The republican form of government now seemed safer than be-re. After the war, southern congressmen such as John C. Calhoun, who later would be the greatest sectionally oriented politician in the South, supported ationalistic legislation.

The legend of the battle of New Orleans was an especially important cultural egacy. From it General Jackson augmented his enormous popularity on the outhern frontier and gained a reputation as one of the great national heroes. olk songs about "The Hunters of Kentucky" and their sharpshooting communicated pride in southern fighting abilities and popularized the phrase "half orse, half alligator" as a description of the bigger-than-life frontiersmen in the egion. (The free blacks, pirates, Creoles, and other defenders did not, however, receive similar cultural immortality for their roles in the battle.) In the 950s the highly popular tune "The Battle of New Orleans," by country singer ohnny Horton, reminded listeners of this heroic event in the southern past.

CHARLES REAGAN WILSON
University of Mississippi

Henry Adams, *The War of 1812* (1999); Carl Benn, *The War of 1812* (2003); Walter R. Borneman, *1812: The War that Forged a Nation* (2004); Roger H. Brown, *The Republic in Peril: 1812* (1964); Gilbert Byron, *The War of 1812 on the Chesapeake Bay* (1964); Donald R. Hickey, *The War of 1812: A Forgotten Conflict* (1989); Reginald Horsman, *The War of 1812* (1969); John K. Mahon, *The War of 1812* (1972); Bradford Perkins, *Prologue of War: England and the United States, 1805–1812* (1961); Robert Remini, *Andrew Jackson and the Course of American Empire, 1767–1821* (1977); John William Ward, *Andrew Jackson: Symbol for an Age* (1955).

World War I

he onset of a seemingly remote war in Europe set in motion forces that would ave great consequences for southern life. The most immediate impact was a harp economic downturn caused when the British blockade of the Central owers denied cotton producers access to the continental market. Abruptly unctuating a period of modest prosperity for southern agriculture, the collapse initially stirred considerable hostility toward the Allies. Even as the United tates moved closer to its own declaration of war, many prominent southern-rs urged President Woodrow Wilson to maintain American neutrality. This ttitude stemmed partly from parochialism, as well as economic concerns, but outhern opposition also drew on the region's strong anticorporate impulse. pokesmen such as Congressman Claude Kitchin and Senator James Vardaman elieved that business interests were eager to turn a profit on a war the United tates did not need to enter. Several southern legislators opposed the president's preparedness program, and a few even voted against his declaration of war. Senator Vardaman's criticism of the war ultimately cost him his political career.

Skeptical though southerners might have been of a foreign conflict, the region nevertheless threw itself into the war effort. Both culturally and ethnically the white South had strong ties to Great Britain, a link the British shrewdly stressed by purchasing huge amounts of cotton. Moreover, the military tradition has been strong in the South, and the patriotic call to arms in 1917 stirred a tide of popular sentiment. Perhaps typical of the attitudes of his fellow southerners was that of Tennessee draftee Alvin C. York, who initially requested deferment on religious grounds but later became America's most decorated combat soldier.

Although individual southerners were eager to seize arms, the region's traditional distrust of centralized federal power and the economic giantism of major corporations sparked opposition to many aspects of the political economy of the war years. Led by Kitchin, southern legislators worked for a revenue policy that fell most heavily on upper-income groups. Others such as Secretary of the Navy Josephus Daniels criticized the growing partnership between big business and big government and alleged that industry was exploiting the crisis to enhance its profits. Whatever their criticisms of the corporate state, however, southern leaders were determined to see that their region got a substantial share of wartime profits. The army placed a majority of its training camps in southern states, and naval contracts stirred new life in the shipbuilding industry. At a time when the government was imposing price controls on many commodities, southern political clout exempted cotton from this list, allowing its price to soar, thereby fueling a burst of regional prosperity.

The war also accelerated important changes in the structure of the southern economy. The federal government began construction of explosives and wood chemical plants, which helped to spur the growth of hydroelectric power and chemical manufacturing after the war. Most important was the nitrate plant and dam at Muscle Shoals, Ala., which represented the idea of cheap, federally sponsored power and later served as the model for the Tennessee Valley Authority projects of the 1930s. Moreover, the war years saw a general rise in regional prosperity, a prosperity that bred optimism about the future for a section long marked as the poorest in the nation.

World War I had enormous human consequences for the South as well. Military service diminished the region's provincialism as thousands of native southerners left Dixie for assignments elsewhere and thousands of nonsoutherners came to the area for training. These masses of people in transit created considerable stress, especially in race relations. The number of lynchings increased markedly during the war years, and blacks occasionally retaliated in kind, as in Houston, Tex., where a black army unit responded to racial harassment by killing 17 civilians. Simultaneously, the war years saw the beginning of the Great Migration, the massive shift of blacks from the rural South to the urban North. With immigration disrupted and the draft under way, industry needed a source of cheap labor, and by 1920 roughly a million blacks had moved north, the beginning of one of the most important demographic shifts in American history. Southern women also saw important changes in their lives as the women's suffrage amendment moved closer to ratification, although only a few state legislatures in the South supported the proposal. Another longtime political goal of many southern women, prohibition, also won ratification shortly after the war.

The Great War left the South an important cultural legacy. The years after the Armistice saw a great flowering of letters known as the Southern Renaissance. "With the war of 1914–1918," Allen Tate wrote in 1945, "the South reentered the world—but gave a backward glance as it stepped over the border: that backward glance gave us the Southern renascence, a literature conscious of the past in the present." Led by William Faulkner, Thomas Wolfe, the Nashville Agrarians, and many others, for the next two decades the South stood at the forefront of American literature. Indeed, the sense of a changing perspective was a hallmark of southern life during the Great War. After a half century of material poverty and political impotence, the South returned to influence in Washington and embraced some of the idealism and internationalism of its native son, Woodrow Wilson, by supporting both his great crusade and his League of Nations.

DAVID D. LEE
Western Kentucky University

Richard M. Abrams, *Journal of Southern History* (November 1956); Howard Allen, *Journal of Southern History* (May 1961); Dewey W. Grantham, *North Carolina Historical Review* (April 1949), *Southern Progressivism: The Reconciliation of Progress and Tradition* (1983); Michael Howard, *The First World War* (2002); John Keegan, *The First World War* (1998); Arthur S. Link, *American Scholar* (Summer 1951), in *Studies in Southern History in Memory of Albert Ray Newsome, 1894–1951*, ed. J. Carlyle Sitterson (1957), *Wilson*, 5 vols. (1947–65); Hew Strachan, *The First World War* (2004); George B. Tindall, *The Emergence of the New South, 1913–1945* (1967); Richard Watson, *Journal of Southern History* (February 1978).

World War II

War is often a great force of change in any society that endures the trials of mobilization and military conflict. The American South during the Second World War provides a dramatic case for this phenomenon. Although the military action occurred overseas, the mobilization process with its rapid industrial development and augmented federal presence signaled a meaningful change in the lives of most southerners. Historians of the recent South have also viewed the war as a watershed event that ushered the region into a distinct modern period.

President Franklin Roosevelt hoped to use the mobilization effort to foster economic development in the South. Under his encouragement, the expansion and construction of new military bases, aircraft, steel, and petrochemical plants, shipyards, and Manhattan Project sites infused billions of federal dollars into the region. With the Selective Service draft and new employment opportunities, the South experienced a profound demographic shift. Over two million southerners served in the military during the war, and many of these men and women left the South for the first time. Expanded job prospects induced over three million persons to leave rural areas, while close to two million southerners moved out of the region entirely. Because the South had the greatest labor surplus of any region in the nation, employers in western and northern states eagerly recruited workers in low-wage southern industries such as farming, lumber, mining, textiles, and food processing. In response to this recruitment, workers across the region utilized a variety of strategies, including job shopping and migration, to improve their own lives. When these migrants and their families moved to defense centers of the North and West, their settlement often forced racial equality to the forefront of a national discourse on democracy.

As an extension of the New Deal, World War II expanded ties between southern people and the federal government. Initially, liberal reformers in the National Resources Planning Board (NRPB) used mobilization to bolster federal planning, housing, health care, social welfare, and technical training services for southerners and their communities. However, conservative politicians and staunch states' rights advocates generally opposed an increased federal presence. In 1943 southern congressmen dismantled New Deal programs such as the Farm Security Administration (FSA), the Works Progress Administration (WPA), and the National Youth Administration (NYA) and created the War Food Administration (WFA) to give county extension agents greater control over rural workers.

While state leaders hoped to use mobilization to gain industries and pro-

Soldier home on furlough with his family outside a service station in Brown Summit, N.C., 1944 (Standard Oil Collection, Photographic Archives, University of Louisville, Ky.)

mote economic development, they were generally unprepared for the social chaos of rapid industrialization and its long-term impact on race and labor relations. The flight of rural workers, especially African Americans, to federal defense projects upset employers in low-wage rural industries, who resented the ensuing labor shortage and the economic leverage it provided laborers. Throughout the war, employers protested the recruitment of southern workers for national defense projects by the War Manpower Commission (WMC). And, with the creation of the Fair Employment Practices Committee (FEPC) in 1941, states' rights leaders such as Alabama governor Frank Dixon vocally opposed federal support of civil rights in the South.

The fair employment question, in many respects, served as a portent of battles over states' rights and civil rights after the war. The wartime rhetoric of patriotism emphasized U.S. commitment to democracy, and in the South the question of racial equality had profound implications. At a time when the slogan "Victory at Home and Abroad" symbolized the black struggle for civil rights, African Americans used the fair employment issue to force the federal government into acting on the promise of equality. In this wartime movement, labor and civil rights organizations in Dallas, New Orleans, and Atlanta pressured local aircraft and shipbuilding industries to hire, train, and upgrade black workers. At the same time, however, white conservatives in southern labor unions generally hoped to preserve segregation in the workplace as a means of maintaining white economic privileges, such as access to defense jobs and training for higher-paying technical trades.

The growth of organized labor in the region during the war also signaled an important shift in southern labor relations. Closed-shop agreements helped expand the presence of the Congress of Industrial Organizations (CIO) in the South. The CIO's nominal support of interracialism presented a symbolic threat to Jim Crow. As a result, many conservative state and federal procurement agencies established contracts with the racially conservative American Federation of Labor (AFL). Ultimately, however, the most powerful CIO unions in petroleum, steel, and aircraft plants across the South refrained from challenging segregation and in doing so gained some conservative political support in Alabama and Texas, where these industries had a large presence.

While historians have debated the long-term impact of the war upon the South, most observers now recognize that the southern experience between the Depression and the Cold War conveyed an intricate mixture of change and continuity, action and reaction, progress and retraction. After V-J Day, southern state legislatures successfully reduced organized labor's political power and returned federal farming, welfare, and employment programs to state control. Yet the war also produced many lasting economic, political, and social changes. The expansion of military facilities, along with the construction of many new industries, transformed the region from what Roosevelt described in 1939 as the "Nation's No. 1 economic problem" into the heralded Sunbelt. The GI Bill and the federal military presence during the Cold War continued to infuse economic development into the region, helping to expand higher education opportunities for a growing middle class and thereby reducing much of the poverty and provincialism that characterized the prewar South. White veterans returning home to the South also initiated a political shift toward racial moderation. For African Americans, the war engendered a commitment to economic and social equality in the region. In the modern civil rights movement of the 1950s and

960s, black labor and military veterans of the Second World War often led the drive for voter registration and equal rights.

CHARLES D. CHAMBERLAIN
Louisiana State Museum

Charles D. Chamberlain, *Victory at Home: Manpower and Race in the American South during World War II* (2003); Neil R. McMillen, ed., *Remaking Dixie: The Impact of World War II on the American South* (1997); Morton Sosna, in *Perspectives on the American South: An Annual Review of American Society, Politics, and Culture,* vol. 4, ed. James Cobb and Charles Wilson (1987).

Beverley, Robert

(c. 1673–1722) VIRGINIA GENTLEMAN AND PLANTER.

Beverley was the first native-born American to write a history of the Virginia colony—*The History and Present State of Virginia* (1705). Educated in England, he returned to Virginia at 19, when he inherited from his father a large estate. In 1697 he married Ursula Byrd, the 16-year-old daughter of Colonel William Byrd I. She died less than a year later in childbirth, and Beverley never remarried. He held various governmental clerkships and was elected to the House of Burgesses in 1699, but his political career ended about 1703 after he criticized Governor Nicholson and his administration for subverting the rights of Virginians. Settled at Beverley Park in King and Queen County, he pursued his studies and speculated in land. He identified strongly with the New World, proclaiming, "I am an Indian," and in spite of his great wealth lived a deliberately simple life, using furniture made on his own plantation and producing wine from his own grapes. He went on Colonel Alexander Spotswood's 1716 expedition over the Blue Ridge Mountains with the group later known as the "Knights of the Golden Horseshoe." Shortly before his death, he prepared a revised version of the *History* (1722) and *An Abridgement of the Public Laws of Virginia*.

His history was characteristically colonial southern in its approach. Whereas Puritan histories explained events in terms of divine providence, Beverley's was secular and rationalistic; the nearest he came to any supernatural wonders was in a story of Indian rainmaking, which he handled with the skeptical amusement of later front-porch, rocking-chair tellers of folktales. He viewed nature not as a wilderness but as a paradise of natural abundance; his descriptions ranged from scientific observation to rhapsodic wonder. He gave extended, sympathetic treatment of Native Americans and indicted white society for the tragic injustice it inflicted on them. Ironically, however, he referred to black slavery in the briefest terms, merely remarking that slaves generally were not overworked. Demonstrating pride in being an American, he was sharply critical of oppressive English economic policies and of mismanagement by royal governors. But he also lamented the indolence and luxury of the colonists themselves and urged them to work to improve the natural garden of Virginia, to diversify their agriculture and develop manufactures, and to live moderately. He thus held forth a pastoral ideal for the American South.

JUDY JO SMALL
University of North Carolina at Chapel Hill

Robert D. Arner, *Southern Literary Journal* (Spring 1976); Robert Beverley, *The History and Present State of Virginia*, ed. Louis B. Wright (1947); Judy Jo Small, *American Literature* (December 1983).

Boone, Daniel

(1734–1820) FRONTIERSMAN.

The idea of the frontier serves as one of the main themes in the American and southern self-images, and it is im-

Daniel Boone (Library of Congress Prints and Photographs Division [LC-USZ62-37338], Washington, D.C.)

possible to discuss the frontier without discussing Daniel Boone. In fact and in myth perhaps no single individual is more central to the frontier experience.

Nearly 70 of his 86 years were involved with the exploration and settlement of the frontier. On 2 November 1734 Boone was born on the western perimeter of European settlement in Berks County, Pa. At the age of 31, he ventured as far south as Pensacola, Fla., in search of a new home. Four years later, on 7 June 1769, after a 37-day trek that he called "a long and fatiguing journey through a mountainous wilderness," he first "saw with pleasure the beautiful level of Kentucke." When he died on 26 September 1820, he was living on the western boundary of frontier settlement in St. Charles County, Mo., one of the outposts for fitting out expeditions to explore the

Rocky Mountains. Boone constantly placed himself upon the advancing edge of settlement and did so with evident relish.

In the popular imagination, Daniel Boone is the prototype of the frontier hero. His life formed a general pattern that was reenacted with certain variations by the next three major heroes of the westward frontier of the 19th century—Davy Crockett, Kit Carson (a distant relative of Boone), and Buffalo Bill Cody—as well as by Natty Bumppo, the protagonist in James Fenimore Cooper's *Leatherstocking Tales*. Boone and Crockett most clearly symbolize the southern phase of the frontier. Like the physical frontier, Boone progressively moved to the west. Indeed, he and others like him were largely responsible for the retreat of the frontier toward the setting sun. Like the frontier, he remained an invaluable spiritual constant. Daniel Boone exemplified both the American way of life and the ideals of frontier independence and virtue, which were embodied in the expanding 19th-century South of yeoman farmers. In a country whose history has been dominated by continuing migration, the majority of early Americans believed themselves to be pioneers to some extent and, as such, identified with Boone as their hero.

Boone also mirrored the conflict between civilization and the wilderness: which was the ideal state? Boone was the pioneer, a man happy to do his part to help civilize the frontier and to praise these improvements, but, equally the hunter and man of nature, he was appalled at the encroachments of civilization and retreated before its corrupting influence to insure his own happiness. His achievements and fame live on for Americans in this dual role of pioneer and preserver because this is the dual role—imagined, desired, or enacted—of the American people as well.

Significantly, Boone still functions as a model worthy of emulation. Dan Beard, the founder of the Boy Scouts of America, a group that influences the lives of millions of young Americans, based his conception of this organization upon the following premise: "A society of scouts to be identified with the greatest of all Scouts, Daniel Boone, and to be known as the Sons of Daniel Boone."

MICHAEL A. LOFARO
University of Tennessee

John Mack Faragher, *Daniel Boone: The Life and Legend of an American Hero* (1992); Michael A. Lofaro, *The Life and Adventures of Daniel Boone* (1978); Richard Slotkin, *Regeneration through Violence: The Mythology of the American Frontier, 1600–1860* (1973).

Byrd, William, II

(1674–1744) VIRGINIA ARISTOCRAT, LAWYER, POLITICIAN, PLANTER, WRITER, AMATEUR SCIENTIST, FOUNDER OF RICHMOND AND PETERSBURG.

Born 28 March 1674 Byrd inherited a large plantation on the James River and the family home, called Westover, from his father, Colonel William Byrd I (1652–1704). Son of a London goldsmith, Colonel Byrd had risen to prominence by inheriting the estate from his uncle and acquiring vast wealth through land speculation, fur trading, and importation of indentured servants and black slaves. Like other wealthy southern colonials, the young Byrd was educated in England, where he developed many of his talents and tastes. He went to grammar school in Essex, studied law at the Middle Temple, was elected to the Royal Society, attended the theater frequently, and moved in London's elite social and literary circles. He lived in England in the years 1681 to 1696, 1697 to 1705, and 1715 to 1726. He married Lucy Parke in 1706, and after her death in 1716 he courted several wealthy women and carried on intrigues with various others before finally marrying Maria Taylor in 1724.

In Virginia, Byrd devoted his time to managing his plantations. He enlarged Westover into a splendid Palladian mansion with luxurious furnishings, improved its gardens, and entertained friends with generous hospitality. He collected one of the best and largest libraries in colonial America and read nearly every day in Latin, Greek, or Hebrew, as well as in modern literature. He also took an active role in public affairs, as a man of his station was expected to, serving in the House of Burgesses briefly and in the Executive Council from 1708 until his death. He was the chief member of the joint commission that traveled in 1728 from the coast to the mountains surveying the disputed boundary line between Virginia and North Carolina. The manner of his life was in some ways modeled after the ideal of the English country gentleman, and the cosmopolitan Byrd sometimes described his world in pastoral terms. In continually buying and selling land, though, he represented a new southern type divergent from the English. Though he was a slaveholder, Byrd disapproved of the institution of slavery because of its inhumanity and its fostering of severity in slaveholders, laziness among whites, and the danger of bloody insurrections. His attitude toward New England Puritans blended admiration for their industriousness with contempt for their hypocritical traffic in rum and slaves.

Byrd's writings, marked by urbane good humor, were diverse. He was author of a scientific treatise for the Royal Society, gallant and witty verses, and *A Discourse Concerning the Plague* (1721), an anonymous pamphlet recommending tobacco as a preventive for plague. He seems to have written part of *The Careless Husband*, a play he also directed at a private house in Virginia, and he contributed to a promotional tract in German, *New-gefundenes Eden* (1737). His letters and three portions of his shorthand diaries have been found and published. Most important are the accounts of his travels—*A Progress to the Mines* (1841), *A Journey to the Land of Eden* (1928), and two versions of the dividing-line expedition. Of these, *The Secret History of the Dividing Line*, a travel journal circulated privately among friends and not published until 1929, is rich in racy humor and satirical caricatures of the commissioners; the much longer *History of the Dividing Line* (1866), evidently intended for London publication, diminishes the personal elements and includes politi-

cal and natural history. Both versions, from the vantage point of a Tidewater Virginian, ridicule the vulgarities of shiftless backwoods Carolinians. Byrd thus inaugurated the southern tradition of literary humor dealing with poor whites.

JUDY JO SMALL
University of North Carolina at Chapel Hill

William Byrd, *The Commonplace Book of William Byrd II of Westover*, ed. Jan Kirsten Gilliam and Kenneth A. Lockridge (2001); Richard Beale Davis, in *Major Writers of Early American Literature*, ed. Everett Emerson (1972); Kenneth A. Lockridge, *The Diary and Life of William Byrd II of Virginia, 1674–1744* (1987); Pierre Marambaud, *William Byrd of Westover, 1674–1744* (1971); Louis B. Wright, ed., *The Prose Works of William Byrd of Westover* (1966).

Calhoun, John C.

(1782–1850) POLITICIAN AND POLITICAL PHILOSOPHER.
Born of Scots-Irish ancestry in the South Carolina Upcountry in the wake of the American Revolution, John Caldwell Calhoun traveled north for his education. He graduated from Yale and read law with Federalist judge Tapping Reeve in Litchfield, Conn. Calhoun returned home, practiced law, won a seat in the legislature, and then represented South Carolina in the U.S. Congress from 1811 to 1817. A devout nationalist during this phase of his career, Calhoun was a war hawk and an avid supporter of the War of 1812. He voted for a protective tariff in 1816 and introduced the bill chartering the Second Bank of the United States in 1817. He served

as secretary of war in James Monroe's cabinet and in 1824 won election as vice president of the United States.

Calhoun was elected vice president again in 1828 and entered the administration of Andrew Jackson as heir apparent to the presidency. Within four years, however, Calhoun and Jackson were bitter enemies; Calhoun had resigned his office, and he had become an ardent sectionalist. Calhoun's *South Carolina Exposition and Protest* was the philosophical underpinning of the nullification movement in South Carolina. During the nullification crisis and after, Calhoun devoted his energies and considerable talents to the minority interests of the South. As South Carolina senator and during a brief term as John Tyler's secretary of state (1844–45), Calhoun was the South's political champion and spokesman.

In a sense, Calhoun's career in public life embodied southern political behavior. A nationalist during the Virginia dynasty, he became a sectionalist when he came to believe that nationalism conflicted with southern interests. To his death in 1850 Calhoun fought the South's political battles with considerable skill. His greatest significance, however, lay in his capacity for political thought and analysis. His prime concern was for minority interests in American democracy. He believed the Union to be a compact; southern states had entered the compact when they ratified the Constitution, and they were free to dissolve the compact and leave the Union if they so chose. However, Calhoun revered the Union and attempted to discover some moderate constitutional course that would preserve both southern interests and the Union, that would offer the minority South some alternatives to submission and secession. He never resolved the dilemma, but in the process of defining and articulating the southern political stance, Calhoun became a constructive critic of American democracy and perhaps the foremost American political thinker of the 19th century.

EMORY THOMAS
University of Georgia

Gerald M. Capers, *John C. Calhoun, Opportunist: A Reappraisal* (1960); Margaret L. Coit, *John C. Calhoun: American Portrait* (1950); Richard N. Current, *John C. Calhoun* (1963); Ross M. Lence, ed., *Union and Liberty: The Political Philosophy of John C. Calhoun* (1992); John Niven, *John C. Calhoun and the Price of Union: A Biography* (1988); Charles M. Wiltse, *John C. Calhoun, Nullifier, 1829–1839* (1949).

Carter, Jimmy

(b. 1924) U.S. PRESIDENT.

"I am a Southerner and an American," Jimmy Carter wrote in his campaign autobiography, *Why Not the Best?* It would be difficult to quarrel with either assertion. Born and reared in the heart of the southwest Georgia Black Belt, James Earl "Jimmy" Carter could trace both his American and southern ancestry back to the early 17th century when the first Carters arrived in Virginia. By the decade of the 1780s, ancestors of the future president had made their way to Georgia, eventually settling in Sumter County, where Jimmy Carter was born and raised.

The son of a moderately wealthy

Jimmy Carter, 39th president of the United States
(Library of Congress [LC-USZ62-13039 DLC],
Washington, D.C.)

landowner and businessman, Carter,
like many of the other progeny of
upper-middle-class southerners, aspired to a military career. After completing his elementary and secondary
education in Plains and matriculating
for a year at Georgia Southwestern College in nearby Americus, he enrolled in
the naval ROTC program at the Georgia Institute of Technology prior to
securing an appointment to the U.S.
Naval Academy in Annapolis. There
the young cadet did well, finishing in
the upper 10 percent of his 1946 graduating class. Thereafter, he entered the
submarine service after completing his
required two years of surface duty.

The young naval officer's promising
military career ended in 1953, however,
when he returned to Plains to manage
the family's business affairs after the

death of his father. Within a few years
of his return, he was deeply involved in
a variety of community affairs and soon
was campaigning for the state senate
seat once held by his father. After two
terms in the Georgia General Assembly, Carter ran unsuccessfully for the
Democratic gubernatorial nomination
in 1966 before succeeding in the same
quest four years later.

On the first day of his governorship,
Carter attracted national attention by
dramatically proclaiming that the time
for racial discrimination in Georgia
had ended. During the next four years
Carter promoted a moderately liberal,
business progressive reform program,
which included state government reorganization, judicial reform, consumer
protection, welfare reform, tax reform,
and environmental concerns. Following through on earlier commitments,
he also appointed numerous black
Georgians and women to important
positions in state government. Unable
to succeed himself in the governorship, Carter in 1974 began laying the
groundwork for a successful run for
the presidency of the United States.
His 1976 campaign focused national
attention on changes in the South in the
previous decade. Carter played a crucial
role within the South in strengthening, at least temporarily, a black-white
coalition in the Democratic Party. He
won black support and also appealed
to the white rural South. For the first
time since 1964, Democratic politicians across the South enthusiastically
supported their party's presidential
nominee.

Once installed in the presidential office, Carter, with less success, sought to push the same type of reforms that he had sponsored during his governorship. Domestic economic programs and international crises contributed to Carter's presidential woes, however, and in 1980 he was repudiated by the same voters, many of them southerners, who had supported him four years earlier. Several weeks later he was back in Plains, from which he had launched his meteoric rise to national prominence a few years earlier.

An unorthodox politician in many ways, Carter nevertheless was clearly a product of the southern culture into which he was born and in which he was raised. An inherited sense of noblesse oblige, which he shared with numerous others in the southern elite, combined in Carter with religious convictions (he was a "born again" Baptist) and a sense of history to produce a code of social ethics that permitted him to transcend the race issue that had been the burden of so many other white southerners. In so doing, symbolically at least, Carter's rise to the presidency represented the ultimate reunification of the South with the rest of the nation.

Since leaving the presidency, Carter has been a freelance ambassador on international missions, monitoring contested elections, negotiating peace agreements, and initiating relief efforts. He founded the Carter Center in Atlanta in 1982 to address issues of democracy and human rights. He received to Nobel Peace Prize in 2002. He has also been a grassroots participant in Habitat for Humanity house-building programs and has authored 14 books, including works on faith, the outdoor life, and a series of memoirs.

GARY M. FINK
Georgia State University

Peter G. Bourne, *Jimmy Carter: A Comprehensive Biography from Plains to Post-Presidency* (1997); Douglas G. Brinkley, *The Unfinished Presidency: Jimmy Carter's Quest for Global Peace* (1998); Jimmy Carter, *An Hour Before Daylight: Memoirs of a Rural Boyhood* (2001), *The Personal Beliefs of Jimmy Carter: Winner of the 2002 Nobel Peace Prize* (2002), *Sources of Strength: Meditations on Scripture for a Living Faith* (1998); Gary M. Fink, *Prelude to the Presidency: The Political Character and Legislative Leadership Style of Governor Jimmy Carter* (1980); David Kucharsky, *The Man from Plains: The Mind and Spirit of Jimmy Carter* (1975); William L. Miller, *Yankee from Georgia: The Emergence of Jimmy Carter* (1978); Kenneth E. Morris, *Jimmy Carter: American Moralist* (1996).

Citizens' Councils

This group and allied organizations—the Virginia Defenders of State Sovereignty and Individual Liberties, the Tennessee Federation for Constitutional Government, the North Carolina Patriots, and the Georgia States' Rights Council—were formed by white supremacists in the South to resist school desegregation. Appearing first in Mississippi in July 1954, this movement of "white-collar" or "country club" Klans spread rapidly into each of the 11 former Confederate states. Dedicated to "states' rights and racial integrity," the council movement, like the Confederacy itself, failed to overcome southern parochialism and thus never forged a united front. Yet a semblance of regional unity was provided in 1956 by the formation of the Mississippi-based Citizens' Councils of America, an informal confederation of the more viable southern organized resistance groups.

The councils' natural habitats were the old plantation areas of the Lower South, where the black population was most heavily concentrated and where white racial fears were highest. Except in Virginia, where organized resistance was endorsed by the Byrd machine, and Little Rock, where Governor Orval Faubus was a supporter, councils or council-like groups enjoyed little success in the so-called rim-South states. In Florida, North Carolina, Tennessee, and Texas, members of the white power structure rarely became closely identified with the groups. But in the Deep South—in Alabama, Louisiana, Mississippi, and South Carolina—councils won the support of high elected officials and of business and professional leaders. Here, where their power and prestige were greatest, Citizens' Councils officially eschewed violence. Individual members were sometimes implicated in terrorist acts, however, and the movement was instrumental in creating a climate of fear and reprisal in which few whites and even fewer blacks dared challenge the status quo. In Alabama and Mississippi, councils functioned as shadow governments.

There are no reliable membership figures, but the Southwide total probably never exceeded 250,000, though non-dues-paying sympathizers surely numbered many thousands more. Having rapidly expanded in the years immediately after *Brown v. Board of Education*, white resistance organizations gradually declined following the federal-state confrontation at Little Rock. In growing numbers whites recognized that some degree of school desegregation was inevitable. Remobilization campaigns in the 1960s failed, and by mid-decade membership even in Mississippi had dwindled to insignificance. Thereafter, diehard movement leaders turned their support to all-white private schools.

NEIL R. MCMILLEN
University of Southern Mississippi

Numan V. Bartley, *The Rise of Massive Resistance: Race and Politics in the South during the 1950s* (1969); Hodding Carter, *The South Strikes Back* (1959); Neil R. McMillen, *The Citizens' Council: Organized Resistance to the Second Reconstruction* (1971).

Clinton, Bill

(b. 1946) U.S. PRESIDENT.
William Jefferson Clinton was born on 19 August 1946 in "a place called Hope," a small town in southwestern Arkansas. His father, William Jefferson Blythe III, died just three months before his birth in a car accident. While his mother, Virginia Cassidy Blythe, studied nursing in Louisiana to help provide for her son, his grandparents, who ran a country store in Hope, cared for him. When Billy, as he was called, was in early grade school, his mother returned, and they moved to Hot Springs, where Virginia married Roger Clinton. Because of Roger's gambling and alcohol addic-

tion, Billy and his younger half brother, Roger Jr., depended even more on the strength and sacrifice of their mother.

Despite his tumultuous childhood, Clinton excelled in leadership roles and academics, and in high school he attended Boys State and met President Kennedy at the White House. He left Arkansas to attend Georgetown University, earning a bachelor's degree in international affairs. He was awarded the Rhodes Scholarship, which took him abroad to study in Oxford at a time when many of his classmates were being drafted to serve in Vietnam. Upon his return, he attended Yale Law School, where he met Hillary Rodham.

After law school, he came back home to Arkansas and began a life of public service. While teaching law at the University of Arkansas, Clinton wed Hillary Rodham in 1975, and their daughter, Chelsea, was born in 1980. Clinton won his first office, attorney general of Arkansas, in 1976. Two years later, at the age of 32, Clinton was elected governor, becoming the youngest governor in the nation at that time. During his tenure, Clinton positioned himself as a moderate Democrat, insisting on balanced budgets while trying to improve key services like public education.

Clinton entered the 1992 presidential race with the same centrist blueprint that guided his six terms as governor. Calling his approach "New Democrat," he aimed to slash the deficit, put a hundred thousand more police officers on the streets, create millions of new jobs, and reform the welfare and health care systems. While Clinton's message reso-

Bill Clinton, 42d president of the United States (Library of Congress [LC-USZ62-107700 DLC], Washington, D.C.)

nated with party loyalists, Democrats were equally interested in selecting a candidate whose appeal could reach conservative white southerners. After emerging victorious in the primaries, Clinton selected Senator Al Gore of Tennessee as his running mate. The addition of Gore, a fellow Southern Baptist, made it the first time in over a century that a major party chose two southerners as nominees. Although they overwhelmed President George H. W. Bush in the electoral count, Clinton and Gore won only a third of the South's electoral votes.

During his first two years in office, Clinton succeeded in getting much of his agenda through the Democratic Congress, including his Family and Medical Leave Act, anticrime bill, and deficit reduction package. By the midterm elections of 1994, however, backlash against his universal health coverage program and tax increases gave Republicans control of both houses of Congress for the first time since the Eisenhower administration. Moreover, Republicans now held a majority of the South's congressional seats, a feat not seen since Reconstruction. Yet Clinton rebounded as the public perception of his handling of the budget battles with the Republican Congress, which caused two government shutdowns in 1995, steered in his favor. Bolstered by an improved national economy, Clinton won another electoral landslide in his 1996 reelection against Senator Bob Dole. During his second term, Clinton worked vigorously to broker and sustain peace agreements in the Balkans, Northern Ireland, and the Middle East.

Accusations of personal indiscretions dogged Clinton throughout his presidency, but none cost him politically or legally until he gave testimony in Paula Jones's sexual harassment suit against him in 1997. Testifying before a grand jury, Clinton lied about his sexual relationship with a White House intern, Monica Lewinsky. The House impeached Clinton on charges of perjury and obstruction of justice, making him the second president, and the first elected president (Andrew Johnson ascended to the presidency following Abraham Lincoln's assassination), to be impeached. Although the Senate failed to convict Clinton, allowing him to serve out his remaining term, the scandal crippled the president's political agenda and did not end his legal troubles. After Clinton settled with Jones, paying her $850,000, a fed-

eral judge found him in contempt of court for lying in a deposition. Rather than face disbarment hearings, Clinton surrendered his law license for five years.

After leaving the White House, the Clintons continued their roles as public servants. New Yorkers elected Hillary to the Senate in 2000, while the former president, through the Clinton Foundation, has worked to promote multilateral solutions to the world's problems, particularly fighting poverty and AIDS in Africa. The Clinton Presidential Library, which houses a museum and archive, opened in Little Rock in November 2004.

C. DALTON LYON
University of Mississippi

Bill Clinton, *My Life* (2004); John F. Harris, *The Survivor: Bill Clinton in the White House* (2005); Joe Klein, *The Natural: The Misunderstood Presidency of Bill Clinton* (2002); David Maraniss, *First in His Class: A Biography of Bill Clinton* (1996); Dewayne Wickham, *Bill Clinton and Black America* (2002).

Confederate Veterans

To the white southerners who fought it, the Civil War remained forever poignant; and even after many years had passed, it dominated their thinking. To be sure, a few veterans regarded the war and all its trappings as having been too horrible; their greatest desire was to forget. But for most of them the memory refused to fade.

Reverence for the Lost Cause, it has been argued, grew into a new civil religion after the war. As long as any of them remained, the actual veter-

"The Conquered Banner"

Copyright 1913
by C. V. Loy

Photo by
Clinkenbeard

Elderly man in uniform looking at canteen in front of Confederate flag
Library of Congress [LC-USZ62-64127], Washington, D.C.)

ans were that religion's living apostles.
And, just as is the case with a religion,
the veterans tended to nurture their
identity institutionally through various
organizations—especially the United
Confederate Veterans (UCV).

Initially, Confederate veterans, impelled by emotional pressures of living
with defeat, associated informally.
The basic psychological impetus was
an intense belief that the world misunderstood both the history and the

people of the South. As time passed, the relationships and organizations they engendered grew more symbolically meaningful. The great episode had "sanctified" its participants, and that sanctification spilled into the UCV's ancillary groups—the United Daughters of the Confederacy, the Sons of Veterans, the Children of the Confederacy, the Confederated Southern Memorial Association, the Order of the Stars and Bars, and the Confederate Choirs of America.

The UCV officially prohibited "the discussion of political or religious subjects" at meetings and forbade taking "any political action." What they meant to avoid was internal controversy. Their activities had considerable religious aspects: prayers, inspirational lectures, memorial ceremonies, even a special funeral service. Although they showed certain clear and strong political preferences, they rationalized such attitudes as not actually being political: any Confederate veteran obviously was more qualified for public office than a nonveteran; and benefits such as state pensions, soldiers' homes, and relief for needy veterans or their families, as well as the financing of hundreds of Civil War monuments, were humanitarian issues transcending politics.

The Confederate veteran wanted his name mentioned in historical writings, and he desired vindication, as well as status and deference within his own society. He certainly managed to get all of that; it might well have come to him even without his efforts. During his more contemplative moments he wished for a "just treatment" in histori-cal interpretation of himself and of his region. He was a powerful force, both a subject of, and a contributor to, the Lost Cause.

HERMAN HATTAWAY
University of Missouri–Kansas City

Herman Hattaway, *Louisiana History* (Summer 1971, Winter 1975); R. B. Rosenberg, *Living Monuments: Confederate Soldiers' Homes in the New South* (1993); William W. White, *The Confederate Veteran* (1962); Charles Reagan Wilson, *Baptized in Blood: The Religion of the Lost Cause, 1865–1920* (1980).

Congress of Racial Equality (CORE)

Rooted in the 1930s pacifist movements, the Congress of Racial Equality (CORE) was formed in Chicago in 1942 to oppose racial discrimination and encourage integration. For many years the group emphasized interracial membership and Gandhian nonviolent direct action. James Farmer served as CORE's first national chairman and as its dynamic national director from 1961 to 1966.

From 1942 to 1961 CORE focused on integration of public accommodations and in 1946 tested compliance with the Supreme Court's ruling of that year declaring unconstitutional Virginia's laws requiring segregation on interstate motor carriers. To do so, CORE launched the Journey of Reconciliation, an integrated bus trip from Washington, D.C., to Kentucky. The ride elicited little attention, but it boosted CORE morale and served as the model for the Freedom Ride of 1961.

Late-1940s efforts to establish affiliates in the Deep South failed because of

Congress of Racial Equality conducts march in memory of African American youngsters killed in Birmingham bombings, All Souls Church, 16th Street, Washington, D.C.
Thomas J. O'Halloran, photographer, Library of Congress [LC-U9-10515-6A], Washington, D.C.)

fear of brutal reprisals, though in southern border states affiliates slowly grew. After the success of the Montgomery bus boycott organized by the Southern Christian Leadership Conference (SCLC), CORE increased its southern projects. Its voter registration campaign in Virginia in the late 1950s proved disappointing, but such projects fared better in South Carolina, where in the 1960s CORE also actively supported efforts to integrate lunch counters.

CORE catapulted to national attention in 1961 when it spearheaded the Freedom Ride, an integrated bus trip from Washington, D.C., through the Deep South to test the South's response to the 1960 Supreme Court decision prohibiting segregation in bus- and train-terminal accommodations. Suffering violent reprisals in Anniston

and Birmingham, Ala., the CORE riders stopped in Birmingham, where Student Nonviolent Coordinating Committee (SNCC) riders resumed the effort. Further violence occurred in Montgomery, and the CORE-SCLC-SNCC Freedom Ride Coordinating Committee recruited thousands of riders, 360 of whom were arrested and jailed in Jackson, Miss. The campaign resulted in the Interstate Commerce Commission's September 1961 ruling prohibiting segregated facilities in interstate travel. Many Deep South locales ignored the ruling, but a major battle had been won.

Subsequently, CORE's leaders played major roles in the surge of direct action in Mississippi, Alabama, Georgia, and Louisiana. More working-class blacks joined CORE, and attention turned to community-development projects. Among civil rights groups CORE's influence waned between 1962 and 1964, partly because CORE-supported activities—such as demonstrations in Gadsden, Ala., and Plaquemine, La.—received little publicity, even when the protesters met with violence.

CORE established a regional office in Louisiana in 1964, but major voter registration campaigns there met with limited success and much harassment. Frustrated black residents armed for self-defense, and CORE accepted such actions as necessary. The murder of CORE workers Michael Schwerner and James Chaney and SNCC volunteer Andrew Goodman in Neshoba County, Miss., in 1964 elicited a national outcry for protection of civil rights workers. Subsequently, CORE established "freedom schools" for black youth, community centers, and political programs throughout Mississippi and supported creation of the Mississippi Freedom Democratic Party.

Problems and schisms within CORE increased; and by the 1965 CORE convention in Durham, N.C., James Farmer had decided to resign and CORE's interracial focus had been rejected. Floyd McKissick replaced Farmer as head of CORE on 3 January 1966, and the organization was well on the way to becoming a militant and uncompromising advocate of the ideology of black power. When McKissick resigned as national director of CORE in 1968, his close friend and then-head of the Harlem chapter, Roy Innis, was elected to the position and continues to hold it as late as 2005. Still in operation,

CORE continues to promote inner-city community-development projects in black neighborhoods.

SHARON A. SHARP
Boone, North Carolina

Inge Powell Bell, CORE *and the Strategy of Nonviolence* (1968); James Farmer, *Lay Bare the Heart: An Autobiography of the Civil Rights Movement* (1985); August Meier and Elliott Rudwick, CORE: *A Study in the Civil Rights Movement, 1942–1968* (1973).

Crockett, Davy

(1786–1836) FRONTIERSMAN, POLITICIAN, HUMORIST.

The life of the historical David Crockett is interesting but in no way as remarkable as the legendary lives of Davy Crockett. Born on 17 August 1786 in Greene County, Tenn., Crockett was a first-rate but relatively obscure backwoods hunter and Indian fighter with a knack for storytelling. He parlayed his local reputation into a state, and then national, political career. He was elected to the Tennessee legislature in 1821 and 1823 and won congressional elections in 1827, 1829, and 1833. In Congress he promoted sale of public land at low prices but was frequently at odds with President Andrew Jackson. Crockett became perhaps the representative symbol of both the noble and the savage aspects of frontier life in Jacksonian America. His death at the Alamo on 6 March 1836 assured him a prominent place in the history of the South and the nation and, more important, opened the cultural floodgates to the boundless expansion of his legendary image in the popular media of his day and ours.

Crockett promoted himself as a

Davy Crockett, frontier humorist and politician (engraving by C. Stuart from the original portrait by
J. G. Chapman, Library of Congress [LC-USZ62-93521], Washington, D.C.)

simple, down-home country boy whose extraordinary marksmanship was a metaphor for his character: he was a straight shooter. By the early 1830s his image had achieved a life of its own, so much so that in 1834 he published his autobiography (*A Narrative of the Life of David Crockett*) to counteract the compilation of tall tales printed under his name a year earlier by Matthew St. Clair Clarke as the *Sketches and Eccentricities of Col. Crockett.*

David was becoming Davy, the screamer and "ring-tailed roarer" who could "run faster, jump higher, squat lower, dive deeper, stay under longer, and come out drier, than any man in the whole country." Davy was not the first to give vent to the backwoods brag, but in the hands of the Boston literary hacks who produced the tall tales for the *Crockett Almanacs* (1835–56), he became its finest practitioner. This fictional Davy was both the Promethean figure who saved the earth by unfreezing the sun from its axis and the "humanitarian" who killed and boiled an Indian to help cure his pet bear's stomach disorder. He was also an ardent advocate of expansionism, with Mexico and Oregon but two of his targets.

The violent, racist, and jingoistic Davy of the almanacs competed with and was eventually subsumed by over 150 years of romantic melodrama. From Nimrod Wildfire, James Kirke Paulding's Crockettesque character in his play *The Lion of the West* (1831), to the Davys played by Fess Parker and John Wayne, 19th-century drama and 20th-century film always presented the hero in the kindest light. Courageous, dashing, and true blue, this nature's nobleman protected his country and those who were helpless with equal fervor.

Both the outrageous and the idealized Davy were firmly grounded in a southern sense of place. Whether as the purveyor of southern or southwestern humor over the full spectrum of good and bad taste or as the gallant southern gentleman, the knight errant of the backwoods, Davy reflected the range of the region whose hero he became and, in the larger context, the diversity and individuality of the entire nation.

MICHAEL A. LOFARO
University of Tennessee

Richard Boyd Hauck, *Crockett: A Bio-Bibliography* (1982); Michael A. Lofaro, ed., *Davy Crockett: The Man, the Legend, the Legacy, 1786–1986* (1985); James A. Shackford, *David Crockett: The Man and the Legend* (1956).

Davis, Jefferson

(1808–1889) POLITICIAN.

"The man and the hour have met," a distinguished secessionist proclaimed when Jefferson Davis became president of the Confederate States of America. In most ways Davis seemed ideally suited to directing the South's struggle for independence. Born in Fairview, Ky., in 1808, Davis moved with his family to Wilkinson County, Miss., when he was still a boy. Experienced in warfare and politics, he had attended the U.S. Military Academy (graduating in 1828), participated in the Black Hawk War, commanded a regiment of Mississippi volunteers and been wounded in the Mexican War, served as President Franklin Pierce's secretary of war, and eaded the U.S. Senate's Military Affairs Committee. A brave, bold, erudite agrarian who believed in slavery and the right of secession, Davis worked tirelessly for the Confederacy. Against the localism of certain governors and congressmen, he advocated measures for the Confederacy such as a military draft, conscription of blacks into the army, impressment of private property, government management of railroads and blockade runners, and an income tax.

But his inability to maintain the support of the Confederate Congress and his unwillingness to delegate authority except in certain areas created problems; so did his direction of military strategy and tactics. Ironically, it may have been in military affairs, where so much was expected of him, that Davis failed. He picked only one outstanding army commander, Robert E. Lee; other commanders proved to be unsuccessful, distrusted by Davis, or both. Squabbles among generals and over military politics hampered the Confederate war effort, and, as Union armies advanced, Confederate morale deteriorated. Davis hoped that his defensive-offensive strategy would save the South, but in practice it became little more than a series of courageous but costly attacks on enemy forces until dwindling manpower forced the Confederates on the defensive after 1863.

Davis may have been "perverse and obstinate" and "an indifferent judge of men," as his critics claimed, but he maintained during the last months of the war an unfailing will to win and even tried to continue the war as the

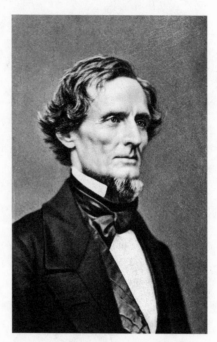

Jefferson Davis, Confederate president, 1861–65 (Mathew B. Brady, photographer, Library of Congress [LC-BH82-2417], Washington, D.C.)

Confederacy collapsed. Captured in May 1865 and imprisoned for two years without a trial, he became in the North the symbol of the South's treasonable sins. In the *Rise and Fall of the Confederate Government*, which he wrote after release from prison, Davis shared much of the blame for Confederate defeat with others. Throughout the remainder of his life he neither repented nor asked forgiveness for himself or for the cause he led.

GRADY MCWHINEY
Texas Christian University

Donald E. Collins, *The Death and Resurrection of Jefferson Davis* (2005); William J. Cooper, *Jefferson Davis, American* (2000); William C. Davis, *Jefferson Davis, The Man and His Hour* (1991); James T. McIntosh,

ed., *The Papers of Jefferson Davis* (1971–);
Dunbar Rowland, ed., *Jefferson Davis*,
10 vols. (1923); Robert Penn Warren,
Jefferson Davis Gets His Citizenship Back
(1980).

Douglass, Frederick

(1808–1895) BLACK LEADER.
Frederick Douglass was the most important black American leader of the
19th century. He was born Frederick
Augustus Washington Bailey, in Talbot
County, on Maryland's Eastern Shore
in 1808, the son of a slave woman and,
in all likelihood, her white master.
Upon his escape from slavery at age 20,
Douglass adopted a new surname from
the hero of Sir Walter Scott's *The Lady
of the Lake*. Douglass immortalized his
formative years as a slave in the first of
three autobiographies, *Narrative of the
Life of Frederick Douglass, an American
Slave*, published in 1845. This and two
subsequent autobiographies, *My Bondage and My Freedom* (1855) and *The
Life and Times of Frederick Douglass*
(1881), mark Douglass's greatest contributions to southern culture. Written
both as antislavery propaganda and as
personal revelation, they are universally
regarded as the finest examples of the
slave narrative tradition and as classics
of American autobiography.

Douglass's public life ranged from
his work as an abolitionist in the early
1840s to his attacks on Jim Crow segregation in the 1890s. Douglass lived the
bulk of his career in Rochester, N.Y.,
where for 16 years he edited the most
influential black newspaper of the mid-
19th century, called successively *The
North Star* (1847–51), *Frederick Doug-*

Frederick Douglass, abolitionist and black leader,
date unknown (Sophia Smith Collection, Smith
College, Northampton, Mass.)

lass' Paper (1851–58), and *Douglass'
Monthly* (1859–63). Douglass achieved
international fame as an orator with
few peers and as a writer of persuasive
power. In thousands of speeches and
editorials Douglass levied an irresistible
indictment against slavery and racism,
provided an indomitable voice of hope
for his people, embraced antislavery
politics, and preached his own brand of
American ideals.

Douglass welcomed the Civil War
in 1861 as a moral crusade to eradicate
the evil of slavery. During the war he
labored as a fierce propagandist of the
Union cause and emancipation, as a
recruiter of black troops, and on two
occasions as an adviser to President
Abraham Lincoln. Douglass made a
major contribution to the intellectual
tradition of millennial nationalism, the

outlook from which many Americans, North and South, interpreted the Civil War. During Reconstruction and the Gilded Age Douglass's leadership became less activist and more emblematic. He traveled and lectured widely on racial issues, but his most popular topic was "Self-Made Men." By the 1870s Douglass had moved to Washington, D.C., where he edited the newspaper the *New National Era* and became president of the ill-fated Freedmen's Bank. As a stalwart Republican, he was appointed marshal (1877–81) and recorder of deeds (1881–86) for the District of Columbia and chargé d'affaires for Santo Domingo and minister to Haiti (1889–91). Douglass had five children by his first wife, Anna Murray, a free black woman from Baltimore who followed him out of slavery in 1838. Less than two years after Anna died in 1882, the 63-year-old Douglass married Helen Pitts, his white former secretary, an event of considerable controversy. Thus by birth and by his two marriages, Douglass is one of the South's most famous examples of the region's mixed racial heritage.

Douglass never lost a sense of attachment to the South. "Nothing but an intense love of personal freedom keeps us [fugitive slaves] from the South," Douglass wrote in 1848. He often referred to Maryland as his "own dear native soil." Brilliant, heroic, and complex, Douglass became a symbol of his age and a unique American voice for humanism and social justice. His life and thought will always speak profoundly to the dilemma of being black in America. Douglass died of heart failure in 1895, the year Booker T. Washington rose to national prominence with his Atlanta Exposition speech suggesting black accommodation to racial segregation.

DAVID W. BLIGHT
Yale University

John W. Blassingame et al., *The Frederick Douglass Papers*, 2 vols. (1979–82); David W. Blight, *Frederick Douglass' Civil War: Keeping Faith in Jubilee* (1989); Philip S. Foner, *Life and Writings of Frederick Douglass*, 4 vols. (1955); August Meier, *Negro Thought in America, 1800–1915* (1963); Benjamin Quarles, *Frederick Douglass* (1948).

Du Bois, W. E. B.

(1868–1963) HISTORIAN, SOCIOLOGIST, EDITOR, NOVELIST.
William Edward Burghardt Du Bois was born 23 February 1868 in Great Barrington, Mass. A New Englander in thought and conduct, as he put it, he entered the South in 1885, after a promising high school career, to attend Fisk University in Nashville, Tenn. He found the South deeply humiliating. "No one but a Negro," he wrote, "going into the South without previous experience of color caste can have any conception of its barbarism." Nevertheless, Fisk itself was challenging, even exhilarating, and summer teaching in rural counties sealed his attachment to the black masses and his determination to champion their cause. Graduating in 1888, he trained further at Harvard University (Ph.D. 1895) and the University of Berlin. His doctoral dissertation on the suppression of the slave trade was published in 1896. He held positions

briefly with the University of Pennsylvania and Wilberforce in Ohio before returning to the South in 1897 to teach sociology, economics, and history at Atlanta University.

His third book, *The Souls of Black Folk* (1903), was a collection of hauntingly beautiful essays on every important aspect of black culture in the South; perhaps its most famous insight concerned the "double-consciousness" of the black American: "One ever feels his twoness—an American, a Negro; two souls, two thoughts, two unreconciled strivings; two warring ideals in one dark body, whose dogged strength alone keeps it from being torn asunder." With this book he secured preeminence among all African American intellectuals and became the leader of those opposed to the powerful and conservative Booker T. Washington of Tuskegee. His yearly (1897–1914) Atlanta University Studies of black social conditions and a biography of John Brown (1909) added to his reputation.

Increasingly controversial, he moved to New York in 1910 to found and edit *The Crisis*, the monthly magazine of the fledgling NAACP. For 24 years he sustained an assault on all forms of racial injustice, especially in the South. In 1934 he published *Black Reconstruction in America*, a grand Marxist-framed reevaluation of the much-maligned role of blacks in the Civil War and its aftermath. That year he returned to Atlanta University after grave disagreements with the NAACP leadership over strategies during the Depression; Du Bois favored a program of voluntary self-segregation stressing economics

that many people found similar to the old program of Booker T. Washington. At Atlanta University he found little support for his projected scheme to organize the study of sociology among black colleges and other institutions in the South. In 1944 he rejoined the NAACP in New York but soon found himself again at odds with the leadership, this time over his growing interest in radical socialism. He left the NAACP finally in 1948. By this time his attitude toward the South had changed somewhat. Influenced no doubt by the aims of the leftist Southern Negro Youth Congress, he declared in 1948 that "the future of American Negroes is in the South. . . . Here is the magnificent climate; here is the fruitful earth under the beauty of the southern sun; and here . . . is the need of the thinker, the worker, and the dreamer." His Socialist activities culminated in his arrest and trial in 1951 as an unregistered agent of a foreign principal; the presiding judge heard the evidence, then directed his acquittal.

Unpopular and even shunned in some quarters, he turned to fiction to express his deepest feelings. In a trilogy set mainly in the South, *The Black Flame (The Ordeal of Mansart)*, 1957; *Mansart Builds a School*, 1959; and *Worlds of Color*, 1961, he told the story of a black southerner, born at the end of Reconstruction, who rises slowly and patiently to the leadership of a small southern school, witnessing in his long lifetime the important events of modern American and world history. In October 1961 Du Bois was admitted to membership in the Communist Party of the United States; that month he left his country to live in Ghana at the invitation of Kwame Nkrumah. In February 1963 he renounced his American citizenship and became a Ghanaian. He had made little progress on the task for which Nkrumah had summoned him, the editing of the *Encyclopedia Africana*, when he died of natural causes 27 August 1963.

ARNOLD RAMPERSAND
Stanford University

Herbert Aptheker, *Annotated Bibliography of the Published Writings of W. E. B. Du Bois* (1973); David Levering Lewis, *W. E. B. Du Bois: Biography of a Race, 1868–1919* (1993); Arnold Rampersand, *The Art and Imagination of W. E. B. Du Bois* (1976); Raymond Wolters, *Du Bois and His Rivals* (2002); Shamoon Zamir, *Dark Voices: W. E. B. Du Bois and American Thought, 1888–1903* (1995).

Evers, Medgar

(1926–1963) CIVIL RIGHTS ACTIVIST. During the 1950s and 1960s Medgar Wiley Evers dedicated his life to the racial integration of Mississippi. He taught black Mississippians about the power of the ballot, and he organized economic boycotts. At his urging, thousands of black customers refused to buy soft drinks, bread, and clothes sold by white-owned businesses that perpetuated segregation in Jackson, Miss. In the guise of a field hand in 1955, he gathered evidence on the lynching of Emmett Till, a black teenager. With force and clarity, Evers spoke out, shaming blacks and whites alike into taking steps to end racial separation.

Born 2 July 1926 Evers grew up in the small, east-central Mississippi town of Decatur. His father worked for a sawmill and on the railroads; his mother was a domestic worker. They raised cows, pigs, chickens, vegetables, and cotton on the small plot of land around their house on the edge of town. As a boy, Medgar learned about self-respect from his father, who did not follow the custom of stepping off the sidewalk when whites approached, and Medgar learned religious values from his mother, who required her children to attend church every Sunday.

Childhood experiences of brutality against blacks embittered Evers, and for a time, after serving in the U.S. Army during World War II, he idolized Jomo Kenyatta of Africa and dreamed of forming a band of fighters, similar to Kenyatta's, who would right the wrongs whites had inflicted on blacks. After the war, he enrolled at Alcorn Agricultural and Mechanical College in southwestern Mississippi. He married Myrlie Beasley on Christmas Eve 1951, and the next year the Magnolia Mutual Life Insurance Company hired him as a salesman. In February 1954 he tried to upgrade his education and break the color barrier at the University of Mississippi Law School but was rejected. Evers decided not to pursue it, although later, in 1962, he assisted James H. Meredith in becoming the first black to enroll in the university. Evers's volunteer work for the National Association for the Advancement of Colored People turned into a full-time job: he was appointed in late 1954 as the first Mississippi field secretary of the NAACP, a post he held until his death.

He eventually rejected his notions of a Kenyatta-style revolution, though he did name one of his sons after Kenyatta. Evers traveled through Mississippi, inspiring blacks to fight segregation in every nonviolent way possible. Myrlie Evers said her husband amazed journalists when he would tell them he stayed in Mississippi because he loved it. "It was part of him," she wrote in *For Us, the Living*, a book about their life together. "He loved to hunt and fish, to roam the fields and woods. . . . He had visited many places . . . but always he came back to Mississippi as a man coming home."

This sense of place and Evers's sense of justice led him to fight for change in Mississippi's capital city of Jackson. During the historic spring of 1963 Evers and other civil rights leaders pushed for blacks to be hired on the Jackson police force and as school crossing guards. Evers wanted public facilities and restaurants to be open to everyone, regardless of race. And he sought an end to the signs that segregated white and black races at drinking fountains and restrooms.

Mass meetings, demonstrations at segregated lunch counters, and boycotts of white businesses in Jackson began to force changes. Police arrested black teenagers who demonstrated and corralled them for days at the fairgrounds. Evers remained at the forefront of the city's boycotts, which were attracting national publicity.

On the night of 11 June 1963 President John F. Kennedy told the nation in a televised address that he was sending a bill to Congress to ensure racial justice. The bill was to become the Civil Rights Act of 1964. After seeing Kennedy's speech, Evers drove to his Jackson home. Just after midnight on 12 June a bullet from a high-powered rifle felled him as he stepped from his car. Within an hour, he died at the University of Mississippi Medical Center, three weeks before his 37th birthday. After services in Jackson, Evers's body was flown to the National Cemetery in Arlington, Va., for a military burial.

Evers's widow moved to California and became active in public administration, serving as the first woman chair of the NAACP, beginning in 1995. The remarried Myrlie Evers-Williams urged the state of Mississippi to reopen the case of Medgar Evers's murder, leading to the conviction in 1994 of Byron De La Beckwith. She established the Medgar Evers Institute in Jackson, Miss.

BERKLEY HUDSON
University of Missouri–Columbia

Myrlie Evers-Williams and Manning Marable, eds., *The Autobiography of Medgar Evers: A Hero's Life and Legacy Revealed through His Writings, Letters, and Speeches* (2005); Cleveland Donald, in *Mississippi Heroes*, ed. Dean Faulkner Wells and Hunter Cole (1980); Mrs. Medgar Evers with William Peters, *For Us, the Living* (1967); John R. Salter Jr., *Jackson, Mississippi: An American Chronicle of Struggle and Schism* (1979).

Farm Security Administration

During the Great Depression the New Deal administration wrestled with the problem of massive and chronic rural poverty. Between 1935 and 1946 the Farm Security Administration (FSA)

as the federal agency that worked
to uplift some of America's poorest
people.

The FSA began as the Resettlement
Administration (RA), created by President
Franklin D. Roosevelt's executive
order in May 1935. The RA consolidated
federal programs for classifying
rural land, retiring submarginal farms,
and resettling their residents. Also
transferred to the RA were rural subsistence
homesteads for surplus industrial
workers, pilot suburban housing
projects, and several cooperative farm
communities started with federal relief
funds. But the largest responsibility
assigned to the new agency was the
rural rehabilitation work of the Federal
Emergency Relief Administration
(FERA). Faced with the urgent needs of
destitute farmers, especially southern
tenants and sharecroppers, the FERA
had attempted to keep them on the
land with a combination of production
and living credit and close supervision
of their farming. Acquiring this
rapidly growing program made the RA
an antipoverty agency.

The RA's responsibilities expanded
in July 1937, when Congress passed
the Bankhead-Jones Farm Tenant Act
providing a modest lending program
to help tenants buy farms. President
Roosevelt assigned this new work to
the RA, which was renamed the Farm
Security Administration.

Even though the FSA never reached
a majority of the poor and often bypassed
the most impoverished, its
programs gave substantial aid to many
farmers during its peak years of 1937–
42. The largest program was always

rural rehabilitation. The FSA's 1941 report,
for example, indicated loans or
grants (typically a few hundred dollars
per case) being received by more than
600,000 southern families. County FSA
supervisors helped clients write farm-
and home-management plans and gave
technical advice. At its best this supervision
improved the farming skills, self-
direction, nutrition, and health of the
poor. Among other programs the FSA
promoted for low-income farmers were
cooperatives for marketing produce and
purchasing supplies, joint ownership of
breeding livestock or machinery, farm-
improvement loans, prepaid health
care plans, and debt-adjustment loans.
However, farm-purchase lending under
the Bankhead-Jones Act was so poorly
funded that the FSA could serve only
a few thousand borrowers per year,
making little impact on tenancy.

Under southern administrators
Will W. Alexander (1936–40) and
Calvin B. Baldwin (1940–43), the FSA
attempted a comprehensive attack on
rural poverty, but its efforts were short-
lived. Congress slashed the FSA's funds
during World War II and disbanded it
in 1946. A few of the FSA's credit functions
survive in a successor agency, the
Farmers' Home Administration.

PAUL E. MERTZ
University of Wisconsin–Stevens Point

Sidney Baldwin, *Poverty and Politics: The
Rise and Decline of the Farm Security Administration*
(1968); Paul E. Mertz, *New
Deal Policy and Southern Rural Poverty*
(1978).

Fitzhugh, George

(1808–1881) SLAVERY ADVOCATE.
Fitzhugh was from Port Royal, Va.,
the descendant of an old southern
family that had fallen on hard times.
He practiced law and struggled as a
small planter but made a reputation
with two books, *Sociology for the South*
(1854) and *Cannibals All!* (1857), which
alarmed northerners like Abraham Lincoln and roused southerners to take
new and higher ground in defense of
slavery.

Fitzhugh insisted that all labor, not
merely black, had to be enslaved and
that the world must become all slave
or all free. He defined slavery broadly
to include all systems of servile labor.
These views had become commonplace
in the South by the 1850s. His origi-
nality lay in the insight that slavery
could only survive and prevail if the
capitalist world market were destroyed.
He understood that organic social
relations and attendant values could
not survive in a world dominated by
capitalist competition and bourgeois
individualism.

His call for war against the modern
world, expressed in a harsh polemical
style, made him a solitary figure. Numerous others agreed that free labor
spelled class war and invited anarchy.
They also agreed that slavery overcame
the "social question" by establishing a
master class that combined interest with
sentiment to offer the masses security.
But, having no confidence in his utopian vision of a reversal of history, they
generally tried, however illogically, to
convince the European and northern

bourgeoisie to restore some form of
slavery in a corporatist order.

Fitzhugh opposed secession until
the last minute, arguing that a slaveholding Confederacy could not survive
until the advanced capitalist countries
had themselves converted. After the
war, which once begun he loyally and
enthusiastically supported, Fitzhugh
sank into obscurity, becoming increasingly negrophobic and idiosyncratic.
For all intents and purposes, he died at
Appomattox.

EUGENE D. GENOVESE
Atlanta, Georgia

Eugene D. Genovese, *The World the Slaveholders Made: Two Essays in Interpretation*
(1969); Harvey Wish, *George Fitzhugh:
Propagandist of the Old South* (1943).

Forrest, Nathan Bedford

(1821–1877) CONFEDERATE GENERAL.
A man of little formal education and
no prior military experience, Nathan
Bedford Forrest became one of three
Confederate soldiers with no military
training to rise to the rank of lieutenant general. Born in Bedford County,
Tenn., Forrest struggled from poverty
to a position of considerable wealth as
a planter and slave dealer. Soon after
the outbreak of the Civil War he raised
and equipped a battalion of cavalry, of
which he was elected lieutenant colonel.
Forrest performed brilliantly at the
battles of Fort Donelson and Shiloh
and as an independent cavalry commander behind enemy lines through
the summer of 1863, rising to the rank
of brigadier general.

In command of the cavalry on the

Nathan Bedford Forrest, Confederate hero
(Photographer and number unavailable,
Library of Congress, Washington, D.C.)

right wing of General Braxton Bragg's
Army of Tennessee during the battle of
Chickamauga, Forrest led his troops,
fighting as mounted infantry, through
some of the most severe fighting of
the war. Afterward he quarreled bitterly with Bragg, was relieved of his
corps, but was granted an independent
command in west Tennessee and north
Mississippi and promoted to major
general.

Operating out of northern Mississippi, Forrest staged several intrepid
and damaging raids against federal
supply links and depots in Tennessee while successfully defending his
base against numerous incursions by
greatly superior Union forces. Forrest
was reassigned to the Army of Ten-

nessee as commander of all cavalry
during John Bell Hood's abortive Tennessee campaign, and only his bold and
skillful rear-guard actions saved that
army from utter annihilation following
the Confederate disasters at Franklin
and Nashville. Although elevated to
the rank of lieutenant general for his
heroic efforts on the retreat from Nashville, Forrest was at last overwhelmed
by vastly superior federal numbers at
Selma, Ala., in April 1865.

Following the collapse of the Confederacy, Forrest served for some years
as president of the Selma, Marion &
Memphis Railroad and was reportedly the principal organizer and first
Imperial Wizard of the Ku Klux Klan.
To many military historians, though,
Nathan Bedford Forrest remains sig--
nificant as the preeminent American
cavalry leader.

Because he was the only unvaryingly
successful Confederate commander in
the western theater and because of the
relative poverty of his origins, Forrest
quickly became the darling of the plain
people of the Old Southwest. Unlike
the Virginia aristocrats, Lee and Stuart,
or the Louisiana Creole, Beauregard,
Forrest was a product of the South's
hardscrabble frontier and an archetypal
example of Jefferson's yeoman class.
Writers in the 20th-century South,
most notably William Faulkner and
the Nashville Agrarians, seized upon
Forrest as a symbol of the best that
the South's frontier culture produced.
Andrew Lytle's biography, *Bedford Forrest and His Critter Company* (1931),
Caroline Gordon's novel *None Shall*

Look Back (1937), and Jesse Hill Ford's *The Raider* (1975) are full-length interpretations of Forrest's character and military career, and the Confederate "Wizard of the Saddle" also provided material for George Washington Cable, who served under him in the war's final year; Stark Young, whose father rode with Forrest; Robert Penn Warren, whose grandfather was one of his captains; and Donald Davidson, who attempted but failed to complete an epic poem based on the great cavalryman's campaigns. To each of these writers Forrest represents the highest emanation of Anglo-Saxon, agrarian democracy on the Old Southwest frontier, an unlettered man of the soil hurling back in confusion the minions of modern industrial, materialistic society. Of the legend of Forrest and his men, William Faulkner wrote that "even seventy-five years afterwards, [it was] still powerful, still dangerous, still coming!"

THOMAS W. CUTRER
Arizona State University

Paul Ashdown, *The Myth of Nathan Bedford Forrest* (2005); R. S. Henry, *"First with the Most" Forrest* (1944); Jack Hurst, *Nathan Bedford Forrest: A Biography* (1993); Andrew Nelson Lytle, *Bedford Forrest and His Critter Company* (1984); James H. Mathes, *General Forrest* (1902); John A. Wyeth, *That Devil Forrest* (1959).

Franklin, John Hope

(b. 1915) HISTORIAN.
Franklin stands in the first rank of professional historians and of those blacks who work actively on behalf of the modern civil rights movement. Born in Rentiesville, Okla., in 1915, Franklin

embodies the ethnic and racial complexities of the South: his family was part Cherokee and part black, and some of its members served as slaves to the Cherokees in the antebellum decades. His father, Buck Franklin, became a successful lawyer in Tulsa and saw his legal offices destroyed in one of the antiblack riots after the armistice of 1918. Buck Franklin quietly rebuilt his legal practice, for a time actually operating inside a tent, and this experience became vital to the spirit of John Hope Franklin's own protests and achievements.

Given the chance to attend college, young Franklin studied at Fisk University (A.B. 1935) and then entered the Harvard University graduate program (A.M. 1936, Ph.D. 1941) at a time when there were few black historians in the country. Between 1942 and 1992 he taught at Fisk University, Howard University, St. Augustine's College, Brooklyn College, the University of Chicago, and Duke University. In the field of civil rights, Franklin was instrumental in integrating the Southern Historical Association, the American Historical Association, and the Mississippi Valley Historical Association (now the Organization of American Historians), eventually serving as president in all of these organizations; he also contributed background research for the National Association for the Advancement of Colored People in the campaign to integrate the public schools, culminating successfully in the legal case *Brown v. Board of Education* (1954).

In the study of black history Frank-

Historian John Hope Franklin (Duke University Archives, Durham, N.C.)

lin published four major works among scores of edited and special studies: *From Slavery to Freedom: A History of African Americans* (1947; 8th ed., 2000) was an encyclopedic mapping of the path of black progress in America, optimistic in its style; *The Militant South, 1800–1861* (1956) was a bolder, more pessimistic interpretation that traced both a self-destructive urge among the antebellum southern leaders who produced the Civil War and a continuing tendency to violence after the war; *Reconstruction after the Civil War* (1963) was one of the early efforts to revise the mythic white view of the horrors of Reconstruction, as embodied in historian William A. Dunning's works, and to focus on black participation and achievement in the post–Civil War period; and *Runaway Slaves; Rebels on the Plantation* (with Loren Schweninger, 1999) was a very sophisticated quantitative analysis of data concerning slave resistance to oppression, which, like his entire oeuvre, emphasizes at once the glorious idea of equality and the sordid facts of inequality even in the best of southern and national venues.

In 1992 Franklin became emeritus professor of legal history at Duke University, but he in no sense retired, publishing a number of scholarly studies, revising earlier studies, and helping to recruit African American scholars in all fields of study to teach at the school. He remained a public figure of importance, serving in the Clinton administration as chairman of the advisory board to the president's initiative on race. In that post, he took occasion, much as he had when far younger, to lecture federal officials, not excluding President Clinton himself, about the continuing failure of the United States to provide adequate educational or job opportunities for black youth. Through the long decades, Franklin has retained a scholar's dignity and a humanist's respect for the opinions of others while working as diligently as any other activist advocate for racial justice in the South and nation.

JOHN HERBERT ROPER
Emory & Henry College

John Hope Franklin, *Free Negroes in North Carolina, 1790–1860* (1943), *Mirror*

to America: The Autobiography of John Hope Franklin (2005), with John Whittingham Franklin, *My Life and an Era* (2000); Earle E. Thorpe, *Black Historians: A Critique* (1971); interviews with August Meier Franklin, C. Vann Woodward, and LeRoy Graf, typescripts in Southern Historical Collection, University of North Carolina, Chapel Hill.

Grimké Sisters

(Sarah, 1793–1874; Angelina, 1805–1879) ABOLITIONISTS.

The Grimké sisters, Sarah and Angelina, were unique in the American antislavery movement. They were southerners, women, and members of a family known to own slaves. Sarah was born in 1793 and Angelina in 1805, the last of 11 Grimké children. Sarah virtually adopted her new baby sister, and they remained close throughout their lives. The Grimké family belonged to Charleston's elite upper class, whose children were reared in luxury and served by many slaves. They were city dwellers, but their large plantation in upper South Carolina and its numerous slaves were an important source of family wealth. The sisters' education in a select girls' academy stressing the social graces was slight and superficial. They were expected to marry well, bear children, and become successful matrons. However, the sisters lost interest in conventional life as each grew into adulthood.

Religion led them both to reject slavery. Though the Grimké family church was St. Philip's Episcopal, each sister experienced conversion in revivals of other churches. Sarah in time

Sarah Moore Grimké (Library of Congress [LC-USZ61-1608], Washington, D.C.)

Angelina Emily Grimké (Library of Congress [LC-USZ61-1609], Washington, D.C.)

became a member of the Society of Friends, Angelina an enthusiastic Presbyterian. Sarah came to know Friends during her father's final illness. In 1821, following his death, she moved to Philadelphia and joined the Friends' Society. She accepted their firm tenet opposing slavery as a sin and eventually won her sister to the Quaker faith and the antislavery conviction. After her efforts failed to convert family and friends, Angelina left Charleston to make her home with Sarah in Philadelphia.

In early 1853 the more activist Angelina began to make contact with the antislavery movement. After William Lloyd Garrison published a letter of hers in the *Liberator*, Angelina began to write her first tract, *Appeal to the Christian Women of the South*. The

American Anti-Slavery Society rushed it into print. The society then urged her to aid the cause by addressing women's groups in "parlor meetings"; Sarah went with her and remained at her side.

They were the only women asked to the "Convention of the Seventy," which met in October of 1836, for the training of new agents to spread abolitionism. Theodore Weld, whom Angelina later married, was the leader in the sessions and gave the sisters special training for their coming lecture tours. They went from this convention to their crowded "parlor meetings," held in churches, and they accepted invitations from other localities. They were swept into preparations for a forthcoming "Convention of American Anti-Slavery Women," held in March of 1837. When it ended, the Grimkés had come to know most of the abolitionist leaders in the East, men and women, and were themselves regarded as belonging to the circle of female leaders. The Grimkés arrived in Boston in May of 1837 and began their historic antislavery crusade. They also increasingly spoke out in favor of women's rights, despite criticism from antislavery leaders.

The spring months of 1838 saw Angelina Grimké's greatest triumphs. Twice in a crowded Massachusetts legislative hall she addressed a committee of the legislature, a sensational occasion headlined in the press. Also, Boston's antislavery women rented the Odeon Theater, and for five meetings, one a week, Angelina addressed an overflowing hall on abolition of slavery. In Philadelphia, she calmly addressed a mass meeting of a Convention of American Anti-Slavery Women with a threatening mob outside.

Angelina and Weld were married the day before the convention. When the sessions ended, Sarah accompanied them to their new home, and she stayed with them for the remainder of her life. Angelina fully expected to return to her work for the antislavery cause but did not do so. She and Sarah assisted Weld on his best-known tract, *American Slavery as It Is* (1839). Three children were born between 1839 and 1844, two boys and a girl.

In the late 1850s both sisters taught in the Eagleswood School, which Weld headed. Later the family lived near Boston, where Weld and Angelina continued to teach. When war came in 1861, Angelina Grimké, at the age of 56, returned to part-time public life.

Garrison had persuaded Weld to lecture again, this time in aid of the war effort. Angelina now rejoined her old friends in forming the organization Loyal Women of the Republic, and once again she was speaking for freedom of the slaves. Sarah was over 70 when the end of the war brought full emancipation. She died in 1874. Angelina suffered two strokes, the first in 1875, and was ill until her death in 1879.

KATHERINE DU PRE LUMPKIN
Chapel Hill, North Carolina

Angelina Emily Grimké, *Walking by Faith: The Diary of Angelina Grimké, 1825–1835*, ed. Charles Wilbanks (2003); Gerda Lerner, *The Feminist Thought of Sarah Grimké* (1997), *The Grimké Sisters from South Carolina: Rebels against Slavery* (1967); Katherine Du Pre Lumpkin, *The Emancipation of Angelina Grimké* (1974); Weld-Grimké Collection, Clements Library, University of Michigan, Ann Arbor.

Hamer, Fannie Lou

(1917–1977) CIVIL RIGHTS ACTIVIST. Fannie Lou Townsend Hamer was the last of 20 children born to Jim and Ella Townsend, sharecroppers in Montgomery County, Miss. The family moved two years after her birth to Sunflower County, where she worked in the cotton fields from the age of six and attended public school through junior high. In 1945 she married Perry Hamer, a tractor driver on the W. D. Marlon plantation, located four miles east of Ruleville. She labored as a field hand on the Marlon plantation until it was discovered that she could read and write. Then she was promoted to timekeeper. She was fired in 1962 be-

Fannie Lou Hamer at the Democratic National
Convention, Atlantic City, N.J., August 1964
(Warren K. Leffler, photographer, Library of Congress
[LC-U9-12470B-17], Washington, D.C.)

cause she had attempted to register to
vote. Forced to leave the plantation, she
received shelter in the home of William
Tucker in Ruleville, but had to flee from
there after the house was attacked and
riddled with bullets.

In 1963 she passed the Mississippi
literacy test and became a registered
voter. She then became a field secretary
for the Student Nonviolent Coordinating Committee, organizing voter
registration campaigns and working to
obtain welfare and other benefits for
underprivileged black families. While
returning by bus from a voter registration workshop, she was arrested
and severely beaten for attempting to
use the restroom in a bus station in

Winona. Meanwhile, she had worked
with the National Council of Churches
in creating Delta Ministry, an extensive
community-development program in
Mississippi.

Because the regular Democratic
Party of Mississippi refused to accept
black members, Hamer joined with
black and white protesters in 1964 to
form the Mississippi Freedom Democratic Party (MFDP). She was a member
that year of the MFDP delegation that
challenged the seating of the regular
Mississippi delegation to the National
Democratic Convention, and in her
testimony before the credentials committee she vividly described the brutal
reprisals she and other blacks had suffered in Mississippi because of their
efforts to vote and to exercise other civil
rights. Her testimony was dramatically
presented to the nation by television.
Thereafter, she was in great demand,
both as a speaker and as a performer of
civil rights songs and spirituals.

The MFDP was unsuccessful in replacing the regular Democratic delegation in 1964, but that convention
pledged that no delegation that barred
blacks would be seated in future conventions. Hamer became a member of
the delegation of the Mississippi Loyal-
ist Democratic Party (the successor of
MFDP), which unseated Mississippi's
regular delegation at the National
Democratic Convention. Meanwhile,
in 1964 she had attempted to run as
the MFDP candidate for the U.S. House
of Representatives from Mississippi's
Second Congressional District, but her
name was not allowed on the ballot.
Consequently, she, along with Victoria

Gray and Annie Devine, on 4 January 1965, challenged the entire Mississippi delegation in the House of Representatives as unrepresentative of the people of the state. Their challenge failed.

In 1965 Hamer was the plaintiff in a suit that resulted in the U.S. Fifth Circuit of Appeals' setting aside the local elections in Sunflower and Moorhead counties because blacks had not been allowed to vote. She served on the Democratic National Committee from 1968 to 1971. In 1969 she founded and became vice president of Freedom Farms Corporation, a nonprofit venture designed to provide social services to help needy black and white families produce food, to promote minority business opportunities, and to provide scholarships. She became chairperson of the board of directors of Fannie Lou Hamer Day Care Center founded in Ruleville by the National Council of Negro Women in 1970. She also served as a director of the Sunflower County Day Care and Family Service and the Garment Manufacturing Plant, as chairperson of the Sunflower County Voter's League, as a member of the policy council of the National Women's Political Caucus, as a trustee of the Martin Luther King Center for Social Change, and as a member of the state executive committee of the United Democratic Party of Mississippi.

Fannie Lou Hamer received honorary degrees from Tougaloo College, Shaw University, Morehouse College, Columbia College, and Howard University. She also received the Mary Church Terrell Award from Delta Sigma Theta Sorority and the Paul Robeson Award from Alpha Phi Alpha Fraternity. In 1976 the mayor of Ruleville declared a Fannie Lou Hamer Day. She died of cancer in Mound Bayou Hospital the following March 14.

CLIFTON H. JOHNSON
Amistad Research Center

Black Enterprise (May 1977); John Egerton, *Progressive* (May 1977); Fannie Lou Hamer, Papers, Amistad Research Center, New Orleans, Louisiana; Susan Johnson, *The Black Law Journal* (Summer 1972); June Jordan, *Fannie Lou Hamer* (1972); Chana Kai Lee, *For Freedom's Sake: The Life of Fannie Lou Hamer* (1999); Kay Mills, *This Little Light of Mine: The Life of Fannie Lou Hamer* (1993); *Never Turn Back: The Life of Fannie Lou Hamer* (Rediscovery Productions film, 1983); *Sojourners* (December 1982); C. J. Wilson, *New South* (Spring 1973).

Hammond, James Henry

(1807–1864) PLANTER AND POLITICIAN.

Hammond was born in 1807 in Upcountry South Carolina. Son of an impecunious schoolmaster who had moved to the South at the turn of the century, young Hammond graduated from South Carolina College in 1825. After several years of teaching while he prepared for the bar, he began the practice of law in Columbia. The excitement of the nullification controversy gave Hammond his initial prominence as a strongly sectionalist newspaper editor. After a fortunate marriage to a Charleston heiress, Hammond left public life to manage the Savannah River plantation and 147 slaves he had acquired as a result of the union. Elected to Congress, Hammond moved to Washington in

1835, but after a dramatic debut attacking the reception of abolition petitions by the House of Representatives, he was stricken with a nervous ailment and resigned his seat in Congress to travel in Europe.

In 1842 Hammond reentered politics as governor of his native state and gained attention during the next few years with an extreme sectionalist position more radical than that of John C. Calhoun. At the end of his term a scandal over charges of improprieties in his relationship with his four nieces, the daughters of the powerful Wade Hampton II, returned Hammond once again to his plantation, where he continued to write on agricultural and political topics and to experiment with agricultural innovations until he was chosen for the U.S. Senate in 1857. More sanguine about the possibilities for the South in the Union than at any previous time of his life, Hammond had profound doubts about its readiness for secession. Upon Lincoln's election, he resigned and privately differed sharply and vociferously with the Davis administration on Confederate policy. His health declined throughout the war years, and he died in November of 1864, just before Sherman began his march through South Carolina.

One of the South's leading intellects, Hammond is perhaps best remembered for his widely distributed tracts defending slavery as a positive good, *Two Letters on Slavery in the United States, Addressed to Thomas Clarkson, Esq.* (1845) and *Letter of His Excellency Governor Hammond to the Free Church of Glasgow on the Subject of Slavery* (1844), as well as for his oft-quoted proslavery "mud-sill" speech to the U.S. Senate in 1858. His extraordinarily rich personal, political, and plantation papers have been extensively used by 20th-century historians of slavery and the South.

DREW GILPIN FAUST
Radcliff Institute for Advanced Study
Harvard University

Carol K. Bleser, ed., *The Hammonds of Radcliffe* (1981); Carol K. Rothrock Bleser and James Henry Hammond, eds., *Secret and Sacred: The Diaries of James Henry Hammond, a Southern Slaveholder* (1988); Drew Gilpin Faust, *James Henry Hammond and the Old South: A Design for Mastery* (1982); James Henry Hammond Papers, Library of Congress; James Henry Hammond Papers, South Carolina Library, University of South Carolina, Columbia.

Jackson, Andrew

(1767–1845) U.S. PRESIDENT, FRONTIERSMAN, PLANTER.
Born near the border of North and South Carolina—the exact spot is in dispute—Andrew Jackson moved to frontier Tennessee in 1788 at the age of 19, an early pioneer in a significant migration pattern that eventually redrew the boundaries of "the South." Tennessee at the time, and throughout Jackson's life, was more western than southern. Although he developed substantial landholdings near Nashville, held slaves, and lived the life of a gentleman planter at "The Hermitage," Jackson as late as the 1840s considered himself a westerner and a nationalist, never a southerner, and he was so perceived by his contemporaries.

Nonetheless Jackson's career was

Andrew Jackson, frontier hero and seventh president of the United States, date unknown (Library of Congress [LC-USZ62-117120], Washington, D.C.)

construction of the Constitution, the party served for decades as a shield for southern slave owners against the rising antislavery clamor. Paradoxically, it also embodied and promoted the democratic impulse whose egalitarian values and reform tendencies were ultimately subversive of the southern slavery system.

Although Jackson's Scots-Irish parents had only recently emigrated at the time of his birth, his formative years in the Upcountry Carolinas doubtless contributed to his fierce combativeness, his attraction to the law and the militia, his love of horses and horse racing, and his patrician style. It was as frontier lawyer and politician, militia leader and military hero, that he rose to fame, an ardent unionist and an instinctive democrat.

RICHARD H. BROWN
Newberry Library
Chicago, Illinois

H. W. Brands, *Andrew Jackson: His Life and Times* (2005); James Curtis, *Andrew Jackson and the Search for Vindication* (1976); Burke Davis, *Old Hickory: A Life of Andrew Jackson* (1977); Robert V. Remini, *The Revolutionary Age of Andrew Jackson* (1976).

rife with consequences for the South. His defeat of the British at New Orleans and of the Seminoles in Florida nailed down southern borders once and for all. He moved carefully on the issue of expansion into Texas while in office, but his passionate interest in the area eventually resulted in extension of the southern frontier westward.

The Democratic Party that he led to the presidency and institutionalized around Jacksonian issues represented an alliance of "Southern Planters and Plain Republicans of the North," as Martin Van Buren put it; it was rooted in the "Old Republican" ideology of Thomas Jefferson and coupled with a strong overlay of western pragmatism. Committed to the Union and to strict

Jackson, Jesse

(b. 1941) CIVIL RIGHTS ACTIVIST, MINISTER, POLITICIAN.
Called "the most famous Black man in America today" by one admiring biographer in the 1980s, a position confirmed at the time by the more scientific conclusions of major national polls, Jesse Louis Jackson was born 8 October 1941 in Greenville, S.C. His mother was Helen Burns, and his father was Noah

Louis Robinson, to whom his mother was never married. Charles Henry Jackson became the husband of Jesse's mother, and young Jackson's stepfather provided him with a comfortable home and stable family life.

Jackson grew up in Greenville, where he was sensitive to the racism and segregation of the times and exhibited an inquisitive mind, street savvy, athletic ability, and discipline. He left the University of Illinois after one year when he was told by coaches that a black man could not play quarterback, and he turned down a professional baseball contract when he was offered less than what would have been offered a white counterpart. He became active in the sit-in demonstrations organized by the Congress of Racial Equality (CORE) in Greensboro, N.C., where he had come to enter all-black North Carolina A & T University on a football scholarship. At A & T, he was a star quarterback, honor student, student body president, and fraternity leader. He was elected president of the North Carolina Inter-Collegiate Council on Human Rights, and by his senior year he assumed broader responsibilities as the southeastern field director of CORE. Jackson accepted a Rockefeller scholarship to the Chicago Theological Seminary, having decided that the pulpit was a better platform than the courtroom to realize his developing ambitions and commitments.

Jackson's prominence in the civil rights movement is tied to his apprenticeship under Dr. Martin Luther King Jr. Jackson met King while in college, but he did not join the staff of the Southern Christian Leadership Conference (SCLC) until 1965, helping to organize the Selma marches and demonstrations just prior to King's Chicago campaign. King later appointed Jackson as director of SCLC's Operation Breadbasket, an economic development coalition of ministers and business people using such direct action tactics as boycotts and mass demonstrations.

The assassination of King on 4 April 1968 led Jackson to assume national leadership, an opportunity he seized with vigor. Jackson emerged as the aggressive spokesperson of a movement in disarray. Operation Breadbasket moved away from its parent organization, SCLC, and proclaimed itself the leading civil rights organization in the nation. After a flurry of boycotts in which "covenants" — agreements to provide jobs, develop businesses, place deposits in black banks, and advertise in the black media — were signed, Operation Breadbasket was renamed Operation PUSH in December 1971. Jackson's tactics were reminiscent of the "Buy Black Campaign" and the "Don't Buy Where You Can't Work" protests of the 1930s in Chicago and other cities.

Jesse Jackson became a well-known political figure after his 1984 presidential campaign. Jackson had run for mayor of Chicago in 1971 and had been active in such national political forums as the National Black Political Assembly in 1972 and 1973. He showed himself in 1984 to be knowledgeable on a wide range of issues, articulate in televised debates, and adept in seizing media attention with such feats as his extrication of a black navy pilot from

Syria. Jackson galvanized black community sentiment, and the results were quite unexpected. With a very small campaign war chest, Jackson gathered almost 20 percent of the vote in the Democratic primaries and won 465.5 convention votes. More important, his campaign spurred voter registration, stirred local debate and activity, and challenged Democratic Party rules that seemed unfair. His achievement led to an invitation to deliver a keynote address to the Democratic National Convention in San Francisco.

Jackson, with his Rainbow Coalition, ran again for president in 1988, winning five Democratic primaries in southern states on 8 March 1988. He became more influential within the party after that and moved to Washington D.C., where he worked against homelessness in the nation's capital. He was elected to a six-year term as "statehood senator" in the District of Columbia.

Jackson has more recently lobbied corporations for minority business and employment opportunities, publicized incidents of racial violence, campaigned against media stereotyping of minorities, and established an international presence as a negotiator for release of captured Americans overseas.

RONALD BAILEY
Northeastern University

Rod Bush, ed., *The New Black Vote: Politics and Power in Four American Cities* (1984); Marshall Frady, *Jesse Jackson: A Biography* (1996); Adolph Reed Jr., *The Jesse Jackson Phenomenon: The Crisis of Purpose in Afro-American Politics* (1986); Barbara A. Reynolds, *Jesse Jackson: America's David* (1985); Hanes Walton, *Invisible Politics: Black Political Behavior* (1986).

Jackson, Stonewall

(1824–1863) CONFEDERATE GENERAL. Born in far western Virginia, at Clarksburg, on 21 January 1824, Thomas Jonathan "Stonewall" Jackson was raised by an uncle after his parents died when he was a child. He graduated from the U.S. Military Academy in 1846, gained renown in the Mexican War, and in 1851 accepted a professional appointment at Virginia Military Institute. He commanded his institution's cadet corps, which was involved in the public hanging of John Brown on 2 December 1859. He served as a field officer in the Confederate army, first as colonel and then, on 17 July 1861, as brigadier general. As commander of a brigade at the first battle of Bull Run (21 July 1861), he and his troops earned everlasting fame when Confederate general Barnard E. Bee praised them for standing "like a stone wall" in battle.

Promoted to major general on 7 October 1861, Jackson assumed command in the Shenandoah Valley on 5 November and led the Shenandoah Valley campaign from March to June 1862. One of the most praised and studied of all American military displays of tactics and strategy, the Valley campaign showed Jackson's ability to use speed, mobility, secrecy, and sheer willpower to distract a larger force. With fewer than 20,000 soldiers, Lieutenant General and Corps Commander Jackson frustrated the movements of over 125,000 Union troops. Jackson was

General T. J. (Stonewall) Jackson (date unknown)
(J. L. Giles, photographer, Library of Congress
[LC-USZ62-93021], Washington, D.C.)

less successful in the Seven Days campaign, but he regained his dominance of northern commanders at Harpers Ferry (15 September 1862), Antietam (17 September 1862), Fredericksburg (13 December 1862), and Chancellorsville (1–2 May 1863). During the night of the Chancellorsville victory, Jackson was wounded by one of his own troops, and he died of pneumonia on 10 May. He was only 39 years old, but Jackson, a lieutenant general when he died, had already become Robert E. Lee's most trusted subordinate.

Jackson was an eccentric personality. Untidy in appearance, rigidly moral and devoutly religious, shy and quiet, Jackson nonetheless was a charismatic figure to the Virginia soldiers he drove relentlessly. His success in the Shenan-

doah Valley made Jackson's name well known to southerners, most of whom apparently regarded him less as Lee's subordinate than as a coinstrument with Lee of God's destiny for the South.

Jackson was a military genius. English biographer George F. R. Henderson claimed in his 1898 study that Jackson's few written maxims "are almost a complete summary of the art of war." But Jackson's importance to southern culture transcended his military significance. He was a stern Calvinist, a spiritual descendant of Cromwell. Southern ministers during and after the war pointed to Jackson as a prophet-warrior on the Old Testament model. They admired his unbending righteousness. The moralistic, hardscrabble South identified with Jackson, the puritanical teetotaler. Henry A. White even included Jackson as an exemplar of his denomination's faith in *Southern Presbyterian Leaders* (1911). Allen Tate's search for the southern heritage in the 1920s led him to write a narrative biography of Jackson, published in 1928. More recently, Bob McDill's country-and-western song "Good Old Boys" refers to the songwriter's childhood, when a picture of Stonewall Jackson hung on the wall, quietly teaching southern lessons.

Jackson was, along with Lee and Jefferson Davis, one of the Confederate trinity of saints. A group of English admirers raised the money to erect a statue of him in Richmond in October of 1875, and another one was later dedicated on that city's Monument Boulevard. A bronze monument marks his grave in Lexington, Va., and a statue by Moses Ezekiel guards the parade grounds at the Virginia Military Institute. VMI's Preston Library displays items from Jackson's life. Elected to the Hall of Fame for Great Americans in 1955, Jackson now has a monument in New York City as well. His image has been carved into the Stone Mountain Memorial in Georgia. The third Monday in January is a Virginia holiday honoring Jackson and Lee.

CHARLES REAGAN WILSON
University of Mississippi

Robert Lewis Dabney, *Life and Campaigns of Lieut.-General Thomas J. Jackson* (1866); Byron Farwell, *Stonewall: A Biography of General Thomas J. Jackson* (1992); James R. Robertson Jr., *Stonewall Jackson: The Man, the Soldier, the Legend* (1997); Allen Tate, *Stonewall Jackson: The Good Soldier* (1928); Frank E. Vandiver, *Mighty Stonewall* (1957).

Jamestown

The founders of Jamestown, Va., had an unrealistic vision of the South's promise. Many imagined a lush, naturally abundant, semitropical paradise replete with exotic fruits ripe for the picking, peopled by friendly natives who would shower them with precious jewels and metals. They also hoped to find the illusory Passage to India, which drew scores of Europeans to America's shores.

By the 19th century, Americans had devised their own myths about the first English settlement to survive in the New World. Some talked of noble Englishmen who carried Christianity and civilization to America and, with the establishment of the House of

Burgesses in 1619, provided the country with democratic self-government. Others, not so generous, noted that the first slave ship also arrived on Virginia's shores in 1619, creating an institution that would tear the nation apart in less than two centuries.

The actual story of Jamestown's settlement was neither romantic nor inspiring. Financed as a short-term joint stock company under the auspices of the Virginia Company, the odd mix of gentlemen, servants, and adventurers sailing to Chesapeake Bay in the spring of 1607 were looking for profit for the company and reward for themselves. They would work for the company for seven years, and then they would be free to make their own fortunes in a bountiful land.

But no one got rich in Virginia. The native Algonquians attacked the colonists almost immediately after they landed, and the fort the adventurers erected to protect themselves from future attacks offered little comfort. Relationships with the natives were tense thereafter, although, without Chief Powhatan's help, the settlement would probably have failed completely. The company did not always send adequate supplies to its New World servants, and the men living in America either would not or could not procure sufficient food for themselves. They were surely not helped by the fact that the area suffered a devastating drought from 1606 to 1612, the worst the Chesapeake region witnessed in over 800 years. Recent archaeological evidence indicates that the colonists were not the "lazy Englishmen" of myth. In fact, they made a valiant effort to help the settlement succeed. There were blacksmiths and brick makers and even a copper works in early Jamestown. Still, the settlers were initially unsuccessful. Indeed, by 1611 only 60 of the original 214 adventurers remained.

Successive charters in 1609, 1612, and 1619 introduced two important innovations—the headright system and the House of Burgesses. The first gave settlers a stake in the country, promising land to those who paid for their own or someone else's transportation to America. The House of Burgesses had very limited powers. Its laws, mere recommendations, became valid only when approved by the company in London. Never particularly democratic, it quickly became the means by which ambitious and ruthless adventurers exploited their less fortunate counterparts. Still, it was the first representative legislative assembly in English America.

In 1619 the first slave ship arrived in Jamestown, although slavery did not take root in Virginia until the end of the century. The mortality rate for new settlers was so high that white servants, often provided gratis by the company, were more economical than chattel slaves.

With the introduction of tobacco, Virginia found itself a profitable crop. But though the "noxious weed" brought riches to a few, it caused the development of what Edmund Morgan has described as a "boom town" mentality. Settlers refused to grow anything but tobacco. Sharp dealing abounded; the streets were filled with men who whored, drank, and gambled away their fortunes. While some settlers became rich, the company's English investors failed to realize any profits. Lack of communication, loss of control over their servants, and the self-interest of the settlers combined to destroy the Virginia Company. An Indian massacre in 1622 demolished any hopes for success that the company's investors may have harbored. In 1624 Virginia became English America's first royal colony. Jamestown remained Virginia's capital until 1698, when its statehouse burned to the ground, and Williamsburg became the new center of government.

A short-term company designed for quick profit had evolved into a permanent society. Unlike New England, Virginia was highly individualistic, at times almost anarchistic. It had few churches and fewer cities; its members lived on widely dispersed farms and developed a distrust of outsiders that to some extent would translate into hostility toward royal interference in the next century. A disappointment to its founders, it nevertheless survived penury, greed, and mismanagement to become England's oldest enduring New World possession.

SHEILA SKEMP
University of Mississippi

Philip L. Barbour, *Pocahontas and Her World: A Chronicle of America's First Settlement in Which Is Related the Story of the Indians and the Englishmen, Particularly Captain John Smith, Captain Samuel Argall, and Major John Rolfe* (1969), *The Three Worlds of Captain John Smith* (1964); Carl Bridenbaugh, *Jamestown, 1544–1699* (1980); Kathleen M. Brown, *Good Wives, Nasty Wenches, and Anxious Patriarchs: Gender,*

Race, and Power in Colonial Virginia (1996); Edmund S. Morgan, *American Slavery, American Freedom: The Ordeal of Colonial Virginia* (1975); Alden T. Vaughan, *American Genesis: Captain John Smith and the Founding of Virginia* (1975).

Jefferson, Thomas

(1743–1826) U.S. PRESIDENT, WRITER, PLANTER, SCIENTIST, ARCHITECT. Thomas Jefferson was born on the edge of the frontier in colonial Virginia. He went on to acquire as fine an education as America offered, graduating from the College of William and Mary in 1726. He studied law under George Wythe and practiced at the bar until the Revolution. He was elected to the Virginia House of Burgesses in 1769. Already the inheritor of large landholdings, he increased his property greatly through the dowry of his wife, Martha Wayles Skelton, whom he married in 1772. They had two daughters who survived to maturity.

In 1774 Jefferson drew political attention with his pamphlet *A Summary View of the Rights of British America*, the best remonstrance against the king and defense of colonial rights that had yet been seen. He carefully controlled his writing style so that any literate reader might follow his argument. Then, in 1776, Jefferson—now a member of the Continental Congress—was chosen to write the Declaration of Independence. It is his masterpiece and America's fundamental political document. In succeeding years he was elected governor of the state of Virginia and member of Congress and was ap-pointed minister to France. From 1790 to 1793 he served under Washington as the first secretary of state.

Jefferson's only book, *Notes on the State of Virginia*, was published in 1785. In it he recorded the milieu of early America. Jefferson was an advocate of the scientific method, and his book included efforts to classify botanical, geological, and paleontological specimens. He showed the confident Enlightenment belief that science could promote progress. His collection and classification of items reflected the practical need of a farmer to know the environment, as well as simply the desire to satisfy his curiosity. He agonized over the question of slavery (he held many slaves), echoing most of the persistent stereotyping of blacks so noticeably American. Controversies over Jefferson's relationship with his slave, Sally Hemings, have reverberated from his time to the contemporary era. Yet he was a true Enlightenment man, also voicing—as in the Declaration—the finest of ideals concerning justice, religious freedom, and equality.

He was paternalistic, not only at home, but in his attitudes toward Indians, blacks, women, and commoners. Thus, his long political service was noblesse oblige. He was elected third president of the United States in 1801 (a second term followed). While president he arranged the Louisiana Purchase (1803), doubling the size of the nation.

Always busy, he designed his mansion, Monticello, the Virginia capitol at Richmond, and, late in life, the University of Virginia. He designed an Epis-

Thomas Jefferson, c. 1898 (Painting by Gilbert Stuart, Library of Congress [LC-USZ62-8195], Washington, D.C.)

copal chapel in Charlottesville, dozens of Virginia country homes, simple and functional courthouses, and even jails in Cumberland and Nelson counties. He accumulated an architectural library of 50 titles in French, Italian, German, and English. His architectural achievement was to adapt classical forms to Virginian and southern needs.

Jefferson personified character, vision, grace, scholarship, and leadership—the qualities of the early southern gentleman that are part of his legacy. Students of southern culture look to him as the exemplar of major themes, ideals, and achievements of the region, as well as the nation.

WILLIAM K. BOTTORFF
University of Toledo

R. B. Bernstein, *Thomas Jefferson* (2003); Julian P. Boyd et al., eds., *The Papers of Thomas Jefferson (1950–)*; Fiske Kimball, ed., *Thomas Jefferson, Architect: Original Designs in the Coolidge Collection of the Massachusetts Historical Society, with an Essay and Notes* (1968); Dumas Malone, *Jefferson and His Time*, 6 vols. (1948–81).

Johnson, Andrew

(1808–1875) U.S. PRESIDENT.
Andrew Johnson was born on 29 December 1808 in Raleigh, N.C. Raised in poverty and informally educated while working as a tailor's apprentice, Johnson left home at a young age, eventually settling in Greeneville, Tenn., and opening his own tailor shop. He married Eliza McCardle on 17 May 1827 and began participating in debates at the local academy. As his business improved, Johnson's tailor shop became a local meeting place for lively discussions on politics. Encouraged by his wife and his debating success, Johnson entered politics.

Within two years Johnson became mayor of Greeneville. By 1835 Johnson was elected to the Tennessee House of Representatives. He lost his reelection in 1837 but was later reelected in 1839. Following his second term Johnson won a seat in the Tennessee Senate. A supporter of free laborers' rights, a champion of the common man, and

an opponent of a law that allowed increased representation to slaves, Johnson also supported a bill that provided farms to the poor. While serving as senator, Johnson motioned to create a new state, to be named Frankland, out of the adjoining Appalachian lands of North Carolina, Virginia, Georgia, and Tennessee. The motion, of course, failed. He went on to win the governorship of Tennessee in 1853 and 1855 and in that position provided his state with a public school system and public libraries.

In 1857 Johnson was elected to the U.S. Senate. He was a steadfast supporter of the Constitution over states' rights. During the crisis over secession, Johnson remained loyal to the Union, and when Tennessee seceded he remained in the Senate (the only southerner to do so), being labeled a traitor by many southerners. Nonetheless, he had supported Stephen Douglas for president in 1860, championed the Fugitive Slave Law, and defended slavery. Uniquely open to both sides' point of view, Johnson warned against secession and abolition, believing that both were threats to the Constitution and the Union.

In 1862 President Lincoln appointed Johnson military governor of Tennessee, and after large parts of the state fell to Union forces Johnson worked to effectively silence anti-Union sentiments. In 1864, sensing an impending end to the Civil War, the Republicans nominated Johnson for vice president in place of Lincoln's first-term vice president, the passionate abolitionist Hannibal Hamlin, even though Johnson was an old-fashioned southern Jacksonian Democrat.

After Lincoln's assassination Vice President Johnson became the 17th U.S. president and was assigned the unenviable tasks of reconciling the North and South and reconstructing a region that remained hostile to the U.S. government. While the Senate was out of session he reconstructed the Confederate states and pardoned all who would take an oath of allegiance, although he required government officials and men of wealth to take a special presidential pardon.

Despite these oaths of allegiance and the abolition of slavery (established by the Thirteenth Amendment), prewar southern leaders initiated "black codes" to restrict freedmen's rights, which Johnson supported, and Radical Republicans in Congress restructured Johnson's program by refusing to seat any prewar southern representative or senator in Congress. Congress also passed the Civil Rights Act of 1866, which forbade discrimination against the newly freed blacks and made them full citizens of the United States. The Fourteenth Amendment was passed soon after. It allowed that no state could "deprive any person of life, liberty, or property, without due process of law," and no southern state but Tennessee consented to its ratification.

The congressional elections of 1866 resulted in an overwhelming victory by the Radical Republicans. The following March, a Radical Republican Congress placed the South under military rule and passed the Tenure of Office Act, which forbade the president to remove civil officers without senatorial consent. The act was an effective attempt to wrest control of Reconstruction from the hands of the president and place it squarely in the control of the largely Republican Senate. When Johnson dismissed the Lincoln-appointed secretary of war, Edwin M. Stanton, Congress voted to impeach him. He was acquitted by one vote.

Johnson completed Lincoln's term but did not receive his party's nomination in 1869. He went home to Greeneville, Tenn., and in 1875 returned to the U.S. Senate. He suffered a stroke later that year, and on 31 July 1875 Andrew Johnson died. As well as the passing of the Thirteenth and Fourteenth Amendments, Johnson's presidential legacy includes the addition of Nebraska as a state and the purchase of the Alaska Territory. His childhood home still remains in Raleigh at the Mordecai Historic Park.

JAMES G. THOMAS JR.
University of Mississippi

Howard Beale, *The Critical Year: A Study of Andrew Johnson and Reconstruction* (1958); Albert Castel, *The Presidency of Andrew Johnson* (1979); Noel Gerson, *The Trial of Andrew Johnson* (1977); Chester G. Hearn, *The Impeachment of Andrew Johnson* (2000); Andrew Johnson, *The Papers of Andrew Johnson* (1979); Eric McKitrick, *Andrew Johnson and Reconstruction* (1967); James Selton, *Andrew Johnson and the Uses of Constitutional Power* (1980); Glenna Schroeder-Lein, *Andrew Johnson: A Biographical Companion* (2001); Brooks Simpson, *The Reconstruction Presidents* (1998); Hans Trefousse, *Andrew Johnson: A Biography* (1989).

Johnson, Lyndon Baines

(1908–1973) U.S. PRESIDENT.
Convinced that a southerner could not
be elected to the presidency in his lifetime, Lyndon Baines Johnson sought
to minimize his southern credentials.
Describing himself as an American, a
westerner, a Texan, and, only lastly, a
southerner, he attempted to divorce
himself from the region and its conservative racial and social image. As
a southerner, a congressional leader
with a mixed civil rights record, and
the successor to a slain president whose
reform image loomed larger in death
than in life, Lyndon B. Johnson sensed a
special need to convince the nation that
he too was dedicated to the cause of
equality and a decent standard of living
for all Americans. Pursuing this goal
during the five years of his presidency
(1963–69), he pushed through the Congress the most significant civil rights
legislation since Reconstruction—the
legislation outlawing discrimination
in education, public accommodations,
voting, employment, and housing.
Armed with authority to cut off federal
funds to segregated public schools, his
administration integrated the schools
at a pace that repeated court decisions
had largely failed to effect. And his 1965
voting rights legislation produced a 50
percent increase in southern black voter
registration by 1966—an increase that
facilitated the election of black officeholders (387 in Mississippi alone by
mid-1980) and ultimately moderated
the region's racial politics.

The administration's War on Poverty
attempted to cope, moreover, with the
plight of the poor in the South and the
rest of the nation. For children, Johnson
created the federal school breakfast,
Head Start, day care, and foster grand-
parent programs; for the elderly, Medi-
care and special housing; for the unemployed, the Job Corps; for the myriad
problems confronting the poor, VISTA
and the Community Action Program.
Nor were such programs intended only
for economic relief. They also provided
a political base for minorities, especially
in the South. Many VISTA volunteers,
for example, became heavily involved in
southern politics; and the Community
Action Program, through which federal
poverty funds were channeled to largely
private, minority-related agencies, was
designed in part to bypass the traditional federal, state, and local power
structures.

While president, Lyndon Johnson
was never able to convince most civil
rights leaders and social activists of his
commitment to reform. For them, as for
his critics on the Right, he was simply
a calculating politician posturing for
liberal and minority votes. More criti-
cally, urban riots, rising inflation, the
growing national preoccupation with
Vietnam, the merging of the civil rights
movement with the antiwar effort, and
the increasingly radical character of
the two movements largely derailed
Johnson's social programs and damp-
ened public enthusiasm for further civil
rights reform. Ironically, too, though he
was a creature of the Solid Democratic
South, his administration probably did
more to drive white southerners into
the ranks of the GOP than all the efforts
of Republican presidents and presidential aspirants. Whatever its direction,

however, his impact on southern politics was to be truly profound. In later years, moreover, liberals would develop a more sympathetic image of his presidency and its role in social reform. That image moved former SNCC leader and caustic Johnson critic Julian Bond to describe the former president in 1972 as "an activist, human-hearted man [who] had his hands on the levers of power and a vision beyond the next election. He was there when we and the Nation needed him, and, oh my God, do I wish he was there now."

TINSLEY E. YARBROUGH
East Carolina University

Robert Dallek, *Flawed Giant: Lyndon B. Johnson, 1960–1973* (1998), *Lone Star Rising: Lyndon Johnson and His Times, 1908–1960* (1991), *Lyndon B. Johnson: Portrait of a President* (2003); Robert A. Divine, ed., *Exploring the Johnson Years* (1981); Ronnie Dugger, *The Politician: The Life and Times of Lyndon Johnson* (1984); Eric Goldman, *The Tragedy of Lyndon Johnson* (1968); Doris Kearns, *Lyndon Johnson and the American Dream* (1976) Nick Kotz, *Judgment Days: Lyndon Baines Johnson, Martin Luther King, Jr., and the Laws That Changed America* (2005).

Church fan depicting civil rights leader Martin Luther King Jr. (Charles Reagan Wilson Collection, Center for the Study of Southern Culture, University of Mississippi, Oxford)

King, Martin Luther, Jr.

(1929–1968) MINISTER AND CIVIL RIGHTS LEADER.
Born on 15 January 1929 in Atlanta, Ga., Martin Luther King Jr. came to symbolize the black freedom struggle that dominated the South from 1955 to 1968. He attended Morehouse College and graduated from Crozer Theological Seminary in June 1951. Emerging at the age of 27 as the principal leader of the Montgomery, Ala., bus boycott that initiated a new era of nonviolent protest against racial discrimination, King brought a strong family heritage in the Baptist Church and excellent graduate training in philosophy and theology at Boston University to his role as spokesman for a movement that in little more than a decade transformed southern life.

In the early years of his public career King stressed two beliefs: that black southerners had to employ mass action as well as lawsuits if they were to win their constitutional rights as American citizens and that many white southerners would respond positively once they were shown that Christian morality supported the goals of the civil rights cause. The tactics of "direct action" led to protest efforts such as the "sit-ins" of 1960, the Freedom Ride of 1961, and the community-based demonstration campaigns that King's Southern Christian Leadership Conference mounted in Albany, Ga.; Birmingham, Ala.; St. Augustine, Fla.; and Selma, Ala., in the years 1962–65. King's early optimism about the white South, and especially the white church, all but vanished as confrontation after confrontation demonstrated that few white southerners would stand up for racial justice.

King's 1963 "I Have A Dream" oration at the March on Washington and his 1964 receipt of the Nobel Peace Prize catapulted him to national and international fame at much the same time that civil rights protests were leading the federal government to enact the landmark Civil Rights Act of 1964 and Voting Rights Act of 1965. Achievement of these milestones and realization of their limitations led King to focus increasingly on the serious problems of his country and world that had not been ameliorated by those racial reform statutes: poverty and economic powerlessness that oppressed many white as well as black Americans, North as well as South; militarism and materialism that led to international violence and economic imperialism. King's desire to attack the former set of problems led him to mount a largely unsuccessful attack upon economic injustice in Chicago's ghettos in 1966; his realization of the need to speak out against international violence and oppression led him in 1967 to denounce America's involvement in Vietnam.

Before his murder, King was articulating a vision far distant from that with which he had begun. America, and the South, required thoroughgoing economic and structural change, and not merely the elimination of racial discrimination, if real human justice were to be attained. That struggle for a more just society would have to employ coercive and disruptive tactics, not simply persuasive ones, for the preceding 12 years had shown that white America was far less interested in social justice than King had imagined in 1956. At the time of his assassination in Memphis on 4 April 1968, Martin Luther King Jr. believed that the road ahead was still far longer than the road he himself had traveled. In January 1986 King's birthday was declared a national holiday, the first such tribute to a black American. The Martin Luther King Jr. Papers Project, under the direction of Clayborne Carson, has produced five edited volumes of King's work.

DAVID J. GARROW
City College of New York
CUNY Graduate Center

Lewis V. Baldwin, ed., with Rufus Burrow Jr., Barbara A. Holmes, and Susan Holmes Winfield, *The Legacy of Martin Luther King Jr.: The Boundaries of Law, Politics, and Religion* (2002), *There Is a Balm in Gilead: The Cultural Roots of Martin Luther King Jr.* (1991); Clayborne Carson, ed., *The Autobiography of Martin Luther King Jr.* (1998); Gaynelle Evans, *The Chronicle of Higher Education* (3 September 1986); David J. Garrow, *Bearing the Cross: Martin Luther King, Jr., and the Southern Christian Leadership Conference, 1955–1968* (1986); Martin Luther King Jr., *Where Do We Go*

From Here: Chaos or Community? (1967); David L. Lewis, *King: A Critical Biography* (1970); Stephen B. Oates, *Let the Trumpet Sound: The Life of Martin Luther King, Jr.* (1982); Kenneth L. Smith and Ira G. Zepp Jr., *Search for the Beloved Community: The Thinking of Martin Luther King, Jr.* (1974); James M. Washington, ed., *A Testament of Hope: The Essential Writings and Speeches of Martin Luther King Jr.* (1991).

Lee, Robert E.

(1797–1870) CONFEDERATE GENERAL.
Robert Edward Lee was born at Stratford, Va., the son of Revolutionary War hero "Light Horse Harry" Lee and Anne Hill Carter. He graduated from West Point in 1829, became an officer in the engineer corps, served with distinction in the Mexican War, was appointed superintendent of West Point in 1852, commanded the marines who captured John Brown in 1859, and became one of the South's preeminent military figures during the Civil War and its most famous hero afterward.

Lee's hero status benefited from the adulation of three seemingly disparate groups: Virginians, other southerners, and other Americans. Each group lauded and idealized many of the same features when viewing Lee. The devoted son of an ailing mother, Lee was a young man of abstemious habits and a model student at West Point. He was the loving, devoted husband of ailing Mary Custis, the "child of Arlington." In his life before the Civil War and thereafter, Lee displayed elements of a gentlemanly, Christian character shared by few others. His life was the epitome of humility, self-sacrifice, and reserve.

Even Robert E. Lee's involvement in the Civil War was viewed as different. Lee was the reluctant rebel who disliked slavery and secession, one whose love for the Union transcended that of other southern officers in 1860 and 1861.

After the Civil War, Lee the Confederate became Lee the American. He refused to prolong conflict by guerrilla warfare; Lee declined as well to flee the South or to keep alive the embers of sectional bitterness. Instead, the Virginian shunned lucrative business offers and accepted the modest post as president of Washington College. There he counseled moderation and acceptance of defeat. By his postwar example, Robert E. Lee thus helped to restore the Union. The consistent repetition of these images is evident first in southern writings and then in general American literature from 1865 until World War I.

The rapid development of the Lee mystique is one of the most remarkable developments in the genre of American heroic symbolism. Evidence from contemporary accounts indicates that Lee's status as a hero did not evolve until after his death in 1870. In wartime he shared popularity with such Confederate notables as Generals Thomas "Stonewall" Jackson, Joseph E. Johnston, and P. G. T. Beauregard. A number of writers criticized Lee's military leadership, particularly his direction of the Gettysburg campaign.

By the 1870s, after the general's death, the tone of Lee historiography changed markedly. A high degree of organization was evident in the commemoration of Lee's exploits, as groups such as the Lee Memorial Association,

Robert E. Lee, Confederate general, April 1865
(Mathew B. Brady, photographer, National Archives [111-B-1564], Washington, D.C.)

Lee Monument Association, and Ladies' Lee Monument Association labored to improve his image. They were aided by the Southern Historical Society, whose papers became the most respected southern outlet of Civil War history in the late 19th century. The society and its papers were dominated totally by Lee devotees such as former generals Jubal Early and Fitzhugh Lee and ex-rebel chaplain John William Jones. For them and scores of others, mainly Virginians, the depiction of the stainless Robert E. Lee became a crusade for the Lost Cause.

The literary dominance of Virginia authors continued in a second generation of writers whose main literary impact was felt in the period between the 1880s and World War I. Although the postwar generation had written mainly for a southern audience, the new authors wrote for the northern public. Virginia authors seemed to dominate the topic of the Civil War in both fiction and nonfiction. For several decades, beginning in the 1880s, the national reading public was fed a version of the war by Virginia writers such as Thomas Nelson Page, Francis Hopkinson Smith, Constance Cary Harrison, Robert Stiles, Philip A. Bruce, Robert E. Lee Jr., Sara Pryor, and many others.

The new generation was attuned to new ideas in American thought, such as social Darwinism and the influence of environmental forces in shaping social values. The environmental argument was a keystone of late-19th-century southern authors. For them the South possessed a two-edged sword of triumph and tragedy. For apologists Lee was the supreme example of the alchemy of the noble and tragic. He was the man of superior virtues entrapped in a civilization beset by environmental faults such as human bondage.

The second generation of southern apologists stressed the postwar Lee—an emphasis that meshed well with the elements of both social Darwinism and New South imagery. Lee the war chieftain was now Lee the nationalist, who stressed reunion, shunned the old issues, and emphasized practical mechanical skills for Washington College students.

Lee, then, was the central focus of two generations of southern authors who used his heroic status for different reasons. The earlier generation coped with a theological dilemma. Defeat had gone against the Calvinistic ideal that success is a sign of God's grace. To replace this, the Lost Cause artists fashioned a complicated image whereby the southern cause became a knightly quest in which the righteous may lose but ultimately endure. Lee, the supreme image of this argument, became almost a Christ symbol, evidence that good men do not always prevail at first.

Henceforth the Lee image would change little, except to be altered in succeeding generations as the national mood demanded. In the 1930s an America faced with economic defeat in the Depression era identified with the imagery of Lee and the defeated South. Later, in the 1950s, a nation approaching the Civil War Centennial and reflecting a new post–World War II nationalism would concentrate more upon the qualities of the post–Civil War Lee. Since then, Lee's image has been at the center of controversies throughout the South about the public display of Confederate symbolism. Lee's birthday, 19 January, is a state holiday in many southern states, the celebration of which is often combined with the Martin Luther King Jr. federal holiday.

THOMAS L. CONNELLY
University of South Carolina

Thomas L. Connelly, *The Marble Man: Robert E. Lee and His Image in American Society* (1977), *Civil War History* (March 1973), with Barbara L. Bellows, *God and General Longstreet: The Lost Cause and the Southern Mind* (1982); Marshall Fishwick, *Lee after the War* (1963); Douglas Southall Freeman, *R. E. Lee*, 4 vols. (1934–

35); Emory M. Thomas, *Robert E. Lee: A Biography* (1995); Dixon Wecter, *The Hero in America: A Chronicle of Hero-Worship* (1941).

Lynch, John Roy

(1847–1939) POLITICIAN AND LAWYER. Lynch was born on 10 September 1847 in Concordia Parish, La., the son of an Irishman, Patrick Lynch, and a slave, Catherine White. His father bought and sought to free his whole family, but death and the treachery of a friend intervened so that Lynch was not freed until 1863 by the Union army in Natchez. Lynch was self-educated, except for four months of formal schooling in 1866. He early became active as a Republican, and in 1869 Governor Adelbert Ames appointed him a justice of the peace. That same year Lynch was elected to the Mississippi House of Representatives. Reelected in 1871, Lynch was chosen as Speaker of the House, which he ruled, according to a unanimously passed resolution, "with becoming dignity, with uniform courtesy and impartiality, and with marked ability." The occasion of the resolution was Lynch's departure from the Mississippi House for the U.S. House of Representatives, where he took his seat in December 1873, after handily defeating the Democratic candidate. In all, he served three terms, though his third term was cut short by the necessity of having to contest the election of his Democratic opponent; Lynch was finally declared the winner.

Following defeat for reelection in 1882, Lynch went home to Adams County to run his plantation. Still active as a Republican, he was a delegate to the Republican National Conventions of 1884, 1888, 1892, and 1900; earlier, in 1872, while a member of the Mississippi House, he was a delegate to the Republican convention of that year. Democrat Grover Cleveland offered Lynch a minor appointive office, which he turned down; but in 1889 he accepted from Republican president Benjamin Harrison the position of fourth auditor of the Treasury and served until the return of Democrats to national power in 1893.

About this time Lynch began the study of law, and in 1896 he was admitted to the Mississippi bar. From 1893 to 1896, though, Lynch largely busied himself with his Adams County plantation and with real estate speculation in Natchez. From 1896 to 1898 he practiced law in Mississippi and in Washington, D.C., with the firm of Robert H. Terrell. With the outbreak of the Spanish-American War in 1898, Republican president William McKinley appointed Lynch as a paymaster of volunteer forces, with the rank of major; in 1901 he was appointed to the same position and rank in the regular army, in which he served until 1911, when he retired.

Lynch then settled in Chicago, where he practiced law and traded in real estate. In 1913 he published his *Facts of Reconstruction*, which is commonly regarded as the best account of Reconstruction by a black participant. His last years were spent writing *Reminiscences of an Active Life*, which was not published until 1970, under the editorship of John Hope Franklin. Lynch was married twice. His 1884 marriage to Ella Somerville, by whom he had one daughter, ended in divorce, and in 1911 he married Cora Williams, who survived him.

CHARLES E. WYNES
University of Georgia

John Hope Franklin, ed., *Reminiscences of an Active Life: The Autobiography of John Roy Lynch* (1970).

Madison, James

(1751–1836) U.S. PRESIDENT, POLITICAL PHILOSOPHER, PLANTER.

Madison defended the interests of Virginia and the South within the framework of the federal government that he helped create. Educated by private tutors at plantation schools in Orange County, Va., and at the College of New Jersey (now Princeton University), he became an effective spokesman for his state and region. In the Continental Congress, 1780–83 and 1787–88, he worked to ensure Virginia's cession of western lands to the Confederation government on conditions favorable to his state. He urged that the United States secure navigation rights to the Mississippi River—then controlled by Spain—which he recognized as crucial for the South's economic development.

At the 1787 Constitutional Convention Madison urged that the federal government be strengthened with delegated powers while the states retained reserved powers. As a congressman he worked to establish the new government while opposing efforts by the Federalist administration to further consolidate national powers. His 1798

James Madison, fourth president of the United States (Gilbert Stuart, photographer, Library of Congress [LC-USZ62-106865], Washington, D.C.)

Virginia Resolutions defended civil liberties and asserted the right of states to interpose their authority to declare unconstitutional the Federalist-sponsored Alien and Sedition Acts. Those resolutions became the foundation of states' rights doctrine for early-19th-century Republicans.

Sectional divisions and his own Republican scruples over legislative supremacy impeded Madison as fourth president of the United States, 1809 to 1817. Long-standing disputes with Great Britain finally erupted in the War of 1812, which was supported in the South but unpopular in the North. In retirement, Madison was embarrassed when—during the 1828–33 South Carolina nullification controversy—states' righters invoked his Virginia Resolutions. He objected that his proposals for interposition meant only cooperation among the states to repeal federal laws or amend the Constitution. He advised President Andrew Jackson and cabinet officers on responding to the nullifiers.

Madison deplored slavery but remained economically dependent on the slave labor of his plantation. He was a founder and president of the American Colonization Society, which worked to return free blacks to Africa. His interests ranged beyond political theory and practice to architecture, the visual arts, and education. Madison supervised additions to Montpelier, his Orange County house, which he filled with his collection of books and paintings. He worked with his lifelong friend and political confidant Thomas Jefferson to establish the University of Virginia, which he served as visitor and second rector. Throughout an extraordinarily long career, Madison advanced the political and cultural life of his state, region, and nation.

THOMAS A. MASON
Indiana Historical Society

Irving Brant, *James Madison*, 6 vols. (1941–61); William T. Hutchinson et al., eds., *The Papers of James Madison*, 26 vols. (1962–); Ralph Ketcham, *James Madison: A Biography* (1971); Drew R. McCoy, *The Last of the Fathers: James Madison and the Republican Legacy* (1991); Robert A. Rutland, *James Madison: The Founding Father* (1987).

Meredith, James

(b. 1933) CIVIL RIGHTS ACTIVIST. James Howard Meredith achieved international renown in 1962 when his admission to the University of Mississippi sparked a nightlong riot during which two people were killed. Meredith's admission to the all-white university climaxed 18 months of legal and political resistance by both university and state officials, particularly from Governor Ross Barnett, who physically barred Meredith's admission on two occasions. The racial tension that accompanied his admission soon subsided, and Meredith graduated from the university in August of 1963. He described his experiences in *Three Years in Mississippi* (1965).

James H. Meredith's parents, Moses and Roxie Meredith, owned an 84-acre farm near Kosciusko, in Attala County, Miss. Meredith was born on that farm on 25 June 1933. After graduating from St. Petersburg, Fla., high school, Meredith enlisted in the U.S. Air Force. While in the air force, he conceived a plan to return to his native state to gain admission to the University of Mississippi and break the color barrier in Mississippi.

In the years following his graduation from the university, Meredith pursued a variety of interests and causes. He took graduate courses in economics at the University of Ibadan, Nigeria, in 1964–65 and received a law degree from Columbia University in 1968. In 1966 Meredith was shot and wounded during a walk from Memphis, Tenn., to Jackson, Miss., which he called a "March Against Fear." He has conducted several unsuccessful political campaigns and has served as consultant and lecturer at colleges and universities in America and Africa. Meredith's business interests are as varied as his social and educational pursuits. He owned an apartment building in the Bronx and was a stockbroker before returning to Jackson, Miss., in the early 1970s. While in Mississippi, he was self-employed and spent much of his time promoting business ties between American black entrepreneurs and black Africa. Meredith is married to Mary Jane Wiggins and has five children, one of whom earned a Ph.D. from the University of Mississippi. He served as visiting professor at the University of Cincinnati during the 1984–85 academic year and has run for public office in Ohio and in Jackson, Miss. He served on the staff of Senator Jesse Helms, beginning in 1989, and Meredith authored a second book, *Mississippi: A Volume of Ten Books*, in 1995. In 1997 he donated his papers to his alma mater that he had forever changed.

DAVID SANSING
University of Mississippi

William Doyle, *An American Insurrection: James Meredith and the Battle for Oxford, Mississippi, 1962* (2001); James W. Loewen and Charles Sallis, eds., *Mississippi: Conflict and Change* (1974); James H. Meredith Papers, Archives, and Special Collections, John Davis Williams Library, University of Mississippi.

Monroe, James

(1758–1831) U.S. PRESIDENT, CONGRESSMAN, SENATOR, GOVERNOR, CABINET MEMBER, DIPLOMAT, OFFICER IN THE CONTINENTAL ARMY. James Monroe was born in Westmoreland County, Va., in 1758. In 1774 he entered the College of William and Mary. When the American Revolution erupted, the young Monroe enlisted in the Third Virginia Infantry in 1776

and soon found himself participating in the fighting in New York, New Jersey, and Pennsylvania. Monroe served with General George Washington and the Continental army until 1778, rising to the rank of major. Following his tour of duty, Monroe returned to Virginia, where he became the military commander for Virginia.

Monroe then left military life and entered politics, first as a state assemblyman in 1782, and then as a congressman from Virginia in the Confederation Congress, where he served from 1783 to 1786. As a member of Congress, Monroe helped to defeat the Jay-Gardoqui Treaty that would have closed the Mississippi River to American commerce. Monroe left Congress to resume his studies and became a successful lawyer in Virginia. He was elected to the House of Delegates in 1787, and he served in the Virginia ratifying convention, which ratified the Constitution in 1788. In 1790, Monroe was elected to the U.S. Senate, where he served until 1794. Monroe worked closely with James Madison and Thomas Jefferson, becoming an important leader and spokesman in the Senate for the developing Republican Party.

Monroe's life and career changed course yet again when President Washington offered him the position of minister to France in 1794. Monroe arrived in France in July 1794 after the overthrow of Robespierre by the Thermidorean reaction and served until 30 December 1796. He returned to Virginia and resumed his life as a small planter and lawyer. Monroe wrote *A View of the Conduct of the Executive in* the Foreign Affairs of the United State Connected with the Mission to the French Republic during the Years 1794, 5 & 6, which appeared in 1798.

Monroe returned to elective politics in 1799, when he was elected governor of Virginia. He remained governor until 1802, when he decided to return to his legal career. Monroe had little time to resume his career because President Jefferson nominated him to be an envoy extraordinary to France to assist in the negotiations for the Louisiana Purchase. Jefferson then appointed Monroe minister to Great Britain, where Monroe served from 1803 to 1807. Monroe made an abortive run for the presidency in 1808, but the Republican caucus in Virginia preferred Madison. Monroe's candidacy caused a split in Republican ranks that took several years to heal. Monroe served in the Virginia Assembly from 1810 to 1811, and he was again elected governor in 1811.

His tenure as governor was brief. Madison nominated him as secretary of state in 1811, to replace Samuel Smith. Monroe served as secretary of state from 1811 to 1817, when he became the fifth president. Monroe had the distinction of serving as secretary of state and acting secretary of war during Madison's second term as president, a period that coincided with the War of 1812.

Monroe's presidency from 1817 to 1825 has been characterized as the "Era of Good Feelings." The Republican Party stood alone as the Federalist Party disintegrated after the War of 1812. This era witnessed a burst of American nationalism as the nation moved westward. Several new states joined the Union, including Mississippi (1817), Illinois (1818), Alabama (1819), Maine (1820), and Missouri (1821). The United States also acquired Florida from Spain in the Transcontinental Treaty. There was nationalism in Supreme Court decisions, such as *McCulloch v. Maryland* (1819), *Cohens v. Virginia* (1821), and *Gibbons v. Ogden* (1824), as the Supreme Court stressed the supremacy of federal law over state law. The Monroe Doctrine of December 1823, though written by Secretary of State John Quincy Adams, warned European powers not to attempt to recolonize the South American republics that had recently gained their independence from Spain. There were problems, though, in these years. The Panic of 1819 plunged many Americans into unemployment or bankruptcy and left a lingering antibank sentiment in the South and West. Slavery became a major issue when Missouri petitioned for statehood in 1818, and the Missouri Crisis of 1819–21 threatened to rend the Union along a North-South line. When Monroe left office in March 1825, he was the last of the "Virginia Dynasty," which had included Washington, Jefferson, and Madison. After his presidency, Monroe returned to private life. He did serve Virginia in one final capacity, as president of the state constitutional convention in 1829. Monroe moved to New York City to live with his daughter and died there on 4 July 1831.

JAMES C. FOLEY
St. Andrew's Episcopal School
Ridgeland, Mississippi

Harry Ammon, *James Monroe: The Quest for National Identity* (1971); *Biographical Directory of the American Congress, 1774–1971* (1971); Noble E. Cunningham Jr., *The Presidency of James Monroe* (1996).

National Association for the Advancement of Colored People (NAACP)

Disheartened by the 1908 Springfield, Ill., race riot, the spread of legalized Jim Crow, and the accommodationist leadership of Booker T. Washington, an interracial group including W. E. B. Du Bois met in New York City in 1910 to establish the NAACP. The organization spent the next few decades in court challenging the 1896 *Plessy v. Ferguson* decision, which sanctioned the separate-but-equal doctrine.

Beginning with *Guinn v. the United States* (1915), the NAACP convinced the Supreme Court to outlaw the use of the "grandfather clause" as a means to disfranchise black voters. In 1917 success came in *Buchanan v. Warley*, which ended municipal ordinances that sanctioned residential segregation. The NAACP attained further success in the 1930s and 1940s in cases that involved the removal of restrictions on blacks' participation in primary elections and compelled some southern and border states to admit blacks to their law and graduate schools. The culmination of these efforts came in 1954 in *Brown v. Board of Education*, which reversed *Plessy* and outlawed racial segregation in public schools.

The NAACP was also an activist organization, especially in its local chapters.

In 1915 various NAACP locals picketed theaters showing the racially demeaning movie *Birth of a Nation*. Most major southern cities including Little Rock, Atlanta, Greensboro, and Montgomery had active NAACP chapters, although southern states like Alabama moved to ban the organization during the 1950s. A few southern chapters were especially militant. The president of the Monroe, N.C., NAACP in 1959 vowed self-defense with arms, if necessary, in response to white segregationist violence. The national office suspended him for this breach of policy.

During the civil rights movement, under the leadership of executive director Roy Wilkins and Washington, D.C., representative Clarence Mitchell, the NAACP played a crucial role in the successful lobbying for the 1964 Civil Rights Act and the 1965 Voting Rights Act. A Memphis judge, minister, and Federal Communications Commission member, Benjamin L. Hooks, succeeded Wilkins in 1977. Myrlie Evers-Williams was the first woman chair of the NAACP, beginning in 1995. Since 1998 Julian Bonds has served as chairman of the board.

DENNIS C. DICKERSON
Rhodes College

John Hope Franklin, *From Slavery to Freedom: A History of Negro Americans* (1947; 5th ed., 1980); Gilbert Jonas, *Freedom's Sword: The NAACP and the Struggle Against Racism in America, 1909–1969* (2004); Charles F. Kellogg, NAACP: *A History of the National Association for the Advancement of Colored People, vol. 1, 1909–1920* (1967); Records of the NAACP, Branch Files,

Library of Congress, Manuscript Division, Washington, D.C.; B. Joyce Ross, *J. E. Spingarn and the Rise of the* NAACP, *1911–1939* (1972); John David Smith, *The Ticket to Freedom: The* NAACP *and the Struggle for Black Political Integration* (2005); Roy Wilkins with Tom Matthews, *Standing Fast: The Autobiography of Roy Wilkins* (1982).

Olmsted, Frederick Law

(1822–1903) TRAVEL WRITER AND ARCHITECT.

Olmsted, born in Hartford, Conn., was nurtured by a tolerant father who encouraged him to explore his various talents, a background that prepared him to be a cultural observer. Like many of his New England generation, Olmsted sought to assist his fellow man, and his opportunity to write about the South proved to be beneficial for his subsequent work. Olmsted left farming to make a tour of England, a trip that became the basis for his book *Walks and Talks of an American Farmer in England* (1852) and the paradigm for much of his travel and cultural observation. Because of that book's success Olmsted was asked to tour the South and do a series of articles for the *New York Daily Times*, a project that began modestly but led to many articles, three books, and the 1861 compilation *Journeys and Explorations in the Cotton Kingdom*, an abridgment of his books about the South.

The process of the development of Olmsted's writings from newspaper accounts to books and rearrangement into *The Cotton Kingdom* is a complicated textual story. It reveals much about the era when Olmsted sought

to become a member of what he described as "the republic of letters." In 1855 he purchased an interest in the company that published his first southern book, *Journey in the Seaboard Slave States* (1856); yet its financial collapse and the sudden death of his brother, John (who had written a considerable portion of Frederick's *A Journey through Texas* [1857] from Olmsted's notes), complicated his life sufficiently to make desirable a shift in 1857 toward landscape architecture.

The urgency of abolition and his free-state interests were reflected in Olmsted's writing. An apparent sympathy for slaveholding dwindled as his articles were rewritten for books, then abridged. He gradually became convinced that a slave economy could not be profitable. Even though predisposed to find the South backward, one of his valuable accomplishments was to reveal that southern states were remarkably more complex than might have been assumed in the North. A desire for objectivity allowed him to provide a documentation of antebellum conditions that present-day historians corroborate.

Olmsted sought to be factual. His two long trips (from 1852 to the spring of 1854) yielded a cumulative record of farms and villages, a way of life that did not support stereotyped views. He showed the real South as culturally diverse; in the German settlements of Texas, for example, he reported the good results of democracy, freedom, and efficiency. *A Journey in the Back Country* (1860) documented many types of living conditions. The artistic design of Olmsted's writing should also be noted.

His southern writings have proven beneficial for over a century. As source material for various studies, as demonstrated in *Olmsted South* (1979), his writings remain valuable. As a landscape architect Olmsted returned to the South in the 1890s and imprinted his vision at places as diverse as Biltmore, the Vanderbilt estate, near Asheville, N.C., and the Druid Hills area of Atlanta, which together are his most important living southern legacies. Druid Hills and the Olmstead Linear Parks, now on the National Register of Historic Places, are valuable today both as examples of Olmstead's legacy in design and as a setting which for a century has enhanced southern culture.

VICTOR A. KRAMER
Georgia State University

Charles Beveridge and Paul R. Rocheleau (photographer), *Frederick Law Olmsted: Designing the American Landscape* (1998); Albert Fein, *Frederick Law Olmsted and the American Environmental Tradition* (1972); Victor A. Kramer and Dana F. White, eds., *Olmsted South: Old South Critic, New South Planner* (1979); Witold Rybczynski, *A Clearing in the Distance: Frederick Law Olmsted and America in the 19th Century* (1999); Elizabeth Stevenson, *Park Maker: A Life of Frederick Law Olmsted* (1977).

Owsley, Frank Lawrence

(1890–1956) HISTORIAN.
Frank Lawrence Owsley, born 20 January 1890, on his maternal grandparents' plantation near Montgomery, Ala., grew up on a large farm where his father rented land to black sharecroppers. He was immersed in the South's Lost Cause mythology, thoroughly inculcated in its class and race values. "The purpose of my life," Owsley wrote a friend in 1932, "is to undermine . . . the entire Northern myth from 1820–1876." His books "will not interest the general reader," he explained. "Only historians will read them, but it is the historians who teach history classes and write text books and they will gradually and without their own knowledge be forced into our position."

Owsley earned his doctorate at the University of Chicago, studying under the southern historian William Edward Dodd. Although he relished Dodd's enthusiasm for southern history, he rejected his mentor's disparagements of the region's aristocracy. Graduating in 1924, Owsley matured into a formidable scholar, eventually publishing three monographs, two textbooks, and 34 articles. He also taught at Vanderbilt University from 1920 to 1949, then relocated to the University of Alabama to nurture its newly created Ph.D. program in history.

Owsley's career as a southern historian and polemicist moved through three phases. The first, bounded by his *State Rights and the Confederacy* (1924) and *King Cotton Diplomacy* (1931), warned that Confederate defeat in 1865 and the South's continuing subjection to the North resulted from internal divisions. "My only comment on all this," he noted, "is that Stonewall Jackson or Bedford Forrest should have seized control and become a Napoleon or a Mussolini and thereby saved the

South from . . . peonage at the hands of the God damn Yankees."

Owsley's association with the Vanderbilt Agrarians colored his career's second phase. Throughout the 1930s this circle of 12 concerned intellectuals argued that the antebellum South's agricultural society created a quality of life for whites of all social classes that was superior to that in a northern industrial system where a few wealthy capitalists exploited the masses. Postbellum southern poverty could be directly traced to Yankee victory in 1865 and the subsequent efforts of northern interests to denude the South of its wealth and its will.

Owsley trumpeted these themes. From his essay "Irrepressible Conflict" in *I'll Take My Stand* (1930) through his presidential address before the Southern Historical Association in 1940, he repeatedly branded northern politicians and publicists as aggressors whose industrial values and abolitionists dogmas forced the South out of the Union in 1861. Believing that descendants of northern moralists similarly threatened the South in the 1930s, Owsley proposed dramatic changes to the U.S. Constitution that would abandon the federal-state system and substitute for it autonomous regional governments sanctioned to define and defend their domestic customs. This arrangement not only would protect the South from northern economic aggression, he maintained, but also would preserve its "social and racial interests as well."

Owsley commenced the third phase of his intellectual endeavors in 1936 by focusing on a project to present his idealized image of the Old South; it culminated in his seminal *Plain Folk of the Old South* (1949). Touting concepts born of his agrarian years, he pictured an antebellum South in which small farmers and planters resided together in democratic felicity. Pioneering in the use of manuscript census records, Owsley was struck by the significant ownership of land across class lines but dismissed wealth statistics that demonstrated planter dominance over the region's weal. When describing the plain folk's lifestyle and social attitudes, Owsley relied exclusively upon elite sources—county and local histories and the autobiographies of lawyers, physicians, and preachers. "The Southern folk . . . were a closely knit people," he thus concluded. "They were not class conscious in a Marxian sense, for with rare exception they did not regard the planters and men of wealth as their oppressors."

Owsley suffered a fatal heart attack on 21 October 1956 while visiting England. Across his controversial career, his efforts resonated with a singular purpose. Pleasuring in the applause of a University of Georgia audience in 1938, he warmed to the thought that "it was the *rebel yell* that [he] heard."

FRED ARTHUR BAILEY
Abilene Christian University

Fred Arthur Bailey, in *Perspectives on the American South: An Annual Review of Society, Politics and Culture* (1987); M. E. Bradford, *Sewanee Review* (1970); Anthony Gene Cary, in *Reading Southern History: Essays on Interpreters and Interpretations*, ed. Glenn Feldman (2001); Grady McWhiney, *Continuity: A Journal of Histor*

(1984); Harriet Chappell Owsley, *Frank Lawrence Owsley: Historian of the Old South* (1990).

Phillips, U. B.

(1877–1934) HISTORIAN.
Ulrich Bonnell Phillips has been described by historian Eugene D. Genovese as perhaps the greatest historian America has produced. Author of six major works and 55 factual articles, Phillips almost single-handedly directed the social and economic history of the antebellum South from pietistic antiquarianism to many of the major concerns of contemporary historians. An indefatigable discoverer and user of primary sources, especially plantation records, Phillips was undoubtedly the preeminent historian of the South in the first half of the 20th century. Still, his pervasive, if paternalistic, racism and his insistence that the plantation system was the social/economic system of the antebellum South caused his work to be virtually unread until his recent rediscovery.

Phillips was born on 4 November 1877 in the small upland Georgia town of LaGrange. He received both his B.A. and M.A. from the University of Georgia and then went to Columbia, where he took his doctorate in 1902 under William Dunning. Phillips taught for short periods at both Wisconsin and Tulane and from 1911 to 1929 at the University of Michigan. On 21 January 1934, four years after leaving Michigan for Yale, Phillips died.

Phillips had four major ideas about the antebellum South: (1) its environment was an essential contributing factor to its development, and Frederick Jackson Turner's hypothesis of the frontier worked perfectly for the South of prewar years; (2) the region's political economy was a combination of geography, economics, politics, social structure, race, and ideology and dominated all aspects of southern life; (3) the key to antebellum political economy was the plantation, which was not a mere economic institution but an entire way of life; and, finally, (4) the plantation was primarily a method of social control of a "stupid," genetically inferior race and the necessary first step in what Phillips unabashedly regarded as the continuing, essential task of preserving the South as "a white man's country."

Phillips incorporated Turner's regionalism into his 1902 dissertation, "Georgia and States Rights," ostensibly a history of Georgia political thought. During the early 1900s he further developed the frontier thesis in numerous articles in major journals, the 13-volume *The South in the Building of the Nation* and his introduction to the documentary collection *Plantation and Frontier*. Phillips's first attempt to view political economy as an interrelated system was his 1908 study of the development of the railroad industry, *A History of Transportation in the Eastern Cotton Belt to 1860*, which showed how the needs of the planter class created the type of railroads built in the South. Phillips then concentrated largely upon a systematic study of the plantation economy and produced two classic and highly influential works, *American Negro Slavery* (1918) and *Life and Labor in the Old South* (1929). In the late 1920s Phillips related his ideas of black social control to political history in such essays as "The Central Theme of Southern History" and was preparing a book on the subject at the time of his death.

MARK SMITH
University of Texas at Austin

Merton Dillon, *Ulrich Bonnell Phillips: Historian of the Old South* (1985); Richard Hofstadter, *Journal of Negro History* (April 1944); John Herbert Roper, *U. B. Phillips: A Southern Mind* (1984); Junius P. Rodriguez, in *Reading Southern History: Essays on Interpreters and Interpretations*, ed. Glenn Feldman (2001); John David Smith and John C. Inscoe, eds., *Ulrich Bonnell Phillips: A Southern Historian and His Critics* (1990).

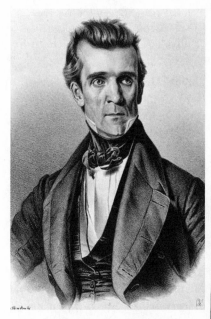

James Knox Polk, 11th president of the United States (Library of Congress [LC-USZ62-23836], Washington, D.C.)

Polk, James Knox

(1795–1849) U.S. PRESIDENT.

For most Americans, James Knox Polk, the 11th president of the United States, is an obscure, historical personality whose administration is remembered because he waged an unpopular war with Mexico — but did little else.

That is unfair to him. He did a great deal more. Surely he is the nation's most unappreciated president. In a single term in office he engineered the annexation of Texas, bluffed the British out of the Oregon Territory, waged the unpopular war with Mexico to win California and New Mexico, and, with all of that, enlarged the nation's landmass by a full third. It was, finally, James Knox Polk who made the United States a continental nation, "from sea to shining sea."

Polk, at a critical moment, also reformed the nation's monetary system.

As he came to office, the country's economic policy was in transitional shambles. He knew it. As a member of Congress and as Speaker of the U.S. House of Representatives, Polk had helped President Jackson, his political guru, win the so-called war against the Second Bank of the United States. "Old Hickory" had stripped from the "Monster" Bank all federal deposits on which the institution had paid no interest and with which it had corruptly influenced politics. Jackson's administration distributed those government funds among what soon became known as "pet banks." Many of them turned out to be as mismanaged and as corrupt as the "Monster." Polk ended all of these problems. As president, he pushed through Congress a measure creating an independent treasury that placed all federal funds in government vaults where they were kept safe and administered only to pay bills and meet payrolls.

Martin Van Buren had first pushed the idea after he succeeded Old Hickory—but he could not sustain it. Polk did. The Independent Treasury remained in place for more than six decades until it ultimately was replaced in 1913 by the present Federal Reserve System.

These were great achievements. But was Polk a great president? Presidential greatness is a notion of elastic and elusive definition. Some may be surprised to learn that American historians, in polls conducted every decade since the 1940s, have consistently ranked Polk somewhere between seventh and twelfth among great and near-great presidents. Harry Truman, the only White House occupant to evaluate his predecessors, listed Polk among his "eight best" chief magistrates. "He was a great president!" said Truman.

Polk's presidency was one thing. His personality was something else again. To read his presidential diary, which he kept with remarkable fidelity over three years, is to confront a brooding and humorless politician. He wrote his diary with effortless clarity and opinionated candor that reveals the shadowed side of a conflicted personality. He seems demanding to the point of unreasonableness, determined to the point of stubbornness, and at times self-righteous to the point of paranoia.

His intense partisanship emerges in the diary. So does his ego. Any member of the Whig opposition party was suspect, reactionary, wedded to money, probably corrupt, and an enemy. Democrats who flirted with Whigs also were castigated in his diary. He branded a Presbyterian minister who had criticized him as "a knave without vital religion or a fanatic without reason."

Secretary of State James Buchanan is repeatedly held up to ridicule by Polk's acidic pen. He also wrote scorching criticisms of his two leading Mexican War generals, Zachary Taylor and Winfield Scott. Outnumbered by Mexican troops, they won battle after battle— but Polk branded them selfish, misguided Whig soldiers eager to use their military success politically. He was right about that, of course. During the 1844 campaign he had pledged that he would not seek reelection—and he kept his word.

It pained him deeply when General Taylor was elected to succeed him as president.

As to his ego, it emerges clearly in the diary's pages. He boasted that he could run the government without the aid of his cabinet and declared himself to be "the hardest working man in the country." He may have been. Without doubt, he was the classic workaholic.

Whatever his flaws of personality (and they are obvious to those who read the diary), there is much to admire in the career of James K. Polk. He loved his country and served it well. Among the 19th-century presidents, only Jefferson, Jackson, and Lincoln exercised the power of the executive as effectively.

Arthur Schlesinger compared Polk favorably with his admirer, Harry

Truman: "Both had the intelligence and courage to accept the challenge of history." Schlesinger added that "history might have broken them, as it broke Buchanan and Hoover. Instead it forced them . . . into the performance of great things."

It hardly seems fair that Polk, who left the White House at age 53, ill and worn from overwork, went home to Nashville and died from cholera three months later.

JOHN SEIGENTHALER
The First Amendment Center, founder

Wayne Cutler, ed., *James K. Polk Correspondence*, vol. 7, January–August 1844 (1989); J. George Harris, *Polk Campaign Biography* (1990); Allan Nevins, ed., *Polk: The Diary of a President—1845–1849, Covering the Mexican War, the Acquisition of Oregon, and the Conquest of California and the Southwest* (1929); Robert V. Remini, *Andrew Jackson and the Course of American Empire*, vol. 1, 1767–1821 (1977); Arthur M. Schlesinger, *The Age of Jackson* (1945); John Seigenthaler, *James K. Polk: 1845–1849* (2003).

Pringle, Elizabeth Allston

(1845–1921) PLANTATION MISTRESS. Elizabeth Allston Pringle exemplified the resourcefulness of elite southern women during and after the Civil War. She was born near Pawleys Island, S.C., to Robert Allston, a successful rice planter and future governor of the state, and Adele Petigru Allston. In her memoir, *Chronicles of Chicora Wood*, Pringle devoted no fewer than 100 pages to her family background, demonstrating the concern with lineage and heritage characteristic of wealthy 19th-century southerners.

Initially taught at home by a governess, Pringle was sent at age nine to join her sister at a small, select Charleston boarding school, which "finished off" young ladies by teaching them the fine arts and French, as well as basic subjects. The Allstons displayed considerable ambivalence about the education of their daughters, insisting that the girls study at home during the summer yet acknowledging that by age 16 "balls, receptions, and dinners" made it "impossible" for a young girl to "keep her mind on her studies." Elizabeth Pringle was too young to attend social events before the Civil War, but she recalled her sister's gowns and beaus and parties with keen interest.

The war, of course, was a central experience in Pringle's life. Through her youthful eyes, the excitement of seeing the men march off with banners waving was a dominant early impression. But she also recalled her father's death, the steady reduction in food and clothing, the looting of the family residence, and tense confrontations with the now-free blacks on the family's various plantations. Clearly Elizabeth Allston derived much of her later strength and independence from watching her mother cope with these trying circumstances and from facing up to them herself.

In the fall of 1865 Elizabeth Allston's mother decided to support herself by opening a school in Charleston. Initially afraid to teach, her daughter was ashamed of her weakness. "Am I really just a butterfly?" she asked herself. "Is my love of pleasure the strongest thing about me? What an awful thought." After three months of teaching, she was ecstatic about her work and confident in her abilities.

In 1868 she accompanied her family back to Chicora Wood, where she married John Julius Pringle two years later. Her memoir is characteristically discreet on the subject of their relationship, but the marriage appears to have been a happy one until Pringle's untimely death in 1876. In a bold move, Elizabeth Pringle acquired her husband's plantation and elected to run it herself, growing rice, fruit, and raising livestock. When her mother died in 1896, she took over Chicora Wood as well. Thus, she became a substantial rice planter, a rare venture for a woman to undertake alone.

Elizabeth Allston Pringle pursued this occupation with vigor. She became deeply involved in agricultural techniques and in the often frustrating management of her workers. While she enjoyed years of prosperity, she succumbed to failure early in the 20th century, when severe weather and competition from other regions ruined many Lowcountry rice planters. But she voiced no regrets. "I have so loved the freedom and simplicity of the life, in spite of its trials and isolation," she asserted, noting too "the exhilaration of making a good income myself." In the last two decades before her death in 1921, she turned to writing, and her gracefully penned recollections add much to the understanding of southern womanhood and southern life during the important transitional period in which she lived.

LAURA L. BECKER
University of Miami

Patience Pennington, *A Woman Rice Planter* (1961); Elizabeth A. Pringle, *Chronicles of Chicora Wood* (1922).

Randolph, John

(1773–1833) POLITICIAN.

John Randolph of Roanoke represented the interests of traditional slaveholding Virginians in Congress and expressed the aristocratic style of the Virginia past in American public life from the early Republic through the Jacksonian period. Randolph entered public life as part of the Jeffersonian opposition to the Adams administration and was a prominent member of the congressional leadership in Jefferson's first administration. He broke with Jefferson and, along with purist Republicans, formed an extreme group called the "tertium quids" within the party.

Beginning with an uncompromising assertion of states' rights, in time they became suspicious of democracy, as well as American nationalism, detecting in the growth of the federal government an ultimate threat to slavery and the plantation way of life. Randolph's career was largely one of opposition, although he sometimes found allies on particular issues. He was probably the first important American statesman to stake out the positions that came to characterize the secessionist southern view of the Union. Although he dismissed Calhoun's metaphysics, he influenced the South Carolinian's development as a sectional leader.

Randolph's notorious, exciting, and eccentric public persona, his witticisms and verbal challenges, and his stinging contempt for the barbarities of American democratic public life contributed to the mythology of southern bluebloods and hot bloods. Randolph seized the American imagination, North and South, in a pattern that would come to characterize the southern hold on the American imagination.

In his antidemocratic and anticommercial conservatism, his states' rights consistency and republican purity, and his prophetic sense of where southern slaveholding interests must lie, Randolph earned his place in the pantheon of southern activists. In his extravagant and dramatic eccentricity, his keen eye for the appetites of the democratic electorate, and his attempt to embody the Virginia heritage, Randolph earned a lasting place as a mythic southerner.

ROBERT DAWIDOFF
Cornell University

Henry Adams and Robert McColley, *John Randolph* (1882, 1995); William Cabell Bruce, *Randolph of Roanoke: A Biography Based Largely on New Material*, 2 vols. (1922); Robert Dawidoff, *The Education of John Randolph* (1979); William R. Taylor, *Cavalier and Yankee: The Old South and American National Character* (1961).

Segregation and Train Travel

Nothing made more clear the lie of segregation in the late-19th-century South than train travel. Now that southern people were moving—taking the train

from small towns to other towns and cities, even walking from a farm to a crossing, flagging down the engine, and ending up far away—strangers became more common even in the smallest places. Trains took traveling pockets of anonymous urban social relations wherever the tracks went. Traveling forced passengers to deal with a world in which other people were not known, in which their identity could only be determined from their outward appearance, and in which lines of division and order, other than who could afford first class and who had to ride coach, became hopelessly confused.

From the 1880s to the 1950s, in magazine articles, essays, court cases, and novels, southerners referred again and again to the figure of the middle-class black, made visible through clothing, educated speech, and often a lightness of skin color, and made increasingly visible by this new ability to travel. In fact, the 1896 Supreme Court decision that upheld the constitutionality of segregation and made "separate but equal" the law of the land, *Plessy v. Ferguson*, turned on a man who perfectly embodied this confusion, Homer Adolph Plessy. Light-skinned and racially mixed, Plessy made a planned challenge to Louisiana's 1890 law requiring segregated streetcars. His lawyer, Albion Tourgee, a northern white Reconstruction official and popular novelist, argued that the government did not have the right to determine the racial identities of its citizens.

Who but Plessy himself should say where the almost white Plessy belonged? The Court, of course, disagreed, reasoning that racial differences lay before and outside the law, in human nature itself. Plessy would have to be placed on one side or the other, would have to be either black or white. The *Plessy* decision fully denied what African American writer Albert Murray later called the "incontestable mulatto" nature of American culture and set this lie at the very center of modern society. The Court simply added its voice to the increasingly racialist and white supremacist thinking that permeated late-19th-century American society, an attempt in part to ground Plessy-like people's mutable identities in a concreteness of blood, bodies, science, and the law.

The middle-class, racially ambiguous person on the train made white southerners fear the possibility of making a mistake in identifying strangers. In 1889 a Tennessee newspaper turned this anxiety into humor. When "a bright and good-looking colored girl (or rather an almost white colored girl)" boarded a train in Nashville, a "flashily dressed white gentleman," usually known as the "car masher," began a flirtation. Wooing his "lady friend" with lunch and witty conversation, he did not realize his mistake until after she got off the train and the other ladies still aboard laughed at him. The joke (and the incident would not have been at all funny to whites if the genders had been reversed) served as a warning about the dangers inherent in the first-class train car's world of anonymous yet intimate social relations. For whites, the middle-class African American, now able and willing to travel—not the ragged riders in second-class cars—made segregation a necessity.

For African Americans, people who identified themselves or were identified by others as black, however, nothing demonstrated the lie of segregation's premise of absolute racial difference, of white supremacy and black inferiority, like the figure on the train. Activists and writers Mary Church Terrell and Anna Julia Cooper described their own encounters with travel in the South, what Cooper called America's "out-of-the-way jungles of barbarism," where young black girls and dignified colored ladies were routinely ejected from first-class cars by tobacco-stained, stinking white men in the years before *Plessy*. In 1885 the white southern writer George Washington Cable took the figure to *Century Magazine*, describing a middle-class mother and child trapped in a car with chained convicts in his passionate plea for African American civil rights. In his 1901 novel *The Marrow of Tradition*, Charles Chesnutt brought his readers along on a train ride from New York to North Carolina, exploring the experience of being "branded and tagged and set apart from the rest of mankind upon the public highways like an unclean thing."

Writer, intellectual, and activist W. E. B. Du Bois referred often to the figure on the train and to his own travels: "I am in the hot, crowded, and dirty Jim Crow car where I belong. . . . I am not comfortable." But he also went further, shaping the figure into one who defined racial identity even as it pointed to the impossibility of any "natural" racial categories. Asked how blacks could be both superior and the salvation of humanity if race was unreal, segregation a lie, he answered: "I recognize it [racial identity] easily and with full legal sanction: the black man is a person who must ride 'Jim Crow' in Georgia." For African Americans and a few dissident whites, the middle-class person on the train made it clear that segregation created the very racial categories it was supposedly enacted to uphold.

GRACE ELIZABETH HALE
University of Virginia

Edward L. Ayers, *The Promise of the New South: Life after Reconstruction* (1992); Grace Elizabeth Hale, *Making Whiteness: The Culture of Segregation in the South, 1890–1940* (1998); David Levering Lewis, ed., *W. E. B. Du Bois, A Reader* (1995); Eric Sundquist, *To Wake the Nations: Race in the Making of American Literature* (1993).

Southern Christian Leadership Conference (SCLC)

The SCLC was founded in 1957 in Atlanta's Ebenezer Baptist Church, which was pastored by the Reverend Martin Luther King Sr. Local protest movements, mostly bus boycotts, had occurred between 1953 and 1956 in such southern cities as Baton Rouge, New Orleans, Montgomery, Tallahassee, and Birmingham. Informal meetings took place among local movement leaders, mostly black ministers, including Joseph Lowery of Mobile, Fred Shuttlesworth of Birmingham, and Martin Luther King Jr. of Montgomery, and among interested northern activists such as A. Philip Randolph, Bayard

Rustin, Ella Baker, and Stanley Levison (the only white); the consensus was that a new federated organization could organize and focus growing black militancy in the South. Moreover, the NAACP had been barred legally from some southern states, and SCLC might fill the void left by this activist civil rights group.

Martin Luther King Jr., largely because of his able leadership of the successful Montgomery bus boycott of 1955–56, became the first president of SCLC. SCLC was synonymous with King. Under the organization's auspices, he became involved in major demonstrations in Albany, Ga. (1961–62), Birmingham, Ala. (1963), St. Augustine, Fla. (1964), and Selma, Ala. (1965). The Birmingham and Selma marches dramatized the need for the Civil Rights Act of 1964 and the Voting Rights Act of 1965. King and SCLC also ventured north to Boston and Chicago to focus attention on racial and urban issues that produced de facto segregation and discrimination for blacks outside the South. He later spoke out strongly against the Vietnam War.

King operated SCLC with able lieutenants, including the Reverends Ralph D. Abernathy, Andrew Young, Wyatt T. Walker, and Jesse Jackson. SCLC grew to 275 affiliates in both the North and South, although in many cases these locals were individual Baptist congregations. SCLC also had a Department of Economic Affairs, which for a time operated tutorial centers in 16 Alabama towns and tried to upgrade the occupational status of black steel-workers at an Atlanta plant. A large foundation grant in 1967 established an SCLC-sponsored educational project for black church leaders in 15 selected cities.

Just before King's assassination in 1968 in Memphis, he led that city's black sanitation workers in a fight for better wages and union recognition. King had hoped this effort would precede a massive Poor People's campaign in Washington, D.C. His successor, Abernathy, carried out the plan. Abernathy was eventually succeeded by a black United Methodist clergyman, the Reverend Joseph Lowery. In 2004 Charles Steele Jr. succeeded Reverend Fred Shuttlesworth as president and CEO of the Southern Christian Leadership Conference.

DENNIS C. DICKERSON
Rhodes College

Adam Fairclough, *To Redeem the Soul of America: The Southern Christian Leadership Conference and Martin Luther King, Jr.* (1987); Grant Files, Southern Christian Leadership Conference, PA67-580, Ford Foundation Archives, Ford Foundation, New York, N.Y.; David L. Lewis, *King: A Critical Biography* (1970); Aldon D. Morris, *The Origins of the Civil Rights Movement: Black Communities Organizing for Change* (1984); Stephen Oates, *Let the Trumpet Sound: The Life of Martin Luther King Jr.* (1982); Southern Christian Leadership Conference Records, Department of Economic Affairs, 1965 folder, 37:2, Martin Luther King Jr. Center for Nonviolent Social Change Archives, Atlanta, Ga.

Southern Historical Association

In November 1934, 18 historians from throughout the South met in Atlanta to form the Southern Historical As-

sociation, a group focusing on "the promotion of interest and research in southern history, the collection and preservation of the South's historical records, and the encouragement of state and local historical societies in that section to vigorous activity." To address these objectives, the founders launched the quarterly *Journal of Southern History*. Historians from the South, such as Charles Knapp of the University of Kentucky, Philip Hamer of the University of Tennessee, Thomas Abernethy of the University of Virginia, and Benjamin Kendrick of the Women's College of the University of North Carolina, led the group's early efforts but encouraged participation by historians nationwide.

Changes in the association's leadership and focus during the next decade largely reflected the fluctuating parochialism and sectionalist fervor of historians throughout the South. E. Merton Coulter, the first president, avoided controversial sectional sentiment, but Frank L. Owsley in a 1940 presidential address indicted the North for an egocentric sectionalism, which he viewed as a principal cause of the Civil War. A South-versus-North focus, rooted partly, too, in disagreements with President Franklin Roosevelt's policies, flourished for several years in the association. According to historian Robert Durden, "[Albert B.] Moore's diatribe of 1942 signaled the high-water mark of polemical bitterness in the presidential addresses . . . and such sectionalist sentiments virtually disappeared from the succeeding addresses."

Some of the other outstanding historians heading the group have been Fletcher M. Green, who in 1945 delivered an influential address on political democracy in the Old South; Ella Lonn, the first female president, who in 1946 examined 20th-century North-South reconciliation; C. Vann Woodward, who in 1952 delivered the widely respected address "The Irony of Southern History"; Francis Butler Simkins, who "in 1954 sounded what may have been the last bugle call . . . for the old-time sectional verities and attitudes" with his address "Tolerating the South's Past"; James W. Silver, who in his 1963 address "Mississippi: The Closed Society" scrutinized the South's white-supremacist policies; Robert Durden, who gave a talk titled "A Half Century of Change in Southern History" during the association's 50th annual meeting in 1984; and Carl N. Degler, who in 1986 dialectically assessed the evolving relationship of the South, the North, and the nation. Among the most recent presidents have been Jacquelyn Dowd Hall of the University of North Carolina at Chapel Hill, Drew Gilpin Faust of the Radcliffe Institute for Advanced Study and Harvard University, and Bertram Wyatt-Brown of the University of Florida. The various leaders have not only mirrored prevailing sentiments of their times regarding sectionalism but also shaped new frameworks for assessing southern history.

Journal of Southern History articles cover a wide range of time periods and subjects, and each May issue contains a selected bibliography of the previous year's coverage of southern history in periodicals. The association's annual meeting focuses on southern history but also includes sessions on American, European, Latin American, and public history. The organization gives awards for outstanding books, presentations, dissertations, and articles on southern history. It maintains an editorial office and Web site at Rice University, plus administrative offices and an associated Web site at the University of Georgia.

SHARON A. SHARP
Boone, North Carolina

John B. Boles and Evelyn Thomas Nolan, eds., *Interpreting Southern History: Historiographical Essays in Honor of Sanford W. Higginbotham* (1987); Robert F. Durden, *Journal of Southern History* (February 1985); *Journal of Southern History* Web site, <http://www.jsh.rice.edu>; Arthur S. Link and Rembert W. Patrick, eds., *Writing Southern History: Essays in Historiography in Honor of Fletcher M. Green* (1965); Southern Historical Association Web site, <http://www.uga.edu/sha>; George B. Tindall, ed., *The Pursuit of Southern History: Presidential Addresses of the Southern Historical Association, 1935–1963* (1964).

Southern Historical Society

In May 1869 a group of Confederate veterans met in New Orleans to establish an organization to collect, preserve, and publish records of the Confederacy. General Braxton Bragg chaired the newly formed group, which planned to establish an affiliate in every southern state. The new group floundered in its first few years, but supporters convened in August 1873 at White Sulphur Springs in West Virginia to reorganize the Southern Historical Society. Headquarters for the group were moved from New Orleans to Richmond, Va., where an archive of Civil War documents was established at the state capitol.

General Jubal A. Early, the reorganized society's first president, served with a group of vice presidents, one from each southern state. Historian E. Merton Coulter noted that the group might well have been called the Confederate Historical Society, because the leaders were "erstwhile warriors turned historians and conservers of history," determined to garner evidence for the tribunal of history. Racing to collect Confederate materials before the federal government completed its congressionally mandated gathering and publication of official Civil War records, the Southern Historical Society members rekindled the flames of Confederate patriotism by exhorting good southerners to contribute to their cause—assembly of the archives of the covenant. Materials collected included wartime correspondence, memoirs, unit rosters, books, newspaper articles, manuscripts, military reports, maps, charts, speeches, ballads, and poetry. Initially the society published materials regularly in Baltimore's *Southern Magazine*.

In 1875 the Reverend J. William Jones, who had been the society's temporary secretary, became the permanent secretary-treasurer and served until 1887. Jones, described by historian Charles Reagan Wilson as "the most influential and well-known clergyman in the cult of the Lost Cause," shaped what became the preeminent publication institutionalizing the preservation of Confederate history, the *Southern Historical Society Papers*. Launched in 1876 as a monthly publication, the papers were published quarterly from 1880 until 1888, when they became annual volumes, then they became occasional publications until 1959. Jones edited 14 of the total 52 volumes of the *Southern Historical Society Papers*, and in so doing shaped and disseminated one of the most valuable and complete bodies of information available on Confederate military history—and its interpretation from a Confederate viewpoint. Some of the state organizations, such as North Carolina's and Kentucky's, separately published materials, too.

After 1900 membership in the society waned, and only a few members in the Richmond area remained by the 1950s. Among the last members was noted journalist and historian Douglas Southall Freeman, whose death in 1953 marked the society's demise. In its heyday, however, the Southern Historical Society had organized the documentation and galvanized the core ideas upon which the vision of the South as a defeated "redeemer nation" flourished for decades.

SHARON A. SHARP
Boone, North Carolina

E. Merton Coulter, *Journal of Southern History* (February 1936); Gaines Foster, *Ghosts of the Confederacy: Defeat, the Lost Cause, and the Emergence of the New South, 1865–1913* (1987); Arthur S. Link and Rembert W. Patrick, eds., *Writing Southern History: Essays in Historiography in Honor of Fletcher M. Green* (1965).

Gen. J. E. B. Stuart's raid around McClellan, June 1862
(H. A. Ogden, photographer, Library of Congress [LC-USZC4-2462], Washington, D.C.)

Stuart, Jeb

(1833–1864) CONFEDERATE GENERAL.
During his short life, James Ewell
Brown "Jeb" Stuart accomplished
much. Born in Patrick County, Va., in
1833, "Jeb" Stuart graduated from West
Point (1854) and served on the western

frontier in the U.S. Army until 1861. He
resigned to serve Virginia and the Confederacy as commander of a regiment
of cavalry. Stuart was conspicuous at
First Manassas (Bull Run) and tireless
in his employment of mounted troops
as scouts and pickets between rival

armies. Promoted to brigadier general in September 1861, Stuart expanded his command and his fame. In June 1862 Stuart rode completely around George B. McClellan's Union army and was able to supply Robert E. Lee with the intelligence upon which Lee based his Seven Days campaign. In July 1862 Stuart became a major general and assumed command of the cavalry component of the Army of Northern Virginia. He led other cavalry raids—Catlett's Station in August 1862, Chambersburg in October 1862, and Dumfries in December 1862—which embarrassed his enemies and enhanced his fame. At Chancellorsville (May 1863) Stuart succeeded Stonewall Jackson in command of an infantry corps and played a key role in the Confederate victory.

The cavalry battle at Brandy Station (June 1863) opened Stuart to criticism because he allowed the Federals to surprise him. His protracted raid during the Gettysburg campaign deprived Lee of his "eyes and ears" and contributed to the Confederate defeat. But when Stuart suffered a mortal wound at Yellow Tavern in May of 1864, he died a southern hero. He had worn a plume in his hat, collected a retinue that included a banjo player, and flirted with women wherever he went. He had sung and danced and laughed; but he had avoided alcohol, remained faithful to his wife, and set an example of Christian piety.

Stuart made himself a legend while he lived, and later his legend grew larger than life. Stuart has stood for southerner as cavalier and knight in the American mind. As symbol he is eter-

nally dashing, romantic, and gallant. Stuart's life may have been brief, but his legacy yet lives.

EMORY THOMAS
University of Georgia

Burke Davis, *Jeb Stuart: The Last Cavalier* (1957); Henry Brainerd McClellan, *I Rode with Jeb Stuart: The Life and Campaigns of Major General J. E. B. Stuart* (1885, 1958); Mark Nesbitt, *Saber and Scapegoat: J. E. B. Stuart and the Gettysburg Controversy* (2002); Emory Thomas, *Bold Dragoon: The Life of J. E. B. Stuart* (1986).

Student Nonviolent Coordinating Committee (SNCC)

Formed in April 1960, the Student Nonviolent Coordinating Committee (SNCC) drew heavily from Nashville student activists committed to nonviolent direct action. In 1961 Congress of Racial Equality (CORE) leaders asked SNCC to help black students who were waging unsuccessful lunch-counter sit-ins in Rock Hill, S.C. Fifteen SNCC members joined the efforts and initiated the "jail—no bail" protest strategy.

SNCC's next major wave of activity came during the CORE-initiated Freedom Ride of 1961. When in the face of violence in Alabama CORE leaders called off the project, SNCC members resumed the trip and traveled to Montgomery, where further violence erupted. SNCC, CORE, and the Southern Christian Leadership Conference (SCLC) formed the Freedom Riders Coordinating Committee, which solicited more participants to extend the rides to Jackson, Miss. Clayborne Carson notes that SNCC workers gained a reputation as the "shock troops" of the civil rights movement.

In 1961 SNCC developed both a protest wing and a voter registration one. Robert Moses headed SNCC's voter registration efforts in Mississippi, and James Forman became the group's new executive secretary. As the Mississippi efforts floundered in the face of resistance, other SNCC staff members launched massive black protests in Albany, Ga., between fall 1961 and summer 1962.

In 1962 and 1963 SNCC staff members became increasingly effective as community organizers, and membership grew. James Forman recruited many notable young black leaders, such as Julian Bond, and activists such as Fannie Lou Hamer joined SNCC's staff. SNCC built support among northerners and expanded its community organization efforts in southwest Georgia and Mississippi. SNCC members increasingly criticized the Kennedy administration and black groups such as the SCLC and only reluctantly supported the coalition that planned the 1963 March on Washington.

In 1964 SNCC leaders initiated the Mississippi Summer Project, a plan to enlist a massive force of white student volunteers as fieldworkers. All of the other major civil rights organizations supported the plan, and SNCC vied to maintain its leadership role. One 1964 effort was formation of the Mississippi Freedom Democratic Party, an alternate Democratic political organization that hoped to challenge the regular party in Mississippi for seating at the Democratic National Convention. Through separate voter registration procedures, over 80,000 blacks participated in the SNCC-organized "freedom vote." Though the MFD Party challenge gained national support, it ultimately failed. The other major thrust of the Summer Project was establishment of "freedom schools" to educate young blacks in Mississippi. Over 2,000 students attended classes in the 41 schools.

After the murder of SNCC volunteer Andrew Goodman and CORE workers James Chaney and Michael Schwerner in Mississippi in 1964, SNCC moved toward approval of armed self-defense and helped black residents near Selma and Montgomery form the Lowndes County Freedom Organization (LCFO), known as the Black Panther Party, headed by Stokely Carmichael.

Ambivalent about SCLC's 1965 voting rights campaign in Selma, Ala., SNCC became active in the Alabama protests after SNCC and SCLC marchers were attacked outside Selma in early spring. Following the Selma-to-Montgomery march led by Martin Luther King Jr., SNCC recruited many black college students in Alabama, strengthened its militant focus, and targeted economic reforms and black pride themes. In 1966 Carmichael became chairman, leaders such as Robert Moses and Julian Bond left, and whites were virtually expelled. A tumultuous period followed, and by 1970 SNCC had disintegrated amidst internal conflict and widespread criticism.

SHARON A. SHARP
Boone, North Carolina

Inge Powell Bell, CORE *and the Strategy of Nonviolence* (1968); Clayborne Carson, *In Struggle:* SNCC *and the Black Awakening of the 1960s* (1981); James Forman, *The Making of Black Revolutionaries: A Personal Account* (1972); Cheryl Lynn Greenberg, ed., *A Circle of Trust: Remembering* SNCC (1998); Howard Zinn, SNCC: *The New Abolitionists* (1964).

Taylor, John

(1753–1824) POLITICAL PHILOSOPHER, WRITER, PLANTER.

Taylor, born in December 1753 in Caroline County, Va., is referred to as "John Taylor of Caroline"; he was one of the fathers of southern politics. He was more famous in his own time than later; his prestige was such that he was several times elected U.S. senator from what was then the most powerful state in the Union without campaigning and against his wishes. He was a soldier in the American Revolution who died regretting that the Revolution had ended in the construction of a federal government more dangerous to the colonies than that of Great Britain. He retired from a lucrative law practice to become not only a highly successful planter and agricultural reformer but the foremost political defender and philosopher that American agriculture ever had. He was an eloquent advocate of economic, political, and religious freedom for the citizen, and an unbending defender of slavery.

Taylor may even be said to have been a pioneer figure in southern literature. His books and pamphlets not only are full of keen political and economic

John Taylor (Virginia), (1753–1824) *(Courtesy U.S. Senate Historical Office)*

analysis but are written in a colloquial style—full of satire, hyperbole, and front-porch digressions—highly suggestive of the oral tradition evident in later southern writers.

Taylor embodied many persistent and recurrent tendencies and themes of southern politics. He represented both a conservative allegiance to local community and inherited ways and a radical-populist suspicion of capitalism, "progress," government, and routine logrolling politics. He was at the same time more radical and more conservative than his friend, admirer, and fellow Virginia planter Thomas Jefferson. Taylor was Jefferson's down-home side—exactly what Jefferson would have been had he been less cosmopolitan and less of a practical politician. In many respects Taylor was a more authentic voice of Jeffersonianism than was Jefferson himself. Taylor's Old Republican defense of states' rights, strict construction, and intelligent farming and his opposition to federal power, judicial oligarchy, paper money, stock jobbing, taxation, and expenditure were reflexive, reluctant defenses of native soil and were based upon the unyielding conviction that an unoppressed and predominantly agricultural population was the only possible basis for free government.

At the core of Taylor's thinking was a belief that the world is divided between producers and parasites. The producers are decent folk who labor in the earth for their daily bread and produce everything of real economic and moral value in society. They are subject to endless depredations from those that Taylor referred to as "aristocrats." By aristocrats he meant not people of good birth but people, mostly northerners, whose main business was manipulating the government for artificial advantages for themselves. This view of the world, as much a folk attitude as a philosophical position, is a recurrent theme in much southern behavior.

Taylor's more important works are *Definition of Parties, or the Political Effects of the Paper System* (1794); *An Enquiry into the Principles and Tendency of Certain Public Measures* (1794); *A Defense of the Measures of the Administration of Thomas Jefferson* (1804); *Arator, Being a Series of Agricultural Essays, Practical and Political: In Sixty-Four Numbers* (1814); *An Inquiry into the Principles and Policy of the Government of the United States* (1814); *Construction Construed, and Constitutions Vindicated*

(1820); *Tyranny Unmasked* (1822); and *New Views of the Constitution of the United States* (1823).

CLYDE N. WILSON
University of South Carolina

M. E. Bradford, introduction to *John Taylor, Arator* (1977 reprint); Charles William Hill, *The Political Theory of John Taylor of Caroline* (1997); Eugene T. Mudge, *The Social Philosophy of John Taylor of Caroline* (1939); Robert E. Shalhope, *John Taylor of Caroline: Pastoral Republican* (1980).

Trail of Tears

In 1838 the U.S. government uprooted some 13,000 Cherokee Indians from their land east of the Mississippi River and forced them westward into the Oklahoma Territory. The 1,000-mile route they took to Oklahoma is called the Trail of Tears because of the hardships of weather, disease, and starvation that accompanied the Native Americans.

The forced migration along the Trail of Tears was a dismal journey, much of which took place in the middle of a harsh winter. Eyewitness accounts by missionaries, soldiers, government officials, and the uprooted Indians themselves describe how natives marched and suffered for hundreds of miles before reaching Oklahoma. Thousands of Native Americans died on the trip, which took them from north Georgia through middle Tennessee, southern Kentucky, and Missouri, and into present-day Oklahoma. The trip itself was only part of the harrowing experience the Indians endured in this stage of the removal. Federal troops held as many as 15,000 Cherokees in detention camps prior to the trip. Many of the detainees died of starvation or disease while in the camps.

The Trail of Tears has become a symbol for the historic oppression of Native Americans by whites, of which the forced removal of Indians to the West between 1820 and 1840 is only a part. Many southern Indians were tricked with unfamiliar legal practices or intimidated into giving up their land. The federal government demoralized the Native Americans by reducing the supply of game and negotiating separate treaties with certain tribesmen who were willing to accept white civilization. The Removal Acts of 1830 proposed the "final solution"—the exile of the southeastern Indians to the territories west of the Mississippi. At the time of the Indian removal, some Cherokees, like John Ross, advocated the move as the natives' only hope of survival; others, like John Ridge, argued for remaining in the Southeast and preserving traditional ways.

Today, the Trail of Tears has become a historic route developed by the Tennessee Department of Conservation in conjunction with the Department of Tourist Development. Along the route the tourist can see the final capitol of the Cherokee nation near Cleveland, Tenn., the only remaining stockade where the Indians were imprisoned before removal, and Andrew Jackson's home outside Nashville. The inclusion of Jackson's home, the Hermitage, is ironic because, as president, Jackson was a staunch advocate of many of the brutal policies against the Indians, and he was instrumental in implementing the forced migration policy. Sixty thousand Indians were relocated west of the Mississippi under Jackson's direction.

KAREN M. MCDEARMAN
University of Mississippi

John Ehle, *Trail of Tears: The Rise and Fall of the Cherokee Nation* (1988); Gloria Jahoda, *The Trail of Tears: The Story of the Indian Removal, 1813–1850* (1975); Vicki Rozema, ed., *Voices from the Trail of Tears* (2003); *Southern Exposure* (November–December 1985).

Turner, Nat

(1800–1831) SLAVE.

Born in Southampton County, Va., Turner was a black American slave who led the Southampton insurrection, which has often been seen as the most effective slave rebellion in the South. In recent years, Turner has been a focus of cultural and historical debate.

Turner is the dominant figure among a trio of insurrectionists who led major uprisings, beginning in 1800 with Gabriel Prosser, continuing with Denmark Vesey in 1822, and ending with Turner in 1831. Famous in the folklore and oral history of black Americans, these rebels expressed the powerful urges of blacks to be free. Called "Ol' Prophet Nat" and leader of the most violent of the rebellions, Turner became an especially vivid figure in the underground history of American slavery.

Turner was born to a black woman owned by a plantation aristocrat also named Turner. Transported from Africa in her youth, Nat Turner's mother imbued in him a passion for freedom. Always dreamy and visionary, he learned to read, probably taught by his master's son, and early displayed strong religious feelings. As an adult he became a preacher among the slaves. Sold by the Turner family to a less prosperous farmer and sold again to a Southampton craftsman named Joseph Travis, Turner bitterly withdrew into religious fantasies marked by omens, signs, and visions. Turner burned for his freedom, but he also saw himself as a savior of his people. Following an eclipse of the sun, taken as a sign from the Lord, Turner and four trusted lieutenants embarked upon the bloody insurrection on the night of 21 August 1831, beginning with the slaughter of the Travis family. By 23 August, when the rebellion was thwarted by militia, Turner's rebels had killed almost 60 white men, women, and children. Turner escaped capture for six weeks but eventually was caught, tried, and executed, as were some 16 others involved with him.

The cultural debate over Turner was sparked in 1967 by the publication of William Styron's novel *The Confessions of Nat Turner*. Though Daniel Panger published *Ol' Prophet Nat* (1967), it was Styron's bestseller that challenged black Americans, historians, and social critics, for it raised questions on Turner, black history, and the "true" character ("Sambo" or "rebel") of the slave in the South. The co-opting of Turner by a white author prompted, for example, a polemical outcry called *William Styron's Nat Turner: Ten Black Writers Respond* (1968). Coming in the midst of the social revolution of the 1960s, Panger's, Styron's, and many others' works devoted to the Southampton revolt soon made Turner a symbol of "Black Power and social liberation."

JAMES M. MELLARD
Northern Illinois University

John B. Duff and Peter M. Mitchell, *The Nat Turner Rebellion: The Historical Event and the Modern Controversy* (1971); Kenneth S. Greenberg, ed., *Nat Turner: A Slave Rebellion in History and Memory* (2003); Thomas Wentworth Higginson, *Black Rebellion: Five Slave Revolts* (1998 reprint); Stephen B. Oates, *The Fires of Jubilee: Nat Turner's Fierce Rebellion* (1975); Henry L. Tragle, *The Southampton Slave Revolt of 1831: A Compilation of Source Material* (1971).

United Daughters of the Confederacy (UDC)

Southern fiction frequently portrays indomitable southern women in the Civil War. Given the late 19th century's predilection for organizations, it was perhaps inevitable that real-life diehard women who saw themselves as guardians of the Lost Cause would create the United Daughters of the Confederacy (UDC) in Nashville in September 1894. The roots of the UDC may be traced back to the wartime Ladies' Aid Societies that sprang up spontaneously throughout the South in 1861 to assist Confederate soldiers. Perhaps the earliest organized voluntarism among Victorian southern women, these societies began as sewing groups, many of them in the churches, to prepare socks, mufflers, gloves, balaclava helmets, uniforms, and blankets for Confederate soldiers. As war took its human toll, some societies changed into Women's

Monument to Gen. John H. Morgan and his men, and some of the members of the UDC Committee
that built it, c. 1911 (R. L. McClure, photographer, Lexington, Ky., Library of Congress
[LC-USZ62-95819], Washington, D.C.)

Hospital Associations, which set up hospitals and convalescent homes for Confederate sick and wounded soldiers.

During the spring of 1866 many of these organizations reorganized as Ladies' Memorial Associations to insure proper interments for hastily buried Confederate dead and to honor their graves on 26 April (Confederate Memorial Day), and then to raise funds for monuments and statues commemorating the Lost Cause in settings ranging from courthouse squares to battlefields.

Many members of the Ladies' Memorial Associations joined the UDC when it was organized, with its founders' declared goal of obtaining an accurate history of the Confederacy.

The UDC was and is a social, literary, historical, monumental, and benevolent association made up of widows, wives, mothers, sisters, and other lineal descendants of men who rendered military, civil, or other personal service to the Confederate cause.

Organized 10 September 1894, the UDC was incorporated in the District of Columbia on 18 July 1919. It has erected numerous memorials, it presents Crosses of Military Service to lineal Confederate descendants who themselves have served in later American wars, and it presents awards to outstanding service academy cadets and midshipmen. At its height in the early 20th century, the UDC totaled some

100,000 members and was a political force to be reckoned with. As the years took their toll and memories faded, its membership dwindled to about 20,000 in the 1950s; but after the Civil War Centennial, interest was slightly, if temporarily, revived. Today there are about 20,000 members, including those in chapters in northern and western states, as well as in Paris and Mexico City. Associated organizations include the Sons of Confederate Veterans (SCV), founded in 1896; the Children of the Confederacy, organized in 1899; and the Military Order of the Stars and Bars (MOSB), begun in 1938 and made up of male descendants of Confederate officers.

CAMERON FREEMAN NAPIER
Montgomery, Alabama

Jerome Francis Beattie, ed., *The Hereditary Register of the United States of America* (1972); Karen L. Cox, *Dixie's Daughters: The United Daughters of the Confederacy and the Preservation of Confederate Culture* (2003); Wallace Evan Davies, *Patriotism on Parade: The Story of Veterans' and Hereditary Organizations in America, 1783–1900* (1955); Mary B. Poppenheim et al., *The History of the United Daughters of the Confederacy* (1956).

Voting Rights Act (1965)

Two things have changed the modern South: air-conditioning and the Voting Rights Act. Unfortunately, Americans have a better understanding of how air-conditioning functions than they do the Voting Rights Act.

Because discriminatory administration of state laws and constitutional amendments undermined federal pro-

tection of the rights of minority voters, Congress passed the Voting Rights Act in 1965. The act changed the landscape of electoral politics in America, overthrowing three generations of disfranchisement. After the Civil War and emancipation, Reconstruction brought to formerly enslaved African Americans freedom, citizenship, and the right to vote under the Thirteenth, Fourteenth, and Fifteenth Amendments. Yet, when Reconstruction ended, these constitutional amendments did not assure a fair and equal vote. Recalcitrant whites, including organizations such as the Ku Klux Klan, used terrorist and fraudulent antisuffrage activities to deny African Americans the right to vote. A series of court cases systematically dismantled the civil and voting rights legislation of the First Reconstruction. Legal methods of disfranchising African Americans included gerrymandering, at-large elections, registration and secret-ballot laws, the poll tax, literacy tests, and the white primary. By the early 20th century, these methods had effectively disfranchised millions of African Americans. In 1958 the Civil Rights Commission reported that there were 44 counties in the Deep South where there was not a single black voter registered. Many of these counties had large African American populations; some had black American majorities.

The 1965 Voting Rights Act banned literacy tests, facilitated lawsuits to prohibit discriminatory laws or practices, and sent federal voting registrars into intractable areas. In addition, Section 5 of the Voting Rights Act required "covered jurisdictions," all initially in the South, to obtain "preclearance" from the U.S. Department of Justice for any change in their electoral procedures. An immediate effect of more minority voters was the replacement of blatant bigotry in electioneering with more subtle racial appeals. A longer-term effect has been the election of minority citizens to almost every level of government.

South Carolina, joined by other southern states, challenged the Voting Rights Act in 1966 in *South Carolina v. Katzenbach*, claiming that the act violated its right to control and implement elections. After the Supreme Court rejected this challenge, Mississippi and Virginia filed *Allen v. Board of Elections* (1969), contending, again unsuccessfully, that the act protected only the right to cast a ballot, not the right to have nondiscriminatory election structures, such as district elections. Congress renewed all the provisions of the Voting Rights Act in 1970 and 1975, amending it in 1975 to include, in Section 203, provisions to protect language minorities, such as Asian, Hispanic, and Native American voters.

After its initial victories in court, the Voting Rights Act began to suffer defeats. In *Beer v. U.S.* (1976), the Supreme Court ruled that Section 5 of the act did not prevent discriminatory election laws generally but only those that resulted in a "retrogression" of minority influence. For instance, after African Americans were enfranchised by the act, a local jurisdiction could shift district lines in order to insure a continuation of all-white government, and the Department of Justice had to allow the change to go into effect. Even more significantly, a four-person plurality of the U.S. Supreme Court ruled in *Mobile v. Bolden* (1980) that no election law violated Section 2 of the act or the Fifteenth Amendment to the U.S. Constitution unless it could be shown that the law had been adopted with a racially discriminatory intent. During the First Reconstruction, in 1874, Mobile, Ala., had instituted at-large elections; after the passage of the act in 1965, many other southern localities switched from district to at-large elections. In such elections, because whites who outnumber minorities generally vote for whites (i.e., racial bloc vote), minorities had a much more difficult time getting elected, and under *Bolden*, minority plaintiffs had a much more difficult time winning lawsuits.

In 1982 Congress not only renewed the preclearance provision of Section 5 for 25 years, it also effectively overturned *Bolden* by making clear that a proof of intent was unnecessary to win a Section 2 case. Moreover, it weakened *Beer* by instructing the Justice Department not to preclear state or local laws that were discriminatory in either intent or effect. Ironically, in view of the heated two-year struggle in Congress, this strongest version of the act passed by much more overwhelming congressional majorities than ever before. Even more surprising, within two days of the signing of the renewed act, the Supreme Court in *Rogers v. Lodge* announced an effect standard for the act that was nearly identical to that just passed by Congress and that implicitly repudiated the *Bolden* decision of 1980.

Along with the one-person, one-vote ruling of the Supreme Court in *Reynolds v. Sims* (1964), the Voting Rights Act has added another dimension to the politics of redistricting following each decadal census. Once a secretive, unchallengeable practice, redistricting is now played out in courtrooms, as well as back rooms, often ending up before the U.S. Supreme Court. The most startling Supreme Court decision was *Shaw v. Reno* (1993). Disfranchisement had prevented African Americans from electing a single member of Congress from North Carolina from 1898 to 1965; after 1965 the state's leaders had repeatedly rearranged district boundaries to keep the 11-member delegation all white in a 23 percent black state. But after the 1982 amendments strengthened the Voting Rights Act, a newer generation of North Carolina leaders, under pressure from the U.S. Department of Justice, drew two districts in which 54 percent of the voters were African American. In order to preserve the seats of white Democratic incumbents, North Carolina legislators drew new black-majority districts in even stranger shapes than the districts they replaced. Ignoring previous prowhite racial gerrymandering in the state, five members of the U.S. Supreme Court denounced the most integrated congressional districts in North Carolina's history as "segregated" and declared them unconstitutional. White-majority districts could take any shape, the same five justices wrote in a later case from Texas (*Bush v. Vera*, 1996), but black-majority

districts could not look "bizarre" to judges. And in a Georgia case, *Miller v. Johnson* (1995), the Supreme Court by the same 5-4 vote announced that black-majority districts could not be drawn with a predominantly racial intent and that white-majority districts could not be challenged under this standard. Finally, in two cases from Bossier Parish, La., the five-person Supreme Court majority ruled that the Justice Department under Section 5 of the act had to preclear any election law change, unless it made minorities worse off than before the change. Bossier's school board could thus remain all white.

The Voting Rights Act rid the country of the most outrageous forms of voter disfranchisement. Equal voting rights has meant representation for a large minority of citizens and has brought a tremendous increase in minority elected officials, particularly Native Americans in the West, Hispanics in California and Texas, and literally the election of thousands of African American officeholders across the old Confederacy. The Voting Rights Act is a success story. Designed to increase minority voter registration, it has done so. It has also reduced election-related violence, increased responsiveness and the provision of services to minorities, made the political resources of the minority community, especially African Americans in the South, more available to society as a whole, made it possible for southern solons to support civil rights, made racial politics unfashionable, and opened opportunities for minorities to pursue careers in politics. Despite its significant weakening by a 5-4 majority of the U.S. Supreme Court in the 1990s, the Voting Rights Act continues to have a tremendous influence on American, and especially southern, political life.

ORVILLE VERNON BURTON
University of Illinois at Urbana-Champaign

Chandler Davidson and Bernard Grofman, eds., *Quiet Revolution in the South: The Impact of the Voting Rights Act, 1965–1990* (1994); David Garrow, *Protest at Selma: Martin Luther King, Jr., and the Voting Rights Act of 1965* (1978); Nick Kotz, *Judgment Days: Lyndon Baines Johnson, Martin Luther King Jr., and the Laws That Changed America* (2005); J. Morgan Kousser, *Colorblind Injustice: Minority Voting Rights and the Undoing of the Second Reconstruction* (1999); Steven F. Lawson, *Black Ballots: Voting Rights in the South, 1944–1969* (1976).

Washington, Booker T.

(1856–1915) EDUCATOR.
Booker Taliaferro Washington was the foremost black educator of the late 19th and early 20th centuries. He also had a major influence on southern race relations and was the dominant figure in black public affairs from 1895 until his death in 1915. Born a slave on a small farm in the Virginia backcountry, he moved with his family after emancipation to work in the salt furnaces and coal mines of West Virginia. After a secondary education at Hampton Institute, he taught an upgraded school and experimented briefly with the study of law and the ministry, but a teaching position at Hampton decided his future career. In 1881 he founded Tuskegee Normal and Industrial Institute on the Hampton model in the Black Belt of Alabama.

Though Washington offered little that was innovative in industrial education, which both northern philanthropic foundations and southern leaders were already promoting, he became its chief black exemplar and spokesman. In his advocacy of Tuskegee Institute and its educational method, Washington revealed the political adroitness and accommodationist philosophy that were to characterize his career in the wider arena of race leadership. He convinced southern white employers and governors that Tuskegee offered an education that would keep blacks "down on the farm" and in the trades. To prospective northern donors and particularly the new self-made millionaires such as Rockefeller and Carnegie he promised the inculcation of the Protestant work ethic. To blacks living within the limited horizons of the post-Reconstruction South, Washington held out industrial education as the means of escape from the web of sharecropping and debt and the achievement of attainable, petit-bourgeois goals of self-employment, landownership, and small business. Washington cultivated local white approval and secured a small state appropriation, but it was northern donations that made Tuskegee Institute by 1900 the best-supported black educational intuition in the country.

The Atlanta Compromise Address, delivered before the Cotton States Exposition in 1895, enlarged Washington's influence into the arena of race relations and black leadership. Washington offered black acquiescence in disfranchisement and social segregation if whites would encourage black progress in economic and educational opportunity. Hailed as a sage by whites of both sections, Washington further consolidated his influence by his widely read autobiography *Up From Slavery* (1901), the founding of the National Negro Business League in 1900, his celebrated dinner at the White House in 1901, and control of patronage politics as chief black adviser to Presidents Theodore Roosevelt and William Howard Taft.

Washington kept his white following by conservative policies and moderate utterances, but he faced growing black and white liberal opposition in the Niagara Movement (1905–9) and the NAACP (1909–), groups demanding civil rights and encouraging protest in response to white aggressions such as lynchings, disfranchisement, and segregation laws. Washington successfully fended off these critics, often by underhanded means. At the same time, however, he tried to translate his own personal success into black advancement through secret sponsorship of civil rights suits, serving on the boards of Fisk and Howard universities, and directing philanthropic aid to these and other black colleges. His speaking tours and private persuasion tried to equalize public educational opportunities and to reduce racial violence. These efforts were generally unsuccessful, and the year of Washington's death marked the beginning of the Great Migration from the rural South to the urban North. Washington's racial philosophy, pragmatically adjusted to the limiting conditions of his own era, did not survive the change.

LOUIS R. HARLAN
University of Maryland

Louis R. Harlan, *Booker T. Washington*, 2 vols. (1972, 1983), *Booker T. Washington in Perspective: Essays of Louis R. Harlan*; Raymond W. Smock, ed., *The Booker T. Washington Papers*, 14 vols. (1972–89); August Meyer, *Negro Thought in America, 1880–1915* (1963).

Washington, George

(1732–1799) U.S. PRESIDENT, FARMER, MILITARY LEADER.

Washington was born into a well-established and prosperous Virginia family in 1732. By his own efforts and by his marriage to Martha Dandridge Custis he entered the ranks of the First Families of Virginia. In youth his loyalties were to Virginia and the British Empire. Convinced that it was wrong for one people to have power to tax and to dominate another, he came to the forefront of the Virginia patriots.

As commander in chief of the Continental army he was one of the first to indicate that he desired independence from Britain. In the fall of 1775 he referred to America as "my country" and "my bleeding country." He gave utter allegiance thereafter to the American Republic. In the 1780s he referred to Virginia as a "middle" state rather than a southern one. He condemned the Articles of Confederation because they gave the central government insufficient power, and he was the most influential

George Washington, 1844 (Painting by Gilbert Stuart, Library of Congress LC-USZ62-7585 DLC], Washington, D.C.)

hampion of the Constitution. As president he steadily and effectively toiled o assure the safety and growth of the ation. He denounced sectionalism of very sort, in particular condemning ll efforts to set the emerging sections, Jorth and South, against each other.

It is fair to say that he was an ardent Federalist in his last years.

Washington was a land speculator and a farmer rather than a planter, for he turned away well before 1775 from emphasis upon tobacco growing to general husbandry. With the years he became increasingly hostile to black slavery. He declared that it ought gradually to be abolished, said that he would vote for emancipation, and arranged in his will to free his slaves and those of his wife.

JOHN R. ALDEN
Duke University

John R. Alden, *George Washington: A Biography* (1984); Joseph J. Ellis, *His Excellency: George Washington* (2004); James T. Flexner, *George Washington*, 4 vols. (1965–72); Paul Johnson, *George Washington: The Founding* (2005); Douglas Southall Freeman, John A. Carroll, and Mary W. Ashworth, *George Washington: A Biography*, 7 vols. (1948–57).

Wells-Barnett, Ida B.

(1862–1931) JOURNALIST AND SOCIAL ACTIVIST.

On 16 July 1862, Ida Bell Wells-Barnett, a future journalist, club woman, and militant antilynching crusader, was born a slave in Holly Springs, Miss. The oldest daughter of slave parents James and Elizabeth (Bowling) Wells, she received her public school education in Holly Springs and attended Rust College, which was founded in 1866 as an industrial school for blacks in Holly Springs. A yellow fever epidemic took the lives of Wells's parents, leaving her, at the age of 14, in charge of her younger brothers and sisters. In order to support herself and her siblings, Wells began teaching at a nearby rural school while attending Rust College.

In 1884 Wells moved her family to Memphis, Tenn., to be near an aunt and to obtain a better-paying teaching position. Before passing the teaching examination for the Memphis public schools, Ida Wells taught at a rural school outside Memphis. In Tennessee she began her lifelong public crusade against injustice and inequality, successfully suing in 1884 the Chesapeake and Ohio Railroad Company for attempting to force her to sit in the smoking car that had been designated for blacks. The lower court decision in Wells's favor was subsequently overruled by the Tennessee Supreme Court.

While in Tennessee, Wells became part owner and editor of a local black newspaper, the *Memphis Free Speech and Headlight* (shortened by Wells to *Free Speech*). Her previous journalistic experience included occasional articles, primarily on race relations in the South, under the pen name "Iola," for religious publications and black newspapers. In 1891 Wells lost her teaching job in Memphis, following the publication in the *Free Speech* of articles critical of the school system's unequal allocation of resources to black schools. The next year a Wells editorial denouncing lynching in general and the lynching of three Memphis blacks in particular resulted in the destruction of the *Free Speech* building and threats on her life.

Although forced thereafter to live outside the South, Wells continued her campaign against racial injustice, especially the lynchings of blacks, as a columnist for the New York *Age*, as an author, and as a prominent lecturer on racial injustice in the United States and abroad. In 1895 she published a pamphlet titled *A Red Record: Tabulate*

Statistics and Alleged Causes of Lynchings in the United States, 1892–1893–1894, which later appeared in London under the title United States Atrocities. In her crusade against lynching, the articulate Wells delivered numerous lectures, aided in the formation of antilynching societies in England, and met with President William McKinley in 1898, along with other blacks, to protest the lynchings of blacks. Her fight against injustice also led to the denunciation of black exclusion from the Chicago World's Fair in 1893. She collaborated with Frederick Douglass, Ferdinand L. Barnett, and I. Garland Penn on a publication titled The Reason Why the Colored American Is Not in the World's Columbian Exposition—The Afro-American's Contribution to Columbian Literature.

In 1895 Ida married Ferdinand Lee Barnett, assistant state's attorney for Cook County and editor of the Chicago Conservator, the first black newspaper in Chicago. Wells then turned her attention to local civic activities. She founded and served as an officer in numerous women's groups, earning the title among some as the "Mother of Clubs." With money provided by some of the organizations she was active in, as well as with her own personal funds, Wells-Barnett traveled to Arkansas and Illinois to investigate race riots during World War I and in the postwar years reported on them for various black newspapers. Up to the time of her death in Chicago on 25 March 1931, Ida B. Wells-Barnett devoted her life to fighting for full equality for blacks and

women throughout the United States, but especially in the South.

SHARON HARLEY
University of Maryland

Alfreda M. Duster, Crusade for Justice: The Autobiography of Ida B. Wells (1970); Patricia Ann Schecter, "To Tell the Truth Freely": Ida B. Wells and the Politics of Race, Gender, and Reform in America, 1880–1913 (1995); Linda O. Murray, To Keep the Waters Troubled: The Life of Ida B. Wells (1998); Ida B. Wells-Barnett, On Lynchings (1969).

Wilson, Woodrow

(1856–1924) U.S. PRESIDENT.
Born in Virginia and raised in Georgia, South Carolina, and North Carolina, Woodrow Wilson was one of the South's most influential leaders in American history. His first memories, he once said, were of the news of Lincoln's election and the outbreak of the Civil War. The most important influence on his early life was his father, Joseph R. Wilson, a prominent Presbyterian minister who helped form the Presbyterian Church in the United States and ardently defended slavery. Woodrow Wilson later declared that "the only place in the country, the only place in the world, where nothing has to be explained to me is the South."

He began his education at Davidson College in North Carolina, completed his undergraduate work at Princeton, and pursued his legal training at the University of Virginia under John B. Minor. For a brief time in Atlanta he practiced law, which he found at odds with his primary interests—history and literature. During this period he

Woodrow Wilson, 28th president of the United States, c. 1916 (Library of Congress [LC-USZ62-107577], Washington, D.C.)

met his first wife, Ellen Axson Wilson, herself the daughter of a distinguished family of southern Presbyterian ministers. He left Atlanta to do doctoral work at the Johns Hopkins University, where he received his Ph.D. for his work *Congressional Government*.

Southern observers watched with pride as Wilson steadily achieved fame and influence as an educator, historian, man of letters, and political commentator, and Wilson's successful campaign for the White House in 1912 was due in great measure to his ability to portray himself paradoxically as both a southerner and a national figure.

In fact, he was both. He retained southern attitudes toward women throughout his life but insisted on a college education for his own daughters. He shared the racist values of American society of his day and as

president (1913–21) presided over the segregation of federal agencies yet never trafficked in blatant racism. In his historical writing he lauded the South for its adherence to principle in fighting the Civil War but described both the institution of slavery and the South's understanding of the Constitution as doomed by the progressive forces of history. He disciplined himself and his wife to drop their southern accents, although his southern political alliances brought him to national power.

Wilson's political achievements include breaking the Republican hold on the White House in the post–Civil War period and bringing the South into national politics. But perhaps the greatest irony is that this son of a region known for its parochialism should have laid the foundations for America's self-understanding in world affairs. Ellen Axson Wilson praised him for being "an infinitely better, more helpful son to her [the South] than any of those who cling so desperately to the past and the old prejudices." "I believe," she said, "you are her greatest son in this generation and also the one who will have the greatest claim on her gratitude."

JOHN M. MULDER
Louisville Presbyterian Theological Seminary

Thomas J. Knock, *To End All Wars: Woodrow Wilson and the Quest for a New World Order* (1992); Arthur S. Link, *Journal of Southern History* (February 1970), *Wilson: The Road to the White House* (1947); John M. Mulder, *Woodrow Wilson: The Years of Preparation* (1978); J. A. Thompson, *Woodrow Wilson: Profiles in Power* (2002).

Woodson, Carter G.

(1875–1950) HISTORIAN.
In 1915 Carter G. Woodson, who was
born in New Canton, Va., a son of
former slaves, organized the Association for the Study of Negro Life and
History. He began publishing the *Journal of Negro History* 1 January 1916 and
remained its editor until his death in
1950. Through the *Journal* and through
his Associated Publishers, in Washington, D.C., he countered the bias perme-
ating many contemporary accounts of
slavery and the black man.

Woodson's 1922 *The Negro in Our
History* went through 10 editions and
was for many years the most widely
used college text on the subject. But as
time went on, Woodson turned more
and more to racial propaganda in an
effort to uplift his people. As one who
had risen from a six-year stint in the
coalfields of West Virginia to study
at Berea College (1896–98), earn B.A.
and M.A. degrees at the University of
Chicago, take a 1912 Harvard Ph.D. in
history, and become dean of liberal
arts at Howard University (1919) and
West Virginia State College (1920), he
had an understandably sure sense of
his own abilities. A self-made man,
he was successful as an academician
and publisher, and he believed in the
need to present successful role models
to black school children. As a result
he wrote race history, emphasizing
examples of individual success. His
program for solving the problems of
blacks in America was not unlike that
of Booker T. Washington, whom he
greatly admired.

Woodson became an entrenched

member of the "black bourgeoisie." He
adopted its mid-19th-century middle-
class (white) values. He never learned
to think in terms of black power—
whether it be labor-union power or
mass voting power.

Whatever his shortcomings as a
historian and as a theorist, Carter G.
Woodson was able to create, through
his *Journal* and his Associated Publishers, vehicles for an alternative definition of the black situation to those
that dominated American publishing
throughout his lifetime.

S. P. FULLINWIDER
Arizona State University

Jacqueline Goggin, *Carter G. Woodson: A
Life in Black History* (1993); Frank Kling-
berg, *Journal of Negro History* (January
1956); Michael Winston, *Journal of Negro
History* (October 1975); James O. Young,
Black Writers of the Thirties (1973).

Woodward, C. Vann

(1908–1999) HISTORIAN.
Born 13 November 1908 in Vanndale,
Ark., to Hugh Allison and Bess Vann
Woodward, Comer Vann Woodward
was the most influential historian of
the 20th-century South. Educated at
Emory University (Ph.B. in philosophy, 1930), Columbia University (A.M.,
political science, 1933), and the University of North Carolina (Ph.D., 1937),
Woodward did not come to the discipline of history by a straight line but
rather through a succession of student
and teaching careers in the humanities,
which produced an undying interest in
creative literature that kept him in the
company of great writers, from Robert
Penn Warren and Cleanth Brooks to

John Updike. After briefly teaching English at Georgia Institute of Technology, he entered the study of history in 1934, was one of the attendees at the first meeting of the Southern Historical Association in that year, and subsequently taught at the University of Florida, Scripps College, the University of Virginia, Johns Hopkins University, and Yale University, where he became Sterling Professor of History and kept an office until very late in the 20th century. Yale University has established a chair in history in honor of Woodward and his son Peter Vincent, a student of political science who, like the historian's wife, Glenn Boyd Macleod, and a number of close friends, succumbed to cancer at an early age.

Woodward showed an unusual blend of activism and detachment, of aristocratic provenance and fascination with the masses, of great privilege conferred by family and friend and iconoclastic rebelliousness, and of professional specialization and an eclectic training. Evoking irony in his writings, he also lived a life of considerable irony, demonstrating what David Minter has called "deep reciprocities" between experiences of his personal life and the history he wrote.

Growing up in Arkansas during a period of racial violence and of grinding regional poverty, Woodward was nurtured by a family of devout Methodists committed to moderate social reform. Forsaking their path, he left an Arkadelphia Methodist college for Emory University, studying philosophy there with LeRoy Loemker, who taught him German existentialism and demonstrated to him a life that successfully combined scholarly excellence with social activism. After brief seasons teaching literature at Georgia Institute of Technology and studying political cal science at Columbia University, Woodward entered the University of North Carolina, studying with Howard Kennedy Beale; there he developed a historical interpretation based on class analysis and economic determinism, writing a dissertation that became his first book and his only biography, a celebration of Georgia Populism titled *Tom Watson: Agrarian Rebel* (1938). In subsequent years, during World War II, he began to integrate his understanding of creative literature with this economic history, producing his most enduring scholarship, *Origins of the New South, 1877–1913* (1951), and his most influential study, *The Strange Career of Jim Crow* (1955; subsequent revisions to 1974), which the Reverend Martin Luther King Jr. called "the Bible of the civil rights movement." In his provocative biography and in his magisterial 1951 study of the region, he established certain themes of interpretation that set historians onto new paths of exploration — and considerable and continuing debate. In these works, and in all later works, he said there was a sharp discontinuity, or break, in southern history caused by the Civil War, with a new group of more bourgeois leaders replacing the old agrarian elite; he also insisted that certain aspects of race relations, especially the legal de jure segregation called Jim Crow, were essentially New South and products neither of Reconstruction nor of the Old South.

In all these works, too, among many other things, he tried to use the tools of irony in his style of writing to belittle those with power and authority and to uplift those, especially black and white allies in the rural countryside, who sought radical economic redress of social injustice.

After distinguishing himself as a professor at Johns Hopkins University and as a visiting professor at Oxford University, he became Sterling Professor at Yale University in 1961. At both Johns Hopkins and Yale, he directed excellent graduate students, three of whom earned the Pulitzer Prize, one of whom became director of the National Endowment for the Humanities, and all of whom made their own impact on the study of southern history. At Yale he became an essayist and an editor, turning out the collections of poignant essays *The Burden of Southern History* (1960) and *American Counterpoint: Slavery and Racism in the North-South Dialogue* (1971), while editing the Pulitzer Prize–winning *Mary Chesnut's Civil War* (1981). He continued to travel to conferences and to work with young scholars, and he continued to turn out essays both provoking and graceful, a number of which were collected usefully in *The Future of the Past* (1989).

His work received the Bancroft and Sydnor awards; and he served as president of the Southern Historical Association, which he worked mightily to integrate, the American Historical Association, and the Organization of American Historians. Inside the profession, his interpretation of history, a subtle melding of lyric determinants,

has been criticized for underestimating the force of racism and understating the longevity of segregation; and many others have scored him for overvaluing the reformism inherent in agrarian movements at the turn of the century. Although he paid attention to women in history in ways unprecedented by the scholars who went before him, it is likely a fair judgment that he failed to appreciate the variety of roles played by women in the South. While his judgments in such controversies may finally be ruled incorrect in every instance by subsequent scholars, he, like Charles Beard, whom he so admired, will be long remembered as the starting point for the major debates in the discipline of history. Outside the profession, his essays, especially *The Strange Career of Jim Crow* and those in *The Burden of Southern History*, attracted and held the attention of nonspecialist readers and thinkers who appreciated his grace, wit, and commitment to moral change and his insistence that "southern intellectual" and "southern reformist" were not oxymorons.

JOHN HERBERT ROPER
Emory & Henry College

John Herbert Roper, ed., *C. Vann Woodward: A Southern Historian and His Critics* (1997), *C. Vann Woodward, Southerner* (1987); "C. Vann Woodward's *Origins of the New South, 1877–1913*: A Fifty-Year Retrospective," *Journal of Southern History* 67 (2001); C. Vann Woodward, *Thinking Back* (1985), ed., *Responses of the Presidents to Charges of Misconduct* (1974); Glenn Weddington Rainey Papers, Manuscript Collections, Library of Emory University, Atlanta, Ga.; C. Vann Woodward

Portrait of Sergeant Alvin York and his wife standing outside a building in Chicago, Ill. (Chicago Daily News Negatives Collection, Chicago Historical Society, Library of Congress [DN-0071461], Washington D.C.)

Papers, Manuscript Division, Library of Yale University, New Haven, Conn.; interview, Charles Crowe with Woodward, tape recording, Southern Historical Collection, Library of the University of North Carolina, Chapel Hill.

York, Alvin C.

(1887–1964) SOLDIER.
In the last days of World War I, Alvin C. York came marching out of the Argonne Forest with 132 German prisoners and a tale of individual daring

unsurpassed in the nation's military annals. One of the least likely heroes in our history, the Tennessee-born York was initially a conscientious objector who was drafted only after his pleas for a deferment on religious grounds were rejected. However, his army superiors persuaded him that America was fighting God's battle in the war, an argument that transformed the pacifist from the Appalachian Mountains into a veritable soldier of the Lord.

During the final Allied offensive

of the conflict, York single-handedly outshot an entire German machine-gun battalion, killing approximately two dozen men and taking 132 prisoners. His explanation that God had been with him during the fight meshed neatly with the popular attitude that American involvement in the war was truly a holy crusade. He returned to the United States in the spring of 1919 amid a tumultuous public welcome and a flood of business offers from people eager to capitalize on the soldier's reputation. In spite of these lucrative opportunities, York decided to return to his native hamlet of Pall Mall, where he spent the rest of his life working to bring schools and other public services to his mountain neighbors.

York's Appalachia heritage was central to his popularity, because the media portrayed him as the archetypal mountain man. At a time of domestic upheaval and international uncertainty, York's pioneerlike skill with a rifle, his homespun manner, and his fundamentalist piety endeared him to millions of Americans as a kind of "contemporary ancestor" fresh from the backwoods of the southern mountains. As such, he seemed to affirm that the traditional virtues of agrarian America still had meaning in the new era. In short, York represented not what Americans were but what they wanted to think they were. He lived in one of the most rural parts of the country at a time when a majority of Americans lived in cities: he rejected riches at a time when the tenor of the nation was crassly commercial; he was pious at a time when secularism was on the rise.

For millions of people, York was the incarnation of their romanticized understanding of the nation's past when men and women supposedly lived plainer, sterner, and more virtuous lives. Ironically, although York endured as a symbol of an older America, he spent most of his adult life working to bring roads, schools, and industrial development to the mountains, changes that irrecoverably altered the society he had come to represent.

DAVID D. LEE
Western Kentucky University

Michael Birdwell, *Celluloid Soldiers: The Warner Brothers Campaign against Nazism* (1999); Samuel K. Cowan, *Sergeant York and His People* (1922); David D. Lee, *Sergeant York: An American Hero* (1985); John Perry, *Sergeant York: His Life, Legend, and Legacy: The Remarkable Untold Story of Sergeant Alvin C. York* (1997); Thomas Skeyhill, ed., *Sergeant York: His Own Life Story and War Diary* (1928).

Page numbers in boldface refer to articles.

infrastructure of, 78; military leaders of, 80

Confederation Congress, 319

Confessions of Nat Turner, The (Styron), 342

Conflict, 1; between classes, 9, 222; North-South, 11, 13, 15, 75, 178, 179; in northern cities, 56; during Depression, 110; Native American, 135; within church denominations, 221

Congressional Government (Wilson), 352

Congress of Racial Equality (CORE), **278–80**, 301, 337

Connally, Tom, 166

Connecticut, 39, 40

Connelly, Thomas L., 190

Conner, Eugene "Bull," 173

Conning, James, 45

Conroy, Pat, 256

Constitution, U.S., 42, 227, 349; civil rights amendments to, 42, 55, 56, 212, 222, 344; Thirteenth Amendment, 79, 82; Bill of Rights, 103; Nineteenth Amendment, 212; Fourteenth Amendment, 309; Convention, 317; Fifteenth Amendment, 344

Contemporary South, **32–34**

Convention of American Anti-Slavery Women, 296

Conwell, Russell, 49, 51

Cooper, Anna Julia, 84, 331

Cooper, James Fenimore, 268

Cornbread, 87, 88, 91

Cornwallis, Charles, 167

Cotton, 4, 13, 101, 102, 113, 114, 127, 152, 168, 232, 257, 259; mills, 23; decline in price of, 28; mechanization of, 180, 234

Cotton gin, 12, 101, 152, 228

Cotton Kingdom, The (Olmsted), 322

Couch, W. O., 112

Couch, W. T., 196

Coulter, E. Merton, 333, 335

Council on Foreign Relations, 97

Crackers, 102

Craft, Ellen, 246

Craven, Avery O., 187

Craven, Wesley Frank, 4

Crews, Harry, 257

Crisis, The, 286

Crisp, James E., 108

Crockett, Davy, 100, 101, 268, **280–82**

Crockett Almanacs, 282

Crops, 4, 47, 126; colonial, 74

Crozer Theological Seminary (Chester, Pa.), 311

Crush, Tex., 216

Cuba, 251

Cultural integration, 3

Cultural programs, New Deal, **194–98**; Federal Music Project, 193, 195, 196; Federal Arts Project, 193, 195, 197; Historical Records Survey, 195; Federal Writers' Project, 195, 196; Federal Theater Project, 195, 196, 197

Culture, 2, 43, 84; national, 43, 63; Anglo-American antebellum, **43–46**, 47; slave, 47, **235–39**; Confederate, 60, 63, 78, 80; Lost Cause, 65, 80; southern colonial, 69, 228; food, 91; black, 286

Cunliffe, Marcus, 187

Cunningham, Ann Pamela, 118

Dabbs, James McBride, 106

Dabney, Robert L., 163

Dallas, Tex., 264

Daniel, John M., 61

Daniels, Josephus, 260

Danville, Ky., 214

Darwin, Charles, 46

Davidson, Donald, 112, 292

Davidson College (N.C.), 351

Davis, James H. "Cyclone," 26, 164

Davis, Jefferson, 19, 21, 62, 63, 78, 164, 177, **282–84**, 303; election of, 76

Dawson, Francis W., 23

De Ayllón, Lucas Vázquez, 4, 146

De Bow's Review, 46

Decatur, Miss., 287

Declaration of Independence, 12, 162, 216, 306

Grimké, Sarah, **294-96**
Groom, Winston, 257
Grundy, Felix, 258
Guerrilla warfare, 313
Guidebooks, state, 195
Gumbo Ya-ya: A Collection of Louisiana Folk Tales (Botkin), 196
Guns, 104
Gunston Hall, 124, 125
Gurganus, Allan, 65

Habitat for Humanity, 273
Hahn, Steven, 82
Hall, Jacquelyn Dowd, 334
Hall, Prince, 40
Hall of Fame for Great Americans, 304
Hall-Rogers, Thomas, 197
Hamburg, S.C., 226
Hamer, Fannie Lou, **296-98**, 338; honorary degrees of, 298; member organizations, 298
Hamer, Philip, 333
Hamilton, Alexander, 161, 228, 229
Hamilton, J. G. de Roulhac, 116
Hamlin, Hannibal, 308
Hammond, James Henry, **298-99**
Hammond, Marcus Claudius Marcellus, 178
Hampton, Wade, II, 299
Hampton Institute (Va.), 347
Hampton Roads, Va., 170
Hannah, Barry, 256
Hargis, Billy Joe, 172
Harkins, George Washington, 153
Harlem Renaissance, 29
Harpers Ferry, Va., 17, 303
Harrison, Benjamin, 316
Harrison, Constance Cary, 315
Hartford, Conn., 322
Harvard University (Cambridge, Mass.), 99, 285, 292; Radcliffe Institute of, 334
Hawley-Smoot Tariff (1930), 111
Haynes, Lemuel, 40
Hazel, John T. "Til," 52
Health, 111, 212, 213; philanthropy for, 206

Helms, Jesse, 175, 254, 255, 319
Hemings, Sally, 12, 165, 306
Henderson, Fletcher, 29
Henderson, George F. R., 303
Henry, John, 217
Henry, Patrick, 14, 227, 229
Hepplewhite, George, 44
Heritage, colonial, **69-75**; frontier, **99-106**
Hermitage, 122
Heroes, 11, 14, 19, 49, 268, 313; Confederate, 80, 313, 337; Mexican War, 178; Spanish-American War, 251
Herrenvolk democracy, 16
Historians, 11, **115-18**, 178, 292; views of Reconstruction, 219; encounter with Redemption, 224
Historic Savannah Foundation, 119
Historie de la Louisiane (Gayarré), 115
Historiography, 116
History: attitudes toward, 14, 73; books of, 115, 116; teaching of, 116; popularity of, 117; central themes of, **126-30**; social, 196; scholarship of Reconstruction, 220, 222
History and First Discovery of Virginia (Stith), 11, 115
History and Present State of Virginia (Beverley), 10, 115, 267
History of South Carolina (Ramsay), 115
History of the Colony and Ancient Dominion of Virginia (Campbell), 115
History of the South, 116
History of Transportation in the Eastern Cotton Belt to 1860, A (Phillips), 325
Hogg, James S., 209
Holly Springs, Miss., 350
Honor, code of, 25, 43, 84, 189, 252, 254
Hood, John Bell, 291
Hook, Benjamin, 321
Hoover, Herbert, 110, 166
Hope, Ark., 274
Hopkins, Harry, 194
Horton, Johnny, 259
Hospitality, 106

Patriotism, 49, 94, 252, 253, 260
Paulding, James Kirke, 282
Pawleys Island, S.C., 328
Peabody, George, 200, 205
Peanuts, 85
Peg Leg Sam, 217
Pember, Phoebe, 61
Penn, J. Garland, 351
Pennsylvania, 11, 39, 40, 49, 105
Pennsylvania Abolition Society, 39
Pensacola, Fla., 216, 258, 268
Pepper, Claude, 96
Perman, Michael, 224
Pershing, John J., 187
Petersburg, Va., 61
Peterson, Merrill D., 162, 163
Phelps-Stokes, Caroline, 200
Philadelphia, Miss., 68
Philadelphia, Pa., 39, 41, 42, 69
Philadelphia Convention, 12
Philanthropy, northern, **198–203**; categories of, 198; agencies and foundations of, 199
Philanthropy, southern, **203–7**; community foundations, 204; establishment of, 204; growth of, 205, 206
Phillips, Jayne Anne, 256
Phillips, U. B., 126, 127, **325–26**
Photographs, 196, 197
Pierce, Franklin, 282
Pike, Albert, 178
Pitts, Helen, 285
Place over Time: The Continuity of Southern Distinctiveness (Degler), 22
Plain Folk of the Old South (Owsley), 324
Plains, Ga., 272, 273
Plantation and Frontier (Phillips), 325
Plantations, 13, 44, 81, 87, 89, 108, 231, 242; idealization of, 21; houses of, 44, 45; during Civil War, 64, 83; colonial, 69, 227; return of freed slaves to, 82, 83, 181; international, 108
Planters, 6, 7, 13, 103, 108; postwar, 22, 23, 26; colonial, 69, 70, 227; after emancipation, 83, 84; fears of, 93, 230, 248

Plants, domestication of by Indians, 137–41
Plaquemine, La., 280
Plessy, Homer Adolph, 330, 331
Plessy v. Ferguson, 24, 31, 321, 330, 331
Poe, Edgar Allan, 45
Policy, foreign, **92–99**
Politics, 26, 32, 211; Civil War, 63; Cold War, 68; primaries, 212; Reconstruction era, 221; colonial era, 228; of secession, 230
Polk, James Knox, 94, 177, 179, **326–28**
Polk, Leonidas, 79, 207
Pollard, Edward A., 61
Poor whites, 23, 108
Population, 42, 52, 112; Indian, 4, 133, 134, 147; slave, 7, 40, 249; of Confederacy, 76; of Union, 76
Populism (People's Party), 159, 162, 164, **207–11**; fusion with Democrats, 164; failure of, 209, 210
Pork, 86
Port Royal, Va., 290
Ports: Edenton, N.C., 167; New Bern, N.C., 167; Norfolk, Va., 167; Savannah, Ga., 167; New Orleans, La., 167, 168, 169; Charleston, S.C., 167, 170; Mobile, Ala., 168; small, 169; Galveston, Tex., 170; Hampton Roads, Va., 170; Houston, Tex., 170; Jacksonville, Fla., 170; Tampa, Fla., 170; Wilmington, N.C., 170
Potter, David M., 160
Poverty, 20, 25, 31, 108, 110, 212, 213, 264, 276, 288, 312, 324; of tenants and sharecroppers, 231, 232, 233
Poverty Point, La., 136
Powhatan, Chief, 304
Presbyterians, 15, 25, 47, 294; southern denomination of, 221, 351
Preservation, historic, 53, **118–22**; organizations dedicated to, 53; of colonial sites, 124; of African American sites, 125
Preservation North Carolina, 120
Preston Library (Virginia Military Institute), 304

Secret History of the Dividing Line, The (Byrd), 270

Seeger, Charles, 196

Segregation, 21, 24, 25, 27, 31, 32, 58, 67, 68, 112, 114, 128, 221, 222, 264, 273, 285, 288, 321; laws, 55, 56; abolition of, 56; residential, 56, 321; after emancipation, 84; resistance to, 171–75; organizations supporting, 172, 273; military, 189; self-segregation, 286, 348; on trains, **330–32**

Selma, Ala., 31, 291, 312, 332; March, 332, 338

Sense of place, 109

September 11, 2001, 98

Servants, indentured, 6, 247, 305

Settlers: European, 3, 4, 9, 43, 47; frontier, 102

Sharecropping and tenancy, 22, 23, 89, 90, 110, 113, 114, **231–35**, 289, 323; lifestyles of, 233

Shawnee interior, 4

Shearer, Thomas, 44

Sheraton, Thomas, 44

Sherman, William Tecumseh, 80, 299

Shiloh, Tenn., 32, 51, 54, 80, 290

Shipbuilding, 167–70; military, 170

Shuttlesworth, Fred, 332, 333

"Siege of Monterrey, The" (Falkner), 178

Silver, James W., 334

Simkins, Francis Butler, 334

Simms, William Gilmore, 45, 106, 178

Sites, historic, 53, 118, 121, **122–26**; African American, 125

Sit-ins, 31, 56, 337

Sketches and Eccentricities of Col. Crockett (Clarke), 282

Slater, John F., 200, 205

Slavery, 44, 46, 48, 79, 81, 93, 94, 127, 128, 220, 283, 305, 313, 320, 322; sentiment against, 12, 14, 15, 227, 240, 270, 294, 318; white guilt over, 64; colonial, 74, 227, 228, 229, **247–50**; foreign colonial, 108; differing views on, 158; Jefferson's views on, 162, 163, 227, 240; western

expansion of, 179, 230; antebellum, **242–47**

Slaves, 6, 8, 14, 20, 47, 51; population of, 5, 7, 40, 249; interaction with whites, 5, 74, 249; work of, 5, 242; culture of, 7, 9, 16, **235–39**, 249; revolts of, 7, 12, 14, 17, 79, 227, **239–42**, 245, 341, 342; trade of, 7, 244; dwellings of, 9, 242, 243, 244; owners of, 12; in literature, 15; laws for, 39, 40, 42, 239; runaway, 39, 42, 237, 239, 246; rescues of, 42; as soldiers, 62; emancipation of, 78, 79, 80, 238; during war, 79, 82; images of North, 82; joining Union ranks, 82; as war contraband, 83; foodways of, 89; frontier, 103; Native American, 148, 24[ ] forced migration of, 179; former, 180; escapees, 180, 238, 239; WPA intervie[w] with, 195, 196; creole, 235; marriage of 235; family groups of, 235, 243, 245; Se[a] Island, S.C., 236; Gullah, 236, 244; lan guage of, 236, 244; religion of, 236, 24[ ] 249; music of, 237; masters' attitudes toward, 242; resistance of, 245

Smith, Francis Hopkinson, 315

Smith, John, 10

Smith, Samuel, 320

Snopes family (Faulkner), 23

Sobel, Mechal, 5

Social classes, 103, 231; aristocratic, 5, 6; middle, 6, 94, 97, 330; poor whites, 6, 95; working, 16; Yeomen, 16; frontier, 102; landowning, 113; on trains, 330

Societies, historical, 116

Sociology for the South (Fitzhugh), 290

Soil, 102, 103, 126

Soldier's Joy (Bell), 257

Somerville, Ella, 316

Sons of Confederate Veterans, 52, 278

Souls of Black Folk, The (Du Bois), 27, 28[ ]

Southampton County, Va., 14, 241, 245, 246, 341, 342

South Carolina, 4, 7, 8, 47, 101, 102, 298; nullification crisis of, 13, 162, 271, 317, 318; colonial, 72, 74, 75; secession of, 7[ ]

Wicker, Tom, 255
Wiener, Jonathan, 23
Wilberforce University (Ohio), 286
Wilkins, Roy, 321
Wilkinson County, Miss., 282
William Styron's Nat Turner: Ten Black Writers Respond (various), 342
Williams, Cora, 316
Williams, John Sharp, 164
Williamsburg, Va., 69, 118, 305; restoration of, 122
Wilson, Charles Reagan, 335
Wilson, James R., 256
Wilson, Woodrow, 27, 95, 116, 162, 164, 208, 259, 261, **351–52**
Wiltse, Charles M., 159
Winterville Mounds (Greenville, Miss.), 143
Wolfe, Thomas, 217, 261
Women, 3, 6, 23, 108; as abolitionists, 41, 42, 295; during Civil War, 62, 63, 64, 79; yeoman, 64; complaisance of, 127; as Southern Alliance members, 208; progressives, 211; suffrage of, 211, 212, 261; home demonstration agents, 213; roles in World War I, 261
Wood, Peter, 3
Woodland Indians, **137–41**

Woodson, Carter G., 84, **353**
Woodward, C. Vann, 17, 22, 52, 117, 128, 129, 219, 224, 334, **353–56**
Works Progress Administration (WPA), 191, 193, 195, 262; subagencies of, 195
Worlds of Color (Du Bois), 286
World War I, 27, 96, 185, **259–61**, 356, 357
World War II, 31, 66, 68, 96, 114, **262–65**
Wright, Richard, 112, 183, 196
Writers, 15, 29, 112, 315; New Deal opportunities for, 194, 196
Wyatt-Brown, Bertram, 43, 334
Wythe, George, 306

Yale University (New Haven, Conn.), 270, 275, 354, 355
Yancey, William Lowndes, 45
Yankees, 24, 84
Yeoman farmers, 16, 64, 90, 158, 159, 160, 162, 163, 222, 291; frontier, 103, 268
Yoknapatawpha County (Faulkner), 103
York, Alvin C., 260, **356–57**
Yorktown, Va., 124, 167, 184
Young, Andrew, 97, 332
Young, Stark, 292

Zelinsky, Wilbur, 104, 128